Sir Isaac Newton Kn.t
President of the Royal Society 1720-1

Pub June 25 1802 by Bunney & Gold 105 Shoe Lane

INTRODUCTION.

ON preſenting to the Public the following Abridgment of the PHILOSOPHICAL TRANSACTIONS, we deem it unneceſſary to dwell long on its utility, or importance. The original work has poſſeſſed a ſettled place in the libraries of the learned in England, and has obtained applauſe among the moſt diſtinguiſhed ſcholars in every part of Europe. And, as the eſtabliſhment of the ROYAL SOCIETY in this country gave birth to ſimilar Inſtitutions in other nations, ſo did the publication of the PHILOSOPHICAL TRANSACTIONS here, prepare the way for ſimilar publications abroad; all containing the moſt intereſting inveſtigations, and the moſt uſeful diſcoveries, purſued, through a ſeries of years, by the moſt enlightened nations. For, though this Society was not the firſt of the kind in Europe, it ſoon became the moſt diſtinguiſhed. To the exertions of individuals, connected with it, we have been indebted for the most ingenious experiments, and the moſt curious inventions; and to the publication of its Tranſactions, that ſuch experiments and inventions were ever made known to the world.

But the circulation of that work would neceſſarily be ſlow and limited, in proportion to its unwieldineſs. For, though a ſingle volume, or a ſingle number of a volume, might occaſionally find its way to ordinary readers, and among perſons more immediately occupied in active life, ſtill the entire work was deſtined to repoſe only with ſpeculative men, or in public libraries. The full benefit of the diſcoveries could not be reaped by the People at large: a few wealthy collectors might be provided with them, but they would be inacceſſible to the greater part of

our countrymen. Hence the importance of an Abridgment, the object of which, is, to reduce the bulk of *ninety-two* volumes to a more manageable size, and to render what would otherwise be of private concern, beneficial to the community.

The general object, then, of an Abridgment may be fairly left to speak for itself. What appears to be our province, is, to give a few historical particulars of the Society, whose labours, by thus contracting them, we are endeavouring to render more popular; to show on what principles this Abridgment is conducted; and in what respects it differs from the preceding.

To begin, then, with the Society. From small beginnings, accidental occurrences, or random hints, have frequently arisen Institutions, the most comprehensive in their character, and permanently useful. And it is useful to notice the infancy of such establishments, and the means, by which they arrived to maturity, as holding out encouragement to the sagacity of writers, and to the exertions of private individuals.

The origin of this Society was as follows:—At the close of the civil wars, a few men of philosophical minds retired to the University of Oxford, to seek repose in the shades of peaceful life, and to enjoy the benefit of literary conversation. To these, as might be expected, a few members of the University were added. It does not appear, that any thing was originally intended, beyond a friendly meeting of literary men, or that they professed any higher aim than their own edification. The subject of their attention was Philosophy, and of that species, which, by tracing causes to their effects, and by renouncing abstract reasonings, for the observations of the senses, and matters of fact, is called Experimental. The persons more particularly mentioned, as the first members of this Society, were Dr. Seth Ward, Bishop of Exeter, Hon. Mr. Boyle, Dr. Wilkins, Sir William Petty, Mr. Matthew Wren, Dr. Wallis, Dr. Goddard, Dr. Willis, Dr. Bathurst, Dr.

Chriſtopher Wren, and Mr. Rook ; perſons all eminently devoted to the ſtudy of Natural Philoſophy.

Their Meetings were held here a conſiderable time ; when, in the year 1658, they were adjourned to the metropolis ; a ſituation likely to give publicity to their plan, and to invite among them people of all ranks and profeſſions. The place, in which they firſt aſſembled, was Greſham College. Here they continued to hold ſtated meetings ; till, through the violence of thoſe civil commotions, which then unhappily diſtracted London, they were obliged to diſperſe. On the return of Charles the Second, however, the great aim of their meetings was reſumed with freſh ardour ; and the Society being then conſiderably augmented by the addition of new members, men of rank, and in high favour with the King, it roſe with new luſtre, and gave promiſe of the moſt durable eſtabliſhment.

And here juſtice requires, that Poetry ſhould have its due portion of commendation. For certain it is, that the original Inſtitution was conſiderably indebted to the genius of Cowley, the poet, who not only after the building was finiſhed gave his high-ſounding Plaudite in an Ode, but alſo furniſhed conſiderable materials for raiſing it. An eſſay of his, publiſhed at this time, extended the views of thoſe learned men now aſſembled ; and to this, as to a model, was the edifice conſiderably indebted.

The ſcheme, indeed, favours ſomewhat too much of the cloiſter, having been formed on the monaſtic plan, and having entailed on it, alſo, the incumbrance of the education of youth. It, however, diſcovers much ingenuity, diſplays great compaſs of thought, and, no doubt, furniſhed thoſe perſons who were the immediate inſtruments of raiſing this infant Society, with many uſeful hints, and many ſteady reſolutions. This eſſay may be ſeen in Cowley's Works, and is entitled A Propoſition for the Advancement of Experimental Philoſophy.

A Society being thus formed, rapidly increafed both in numbers and refpectability ; and the King, in the year 1665, beftowing on it his Letters Patent, it appeared under a new character, the ROYAL SOCIETY.

It has been maintained by fome writers, that Philofophy fhould be wholly left to its own energies, and to the exertions or encouragements of private individuals. In confirmation of their opinion, they appeal more particularly to the Athenian republic, where, it muft be acknowledged, Philofophy rofe into great confideration, and the Arts were fo foftered, that they never arrived to fuch eminence in any other country. On the other hand, it has been urged, that the interefts of Science are beft promoted by the united efforts of many ;—Becaufe union holds out encouragement, and brings together the fcattered rays of genius into one focus ;—that Science requires every fupport from opulence and power ;—Becaufe where great expences are incurred, private means are inadequate. The truth in this matter feems to be,—that though Societies have fometimes failed in their object, originally avowed, of making experiments, and purfuing difcoveries in a body, yet individuals have generally received benefit, and their refearches been more readily forwarded ;—that States are affected by literature according to the different principles of their governments. In Republics, properly conceived and wifely matured, Art and Science, perhaps, will be more generally diffufed. In Monarchies, ftrictly fo called, there will be a few more tranfcendently eminent. In limited Monarchies, we fhall behold a mixture of the extremes ; the many will be moderately informed, and a few extraordinarily enlightened.

But, leaving thefe matters, as more particularly belonging to queftions about civil government, and not undertaking to fettle political controverfies, we now only obferve, that, in the prefent inftance,—(and we are fpeaking of the ROYAL SOCIETY hiſtorically,)—it was by union it gained ſtrength; and that the Royal Patronage did eſſentially contribute to lift it into conſequence, by inviting ſome of the moſt diſtinguiſhed nobility of thoſe times, and the moſt ſcientific men in the different profeſſions, to think well of its pretenſions, and to become its members.

The Society being thus incorporated by Royal Charter, continued to receive freſh ſupplies of nutriment and ſtrength from all quarters: for the bond of union being Natural Science, which addreſſes itſelf, viſibly, as it were, to all mankind; and political diſquiſitions, metaphyſical ſubtleties, and theological diſtinctions, being wholly excluded, the way was thrown open to the freeſt communication, to the moſt generous and manly confidence. For though, in ſtating the qualities of members, the charter, being made at the beginning of the new Government, gave a preference to ſuch as were diſtinguiſhed for their loyalty, ſtill it held out no excluſive privileges; it authorized no objections againſt men of philoſophical minds, for differences about forms of government, or the doctrines and rites of religion. For, as men at variance about politics may harmonize over experiments; and ſuch as view with different eyes articles of faith, may yet, with organs more congenial, behold the works of Nature; Churchmen, Diſſenters, and learned men attached to no party, have united as Philoſophers, and become Members of the Royal Society.

Hence, by a union of the talents of men of all ſentiments, ſuch a combination of the moſt diſpaſſionate inquirers was formed, as was never ſeen till this period in England. Nor did it ſo excluſively conſiſt of the nobility and gentry of the country, as to keep out, with an invidious faſtidiouſneſs, even the mechanic. For the uſeful arts of life, and ſuch as fall under every day's practice, and the obſervation of the ſenſes, being made frequently the ſubject of their experiments, it was but reaſonable, that ſuch ſhould be allowed to be members, whofe profeffions might qualify them for ufeful obfervation, and whofe habits were formed by genuine experiment. Nay, the Society extended its regard ftill further, to diftant nations; it enrolled among its members many eminent foreigners; and correfpondencies were promoted among enlightened men in every part of the civilized world. Thus extenfive was the object of the Society; acceffible to people of every religious denomination, to men of any profeffion or rank, and to Philofophers, refiding in any quarter of the world!

And here let us trace back the state of Philofophy in different periods, and in different parts of the world; fo fhall we more clearly underftand the fuperior defignation of the ROYAL SOCIETY.

That the Arts and Sciences had their origin in the Eaft, is univerfally acknowledged; though, how far they had advanced in that immenfe tract of country, is not accurately known; as well on account of the difingenuoufnefs of the Grecians, who would be thought to have invented what they only borrowed from the Eaft; as of that myfterious way of teaching adopted by the Afiatics:—For, as may be collected from all quarters, the religion and philofophy of the Eaft were both alike involved in much obfcurity; the former converfant about innumerable natures, the different orders of fupernatural and incomprehenfible beings; the latter, about the various divinations from natural objects. Thus much may be faid with fafety, that the Afiatics had among them much Art and Science, but excelled not in the talent of communicating them to the world. Their wifdom, inftead of rendering perplexed things fimple, and of directing the great movements of the world to ufeful purpofes, was too much occupied in giving an air of myftery to what was plain. Their wife men retained for particular purpofes what knowledge they poffeffed, inftead of bringing it into a public ftock;—they appealed to latent qualities and imaginary beings, inftead of calling forth the powers of

Nature by experiment, and of eſtabliſhing her laws on the evidence of facts.

In Greece we may trace Philoſophy without the danger of miſſing it. For under whatever diſguiſe the Grecians found it in more eaſtern countries, they ſoon rendered it conſpicuous in their own, by arraying it in the moſt winning attire, and by holding it out thus adorned, to the notice and admiration of the world. In Logic and Metaphyſics, too, they made great advances. Among the Stoics we find all our ideas traced to ſenſation, as clearly as in Locke; among the Peripatetics we perceive the doubts of Des Cartes: the doctrine of innate ideas, as held by Leibnitz and Mallbranche, may be ſeen in Plato; and all that has been delivered in thoſe French Philoſophers on Entities, really exiſting, the Eternal Images of Univerſal Natures, are but thoſe divine ideas, the exemplars of the intellectual and material worlds, as held by Heraclitus, Democritus, and Plato.

In Phyſics, too, the Grecians made conſiderable proficiency. Natural Hiſtory and Mathematics, Aſtronomy, Optics, and Mechanics; Botany, and Medicine, Anatomy, and Phyſiognomy, were familiar to the Grecians. There are but few of thoſe improvements in Science, which the Moderns have claimed as their diſcoveries, of which ſketches, at leaſt, may not be found in the writings of antiquity. The laws of Gravitation, the doctrine of Colours, and in part, the Planetary Syſtem, as demonſtrated by Newton, were held by Plato and Pythagoras. The Circulation of the Blood was known to Hippocrates; Botany, Anatomy, and Phyſiognomy, had been ſtudied by Ariſtotle.

Thus far the Grecians ſucceeded: they brought much from the Eaſt, and knew how to ſet it off to advantage; they were ſtudious over other peoples diſcoveries, and were fruitful in theories and hypotheſes. Still the Grecians were deficient in EXPERIMENTAL Philoſophy.

The fact is, Philosophy having, at length, settled itself in Greece, did not combine men in one pursuit, but contributed rather, from various causes, to divide them into numerous parties. The most distinguished Philosophers became the heads of sects, and formed schools—each became a kind of master—their scholars, as well as themselves, were disputers rather than inquirers, believers rather than experimentalists. They looked with the eyes of their mind, not with their material organs; they worked more with their heads than their hands; and to such a Philosophy their fondness for Metaphysics was favourable: for this rendered them familiar with obscurity, and not greatly out of humour with uncertainty. It should be observed, too, that these Ancients were not so favourably provided with means for observation and experiment, as the Moderns. The art of printing, and many other useful inventions, were unknown: Astronomy had, as yet, derived no aid from the telescope, and Navigation had not been indebted to the compass. And hence, some parts of Science, which the Grecians could know only as matters of opinion, have been demonstrated by the Moderns; for though the former were always distinguished for genius and talent, the latter have possessed the advantages of experiment and practice.

Of the method of philosophizing among the Romans, little need be said; for it was late in the Republic before the Romans attached themselves to Philosophy; they had been studying the art of government, not making experiments; conquering rather than philosophizing; and when, at length, they sat down to Philosophy, they took the systems of the Grecians ready made to their hands. Still less need be said of that period between the decline of the literature and the Republic of the Romans, and the revival of letters in Italy. For though religion might flourish in some of those periods, still Philosophy was on the decay; and what remained of the latter was, for the most part, composed of the more poetical fancies of Plato, or the abſtruſer parts of Ariſtotle's Metaphyſics. To theſe periods, too, must be referred ages, then only awake, when ſpirited up by ſubtle arguments, or rouſed by the violence of controverſy. Theſe have, therefore, been called the dark ages; and theſe were not ages of Experiment.

Philoſophy, after a long exile, was to return to the world in a character more favourable to all the purpoſes of human life. But it was thought expedient by the revivers of literature to recover the letter, before they followed the ſpirit of Science. The activities of ingenious men were accordingly occupied in ranſacking monaſteries, in poring over manuſcripts, in recovering ancient authors, and in fixing their ſenſe, or eſtabliſhing their authority. The experiments firſt made were moſtly on doubtful paſſages in Greek or Latin writings, or on thoſe branches of Science, which tended to their eclairciſſement, Grammar, Criticiſm, Rhetoric, and Poetry. Societies, however, were ſoon formed in Italy, though at firſt more for the elegant Arts, for polite Literature, and the theoretical parts of Philoſophy, than for the practical part, that conſiſts in experiments; that method which, at length, brought Philoſophy within the reach of the ſenſes, and left no room for faith, beyond what was founded in evidence.

Theſe obſervations have been made, in order to place the leading view of the Royal Society in the cleareſt light. There will, therefore, be leſs occaſion to dwell on the dreams of ſchoolmen, the credulity of viſioniſts, the ſuperſtitions of the implicit followers of the Ancients, or the raſhneſs and impetuoſity of modern dogmatiſts. Suffice it to ſay, that they all followed a method of philoſophizing contrary to the order of Nature, and repulſive to the common ſenſe of mankind.

Experimental inquiry, which now began its reſearches, took the oppoſite courſe. It was exerciſed in breaking the ſhackles of opinion, in burſting from the tyranny of authority, and the yoke of ſuperſtition. It kept aloof from theories and hypotheſes, and paid little regard to the ſubtleties of logic, the wantonneſs of metaphyſics, and the faſcinations of eloquence; it called man to conſider his own importance, to aſſert his proper dignity, and to employ his genuine powers; it directed his obſervation to the air, the earth, the ſea, the ſkies; and, through the vaſt extent, to become acquainted with their different inhabitants, their numerous properties, and their diſtinct uſes;—to aſcertain their mighty wonders, their various movements, and their regular laws. It placed him, as it were, in the centre of the univerſe, with no other limits, but the circumference; and with no other reſtraints, but the laws of his own underſtanding. In a word, it furniſhed him with thoſe principles of philoſophizing, and that perſeverance of reſearch, that have formed the greateſt maſters in all the Arts and Sciences, and given the world ſuch men, as Bacon, and Boyle, and Newton.

Such then were the views, and ſuch is the courſe of inquiry, that was profeſſed by the ROYAL SOCIETY. It comprehended, for we can ſpeak only in general terms, that vaſt diverſity of ſubjects which the human body, its health, its ſtrength, and its duration, compriſes; which embraces Arts and Manufactures, whether they adminiſter to the wants and comforts, or to the juſt and natural pleaſures of life; and which is concerned in a general ſurvey of the works of Nature, both as they are in themſelves curious and intereſting, full of beauty, variety, and wonder; and as brought forward into real life for the multifarious ſervices of mankind.

That our readers may form an accurate idea of the internal policy of the Society, we ſhall here ſubjoin an extract of the Statutes.

"Whatever Statute ſhall be made or repealed, the making or repealing of it ſhall be voted twice, and at two ſeveral Meetings of the Council.

This obligation ſhall be ſubſcribed by every Fellow; or his election ſhall be void.

We, who have hereto ſubſcribed, do promiſe each for himſelf, that we will endeavour to promote the good of the ROYAL SOCIETY of London, for the improvement of Natural Knowledge, and to purſue the ends for which the ſame was founded; that we will be preſent at the Meetings of the Society, as often as we conveniently can; eſpecially at the anniverſary Elections, and upon extraordinary occaſions; and that we will obſerve the Statutes and Orders of the ſaid Society; provided, that whenever any of us ſhall ſignify to the Preſident, under his hand, that he deſires to withdraw from the Society, he ſhall be free from this obligation for the future.

Every Fellow ſhall pay his admiſſion money, and afterwards contribution, towards the defraying the charges of obſervations and experiments, &c.

The ordinary Meetings of the ROYAL SOCIETY ſhall be held once a week, where none ſhall be preſent beſides the Fellows, without the leave of the Society, under the degree of a Baron in one of his Majeſty's three kingdoms, or of his Majeſty's Privy Council, or unleſs he be an eminent Foreigner; and theſe only without the leave of the Preſident.

The buſineſs of their Weekly Meetings ſhall be to order, take account, conſider, and diſcourſe of, Philoſophical experiments and obſervations; to read, hear, and diſcourſe upon, letters, reports, and other papers, containing philoſophical matters, as alſo to view and diſcourſe upon the productions and rarities of Nature and Art, and to conſider what to reduce from them, or how they may be improved for uſe and diſcovery.

The experiments ſhall be made at the charge of the Society; two Curators, at leaſt, ſhall be appointed for the inſpection of thoſe which cannot be performed before the Society; by them the bare report of matter of fact ſhall be ſtated and returned.

The Election of Fellows ſhall be made by way of ballot; and their admiſſion by a ſolemn declaration made by the Preſident of their election.

The election of the Council and Officers ſhall be made once a year; eleven of the preſent Council ſhall be continued, by lot, for the next year, and ten new ones choſen in like manner. Out of this new

b 2

5

Council ſhall be elected a Preſident, Treaſurer, and two Secretaries in the ſame way.

The Preſident ſhall preſide in all Meetings, regulate all debates of the Society and Council; ſtate and put queſtions; call for reports and accounts from Committees, Curators, and others; ſummon all extraordinary meetings upon urgent occaſions, and ſee to the execution of the ſtatutes. The Vice-Preſident ſhall have the ſame power in the absence of the Preſident.

The Treaſurer or his Deputy ſhall receive and keep accounts of all money due to the Society, and diſburſe all money payable to the Society. He ſhall pay ſmall ſums by order of the Preſident under his hand; but thoſe that exceed five pounds by order of the Council. All bills of charges for experiments ſhall firſt be ſigned by the Curators. The accounts of the Treaſurer ſhall be audited four times a year, by a Committee of the Council, and once a year by a Committee of the Society.

The Secretaries are to take notes of the orders and material paſſages of the Meetings; to take care of the books, papers, and writings of the Society; to order and direct the Clerks in making entries of all matters in the Register and Journal Books of the Society or Council; to draw up ſuch letters as ſhall be written in their name, which ſhall be approved at one of their meetings; to give notice of the Candidates propounded in order to election.

The Curators by office ſhall have a ſufficient allowance for their encouragement, which ſhall increaſe proportionally with the revenues of the Society, provided that it exceed not two hundred pounds a year. They ſhall be well ſkilled in Philoſophical and Mathematical learning, well verſed in obſervations, inquiries, and experiments of nature and art. They ſhall take care of the managing of all experiments and obſervations appointed by the Society or Council, and report the ſame, and perform ſuch other taſks as the Society or Council ſhall appoint; ſuch as the examination of the Sciences, Arts, and Inventions now in use; and the bringing in hiſtories of natural and artificial things, &c. They ſhall be propounded at leaſt a month before they are choſen. They ſhall be examined by the Council before the election. To their election every Member of the Society ſhall be ſummoned. They ſhall at firſt be only elected for a year of probation, except they be of known merits; at the end of the year they shall be either elected for perpetuity, or for a longer time of probation, or wholly rejected. The causes of ejecting a Curator shall be the same with ejecting a fellow, or for fraudulent dealing and negligence in the affairs of the Society, provided that he shall receive three respective admonitions. If any Curator shall be disabled by age, infirmity, or any casualty, in the service of the Society, some provision shall be made for him during life, if his condition requires, according as the Council shall think fit.

The Clerk shall constantly attend at the Meetings; he shall follow the directions of the Secretaries, in registering and entering all matters that shall be appointed: he shall not communicate any thing contained in their books to any that is not a Fellow. He shall have a certain rate for what he copies, and a yearly stipend for his attendance.

The Printer shall take care for the printing of such books as shall be committed to him by order of the Society or Council; and therein he shall observe their directions, as to the correction of the edition, the number of copies, the form, or volume, &c.

The Operators of the Society, when they have any of their work under their hands, shall not undertake the work of any other person, that may hinder the business of the Society. They shall have salaries for their attendance.

The Common Seal of the Society shall be kept in a chest with three locks, and three different keys, by the President, Treasurer, and one of the Secretaries. The deeds of the Society shall be passed in Council, and sealed by them and the President.

The Books, that concern the affairs of the Society, shall be the Charter Book, Statute Book, Journal Books, Letter Books, and Register Books, for the entering of Philosophical Observations, Histories, Discourses, Experiments, Inventions.

The names of Benefactors shall be honourably mentioned in a book provided for that purpose.

In case of death, or recess of any Fellow, the Secretaries are to note it in the margin of the Register, over against their names.

The causes of ejection shall be contemptuous disobedience to the Statutes and Orders of the Society; defaming or malicious damnifying of the fame. This fhall be declared by the Prefident at one of the Meetings, and the ejection recorded."

And thus much for a few general outlines of the Hiftory, the objects of Inveftigation, and the internal Policy, of the ROYAL PHILOSOPHICAL SOCIETY.

It only remains, that we lay before our Readers, in few words, the principles on which this Abridgment of the PHILOSOPHICAL TRANSACTIONS proceeds, and in what refpects it differs from the preceding.

The idea of Abridgment includes that of difpatch; for felections from valuable works are intended to fhorten labour, and to fave time, as well as expence. We have kept this idea in view throughout thefe volumes. Perhaps no work admits of an Abridgment more readily than the PHILOSOPHICAL TRANSACTIONS. A large part of the earlier volumes is now quite uninterefting, on account of more recent difcoveries, or of fucceeding writers, who have written more clearly and fcientifically on the fame fubjects. Of courfe, we have thought ourfelves juftified in wholly omitting many entire Effays. We retain fuch only as ftill preferve their importance; and fuch papers as contain matters that fucceeding writers have treated fo much better, we have curtailed. The titles of fuch Treatifes as are wholly omitted, will either be noticed in their refpective places, or be thrown into an Appendix, at the end of each volume.

We retain the original words of the Authors, but as the mode of fpelling in fome inftances is now obfolete, we fpell them in the modern way. Thus we preferve the air and fhape of the work, but drefs it after the more approved fafhion.

We fhall differ in our arrangement from all thofe that preceded; but fo differ, as to render, we hope, our work more agreeable to the prefent times. Mr. *Lowthorp's* Abridgment in 1705, Mr. *Motte's* in 1720, Mr. *Jones's* in 1721, Mr. *Martin's* in 1733, &c. all follow one method, which was not in the way, in which they were delivered, in the form of independent ſubjects; but in the way of arrangement, bringing together the different papers on the ſame ſubject under one head. We have rather choſen to purſue the order, in which the ſeveral papers were delivered; conceiving, that this variety will be infinitely more agreeable to the generality of readers, and better adapted to the preſent taſte. The increaſe of periodical publications has rendered us familiar with this ſort of variety; the Public expect it; and the expectation is reaſonable. For, as one Number of the Work will appear every week, in the form of a periodical publication, who does not ſee the inconvenience of having one Art or Science continued through ſo many numbers, and broken, as it were, into a variety of disjointed pieces? This method, as it falls in the natural order of the original experiments, ſo will it, we doubt not, meet the approbation of the generality of our readers.

We have only to add, that as this difference in our plan, is, we apprehend, a very conſiderable improvement on the method of preceding Abridgments, ſo, from the very nature of a work greatly enlarged, will the preſent volumes carry with them a recommendation, on which it is unneceſſary for us to dwell. Suffice it to ſay, that as there has been no Abridgment of the PHILOSOPHICAL TRANSACTIONS for nearly fifty years, and as we mean to comprehend the Experiments, Inventions, and Diſcoveries made during that long period, our Work profeſſes to be a Selection of the moſt important, edifying, and entertaining ſubjects diſcuſſed by the ROYAL SOCIETY, from its commencement to the preſent day. We have not, we truſt, been defective in our duty; but have made it our ſerious ſtudy, to render the work every way worthy of the public encouragement.

THE

PHILOSOPHICAL TRANSACTIONS ABRIDGED.

A. D. 166$\frac{4}{5}$.

The Motion of the late Comet predicted.

THERE was lately ſent to one of the Secretaries of the ROYAL SOCIETY a packet, containing ſome copies of a printed paper, entituled, "The Ephemerides of the Comet," made by the ſame perſon who ſent it, called Monſieur Auzout, a French gentleman of no ordinary merit and learning, who deſired that a couple of them might be recommended to the ſaid Society. The end of the communication of this paper was, that the motion of the Comet that hath lately appeared, having been predicted by the ſaid Monſieur Auzout, after he had ſeen it, as he himſelf affirms but four or five times, the virtuoſi of England might among others, alſo compare their obſervations with his Ephemerides, either to confirm the hypotheſis upon which the Author had before hand calculated the way of this Star, or to undeceive him, if he be in a miſtake. The ſaid Author dedicateth theſe his conceptions to the Moſt Chriſtian King, telling him that he preſents him with a deſign, which never yet was undertaken by any Aſtronomer; all the world having been hitherto perſuaded, that the motions of Comets were ſo irregular that they could not be reduced to any laws; and men having contented themſelves, to obſerve exactly the places through which they *did* paſs; but no man, that he knows, having been ſo bold as to venture to foretel the places through which they *ſhould* paſs, and where they ſhould ceaſe to appear: whereas he exhibits here the Ephemerides, determining day by day, in what place of the heavens this Comet ſhall be, at what hour it ſhall be in its meridian, and at what hour it ſhall ſet; until its too great remoteneſs, or the approach of the ſun, hide it from our eyes. Deſcending to particulars, he ſaith, that this ſtar, being diſengaged from the beams of the ſun, might have been obſerved, if his conjectures be good, ever ſince it hath been of 17 or 18 degrees ſouthern latitude, and that about the middle of November laſt, and ſooner, unleſs it had been too ſmall; that however it hath been ſeen in Holland ever ſince the ſecond of December laſt, at which time, according to his reckoning, the diurnal motion of the Comet ſhould already amount to 17 or 18 minutes. He finds that this Star moveth juſt enough in the plan of a *great circle*, which inclineth to the equinoctial about 30 degrees, and to the ecliptic 49 degrees, or $49\frac{1}{25}$, cutting the equator at about 45 degrees $\frac{1}{25}$, and the ecliptic at the 28th degree of Aries, or a little more. He ſaith juſt enough, becauſe he thinks there may perhaps be ſome parallax; which he wiſheth could be determined.

Hence every one who pleaſeth may ſee, in tracing the Comet upon the globe, through, or by which Stars it hath paſſed and ſhall paſs; adding, that there will be *neither* cauſe to wonder, that having deſcended to about ſix degrees beneath the tropic of Capricorn, he hath remounted afterwards, and ſhall go on aſcending ſo, as to paſs the equinoxial, and perhaps proceed to 15 degrees northern declination, if it do not diſappear before that time, by reaſon of its remoteneſs: *Nor* to believe that there have been two Comets, upon its being ſeen again on the 31ſt of December, ſince it ought to have been ſo, if it continued to move in a great circle.

Having hereupon ſhewn, how the motion is to be traced upon the *globe*, he finds that, according to his calculation, this Comet was to paſs the tropic of Capricorn about the 16th of December, and being entered into the ſign of Virgo on the 20th of the ſame month, and having been in quadrate with the Sun, it ſhould ſtill deſcend until the 26th of December in the morning, and then enter into *Leo*; that having entered, the 28th of the ſame month, into Cancer, and being a little after that time in its greateſt inclination to the ecliptic, *viz.* in the 28th degree of Leo, it was to repaſs the ſouthern tropic, over againſt the Little Dog, on the 29th of December, about nine or ten of the clock in the morning, after it had been oppoſite to the Sun about two or three hours before; and that on the 29th of December in the evening it ſhould be in Gemini, and at the very beginning of the new year, enter into Taurus.

After this, our Author finds that this Comet ſhould paſs the Equator on the fourth of January before noon, and that about five or ſix of the clock in the evening of that day, it was to come into the Jaw of the Whale, and the ninth of the ſame, at ſix of the clock, it ſhould come cloſe to the ſmall ſtar of the Whale, which is in its way, a little below. At length, he finds that it was to enter into Aries on the 12th of January, and to cut the ecliptic on the 16th of the ſame month about noon, at which time it was to be again in quadrate with the Sun, whence drawing a little above the northern line of Piſces, it ſhould in his opinion ceaſe to appear a little beyond that place, without going as far as to the middle of Aries, if ſo be that its remoteneſs make it not diſappear ſooner.

He continueth, that this Comet ſhall not arrive to the place over againſt the line of Piſces till the 10th of February, and that then its diurnal motion ſhall not exceed eight minutes, and not five minutes about the 20th of the ſame month: and that then in the beginning of March, if we ſee it ſo long, the ſaid motion ſhall not exceed four minutes, and ſo ſhall be ſtill diminiſhing; except the Comet become retrograde, which, as very important, he would have well obſerved; as alſo whether its motion will be about the end more or leſs ſwift, than he has yet calculated it.

He ſubjoins, that the greateſt way which this Star could make in 24 hours, hath been 13 degrees 25 minutes; and in one hour, about 34 minutes; and thinking it probable that about the time when it made ſo much way it ſhould be neareſt to the Earth, he concludes that its motion in 24 hours muſt be in its leaſt diſtance from the Earth, as about 3 to 14, or 1 to 4$\frac{2}{3}$ds, and that its motion in one hour was to be the ſame leaſt diſtance, as about 1 to 102$\frac{1}{7}$th.

But that, which he judgeth moſt remarkable is, that he found by his calculation that the ſaid leaſt diſtance ſhould be on the 29th of December, when the Comet was oppoſite to the Sun, which he does not know whether it may not ſerve to decide the grand queſtion concerning the *Motion of the Earth.*

He taketh further notice, that the tail of the Comet was to turn weſtward, with a point to the north, until the 29th of December, at which time it was to be oppoſite to the Sun, and that then the ſaid tail was to look directly north; but that, after that time, the tail was to turn eaſtward, and continue to do ſo until it diſappear; and that it ſhall draw a little towards the north, until the eighth or tenth of February, at which time the tail is to be parallel to the Equator, and if the Comet be yet ſeen for ſome time after, the tail ſhall go a little lower towards the ſouth, but grow ſmaller.

He finds by this hypotheſis, that on the ſecond of December, which is the firſt obſervation that he hath heard of, this Star was to be about ſeven times more remote from the Earth, than when it was in its perigeum; and that it will be again in an equal remoteneſs from the Earth on the 27th of January; ſo that he is of opinion, that in caſe this Comet have not been ſeen before the ſecond of December, it will not be ſeen any more after the 27th of January.

He wiſhes above all things that it might be very exactly obſerved at what angle the way of the Comet cuts the Equator, and moſt of all the Ecliptic, that ſo it may be ſeen, whether there hath not been ſome parallax in the circle of his motion, as alſo, that ſome obſervations could be had of its greateſt deſcent beneath the tropic of Capricorn in the more ſouthern parts, where he ſays it would have been without refraction; moreover, of the time when it hath been in quadrate with the Sun about the 20th of December, and that alſo very exact obſervations might be made of the time of its being again in quadrate with the Sun, which, according to him, was to be January the 16th.

He wiſhes alſo that ſome in Madagaſcar may have obſerved this Star; ſeeing that it began to appear over the middle of that iſland, and paſſed twice over their heads; he judgeth that they have ſeen it before us. And he wiſhes, laſtly, that there were ſome intelligent perſon in Guiana to obſerve it there, ſeeing that within a few days, according to his reckoning, it will paſs over their heads, and will not remove from thence but eight or ten degrees northward, where he ſaith, it will diſappear, thinking it improbable that it can ſtill appear after the Sun ſhall have paſſed it.

This account bears date the ſecond of January, new ſtyle, 1665, and the Author adds this Note, that ſeeing it could not be printed or diſtributed ſo ſoon as he deſired, he hath had the opportunity to verify it by ſome obſervations from which he affirms he hath found no ſenſible difference, or, if there be, that it proceeds only from thence, that the Stars have advanced ſince his globe was made. He concludes, that if this continue, and the firſt obſervations do likewiſe agree, or that the differences do arrive within the times gueſſed by him, that he hopes he ſhall determine both the diſtance and the magnitude of this Comet, and that perhaps one may be enabled to decide the queſtion of the Motion of the Earth. In the interim, he aſſureth that he hath not changed the leaſt number in his calculations, and that Monſ. Huygens, and ſeveral French gentlemen, to whom he ſaith he hath given them long ſince, can bear witneſs that he hath done ſo; as alſo many other friends, who ſaw upon his globe ſeveral days before, the way of the Comet from day to day.

Thus far the Pariſian account of the Comet, which is here inſerted at large, that the intelligent and curious in England may compare their obſervations therewith, either to verify theſe predictions, or to ſhew wherein they differ; which is (as was hinted above) the deſign of this Philoſophical Prophet in diſperſing his conceptions, who declares himſelf ready, in caſe he be miſtaken in his reckoning, to learn another hypotheſis, to explicate theſe admirable appearances by.

An Account of a very odd monſtrous Calf.

THERE was lately communicated to the ROYAL SOCIETY, by Mr. Boyle, an account of a very odd *monſtrous Birth,* produced at Hemmington, in Hampſhire, where a butcher, having cauſed a cow (which caſt her calf the year before) to be covered, that ſhe might the ſooner be fatted, killed her when fat, and opening the womb, which he found heavy to admiration, ſaw in it a calf, which had begun to have hair, whoſe hinder-legs had no joints, and whoſe tongue was Cerberus-like, *triple,* to each ſide of his mouth one, and one in the middle. Between the fore-legs and the hinder-legs was a great *ſtone,* on which the calf rid. The ſternum, or that part of the breaſt where the ribs lie, was alſo perfect ſtone; and the ſtone, on which it rid, weighed twenty pounds and a half; the outſide of the ſtone was of a greeniſh colour, but ſome ſmall parts being broken off, it appeared a perfect freeſtone. The ſtone according to the letter of Mr. David Thomas, who ſent this account to Mr. Boyle, is with Doctor Haughteyn of Saliſbury, to whom he alſo referreth for further information.

Of the new American Whale-fiſhing about the Bermudas.

THE following Relation is about the new Whale-fiſhing about the Bermudas, as it was delivered by an underſtanding and hardy Seaman, who affirmed he had been at the killing work himſelf. His account, as far as remembered, was this; though hitherto all attempts of maſtering the Whales of thoſe ſeas had been unſucceſsful, by reaſon of the extraordinary fierceneſs and ſwiftneſs of theſe monſtrous animals, yet the enterprize being lately renewed, and ſuch perſons choſen and ſent thither for the work, as were reſolved not to be baffled by a ſea monſter; they did proſper ſo far in this undertaking, that, having been out at Sea, near the ſaid Iſland of Bermudas, ſeventeen times, and faſtened their weapons a dozen times, they killed in theſe expeditions two old female Whales and three cubs, whereof one of the old ones, from the head to the extremity of the tail, was 88 feet in length, by meaſure; its tail being 23 feet broad, the ſwimming fin 26 feet long, and the gills three feet long: having great bends underneath from the noſe to the navel; upon her after part a fin on the back, being within paved (this was the plain Seaman's phraſe) with fat, like the cawl of a hog.

The other old one, he ſaid, was ſome 60 feet long. Of the cubs, one was 33, the other two, much about 25 or 26 feet long.

The ſhape of the fiſh, he ſaid, was very ſharp behind, like the ridge of a houſe: the head pretty bluff, and full of bumps on both ſides, the back perfectly black, and the belly white.

Their celerity and force he affirmed to be wonderful, inſomuch that one of thoſe creatures, which he ſtruck himſelf, towed the boat wherein he was, after him, for the ſpace of ſix or ſeven leagues in a quarter of an hour's time. Being wounded, he ſaith they make a hideous roaring, at which, all of that kind that are within hearing come towards the place where the animal is, yet without ſtriking or doing any harm to the wary.

He added, that they ſtruck one of a prodigious bigneſs, and by gueſs of above 100 feet long. He is of opinion that this fiſh comes neareſt to that ſort of Whales, which they call the *Jubartes*; they are without teeth, and longer than the Greenland Whales, but not ſo thick.

He ſaid further, that they fed much upon graſs growing at the bottom of the ſea, which, he affirmed, was ſeen by cutting up the great bag or maw, wherein he had found in one of them about *two* or *three hogſheads* of a greeniſh graſſy matter. As to the quantity and nature of the oil which they yield, he thought the largeſt of theſe Wales might afford ſeven or eight tuns if well huſbanded, although they had loſt much this firſt time, for want of a good cooper, having brought home but 11 tuns. The cubs by his relation do yield but little, and that is but a kind of jelly. That which the old ones render, doth candy like pork's-greaſe, yet burneth very well. He obſerved that the oil of the blubber is as clear and fair as any whey; but that which is boiled out of the lean, interlarded, becomes as hard as tallow, ſpattering in the burning; and that which is made of the cawl reſembleth hog's greaſe.

One, but ſcarcely credible, quality of this oil he affirms to be, that though it be boiling, yet one may run one's hand into it *without ſcalding*; to which he adds, that it hath a very healing virtue for cuttings, lameneſs, &c. the part affected being anointed therewith. One thing more he related, not to be omitted, which is, that having told that the time of catching theſe fiſhes was from the beginning of March to the end of May, after which time they appeared no more in that part of the ſea; he did, when aſked whither they then retired, give this anſwer; that it was thought they went into the weed beds of the Gulf of Florida, it having been obſerved that upon their fins and tails they have ſtore of clams or barnacles, upon which, he ſaid, rock weed or ſea tangle did grow a yard long, many of them having been taken off them, of the bigneſs of great oyſter ſhells, and hung upon the Governor of Bermudas' pales.

Of a peculiar Lead Ore of Germany, and the Uſe thereof.

THERE was, not long ſince, ſent hither out of Germany from an inquiſitive Phyſician, a liſt of ſeveral minerals and earths of that country and Hungary, together with a ſpecimen of each of them; among which there was a kind of Lead Ore, which is more conſiderable than all the reſt, becauſe of its ſingular uſe for eſſays upon the coppell, ſeeing that there is not any other metal mixed with it. It is found in the Upper Palatinate, at a place called *Freyung*, and there are two ſorts of it, whereof one is a kind of cryſtalline ſtone, and almoſt all good lead, the other not ſo rich, and more farinaceous. By the information coming along with it, they are fetch'd, not from under the ground, but, the mines of that place having lain long neglected, by reason of the wars of Germany and the increase of waters, the people living thereabout, take it from what their forefathers had thrown away, and had lain long in the open air.

A Narrative concerning the Success of Pendulum Watches at Sea for the Longitude.

THE relation lately made by Major Holmes, concerning the success of the Pendulum Watches at sea, (two whereof were committed to his care and observation in his last voyage to Guinea, by some of our eminent virtuosi and grand promoters of navigation) is as followeth:

The said Major having left that coast, and being come to the Isle of St. Thomas under the line, accompanied with four vessels, having there adjusted his Watches, put to sea and sailed westward, 7 or 800 leagues, without changing his course, after which finding the wind favourable, he steered towards the coast of Africa north north east. But having sailed upon that line a matter of 2 or 300 leagues, the masters of the other ships under his conduct, apprehending they should want water before they could reach that coast, did propose to him to steer their course to the Barbadoes, to supply themselves with water there. Whereupon the said Major having called the masters and pilots together, and caused them to produce their journals and calculations, it was found that those pilots did differ in their reckoning from that of the Major, one of them 80 leagues, another about 100, and the third more; but the Major judging by his Pendal Watches that they were only some thirty leagues distance from the Isle of Fuego, which is one of the Isles of Cape Verd, and that they might reach it next day, and having a great confidence in the said Watches, resolved to steer their course thither; and having given orders so to do, they got the very next day about noon a sight of the said Isle of Fuego, finding themselves to sail directly upon it, and so arrived at it that afternoon as he had said. These Watches having been first invented by the excellent Monsieur Christian Hugens of Zulichem, and fitted to go at sea by the Right Honourable the Earl of Kincardin, both Fellows of the ROYAL SOCIETY, are now brought by a new addition to a wonderful perfection. The said Monf. Hugens having been informed of the succefs of the experiment made by Major Holmes, wrote to a friend at Paris a letter to this effect:

" Major Holmes, at his return, hath made a relation concerning the ufefulnefs of Pendulums, which furpaffeth my expectation. I did not imagine that the Watches of this firft ftructure would fucceed fo well, and I had referved my main hopes for the new ones; but feeing that thofe have already ferved fo fuccefsfully, and that the others are yet more juft and exact, I have the more reafon to believe that the invention of *Longitudes* will come to its perfection. In the mean time I fhall tell you that the *States* did receive my propofition when I defired of them a patent for thefe new Watches, and the recompenfe fet apart for the invention in cafes of fuccefs; and that without any difficulty they have granted my requeft, commanding me to bring one of thefe Watches into their Affembly, to explicate unto them the invention, and the application thereof to the Longitudes; which I have done to their contentment. The fame objection that hath been made in your parts againft the exactnefs of thefe *Pendulums*, hath alfo been made here; to wit, that though they fhould agree together, they might fail both of them, by reafon that the air might at one time be thicker than at another. But I have anfwered that this difference, if there be any, will not be at all perceived in the Pendulums, feeing that the continual obfervations, made in winter, from day to day, until fummer, have fhewed me that they have always agreed with the Sun."

The Character, lately publifhed beyond the Seas, of an eminent Perfon, Monf. de Fermat, not long fince dead at Tholoufe, where he was a Councellor of Parliament.

IT is the defervedly famous Monfieur de FERMAT, who was (fays the Author of the Letter) one of the moft excellent men of his age, a genius fo univerfal, and of fo vaft an extent, that if very knowing and learned men had not given teftimony of his extraordinary merit, what can with truth be faid of him would hardly be believed. He entertained a conftant correfpondence with many of the moft illuftrious mathematicians in Europe, and did excel in all parts of mathematical fcience: a teftimony whereof he hath left behind him in the following books.

A Method for the Quadrature of *Parabolas* of all Degrees.

A Book de *Maximis et Minimis*, which ferveth not only for the Determination of Problems of *Plains and Solids*, but alfo for the Invention of *Tangents and Curve Lines*, and of the Centres of Gravity in Solids; and likewife for Numerical Queftions.

An Introduction to the Doctrine of *Plains and Solids*, which is an Analytical Treatife concerning the Solution of Plains and Solids, which had been feen, (as the Advertifer affirms) before Monf. *Des Cartes* had publifhed any thing on the Subject.

A Treatife de *Contactibus Sphæricis*, where he hath demonftrated in Solids what Mr. Viet, Mafter of Requefts, had but demonftrated in Plains.

Another Treatife, wherein he eftablifhes and demonftrates the two Books of *Apollonius Pergæus, of Plains*.

And a General Method for the *Dimenfion of Curve Lines*, &c.

Befides having a perfect knowledge in antiquity, he was confulted from all parts upon the difficulties that did emerge therein: he hath explained abundance of obfcure places, that are found in the ancients. There have been lately printed fome of his obfervations upon Athenæus; and he that hath interpreted Benedetto Caftelli, of the Meafure of Running Waters, hath thence inferted in his work a very handfome one upon an Epiftle of Synefius, which was fo difficult, that the Jefuit Petavius, who hath commented upon this Author, acknowledges that he could not underftand it.

He hath alfo made many obfervations upon Theon of Smyrna, and upon other ancient authors: but moft part of them are not found but fcattered in his Epiftles, becaufe he did not write much upon thefe kinds of fubjects, but to fatisfy the curiofity of his friends.

All thefe Mathematical Works, and all thefe curious Searches in Antiquity, did not hinder this great Virtuofo from difcharging the duties of his place with much affiduity; and with fo much ability, that he hath had the reputation of one of the greateft Civilians of his age.

But that which is moft of all furprifing to many, is, that with all that ftrength of underftanding, which was requifite to make good thefe rare qualities lately mentioned, he had fo polite and delicate parts, that he compofed Latin, French, and Spanifh verfes, with the fame elegance as if he had lived in the time of Auguftus, and paffed the greateft part of his life at the courts of France and Spain.

4

Extract of a Letter, lately written from Rome, touching the late Comet, and a new one.

I CANNOT enough wonder at the ſtrange agreement of the thoughts of that acute French gentleman, Monſieur Auzout, in the Hypotheſis of the Comet's Motion, with mine; and particularly at that of the Tables. I have with the ſame method, whereby I find the motion of this Comet, eaſily found the principle of that Author's Ephemerides, which he then thought not fit to declare; and 'tis this, that this Comet moves about the Great Dog, in ſo great a circle, that that portion, which is deſcribed, is exceeding ſmall in reſpect to the whole circumference thereof, and hardly diſtinguiſhable by us from a ſtraight line.

Concerning the new Comet you mention, I ſaw it on the 11th of February, about the 24th degree of Aries, with a northern latitude of 24 degrees 40 minutes. The cloudy weather hath not yet permitted me to ſee it in Andromeda, as others affirm to have done.

Extract of a Letter, written from Paris, containing ſome Reflections on Part of the precedent Roman Letter.

AS to the Hypotheſis of Geo. Domenico Caſſini, touching the motion of the Comet about the Great Dog in a circle, whoſe centre is in a ſtraight line drawn from the Earth through the ſaid Star, I believe it will ſhortly be publiſhed in print, as a thought I lighted upon in diſcourſing with one of my friends, who did maintain, that it turned about a centre, becauſe that its perigee had been over againſt the Great Dog, as I had noted in my Ephemerides. This particular I did long ſince declare to many of my acquaintance, whereof ſome or other will certainly do me the right, as to let the world know it by the preſs. I have added an obſervation, which I find Signior Caſſini hath not made, *viz.* that there was ground to think, that the Comet of 1652 was the ſame with the preſent, ſeeing that, beſides the parity of the ſwiftneſs of its motion, the perigee thereof was alſo over againſt the Great Dog, if the obſervations extant thereof, deceive not. But, to make it out what ground I had for theſe thoughts, I ſaid, that if they were true, the Comet muſt needs accompliſh its revolution from 12 to 12 years, or thereabouts. But, ſeeing it appears not by hiſtory, that a Comet hath been ſeen at thoſe determinate diſtances of time, nor that over againſt the perigee of all the other Comets, whereof particular obſervations are recorded, are always found ſtars of the firſt magnitude, or ſuch others as are very notable, beſides other reaſons that might be alleged, I ſhall not purſue this ſpeculation; but rather ſuggeſt what I have taken notice of in my reflections upon former Comets, which is, that more of them enter into our ſyſtem by the ſign of Libra and about Spica Virginis, than by all the other parts of the heavens. For both the preſent Comet, and many others regiſtered in hiſtory, have entered that way, and conſequently paſſed out of it by the ſign Aries; by which alſo many have entered.

I did found my Hypotheſis upon three obſervations only, *viz.* thoſe of the 22d, 26th, and 31ſt of December; nor have I done, as ſome have fancied of me, who have been able to obſerve the Comet, the 27th, 28th, 29th, 30th, and 31ſt of December, and to ſee the diminution of its motion, have judged, that I had only determined that diminution for the time to come, conformable to the augmentation thereof in time paſſed until the 29th of December. For January 1ſt, (on which day I compoſed my Ephemerides) I knew not, (nor any perſon here) that the motion of the Comet did diminish; but on the contrary, moſt men believed it was not the ſame Comet. But Signior Caſſini knows very well, that that was not neceſſary, ſeeing that two portions of the tangent being given, and the angles anſwering thereunto, 'tis eaſy to find the poſition and magnitude of its circle. The reaſon which I think the true one, of the diminution of its motion in longitude, and of its retrogradation by me conjectured in my Ephemerides, I began to be aſſured of February the 10th. For until the 6th, the Comet had always advanced, as Signior Caſſini alſo hath very well noted; but after that day, I found that it returned in augmenting always its latitude. And I have conſtantly obſerved it until March the 8th, between many ſtars, which muſt be the ſame with thoſe mentioned by Caſſini, whereof the number was ſo great, that I think I ſaw of them, March the 6th, with one aperture of my glaſs, more than 40 or 50, and eſpecially above the head of Aries; but I did not particularly note the ſituation of more than 12 or 15; amongſt which I have obſerved the poſition of the Comet ſince

January 28th, every day, when the weather did permit, *viz.* January 29th, February 3d, 6th, 10th, 17th, 19th, 24th, 26th, 27th, and March the 6th, 7th, 8th. I left it on March 8 at the 18. of the horn of Aries, almoſt in the ſame latitude; and I am apt to believe it will be eclipſed, which I wiſh I may be able to obſerve this evening, if it be not already paſſed.

If Signior Caſſini hath obſerved it on thoſe days that I have, he will be glad to find the conformity of our obſervations. I ſhall only add, that on February the 3d we were ſurpriſed to ſee the Comet again much brighter than ordinary, and with a conſiderable train. Some did believe that it approached again to us. But having beheld it with a teleſcope, I ſoon ſaid that it was joined with two ſmall ſtars, whereof one was pretty bright, which I had already ſeen, on February the 28th and 29th; and this conjunction gave the Comet that brightneſs, as it happens to moſt of the ſtars of the fifth and ſixth magnitude, where two or three or more are conjoined, which perhaps would ſhow but faintly ſingle, though by reaſon of their proximity to one another they appear but one ſtar. Hence it was that I aſſured my friends here, that the following days we ſhould no more ſee it ſo bright, becauſe I knew that there were none ſuch ſmall bright ſtars in the way, which, by my former obſervations, I conjectured it was to move.

Extract of a Letter, lately written from Venice, by the learned Doctor Walter Pope, to the Reverend Dean of Rippon, Doctor John Wilkins, concerning the Mines of Mercury in Friuli; and a Way of producing Wind by the Fall of Water.

THE Mines of Mercury in Friuli, a territory belonging to the Venetians, are about a day's journey and a half diſtant from Goritia northwards, at a place called Idria, ſituated in a valley of the Julian Alps. They have been, as I am informed, theſe 160 years in the poſſeſſion of the Emperor, and all the inhabitants ſpeak the Sclavonian tongue. In going thither, we travelled ſeveral hours in the beſt wood I ever ſaw before or ſince, being very full of firs, oaks, and beeches, of an extraordinary thickneſs, ſtraightneſs, and height. The town is built, as towns in the Alps uſually are, all of wood, the church only excepted, and another houſe wherein the overſeer liveth. When I was there, in Auguſt laſt, the valley, and the mountains too, out of which the Mercury was dug, were of as pleaſant a verdure as if it had been in the midſt of ſpring, which they there attribute to the moiſtneſs of the Mercury; how truly, I diſpute not. That mine which we went into, the beſt and the greateſt of them all, was dedicated to Saint Barbara, as the other mines are to other Saints. The depth of it was 125 paces, every pace of that country being, as they informed us, more than five of our feet. There are two ways down to it; the ſhorteſt perpendicular way is that whereby they bring up the mineral in great buckets, and by which, oftentimes, ſome of the workmen come up and go down. The other, which is the uſual way, is at the beginning not difficult, the deſcent not being much; the greateſt trouble is, that in ſeveral places you cannot ſtand upright; but this holds not long, before you come to deſcend in earneſt by perpendicular ladders, where the weight of one's body is found very ſenſible. At the end of each ladder there are boards acroſs, where we may breath a little. The ladders, as was ſaid, are perpendicular, but being *imagined produced*, (the words of the Author) do not make one ladder, but ſeveral parallel ones. Being at the bottom, we ſaw no more than what we ſaw before, only the place whence the mineral came. All the way down, and the bottom, where there are ſeveral lanes cut out in the mountain, is lined and propt with great pieces of fir trees, as thick as they can be ſet. They dig the mineral with pickaxes, following the veins: 'tis for the moſt part as hard as a ſtone, but more weighty; of a liver-colour, or that of crocus metallorum. I hope ſhortly to ſhow you ſome of it. There is alſo ſome ſoft earth, in which you plainly ſee the Mercury in little particles. Beſides this, there are oftentimes found in the mines round ſtones like flints, of ſeveral bigneſſes, very like thoſe globes of hair, which I have often ſeen in England, taken out of oxes bellies. There are alſo ſeveral marcaſites and ſtones, which ſeem to have ſpecks of gold in them, but contain none. The manner of getting the Mercury is this: they take of the earth, brought up in baſkets, and put into a ſieve, whoſe bottom is made of wires at ſo great a diſtance, that you may put your finger betwixt them: it is carried to a ſtream of running water, and waſhed as long as any thing will paſs through the ſieve. That earth which paſſeth not, is laid aſide upon another heap: that which paſſeth, reſerved in the hole G, in fig. 1, and taken up again by the ſecond man, and ſo on, to about ten or twelve ſieves proportionably leſs. It often happens in the firſt hole, where the ſecond man takes up his earth, that there is Mercury at the bottom; but towards the farther end, where the intervals of the wires are leſs, 'tis found in very great proportion. The earth laid aſide is pounded, and the ſame operation repeated. The fine ſmall earth, that remains after this, and out of which they can waſh no more Mercury, is put into iron retorts and ſtopt, becauſe it ſhould not fall into the receivers, to which they are luted. The fire forces the Mercury into the receivers: the officer unluted ſeveral of them to ſhow us; I obſerved in all of them, that he firſt poured out perfect Mercury, and after that came a black duſt, which being wetted with water diſcovered itſelf to be Mercury, as the other was. They take the caput mortuum and pound it, and renew the operation as long as they can get any Mercury out of it.

This is the way of producing the Mercury, they call ordinary, which exceeds that which is got by waſhing, in a very great proportion, as you will perceive by the account annexed. All the Mercury got without the uſe of fire, whether by waſhing, or found in the mines, (for in digging, ſome little particles get together, ſo that in ſome places you might take up two or three ſpoonfuls of pure Mercury) is called by them Virgin-Mercury, and eſteemed above the reſt. I enquired of the officer what virtue *that* had more than the other; he told me that making an amalgama of gold and Virgin-Mercury, and putting to the fire, that Mercury would carry away all the gold with it, which common Mercury would not do.

The engines employed in theſe mines are admirable; the wheels, the greateſt that I ever ſaw in my life; one would think as great as the matter would bear: all moved by the dead force of the water, brought thither in no chargeable aqueduct from a mountain, three miles diſtant: the water pumped from the bottom of the mine by 52 pumps, 26 on a ſide, is contrived to move other wheels, for ſeveral other purpoſes.

The labourers work for a julio a day, which is not above ſix or ſevenpence, and endure not long; for, although none ſtay under ground above ſix hours, all of them in time (ſome later, ſome ſooner) become paralytic and die hectic.

We ſaw there a man, who had not been in the mines for above half a year before, ſo full of Mercury, that putting a piece of braſs in his mouth, or rubbing it in his fingers, it immediately became white like ſilver; I mean, he did the ſame effect as if he had rubbed Mercury upon it, and ſo paralytic that he could not, with both his hands, carry a glaſs, half full of wine, to his mouth, without ſpilling it, though he loved it too well to throw it away.

I have been ſince informed, that here in Venice, thoſe that work on the back-ſide of looking-glaſſes are alſo very ſubject to the palſy. I did not obſerve that they had black teeth; it may be, therefore, that we accuſe Mercury unjuſtly for ſpoiling the teeth, when given in venereal diſeaſes. I confeſs I did not think of it upon the place; but black teeth being ſo very rare in this country, I think I could not but have marked it, had theirs been ſo.

They uſe an exceeding great quantity of wood, in making and repairing the engines, and in the furnaces (whereof there are 16, each of them carrying 24 retorts), but principally in the mines, which need continual reparation, the fir trees laſting but a ſmall time under ground. They convey their wood thus: about four miles from the mines, on the ſides of two mountains, they cut down the trees, and draw them into the interjacent valley, higher in the ſame valley, ſo that the trees, according to the deſcent of the water, lie betwixt it and Idria: with vaſt charges and quantities of wood they make a lock or dam, that ſuffers not any water to paſs; they wait afterwards till there be water enough to float theſe trees to Idria: for if there be not a ſpring (as generally there is), rain, or melting of the ſnow, in a ſhort time afford ſo much water, as is ready to run over the dam, and which (the flood-gates being opened) carries all the trees impetuouſly to Idria, where the bridge is built very ſtrong, at very oblique angles to the ſtream, on purpoſe to ſtop them, and throw them on ſhore near the mines.

Theſe mines coſt the Emperor heretofore 70,000 or 80,000 florins yearly, and yielded leſs Mercury than at preſent, although it coſts him but 28,000 florins now. You may ſee what his Imperial Majeſty gets by the following account of what the mines of Idria have produced theſe laſt three years.

1661.		℔	1662.		℔
Ordinary Mercury	-	198,481	Ordinary Mercury	-	225,066
Virgin Mercury	-	6,194	Virgin Mercury	-	9,612
		2574,60			234,678

Fig I. page 17.

Fig. II. page 17.

Fig. III. page 26.

Fig IV. page 27.

Pl. II. Vol. I.

Published as the Act directs by Bunney & Gold, 103, Shoe Lane, 5th June 1802.

1663.		℔
Ordinary Mercury	- - -	244,119
Virgin Mercury	- -	11,862
		255,981

There are always at work 280 perfons, according to the relation I received from a very civil perfon, who informed me alfo of all the other particulars above mentioned, whofe name is Achatio Kappenjager; his office, Contra ferivano per fua Maestà Cefarea in Idria del Mercurio.

To give fome light to this narrative, take this diagramme: A. is the water, C. B. a veffel, into which it runs, D. G. E. H. F. I. are ftreams perpetually iffuing from that veffel; D. E. F. three fieves, the diftance of whofe wires at bottom leffen proportionably; G. the place wherein the earth that paffed through the fieve D. is retained, from whence it is taken by the fecond man, and what paffes through the fieve E. is retained in H. and fo of the reft; K. L. M. wafte water, which is fo much impregnated with Mercury, that it cureth itches and fordid ulcers. See Fig. 1.

I will trefpafs a little more upon you, in defcribing the contrivance of blowing the fire in the brafs-works of Tivoli, near Rome (it being new to me), where the water blows the fire, not by moving the bellows (which is common), but by affording the wind. See Fig. 2. where A. is the river, B. the fall of it, C. the tube into which it falls, L. G. a pipe, G. the orifice of the pipe, F. a ftopper to that hole, D. a place under ground, by which the water runs away. Stopping the hole E. there is a perpetual ftrong wind iffuing forth at G.; and G. being ftopped, the wind comes out fo vehemently at E. that it will, I believe, make a ball play, like that at Frefcati.

An Account of Micrographia, or the Phyfiological Defcriptions of Minute Bodies, made by Magnifying Glaffes.

THE ingenious and knowing author of this treatife, Mr. Robert Hook, confidering with himfelf of what importance a faithful hiftory of Nature is to the eftablifhing of a folid fyftem of Natural Philofophy, and what advantage experimental and mechanical knowledge hath over the philosophy of discourse and disputation, and making it, on that account, his constant business to bring into that vast treasury what portion he can, hath lately published a specimen of his abilities in this kind of study, which certainly is very welcome to the learned and inquisitive world, both for the new *discoveries* in *Nature*, and the new *inventions* of *art*.

As to the former, the attentive reader of this book will find, that there hardly being any thing so small, as by the help of Microscopes to escape our enquiry, a new visible world is discovered by this means, and the earth shows quite a new thing to us, so that in every little particle of its matter we may now behold almost as great a variety of creatures as we were able before to reckon up in the whole universe itself. Here our author maketh it not improbable, but that, by these helps, the subtility of the composition of bodies, the structure of their parts, the various texture of their matter, the instruments and manner of their inward motions, and all the other appearances of things, may be more fully discovered; whence may emerge many admirable advantages towards the enlargement of the active and mechanic part of knowledge, because we may perhaps be enabled to discern the secret workings of Nature, almost in the same manner as we do those that are the productions of art, and are managed by wheels, and engines, and springs, that were devised by human wit. To this end, he hath made a very curious survey of all kinds of bodies, beginning with the point of a needle, and proceeding to the microscopical view of the edges of razors, fine lawn, tabby, watered silks, glass canes, glass drops, fiery sparks, fantastical colours, metalline colours, the figures of sand, gravel in urine, diamonds in flints, frozen figures, the kettering stone, charcoal, wood, and other bodies petrified, the pores of cork, and of other substances; vegetables growing on blighted leaves, blue mould, and mushrooms; sponges and other fibrous bodies, sea-weed, the surfaces of some leaves, the stinging points of a nettle, cowage, the beard of a wild oat, the seed of the corn violet, as also of thyme, poppy, and purslane. He continues to describe hair, the scales of a soal, the sting of a bee, feathers in general, and in particular those of peacocks, the feet of flies and other insects, the wings and head of a fly, a water insect, the teeth of a snail, the eggs of silk-worms, the blue fly, a water insect, the tufted gnat, a white moth, the ſhepherd's ſpider, the hunting ſpider, the ant, the wandering mite, the crab-like inſect, the book-worm, the flea, the louſe, mites, vine mites. He concludeth with taking occaſion to diſcourſe of two or three very conſiderable ſubjects, viz. the inflection of rays of lights in the air; the fixed ſtars; the moon.

In repreſenting theſe particulars to the Reader's view, the author hath not only given proof of his ſingular ſkill in delineating all ſorts of bodies (he having drawn all the ſchemes of theſe 60 microſcopical objects with his own hand), and of his extraordinary care of having them curiouſly engraven by the maſters of that art, but he hath alſo ſuggeſted in the ſeveral reflections made upon theſe objects, ſuch conjectures as are likely to excite and quicken the philoſophical heads to very noble contemplations. Here are found inquiries concerning the *Propagation* of *Light* through differing mediums, concerning gravity, the roundneſs of fruits, ſtones, and divers artificial bodies; concerning ſpringineſs, and tenacity; concerning the original of fountains, the diſſolution of bodies into liquors, filteration, the aſcent of juices in vegetables, and the uſe of their pores. Here an attempt is made to ſolve the ſtrange phænomena of graſs-drops; experiments are alleged to prove the expanſion of glaſs by heat, and the contraction of heated glaſs upon cooling. Des Cartes's hypotheſis of colours is examined; the cauſe of colours, moſt likely to the author, is explained; reaſons are produced, that reflection is not neceſſary to produce colours, nor a double refraction; ſome conſiderable hypotheſes are offered for the explication of light by motion, for the producing of all colours by refraction, for reducing all ſorts of colours to two only, yellow and blue, for making the air a diſſolvent of all combuſtible bodies, and for the explicating of all the regular figures of ſalt, where he alleges many notable inſtances of the mathematics of Nature, as having even in thoſe things which we account vile, rude, and coarſe, ſhewed abundance of curioſity, and excellent geometry and mechaniſm. And here he opens a large field for inquiries, and propoſes models for proſecuting them, &c. &c. And laſtly the author concludes theſe, and many other his curious and extenſive inveſtigations, by obſerving, that there may be found many mechanical inventions to improve our ſenſes of hearing, ſmelling, taſting, and touching, as well as we have improved that of ſeeing by optic glaſſes.

Some Obſervations and Experiments upon May-Dew.

THAT ingenious and inquiſitive gentleman, Maſter Thomas Henſhaw, having had occaſion to make uſe of a great quantity of May-Dew, did by ſeveral caſual eſſays on the ſubject, make the following obſervations and trials, and preſent them to the ROYAL SOCIETY.

That dew newly gathered and filtered through a clean linen cloth, though it be not very clear, is of a yellowiſh colour, ſomewhat approaching to that of urine. That having endeavoured to putrefy it by putting ſeveral proportions into glaſs bottles, with blind heads, and ſetting them in ſeveral heats, as of dung, and gentle baths, he quite failed of his intention: for heat, though never ſo gentle, did rather clarify and preſerve it ſweet, though continued for two months together, than cauſe any putrefaction or ſeparation of parts.

That expoſing of it to the ſun for a whole ſummer, in glaſſes that hold about two gallons, with narrow mouths, that might be ſtopped with cork, the only conſiderable alteration he obſerved to be produced in it, was, that ſtore of green ſtuff (ſuch as is ſeen in ſummer in ditches and ſtanding waters) floated on the top, and, in ſome places, grew to the ſides of the glaſs.

That putting four or five gallons of it into a half tub, as they call it, of wood, and ſtraining a canvas over it, to keep out duſt and inſects, and letting it ſtand in ſome ſhady room for three weeks or a month, it did of itſelf putrefy, and ſtink exceedingly, and let fall to the bottom ſediment like mud.

That, coming often to ſee what alterations appeared in the putrefaction, he obſerved, that at the beginning, within twenty-four hours, a ſlimy film floated on the top of the water, which after a while falling to the bottom, there came another ſuch film in its place.

That if Dew were put into a long narrow veſſel of glaſs, ſuch as formerly were uſed for receivers in diſtilling of aqua fortis, the ſlime would riſe to that height, that he could take it off with a ſpoon; and when he had put a pretty quantity of it into a drinking glaſs, and that it had ſtood all night, and the water drained from it, if he had turned it out of his hand, it would ſtand upright in figure of the glaſs, in ſubſtance like buoyed white ſtarch, though ſomething more tranſparent.

That having once gotten a pretty quantity of this jelly, and put it into a glaſs-body and blind head, he ſet it into a gentle bath, with an intention to have putrefied it; but after a few days he found the head not being well luted on, and that the moiſture exhaling, the jelly was grown almoſt dry, and a large muſhroom grown out of it within the glaſs. It was of a looſe wateriſh contexture, ſuch an one as he had ſeen growing out of rotten wood.

That having ſeveral tubs with good quantity of dew in them, ſet to putrefy in the manner aboveſaid, and coming to pour out one of them to make uſe of it, he found in the water a great bunch, bigger than his fiſt, of thoſe inſects, commonly called hog-lice or millepedes, tangled together by their long tails, one of which came out of every one of their bodies, about the bigneſs of horſe-hair: the inſects did all live and move after they were taken out.

That emptying another tub, whereon the ſun, it ſeems, had uſed ſometimes to ſhine, he found, upon ſtraining it through a clean linen cloth, two or three ſpoonfuls of green ſtuff, though not ſo thick nor ſo green as that above mentioned, found in the glaſſes purpoſely expoſed to the ſun. He put this green ſtuff in a glaſs, and tied a paper over it, and coming ſome days after to view it, he found the glaſs almoſt filled with an innumerable company of ſmall flies, almoſt all wings, ſuch as are uſually ſeen in great ſwarms in the air in ſummer evenings.

That ſetting about a gallon of this dew, which had been firſt putrefied and ſtrained, in an open jar-glaſs with a wide mouth, and leaving it for many weeks ſtanding in a ſouth window, on which the ſun lay very much, but the caſements were kept very cloſe ſhut; after ſome time, coming to take account of his dew, he found it very full of little inſects with great heads and ſmall tapering bodies, ſomewhat reſembling tadpoles, but very much leſs. Theſe on his approach to the glaſs would ſink down to the bottom, as it were to hide themſelves, and upon his retreat wriggle themſelves up to the top of the water again. Leaving it thus for ſome time longer, he afterwards found the room very full of gnats, though the door and windows were kept ſhut. He adds, that he did not at firſt ſuſpect that thoſe gnats had any relation to the dew, but after finding the gnats to be multiplied, and the little watery animals to be much leſſened in quantity, and finding great numbers of their empty ſkins floating on the face of his dew, he thought he had juſt reaſon to perſuade himſelf, the gnats were by a ſecond birth produced of thoſe little animals.

That vapouring away great quantities of his putrefied dew in glaſs baſons and other earthen glaſed veſſels, he did at laſt obtain above two pounds of grayiſh earth, which, when he had waſhed with more of the ſame dew out of all his baſons into one, and vapoured to ſiccity, lay in leaves one above the other, not unlike ſome kind of brown paper, but very friable.

That taking this earth out, and after he had well ground it on a marble, and given it a ſmart fire, in a coated retort of glaſs, it ſoon melted and became a cake in the bottom when it was cold, and looked as if it had been ſalt and brimſtone, in a certain proportion, melted together; but was not at all inflammable. This ground again on a marble, did turn ſpring water of a reddiſh purple colour.

That by often calcining and filtering this earth, he did at laſt extract about two ounces of a fine ſmall white ſalt, which, looked on through a microſcope, ſeemed to have ſides and angles in the number and figure, as rochpetre.

A Way of killing Rattleſnakes.

THERE being not long ſince occaſion given at a meeting of the ROYAL SOCIETY to diſcourſe of Rattleſnakes, that worthy and inquiſitive gentleman, Captain Silas Taylor, related the manner how they were killed in Virginia, which he afterwards was pleaſed to give in writing, atteſted by two credible perſons, in whoſe preſence it was done; which is as follows:—

The wild *pennyroyal* or dittany of Virginia, groweth ſtraight up about one foot high, with the leaves like pennyroyal, with little blue tufts at the joining of the branches to the plant, the colour of the leaves being a reddiſh green, but the water diſtilled of the colour of brandy, of a fair yellow; the leaves of it bruiſed, are very hot and biting upon the tongue, and of thoſe ſo bruiſed, they took ſome, and having tied them in a cleft of a long ſtick, they held them to the noſe of the Rattleſnake, who, by turning and wriggling laboured as much as ſhe could to avoid it; but ſhe was killed with it in leſs than half an hour's time, and, as was ſuppoſed, by the ſcent thereof;

which was done anno 1657, in the month of July, at which ſeaſon they repute thoſe creatures to be in the greateſt vigour for their poiſon.

It is alſo obſerved that where the wild *pennyroyal* or dittany grows, no Rattleſnakes are obſerved to come.

A Relation of ſome extraordinary Tides in the Weſt Iſles of Scotland, Communicated by Sir Robert Moray.

IN that tract of iſles on the weſt of Scotland, called by the inhabitants the Long Iſland, as being about 100 miles long, from north to ſouth, there is a multitude of ſmall iſlands, ſituated in a fretum or frith, that paſſes between the iſland of Euſt and the Herries; among which there is one called Berneray, ſome three miles long and more than a mile broad, the length running from eaſt to weſt as the frith lies. At the eaſt end of this iſland, where I ſtaid ſome 16 or 17 days, I obſerved a very ſtrange reciprocation of the flux and reflux of the ſea, and heard of another no leſs remarkable.

Upon the weſt ſide of the Long Iſland, the Tides which came from the ſouth-weſt run along the coaſt northward, ſo that during the ordinary courſe of the Tides, the flood runs eaſt in the frith where Berneray lies, and the ebb weſt; and thus the ſea ebbs and flows orderly, ſome four days before the full moon and change, and as long after (the ordinary Spring Tides riſing from 14 or 15 feet upright, and all the reſt proportionably, as in other places), but afterwards, ſome four days before the quarter moons, and as long after, there is conſtantly a great and ſingular variation. For then (a ſoutherly moon making there a full ſea), the courſe of the Tide being eaſtward when it begins to flow, which is about half paſt nine of the clock, not only continues ſo till about half paſt three in the afternoon, that it be high water, but after it begins to ebb, the current runs on ſtill eaſtward during the whole ebb; ſo that it runs eaſtward 12 hours together, that is all day long, from about half paſt nine in the morning till half paſt nine at night. But when the night Tide begins to flow, the current turns, and runs weſtward all night, during both flood and ebb, for ſome 12 hours more, as it did eaſtward the day before. And thus the reciprocations continue, one flood and ebb running 12 hours eaſtward, and another 12 hours weſtward, till about four days before the new and full moon; and then they reſume their regular ordinary courſe as before, running eaſt during the ſix hours of flood, and weſt during the ſix of ebb. And this I obſerved curiouſly, during my abode upon the place, which was in the month of Auguſt, as I remember.

But the gentleman to whom the iſland belongs at preſent, and divers of his brothers and friends, knowing and diſcreet perſons, and expert in all ſuch parts of ſea matters as other iſlanders commonly are, though I ſhrewdly ſuſpected their ſkill in Tides, when I had not ſeen what they told me and have now related, of the irregular courſes of the Tides, did moſt confidently aſſure me, and ſo did every body I ſpake with about it, that there is yet another irregularity in the Tides, which never fails, and is no leſs extraordinary than what I have been mentioning; which is, that whereas between the vernal and autumnal equinoxes, that is for ſix months together, the courſe of irregular Tides about the quarter moons is to run all day, that is 12 hours, as from about $9\frac{1}{2}$ to $9\frac{1}{13}$, $10\frac{1}{4}$ to $10\frac{1}{4}$, &c. eaſtward, and all night, that is 12 hours more, weſtward; during the other months from the autumnal to the vernal equinox, the current runs all day weſtward, and all night eaſtward.

Of this, though I had not the opportunity to be an eye witneſs as of the other, yet I do not at all doubt, having received ſo credible information of it.

To penetrate into the cauſes of theſe ſtrange reciprocations of the Tides would require exact deſcriptions of the ſituation, ſhape, and extent of every piece of the adjacent coaſts of Euſt and Herries; the rocks, ſands, ſhelves, promontories, bays, lakes, depths, and other circumſtances, which I cannot now ſet down with any certainty or accurateneſs, ſeeing they are to be found in no map, neither had I any opportunity to ſurvey them; nor do they now occur to my memory, as they did ſome years ago, when upon occaſion, I ventured to make a map of this whole frith of Berneray, which, not having copied, I cannot adventure to beat it out again.

An Account how Adits and Mines are wrought at Liege, without Air Shafts. Communicated by Sir Robert Moray.

IT is well known to thoſe converſant in mines, that there is nothing of greater inconvenience in working, or driving, as they call it, of Mines or Adits under ground for carrying away of water, or ſuch minerals as the Mine affords, than the damp, want, and impurity of air that occur, when ſuch Adits are wrought or driven inward upon a level, or near it, 20, 30, or 40 fathom, more or leſs; as well becauſe of the expence of money, as of time alſo, in the ordinary way of preventing or remedying theſe inconveniences; which is, by letting down Shafts from the *day* (as miners ſpeak), to meet with the Adit; by which means the Air hath liberty to play through the whole work, and ſo takes away bad vapours and furniſhes good Air for reſpiration. The expence of which Shafts, in regard to their vaſt depth, hardneſs of the rock, drawing of water, &c. doth ſome times equal, yea exceed, the ordinary charge of the whole Adit.

Amongſt the expedients that have been deviſed to remedy this, there is one practiſed in the Coal Mines near the town of Liege (or Luyck), that ſeems preferable to all others for efficacy, eaſe, and cheapneſs; the deſcription whereof followeth:—

At the mouth or entry of the Adit there is a ſtructure raiſed of brick, like a chimney, ſome 28 or 30 foot high in all, at the bottom two oppoſite ſides are (or may be), ſome five foot and half broad; and the other two five foot, the wall one brick and a half thick. At the lower part of it is a hole ſome nine or ten inches ſquare, for taking out the aſhes, which, when it is done, this aſh-hole is immediately ſtopped ſo cloſe, as air cannot poſſibly get in at any part of it. Then, ſome three foot above ground or more, there is on that ſide that is next to the Adit or Pit, a ſquare hole of eight or nine inches every way, by which the air enters to make the fire burn; into this hole there is fixed a ſquare tube or pipe of wood, whereof the joints and clinks are ſo ſtopped with parchment, paſted or glued upon them, that the air can no where get into the pipe but at the end; and this pipe is ſtill lengthened as the Adit or Pit advanceth, by fitting the new pipes ſo, as one end is always thruſt into the other, and the joints and chinks ſtill carefully cemented and ſtopped as before. So the pipe or tube being ſtill carried on as near as is neceſſary, to the wall or place where freſh Air is requiſite, the fire within the chimney doth ſtill attract (ſo to ſpeak), Air through the tube, without which it cannot burn, which yet it will do, as is obvious to conceive (all illuſtrations and philoſophical explications being here ſuperfluous), and ſo, while the Air is drawn by the fire from the fartheſt or moſt inward part of the Mine or Adit, freſh Air muſt needs come in from without to ſupply the place of the other, which by its motion doth carry away with it all the ill vapours that breath out of the ground; by which means the whole Adit will be always filled with fresh Air, so that men will there breathe as surely as abroad, and not only candles burn, but fire, when upon occasion there is use for it for breaking of the rock.

Now that there may be no want of such fresh Air, the fire must always be kept burning in the chimney, or at least as frequently as is necessary; for which purpose there must be two of the iron grates or chimnies, that when any accident befalls the one, the other may be ready to be in its place, the coals being first well kindled in it, but when the fire is near spent, the chimney or grate being hauled up to the door is to be supplied with fresh fuel.

The figure of the fabrick, chimney, and all the parts thereof, being hereunto annexed, the rest will be easily understood.

FIGURE 3. *Plate* II.

A. The hole for taking out the ashes.

B. The square hole into which the tube or pipe for conveying the Air is to be fixed.

C. The border or ledge of brick or iron, upon which the iron grate or cradle that holds the burning coals is to rest, the one being exactly fitted to the other.

D. The hole where the cradle is set.

E. The wooden tube through which the air is conveyed towards the cradle.

F. The door by which the grate or cradle is let in, which is to be set eight or ten foot higher than the hole D, and the shutter made of iron or wood that will not shrink, that it may shut very close; this door being made large enough to receive the cradle with ease.

G. The grate or cradle, which is narrower below than above, that the ashes may the more easily fall and the air excite the fire, the bottom being barred as the sides.

H. The border or ledge of the cradle that rests upon the ledge C.

I. Four chains of iron fastened to the four corners of the cradle, for taking it up and letting it down.

K. The chain of iron to which the others are fastened.

L. The pulley of iron or brass through which the chain passeth.

M. A hook on which the end of the chain is faftened by a ring, the hook fixed being placed in the fide of the door.

N. A bar of iron in the wall, to which the pulley is faftened.

The higher the fhaft of the chimney is, the fire draws the air the better; and this invention may be made ufe of in the Pits or Shafts that are perpendicular, or anywife inclining towards it, when there is want of frefh Air at the bottom thereof, or any moleftation by unwholefome fumes or vapours.

Obfervables upon a Monftrous Head (*Fig.* 4.)

THIS was the *Head of a Colt*, reprefented in Fig. 4. firft viewed by Mr. Boyle, who went into the ftable where the Colt lay, and got the Head haftily and rudely cut off, the body thereof appearing to his eye completely formed, without any monftrofity to be taken notice of in it. Afterwards he caufed it to be put into a veffel, and covered with fpirits of wine, thereby chiefly intending to give good example, together with a proof, that by the help of the faid fpirit (which he had recommended for fuch properties in one of his Effays of the Ufefulnefs of Natural Philofophy), the parts of animals, and even monfters, may, in fummer itfelf, be preferved long enough to afford anatomifts the opportunities of examining them.

The head being opened and examined, it was found:

Firft, That it had no fign of any nofe in the ufual place, nor had it any, in any other place of the head, unlefs the double bag C. C. that grew out of the midft of the forehead, were fome rudiment of it.

Next, that the two eyes were united into one double eye, which was placed juft in the middle of the brow, the nofe being wanting, which fhould have feparated them, whereby the two eye-holes in the fcull were united into one very large round hole, into the midft of which, from the brain, entered one pretty large optic nerve, at the end of which grew a great double eye; that is, that membrane called felcrotis, which contained both, was one and the fame, but feemed to have a feam by which they were joined, to go quite round it, and the fore, or pellucid part, was diftinctly feparated into two corners by a white feam that divided them. Each corner feemed to have its iris (or rainbow-like circle), and apertures or pupils, diftinct; and upon opening the corner, there was found within it, two balls or cryſtalline humours, very well ſhaped, but the other parts of it could not be ſo well diſtinguiſhed, becauſe the eye had been much bruiſed by the handling, and the inner parts confuſed and diſlocated. It had four eye-brows, placed in the manner expreſſed in Fig. 4. by *a a*, *b b*; *a a*, repreſenting the lower, and *b b*, the upper eye-lids.

Laſtly, That juſt above the eyes, as it were, in the midſt of the forehead, was a very deep depreſſion, and out of the midſt of that grew a kind of double purſe or bag, C C, containing little or nothing in it; but to ſome it ſeemed to be a production of the matter deſigned for the noſe, but diverted by this monſtrous conception; perhaps the proceſſus mammillares joined into one, and covered with a thin hairy ſkin.

Of the Nature of a certain Stone found in the Indies in the Head of a Serpent.

THERE was ſome while ago ſent by Sir Philiberto Vernatti from Java Major, where he reſides, to Sir Robert Moray, for the Repoſitory of the ROYAL SOCIETY, a certain ſtone, affirmed by the preſenter to be found in the head of a Snake, which laid upon *any* wound made by *any* venomous creature, is ſaid to ſtick to it, and draw away all the poiſon; and then being put in milk, to void its poiſon therein, and to make the milk turn blue, in which manner it muſt be uſed till the wound is cleanſed.

The like relations having been made by ſeveral others, of ſuch a ſtone, and ſome alſo in this city affirming to have made the experiment with ſucceſs, it was thought worth while to enquire further into the truth of this matter; ſince which time nothing hath been met with but an information delivered by that ingenious Pariſian Monſieur *Thevenot*, in his ſecond tome of the Relations of divers conſiderable Voyages, whereof he lately preſented ſome examples to his friends in England. The book being in French, and not common, it is conceived it will not be amiſs to inſert here the ſaid information, which is to this effect:—

" In the Eaſt Indies, and in the kingdom of Quamſy, in China, there is found a ſtone in the head of certain ſerpents (which they call by a name ſignifying *Hairy Serpents*), which heals the bitings of the ſame ſerpent, that elſe would kill in 24 hours. This ſtone is round, white in the middle, and about the edges blue or greeniſh. Being applied to the wound it adheres to it of itſelf, and falls not off but after it hath ſucked the poiſon. Then they waſh it in milk, wherein it is left awhile till it return to its natural condition. It is a rare ſtone, for if it be put a ſecond time upon the wound, and ſtick to it, it is a ſign it had not ſucked all the venom during its firſt application; but if it ſtick not, it is a mark that all poiſon was drawn out at firſt." So far our French author, wherein there appears no conſiderable difference from the written relation before mentioned.

An Experiment of a Way of preparing a Liquor that ſhall ſink into and colour the whole Body of Marble; cauſing a Picture drawn on the Surface to appear alſo in the inmoſt Parts of the Stone.

THIS Experiment is taken from the *Mundus Subterraneus,* of Athanaſius Kircher, who having ſeen ſome ſtones reputed to be natural, that had moſt lively pictures not only upon them, but paſſing through their whole ſubſtance, and finding an artiſt ſkilful to perform ſuch rare workmanſhip, did not only pronounce ſuch ſtones to be artificial, but when that artiſt was unwilling to communicate to him his ſecret, did join his ſtudies and endeavours with one Albertus Gunter, a Saxon, to find it out themſelves; wherein having ſucceeded, it ſeems they made the experiments, which this induſtrious and communicative Jeſuit delivers in this manner:—

The colours, ſaith he, are thus prepared: I take of aqua fortis and aqua regis, two oz. ana; of ſal ammoniac, one oz. of the beſt ſpirits of wine, two drachms; as much gold as can be had for nine julios (a julio being about ſixpence Engliſh); of pure ſilver, two drachms. Theſe things being provided, let the ſilver, when calcined, be put into a phial; and having poured upon it the two drachms of aqua fortis, let it evaporate, and you ſhall have a water yielding firſt a blue colour and afterwards a black. Likewiſe put the gold when calcined, into a phial, and having poured the aqua regis upon it, ſet it by to evaporate; then put the ſpirit of wine upon the ſal ammoniac, leaving it alſo to be evaporated; and you will have a golden coloured water, which will afford you divers colours. And after this manner you may extract many tinctures of colours out of other metals. This done you may by the means of theſe two waters, paint what picture you pleaſe upon white marble of the ſofter kind, renewing the figure every day for ſeveral days, with ſome freſh ſuperadded liquor, and you ſhall find in time that the picture hath penetrated the whole ſolidity of the ſtone, so that cutting it into as many parts as you will, it will always represent unto you the ſame figure on both ſides.

So far he, which how far it anſwers expectation is referred to the trial of ingenious artiſts; in the mean time there are not wanting experienced men who ſcruple the effect; but yet are far from pronouncing any thing poſitively againſt it, ſo that they do not diſcourage any that have conveniences, from trying.

But whether the way there mentioned, will ſucceed or not, according to expectation; ſure it is, that a ſtone-cutter in Oxford, Mr. Bird, hath many years ſince found out a way of doing the ſame thing in effect that is here mentioned, and hath practiſed it for many years. That is, he is able ſo to apply a colour to the outſide of poliſhed marble, as that it ſhall ſink a conſiderable depth into the body of the ſtone, and there repreſent like figures or images as thoſe are on the outſide (deeper or ſhallower according as he continues the operation a leſſer or a longer while), of which kind there be divers pieces to be ſeen in Oxford, London, and elſewhere, and ſome of them being ſhowed to his Majeſty ſoon after his happy reſtoration, they were broken in his preſence, and found to anſwer expectation; and others may be daily ſeen by any who is curious or deſirous to ſee it.

An Account of the Riſe and Attempts of a Way to convey Liquors immediately into the Maſs of the Blood.

WHEREAS there have lately appeared in public ſome books, printed beyond the ſeas, treating of the injecting Liquors into Veins; in which books the original of that invention ſeems to be aſcribed to others beſides him to whom it really belongs. It will ſurely not be thought amiſs, if ſomething be ſaid whereby the true inventor's right may, beyond exception, be aſſerted and preſerved; to which end, there will need no more than barely to repreſent the *time when*, and the *place where*, and amongſt *whom*, it was *firſt* ſtarted and put to trial. To join all theſe circumſtances together, it is notorious, that at leaſt ſix years ſince (a good while before it was heard of that any one did pretend to have ſo much as thought of it), the learned and ingenious Doctor Chriſtopher Wren, did propoſe, in the Univerſity of Oxford (where he now is the worthy Savilian Profeſſor of

Aſtronomy, and where very many curious perſons are ready to atteſt this relation), to that noble benefactor to Experimental Philoſophy, Mr. Robert Boyle, Doctor Wilkins, and other deſerving perſons, that he thought he could eaſily contrive a way to convey any liquid thing immediately into the Maſs of Blood: *viz.* by making ligatures on the veins, and then opening them on the ſide of the ligature towards the heart, and by putting into them ſlender ſyringes or quills, faſtened to bladders (in the manner of clyſter-pipes), containing the matter to be injected; performing that operation upon pretty big and lean dogs, that the veſſels might be large enough and eaſily acceſſible.

This propoſition being made, Mr. Boyle ſoon gave order for an apparatus to put it to experiment; wherein at ſeveral times, upon ſeveral dogs, opium and the infuſion of crocus metallorum, were injected into that part of the hind-legs of thoſe animals, whence the larger veſſels that carry the blood, are moſt eaſy to be taken hold of. Whereof the ſucceſs was, that the opium being ſoon circulated into the brain, did within a ſhort time ſtupify, though not kill the dog; but a large doſe of crocus metallorum made another dog vomit up life and all. All which is more amply and circumſtantially delivered by Mr. Boyle, in his excellent book of the *Uſefulneſs* of *Experimental Philoſophy*, Part II. Eſſay 2. page 53, 54, 55. Where it is alſo mentioned, that the fame of this invention and of the ſucceeding trials being ſpread, and particularly coming to the knowledge of a foreign *Ambaſſador* that was curious, and then reſided in London, it was by him tried with ſome crocus metallorum upon a malefactor, that was an inferior ſervant of his, with this ſucceſs, that the fellow, as ſoon as ever the injection was began to be made, did, either really or craftily, fall into a ſwoon: whereby, being unwilling to proſecute ſo hazardous an experiment, they deſiſted, without ſeeing any other effect of it, ſave that it was told the Ambaſſador that it wrought once downwards with him. Since which time it hath been frequently practiſed both in Oxford and London, as well before the ROYAL SOCIETY, as elſewhere. And particularly that learned phyſician Doctor Timothy Clerk, hath made it part of his buſineſs to purſue thoſe experiments with much induſtry, great accurateneſs, and conſiderable obſervations thereon; which above two years ſince were by him produced and read before the ROYAL SOCIETY, who thereupon deſired him, as one of their Members, to complete what he had propofed to himfelf upon that fubject, and then to publifh the fame; the effect whereof, it is hoped, will now fhortly appear, and not prove unwelcome to the curious. Some whereof, though they may conceive that liquors thus injected into veins without preparation and digeftion, will make odd commotions in the blood, difturb nature, and caufe ftrange fymptoms in the body, yet they have other thoughts of liquors, that are prepared of fuch things as have paffed the digeftion of the ftomach; for example, of fpirit of wine, of hartfhorn, of blood, &c. And they hope likewife, that befide the medical ufes that may be made of this invention, it may alfo ferve for anatomical purpofes, by filling, after this way, the veffels of an animal as full as they can hold, and by exceedingly diftending them, difcover *new* veffels, &c. But now, to enlarge upon the ufes, the reader may fecurely take this narrative, as the naked and real matter of fact, whereby it is clear as noon day (both from the time and irrefragible teftimony of very many confiderable perfons in that Univerfity, who can jointly atteft it, as well as from that particular unqueftionable one of Mr. Boyle and his worthy company, who were the firft eye-witneffes of the trials made), that to Oxford, and in it, to Doctor Chriftopher Wren, this invention is due, and confequently, that all others who difcourfe or write of it, do either derive from him, or are fallen upon the fame device feveral years after him.

Some Obfervations of Swarms of ftrange Infects, and the Mifchiefs done by them.

A GREAT obferver, who hath lived long in New England, did, upon occafion, relate to a friend of his in London, where he lately was, that fome few years fince there was fuch a fwarm of a certain fort of Infects in that Englifh colony, that for the fpace of 200 miles they poifoned and deftroyed all the trees of that country; there being found innumerable little holes in the ground, out of which thofe Infects broke forth in the form of maggots, which turned into flies that had a kind of tail or fting, which they ftuck into the tree, and thereby envenomed and killed it.

The like plague is faid to happen frequently in the country of the Cofacks, or Ukrani, where, in dry fummers, they are infefted with fuch fwarms of locufts, driven thither by an eaft or fouth-eaft wind, that they darken the air in the faireft weather, and devour all the corn of that country; laying their eggs in autumn and then dying; but the eggs, of which every one layeth 2 or 300, hatching the next fpring, produce again fuch a number of locufts, that then they do far more mifchief than afore, unlefs rains do fall, which kill both eggs and the infects themfelves, or unlefs a ftrong north or north-weft wind arife, which drives them into the Euxine Sea. The hogs of that country, loving thefe eggs, devour alfo great quantities of them, and thereby help to purge the land of them, which is often fo molefted by this vermin, that they enter into their houfes and beds, fall upon their tables, and into their meat, infomuch that they can hardly eat without taking down fome of them; in the night when they repofe themfelves upon the ground, they cover it three or four inches think, and if a wheel pafs over them, they emit a ftench hardly to be endured; all which, and much more may be feen in the French Defcription of the Countries of Poland, made by Monf. de Beauplan, and by Monf. Thevenot, in his Relation of the Cofacks, contained in the firft part of his curious Voyages.

Some Obfervations of Vipers.

A CURIOUS Italian, called Francefco Redi, having lately had an opportunity by the great number of Vipers brought to the Grand Duke of Tufcany, for the compofing of *Theriac* or Treacle, to examine what is vulgarly delivered and believed concerning the poifon of thefe creatures, hath (according to the account given of it in the French Journal des Sçavans, printed January 4, 166⅚,) performed his undertaking with much exactnefs, and publifhed in an Italian tract, not yet come into England, thefe obfervations.

1. He hath obferved that the poifon of Vipers is neither in their *Teeth*, nor in their *Tail*, nor in their *Gall*; but in the two *Veficles or Bladders*, which cover their teeth, and which, coming to be compreffed when the Vipers bite, do emit a certain yellowifh liquor, that runs along the teeth and poifons the wound. Whereof he gives this proof, that he hath rubbed the wounds of many animals with the gall of Vipers and pricked them with

with their teeth, and yet no confiderable ill accident followed upon it, but that as often as he rubbed the wounds with the faid yellow liquor, not one of them efcaped.

2. Whereas commonly it hath hitherto been believed that the poifon of Vipers being fwallowed was prefent death; this Author after many reiterated experiments is faid to have obferved, that in Vipers, there is neither humour, nor excrement, nor any part, nor the *Gall* itfelf, that, being taken into the body, kills. And he affures that he hath feen men eat, and hath often made brute animals fwallow all that is efteemed moft poifonous in a Viper, yet without the leaft mifchief to them. Whence he fhews that it needs not fo much to be wondered at that certain empirics fwallow the juice of the moft venomous animals without receiving any harm thereby, adding, that, which is afcribed to the virtue of their antidote, ought to be attributed to the nature of thofe kinds of poifons, which are no poifons when they are fwallowed, but only when they are put into wounds, for which doctrine he alleges Celfus, which has alfo been noticed by Lucan, who introduces Cato thus fpeaking:

> Noxia Serpentum eft admifto Sanguine Peftis,
> *Morfu* Virus habent, et fatum *dente* minantur;
> *Pocula* Morte carent.

And what alfo fome authors have affirmed, *viz.* that it is mortal to eat of the flefh of creatures killed by Vipers, or to drink of the wine wherein Vipers have been drowned, or to fuck the wounds that have been made by them, is by this author obferved to be wide of truth. For he affures that many perfons have eaten pullets and pigeons bitten by Vipers without finding any alteration from it in their health. On the contrary, he declares it a fovereign remedy againft the biting of Vipers to fuck the wound; alleging an experiment made upon a dog, which he caufed to be bitten by a Viper at the nofe, who, by licking his own wound, faved his life: which he confirms by the example of thofe people celebrated in hiftory by the name of *Marfi* and *Pfilli*, whofe employment it was to heal thofe that had been bitten by ferpents by fucking their wounds.

3. He adds, that though Galen and many modern phyficians do affirm that there is nothing which caufeth fo much thirft as Viper's flefh, yet he hath experimented the contrary, and known divers perfons who did eat

the flesh of Vipers at all their meals, and yet did assure him they never were less dry than when they observed that kind of diet.

4. As for the Salt of Vipers, whereof some chemists have so great esteem, he saith it hath no purging virtue at all in it, adding, that even of *all Salts* none hath more virtue than another, as he pretends to shew in another book of his De Naturâ Salium, which hath also not been transmitted into these parts.

5. He denies what Aristotle assures, and what Galen saith to have often tried, that the spittle of a fasting person kills Vipers, and he laughs at many other particulars that have been delivered concerning the antipathy of Vipers unto certain things, and their manner of conception and generation, and several other properties commonly ascribed to them, which the French author affirms to be refuted by so many experiments made by this Italian philosopher, that it seems to him there is no place left for doubting after so authentic a testimony.

Note. Several have taken notice that there is a difference between the brooding of Snakes and Vipers, those laying their eggs in dunghills, by whose warmth they are hatched; but these (Vipers) brooding their eggs within their bellies and bringing forth live Vipers. To which may be added, that some affirm to have seen snakes lie upon their eggs as hens do upon theirs.

Extract of a Letter, written from Holland, about preserving of Ships from being Worm eaten.

THIS Extract is borrowed from the French Journal des Sçavans, of Feb. 15, 1666, and is here inserted to excite inventive here to overtake the Proposer in Holland.—The letter runs thus:—

Although you have visited our port (Amsterdam) I know not whether you have noted the ill condition our Ships are in that return from the Indies. There is in those seas a kind of small Worms, that fasten themselves to the timber of the Ships, and so pierce them that they take water every where, or if they do not altogether pierce them through, they so weaken the wood, that it is almost impossible to repair them.—We have at present a man here that pretends to have found an admirable secret to remedy this evil. That which would render this secret the more important is, that hitherto very many ways have been uſed to effect it, but without ſucceſs. Some have employed deal and hair, and lime, &c. and therewith lined their Ships; but beſides that this does not altogether affright the Worms, it retards much the Ships courſe. The Portugals ſcorch their Ships, inſomuch that in the quick works there is made a coaly cruſt of about an inch thick; but as this is dangerous, it happening not ſeldom that the whole veſſel is burnt, ſo the reaſon why Worms eat not through Portugal Ships is conceived to be the exceeding hardneſs of the timber employed by them.

We expect with impatience the nature and effect of this propoſition. Many have already ventured to give their thoughts concerning it. Some ſay there needs no more than to build Ships of a harder wood than uſual. Others, having obſerved that theſe Worms faſten not to a kind of wild Indian pear tree, which is highly bitter, do thereupon ſuggeſt that the beſt expedient would be to find out a wood having that quality. But certainly there being now no timber fit for Ships that is not known, it is not likely that any will be found either more hard or more bitter than which has been hitherto employed. Some do imagine that the Propoſer will, by certain lixiviums, give to the ordinary wood ſuch a quality and bitterneſs as is found in the already mentioned Indian pear tree. But this alſo will hardly ſucceed, ſince it will be neceſſary not only to make lixiviums in great quantities at an eaſy rate, and ſtrong enongh to penetrate the thick ſides of a Ship, but alſo to make them durable enough not to be waſhed out by the ſea. Yet notwithſtanding in theſe matters one ought to ſuſpend one's judgment until experience do ſhew what is to be believed of them.

So far the extract; to which it may perhaps not be unreaſonable to add, that a very worthy perſon in London ſuggeſts the pitch drawn out of ſea coals for a good remedy to ſcare away theſe noiſome inſects.

Obſervations about Shining Worms in Oyſters.

THESE obſervations occur in the French Journal of April 12, 1666, in two Letters written by Monſ. Azout to Monſ. De la Voye, whereof the ſubſtance may be reduced to the following particulars:—

1. That M. De la Voye having obſerved, as he thought, ſome Shining Worms in Oyſters, Monſ. Azout having been made acquainted with it, did

firſt conceive they were not Worms (unleſs they were cruſhed ones) that ſhined, as having not been able then to diſcern any parts of a Worm, but only ſome ſhining clammy moiſture, which appeared indeed like a little ſtar of a bluiſh colour, and ſtuck to the Oyſter ſhell; being drawn out, ſhone in the air its whole length, (which was about four or five lines) and when put upon the obſerver's hand continued to ſhine there for ſome time.

2. That M. Azout afterwards, cauſing more than 20 dozen of Oyſters to be opened at candle light, really ſaw in the dark ſuch ſhining Worms in them; and thoſe of three ſorts.—*One* ſort was whitish, having 24 or 25 feet on each ſide, forked; a black ſpeck on one ſide of the head (taken by him for a chryſtallin), and the back like an eel ſtript of her ſkin.—The *ſecond*, red and reſembling the common Glow Worms found at land, with folds upon their backs, and feet like the former, and with a noſe like that of a dog, and one eye in the head. The *third* ſort was ſpeckled, having a head like that of a ſole, with many tufts of whitiſh hair on the ſides of it.

3. That beſides theſe, the obſerver ſaw ſome much bigger, that were grayiſh, with a big head and two horns on it, like thoſe of a ſnail, and with ſeven or eight whitiſh feet, but theſe, though kept by him in the night, ſhined not.

4. That the two firſt ſorts are made of a matter eaſily reſoluble, the leaſt ſhaking or touch turning them into a viſcous and aqueous matter; which, falling from the ſhell ſtuck to the obſerver's fingers, and ſhone there for the ſpace of 20 ſeconds: and if any little part of this matter, by ſtrongly ſhaking the ſhell, did fall to the ground, it appeared like a little piece of a flaming brimſtone; and, when ſhaken off nimbly, it became like a ſmall ſhining line, which was diſſipated before it came to the ground.

5. That this ſhining matter was of different colour; ſome whitiſh, ſome reddiſh, but yet that they afforded both a light, which appeared a violet to his eye.

6. That it is very hard to examine theſe Worms entire (eſpecially the white ones), becauſe, at the leaſt touch, they do burſt and reſolve into a glutinous moiſture, whence alſo, if it were not for their feet, that are diſcovered in their matter, none would judge them to be Worms.

7. That among thoſe which he obſerved, he ſaw two more firm than the reſt, which ſhone all over, and when they fell from the Oyſter twinkled like a great ſtar ſhining ſtrongly, and emitting rays of a violet light, by turns,

for the ſpace of 20 ſeconds: which ſcintillation the obſerver imputes to this, that thoſe Worms being alive, and ſometimes raiſing their head, ſometimes their tail, like a carp, the light increaſed and leſſened accordingly, ſeeing that when they ſhone not, he did, viewing them by a candle, find them dead.

8. That forcibly ſhaking the Oyſter ſhell in the dark, he ſometimes ſaw the whole ſhell full of lights, now and then as big as a finger's end, and abundance of this clammy matter, both red and white, (which he judges to have been Worms) burſt in their holes.

9. That in the ſhaking he ſaw all the communications of theſe little verminulous holes, like to the hole of Worms in wood.

10. That in more than 20 dozen of Oyſters he ſhook no ſhell, (10 or 12 excepted) but it emitted light; and found ſome of this light in 16 of the Oyſters themſelves.

11. That this light occurs more frequently in big than ſmall Oyſters, in thoſe that are pierced by the Worm oftener than in thoſe that are not, and rather upon the convex ſide than the other; and more in freſh ones, than in the ſtale.

12. That having ſomewhat ſcaled the convex ſide of the ſhell and diſcovered the communication of the holes, wherein the often mentioned viſcous moiſture that has any form of inſects is found; he ſmelt a ſcent that was like the water of a ſqueezed Oyſter.

13. That the Worms give no light when irritated, but if they do, the light laſts but a very little time, whereas that which appears in thoſe that were not angered before continues a great while; the obſerver affirming to have kept of it above two hours.

So far the Journal des Sçavans, which intimates withall that if the obſervers had had better microſcopes, they could have better examined this matter.

But ſince the curious here in England are ſo well furniſhed with good ones, it is hoped that they will employ ſome of them for further and more minute obſervations of theſe Worms; it being a matter, which joined with other obſervations already made by ſome excellent perſons here (eſpecially Mr. Boyle) upon this ſubject of light, may prove very luciferous to the doctrine of it, ſo much yet in the dark.

Some Obſervations of the Effects of Touch and Friction.

THE operations and effects of Touch and Friction having lately been much taken notice of, and being looked upon by ſome as a great medical branch for the curing of many diſeaſes and infirmities, it will perhaps not be unreaſonable to mention here alſo ſome obſervations relating thereto, which may give occaſion to others to conſider this ſubject more than has been done, and to make further obſervations and trials concerning the ſame.

And firſt, the illuſtrious Lord of Verulam, in his Hiſtory of Life and Death, Hiſt. 6. ſ. 3, obſerves, that motion and warmth (of which two Friction conſiſts) draws forth into the parts new juice and vigour; and, Canon 13, he affirms, that Frictions conduce much to longevity.

Secondly, The Honourable Robert Boyle, in his *Uſefulneſs of Experimental Philoſophy*, ſect. 2. c. 15, conſidering the body of a living man, or any animal, as an engine ſo compoſed, that there is a conſpiring communication betwixt its parts, by virtue whereof a very ſlight impreſſion of adventitious matter upon ſome one part, may be able to work on ſome other diſtant part, or perhaps on the whole engine, a change far exceeding what the ſame adventitious matter could do upon a body not ſo contrived; repreſenting I ſay an animal in this manner, and thence inferring how it may be altered for the better or worſe by motions or impulſes, confeſſedly mechanical, obſerves, how ſome are recovered from ſwooning fits by pricking, others grow faint and do vomit by the bare motion of a coach; others fall into a troubleſome ſickneſs by the agitation of a ſhip, and by the ſea air (whence they recover by reſt and by going aſhore). Again, how in our ſtables, a horſe well curried, is half fed: how ſome can tell by the milk of their aſſes, whether that day they have been well curried or not: arguing hence, that if in milk the alteration is ſo conſiderable, it ſhould be ſo likewiſe in the blood, or other juices of which the blood is elaborated, and conſequently in divers of the principal parts of the body. Where alſo (upon the authority of Piſo) he refers the reader to the Braſilian empirics, whoſe wild Frictions, as unſkilfully as they order them, do ſtrange things, both in preſerving health and curing diſeaſes; curing cold and chronical ones by Friction, as they do acute ones by unction.

Thirdly, The learned Doctor John Beale did not long ſince communicate by ſome letters; firſt, that he could make good proof of the curing or killing a very great and dangerous wen (that had been very troubleſome for two or three years) by the application of a dead man's hand, whence the patient felt ſuch a cold ſtream paſs to the heart, that it did almoſt cauſe in him a fit of ſwooning. Secondly, that upon his brother's knowledge, a certain cook in a noble family of England, (wherein that brother of his then lived) having been reproached for the uglineſs of his warty hands, and returned for anſwer that he had tried many remedies, but found none, was bid by his Lord to rub his hand with that of a dead man; and that his Lord dying ſoon after, the cook made uſe both of his Lord's advice and hand, and ſpeedily found good effects; (which is alſo confirmed by what Mr. Boyle relates in his lately mentioned book of Dr. Harvey's frequently ſucceſsful trial of curing ſome tumors or excreſcencies by holding on them ſuch a hand). Here is Friction or Touch to mortify wens, to drive away ſwellings and excreſcencies; and why not to repel or diſſipate ſpirits that may have a dangerous influence upon the brain or other parts, as well as to call forth the retired ones into the habit of the body for invigoration? Thirdly, that a gentleman who lately came out of Ireland, lay at his houſe, and informed him of an aged Knight there, who having great pain in his feet, inſomuch that he was unable to uſe them, ſuffered, as he was going to bed, a loving ſpaniel to lick his feet, which was for the preſent very pleaſing to him, ſo that he uſed it mornings and evenings till he found the pain appeaſed, and the uſe of his feet reſtored. This, ſaith the relator, was a gentle touch and tranſpiration; for he found the ſpirits tranſpire with a pleaſing kind of titillation. Fourthly, that he can aſſure of an honeſt blackſmith, who by his healing hand converted his bars of iron into plates of ſilver; and had this particular faculty, that he cauſed vomitings by ſtroking the ſtomach; gave the ſtool by ſtroking the belly; appeaſed the gout and other pains, by ſtroking the parts affected.

An Eſſay of Dr. John Wallis, exhibiting his Hypotheſis about the Flux and Reflux of the Sea.

HOW abſtruſe a ſubject in philoſophy the Flux and Reflux hath proved hitherto, and how much the ſame hath in all ages perplexed the minds even of the beſt of naturaliſts, when they have attempted to render an account of the cauſe thereof, is needleſs here to repreſent. It may perhaps be to more purpoſe to take notice, that all the deficiencies found in the various hypotheſes, formerly invented for that end, have not been able to deter the ingenious of this age from making further ſearch into that matter: among whom that eminent mathematician Dr. John Wallis, following his happy genius for advancing real philoſophy, hath made it a part of his latter enquiries and ſtudies, to contrive and deduce a certain hypotheſis concerning that phenomenon, taken from the conſideration of the *common centre of gravity of the earth and moon.* This being by ſeveral learned men looked upon as a very rational notion, it was thought fit to offer it to the public, that other intelligent perſons alſo might the more conveniently at their leiſure examine the conjecture, (the author, ſuch is his modeſty, preſenting it no otherwiſe) and thereupon give in their ſenſe, and what difficulties may occur to them about it, that ſo it may be either confirmed or laid aſide accordingly; as the propoſer himſelf expreſsly deſires in the diſcourſe, we now without any more preamble are going to ſubjoin, as it was by him addreſſed, by way of letter, from Oxford, to Mr. Boyle, April 25th, 1666, and afterwards communicated to the ROYAL SOCIETY as follows:

"You were earneſt with me when we laſt went from hence, that I would put in writing ſomewhat of that, which at divers times theſe three or four years laſt paſt I have been diſcourſing with yourſelf and others, concerning the common centre of gravity of the *earth and moon,* in order to ſolving the phenomena, as well of the ſea's ebbing and flowing, as of ſome perplexities in aſtronomical obſervations of the places of the celeſtial bodies.

"How much the world, and the great bodies therein are managed, according to the laws of motion and ſtatick principles, and with how much more of clearneſs and ſatisfaction many of the more abſtruſe phenomena have been ſolved on ſuch principles within this laſt century of years than formerly they had been, I need not diſcourſe to you, who are well verſed in it. For, ſince that Galileo, and after him Porricellio, and others, have applied mechanic principles to the ſolving of philoſophical difficulties; natural philoſophy is well known to have been rendered more intelligible, and to have made a much greater progreſs in leſs than 100 years, than before for many ages.

" The ſea's ebbing and flowing hath ſo great a connection with the moon's motion, that in a manner all philoſophers (whatever cauſes they have joined with it) have attributed much of its cauſe to the moon; which either by ſome occult quality, or particular influence, which it hath on moiſt bodies, or by ſome magnetic virtue, drawing the water towards it, (which ſhould therefore make the water there higheſt where the moon is vertical) or by its gravity and preſſure downwards upon the terraqueous globe, (which ſhould make it loweſt where the moon is vertical) or by whatever other means (according to the ſeveral conjectures of inquiſitive perſons) hath ſo great an influence on, or at leaſt a connection with the sea's Flux and Reflux, that it would ſeem very unreaſonable to ſeclude the conſideration of the moon's motion from that of the ſea: the periods of tides (to ſay nothing of the greatneſs of them near the new moon and full moon) ſo conſtantly waiting on the moon's motion, that it may be well preſumed that either the one is governed by the other, or at leaſt both from ſome common cauſe.

" But the firſt that I know of, who took in the conſideration of the Earth's Motion (diurnal and annual), was Galileo; who in his Syſtem of the World, hath a particular diſcourſe on this ſubject, which, from the firſt time I ever read it, ſeemed to me ſo very rational, that I could never be of other opinion, but that the true account of this great phenomenon was to be referred to the earth's motion, as the principal cauſe of it; yet that of the moon (for the reaſons above mentioned) not to be excluded, as to the determining the periods of tides, and other circumſtances concerning them. And though it be manifeſt enough, that Galileo, as to ſome particulars, was miſtaken in the account which there he gives of it, yet that may be very well allowed, without any blemiſh to ſo deſerving a perſon, or prejudice to the main hypotheſis; for that diſcourſe is to be looked upon only as an eſſay of the general hypotheſis, which, as to the particulars, was to be afterwards adjuſted, from a good general Hiſtory of Tides; which, it is manifeſt enough that he had not; and which is in a great meaſure yet wanting. For were the matter of fact well agreed on, it is not likely that ſeveral hypotheſes ſhould ſo far differ, as that one ſhould make the water then and there at the higheſt, where and when the other makes it at the loweſt, as when the moon is vertical to the place.

" And what I ſay of Galileo, I muſt in like manner deſire to be underſtood of what I am now ready to ſay to you. For I do not profeſs to be ſo well ſkilled in the Hiſtory of Tides, as that I will undertake preſently to accompliſh my general hypotheſis to the particular caſes, or that I will indeed undertake for the certainty of it, but only, as an eſſay, propoſe it to further conſideration, to ſtand or fall, as it ſhould be found to anſwer matter of fact. And truly had not your importunity (which is to me a great command) required me to do it, I ſhould not ſo eaſily have drawn up any thing about it, till I had firſt ſatisfied myſelf how well the hypotheſis would anſwer obſervation; having for divers years neglected to do it, waiting a time when I might be at leiſure thoroughly to proſecute this deſign.

" But there be two reaſons, by which you have prevailed on me at leaſt to do ſomething: firſt, becauſe it is the common fate of the Engliſh, that out of a modeſty, they forbear to publiſh their diſcoveries, till proſecuted to a certain degree of certainty and perfection, yet are not ſo wary, but that they diſcourſe of them freely enough to another, and even to ſtrangers, upon occaſion; whereby others, who are more haſty and venturous, coming to hear of the notion, preſently publiſh ſomething of it, and would be reputed thereupon to be the firſt inventors thereof, though even that little which they can ſay of it be perhaps much leſs, and more imperfect, than what the true authors could have publiſhed long before, and what they had really made known (publicly enough, though not in print) to many others; as is well known amongſt us as to the buſineſs of the lymphatic veſſels in anatomy; the injection of liquors into the veins of living animals; the exhibiting of a ſtraight line equal to a crooked; the ſpot in Jupiter, whence his motion about his own axis may be demonſtrated; and many other the like conſiderable inventions.

" The other reaſon (which, with me, is more really of weight, though even the former be not contemptible) is, becauſe, as I have been already, for at leaſt three or four years laſt paſt, diverted from proſecuting the inquiry, or perfecting the hypotheſis, as I had thought to do, ſo I do not know but like emergencies may divert me longer; and whether I ſhall ever ſo do it, as to bring it to perfection, I cannot determine; and therefore, if, as to myſelf, any thing ſhould *humanitus accidere*, yet poſſibly the notion may prove worth the preſerving, to be proſecuted by others, if I do not.

And therefore I ſhall, at leaſt to yourſelf, give ſome general account of my preſent imperfect and undigeſted thoughts.

"I conſider, therefore, that in the Tides, or the Flux or Reflux of the Sea, beſides extraordinary extravagancies or irregularities, whence great inundations or ſtrangely high tides do follow (which it perhaps may prove not to be ſo merely accidental as they have been thought to be, but might, from the regular laws of motion, if well conſidered, be both well accounted for, and even foretold), there are theſe three notorious obſervations made of the reciprocation of Tides: firſt the diurnal reciprocation, whereby twice in ſomewhat more than twenty-four hours we have a flood and an ebb, or a high water and low water: ſecondly, the immenſtrual; whereby, in one ſynodical period of the moon, ſuppoſe from full moon to full moon, the time of thoſe diurnal viciſſitudes, doth move round through the whole compaſs of the Νυχθήμερον, or natural day of twenty-four hours; as for inſtance, if at the full moon the full ſea be at ſuch or ſuch a place juſt at noon, it ſhall be the next day (at the ſame place), ſomewhat before one of the clock; the day following between one and two, and ſo onward, till at the new moon it ſhall be at midnight (the other tide, which in the full moon was at midnight, now at the new moon coming to be at noon), and ſo forward, till at the next full moon, the full ſea ſhall (at the ſame place) come to be at noon again; again, that of the Spring Tides, and Neat Tides (as they are called), about the full moon, and new moon, the Tides are at the higheſt; at the quadratures, the tides are at the loweſt; and at the times intermediate, proportionably. Thirdly, the annual; whereby it is obſerved, that at ſome times of the year the Spring Tides are yet much higher than the Spring Tides at other times of the year; which times are uſually taken to be at the ſpring and autumn, or the two equinoxes; but I have reaſon to believe (as well from my own obſervations for many years, as of others who have been much concerned to heed it, whereof more will be ſaid by and by) that we ſhould rather aſſign the beginnings of February and November than the two equinoxes.

"Now in order to the giving account of theſe three periods, according to the laws of motion and mechanic principles, we ſhall now take for granted, what is now-a-days pretty commonly entertained by thoſe who treat of ſuch matters, that a body in motion is apt to continue its motion, and that in

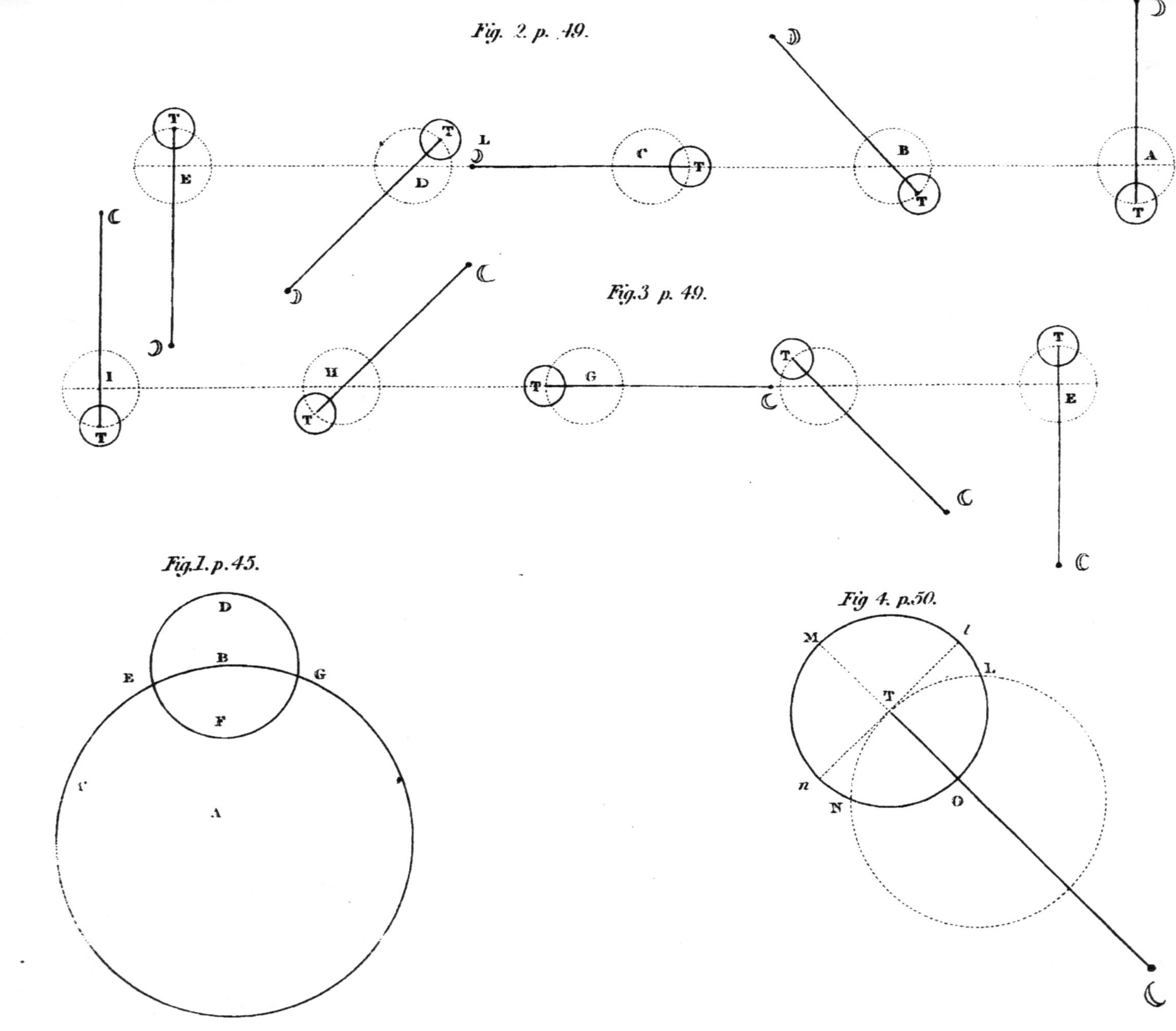

Fig. 2. p. 49.

Fig. 3 p. 49.

Fig. 1. p. 45.

Fig 4. p. 50.

the ſame degree of celerity, unleſs hindered by ſome contrary impediment (like as a body at reſt to continue ſo, unleſs by ſome ſufficient mover put into motion); and accordingly (as daily experience teſtifies), if, on a board or table, ſome looſe incumbent weight be for ſome time moved, and have there contracted an impetus to motion at ſuch a rate, if that board or table chance by ſome external obſtacle, or otherwiſe, to be ſtopped, or conſiderably retarded in its motion, the incumbent looſe body will ſhoot forward upon it: and contrarywiſe, in caſe the board or table chance to be accelerated or put forward with a conſiderably greater ſpeed than before, the looſe incumbent body (not having yet obtained an equal impetus with it) will be left behind, or ſeem to fly backward upon it. Or, (which is Galileo's inſtance) if a broad veſſel of water for ſome time evenly carried forward with the water in it, chance to meet with a ſtop, or to ſlack its motion, the water will daſh forward and riſe higher at the fore part of the veſſel: and contrarywiſe, if the veſſel be ſuddenly put forward faſter than before, the water will daſh backwards and riſe at the hinder part of the veſſel. So that an acceleration or retardation of the veſſel which carries it, will cauſe the riſing of the water in one part, and a falling in another (which yet by its own weight will again be reduced to a level, as it was before); and conſequently, ſuppoſing the ſea to be but as a looſe body, carried about with the earth, but not ſo united to it, as neceſſarily to receive the ſame degree of impetus with it, as its fixed parts do; the acceleration or retardation in the motion of this or that part of the earth will cauſe (more or leſs, according to the proportion of it) ſuch a daſhing of the water or riſing at one part, with a falling at another, as is that which we call the Flux and Reflux of the Sea.

" Now this premiſed, we are next, with him, to ſuppoſe the earth carried about with a double motion; the one annual, as (Fig. 1, *Plate* III.) in B. E. C. the great orb in which the centre of the earth B. is ſuppoſed to move about the Sun, A.

" The other diurnal, whereby the whole moves upon its own axis, and each point in its ſurface deſcribes a circle, as D. E. F. G.

" It is then manifeſt, that if we ſuppoſe that the earth moved but by any one of theſe motions, and that regularly (with an equal ſwiftneſs), the water, having once attained an equal impetus thereto, would ſtill keep equal pace with it, there being no occaſion, from the quickening or ſlackening of the earth's motion (in that part where the water lyeth) for the water thereon to be either cast forward or fall backward, and thereby to accumulate on the other parts of the water; but the true motion of each part of the earth's surface being compounded of those two motions, the annual and diurnal, the annual in B. E. C. being, as Galileo there supposeth, about three times as fast as a diurnal motion in a great circle, as D. E. F. whilst a point in the earth's surface moves about its centre B. from G. to D. and E. and at the same time, its centre B. be carried forward to C. the true motion of that point forwards is made up of both these motions, to wit, of B. to C. and of G. to E.; but while G. moves by D. to E., E. moves backward by F. to G. contrary to the motion of B. to C. so that the true motion of E. is but the difference of B. C. and E. G. (for, beside the motion of B. the centre G. is also put forward as much as from G. to E. and E. put backward as much as from E. to G.); so that the diurnal motion in that part of the earth which is next to the Sun, as E. F. G. doth abate the progress of the annual (and most of all at F.), and in the other part, which is from the Sun, as G. D. E. it doth increase it (and most of all at D.). that is, in the day-time there is abated, in the night-time is added to the annual motion, about as much as is G. E. the earth's diameter, which would afford us a cause of two tides in 24 hours, the one upon the greatest acceleration of motion, the other upon its greatest retardation.

"And thus far Galileo's discourse holds well enough; but then in this it comes short, that as it gives an account of two Tides, so these two Tides are always to be at F. and D. that is, at noon and midnight, whereas experience tells us, that the time of Tides moves in a *month's* space through all the 24 hours; of which he gives us no account. For though he doth take notice of a menstrual period, yet he doth it only as to the quantity of the Tides, greater or less; not as to the *time* of the *Tides*, sooner or later.

"To help this there is one (viz. Jo. Baptista Balianus) who makes the earth to be but a *secondary* planet; and to move, not directly about the sun but about the moon, the moon meanwhile moving about the sun, and the moon about it.

"But this, though it might furnish us with the foundation of a menstrual period of accelerations and retardations in the compound motion of several parts of the earth's ſurface; yet I am not at all inclined to admit this as a true hypotheſis, for divers reaſons, which, if not demonſtrative, are yet ſo conſonant to the general *ſyſtem* of the world, as that we have no good ground to diſbelieve them. For firſt, the earth being undeniably the greater body of the two, (whereof there is no doubt to be made) it cannot be thought probable that this ſhould be carried about by the moon, which is ſo much leſs than itſelf: the contrary being ſeen, not only in the ſun, which is bigger than any of the planets, which it carries about; but in Jupiter, bigger than any of his ſatellites; and Saturn bigger than his. 2d. As the ſun by its own motion about its own axis, is with good reaſon judged to be the phyſical cauſe of the primary planets moving about it; ſo there is the like reaſon to believe that Jupiter and Saturn, moving about their axis, are the phyſical cauſe of their ſatellites moving about them, which motion of Jupiter hath been of late diſcovered, by the help of a *fixt* ſpot diſcerned in him; and we have reaſon to believe the like of Saturn. Whether Venus and Mercury (about whom no ſatellites have been yet obſerved) be likewiſe ſo moved, we have not yet the like ground to determine; but we have of Mars, from the obſervations of Mr. Hook, made in February and March laſt, and by him communicated to the ROYAL SOCIETY. Now that the earth hath ſuch a motion about its own axis (whereby it might be fitted to carry about the moon) is evident by its diurnal motion, and it ſeems as evident that the moon hath not; becauſe of the ſame ſide of the moon always turned toward us, which could not be if the moon carried the earth about; unleſs we ſhould ſay, that it carries about the earth in juſt the ſame period in which it turns upon its own axis; which is contrary to that of the ſun carrying about the Planets; the ſhorteſt of whoſe periods is yet longer than that of the ſun's moving about his own axis. And the like of Jupiter, ſhorter than the period of any of his own ſatellites; if at leaſt the period of his converſion about his axis, lately ſaid to be obſerved, prove true. (Of Saturn we have not yet any period aſſigned; but it is likely to be ſhorter than that of his ſatellites.) And therefore we have reaſon to believe, not that by the moon's motion about its axis the earth ſhould be carried by a contemporary period (whereby the ſame face of the moon ſhould be ever towards us); but that by the earth's revolution about its axis in 24 hours, the moon ſhould be carried about it in 29 days, without any motion on its own axis: and accordingly, that the ſecondary planets about Jupiter and Saturn are not (like their principals) turned about their own axis. And therefore I am not at all inclined to believe, that the menſtrual period of the Tides with us is to be *ſolved* by ſuch an hypotheſis.

" Inſtead of this, that ſurmiſe of mine (for I dare not yet with confidence give it any better name) of what I have ſpoken to you before, (and which hath occaſioned this preſent account which I am now giving you) is to this purpoſe.

" The earth and moon being known to be bodies of ſo great connection (whether by any magnetic, or what other tie, I will not determine, nor need I, as to this purpoſe,) as that the motion of the one follows that of the other; (the moon obſerving the earth as the centre of its periodic motion,) may well enough be looked upon as *one body*, or rather one aggregate of bodies, which have one common centre of gravity; which centre (according to the known laws of ſtatics) is in a ſtraight line connecting their reſpective centres, ſo divided as that its parts be in reciprocal proportion to the gravities of the two bodies. As for example, ſuppoſe the magnitude (and therefore probably the gravity) of the moon to be about a one and fortieth part of that of the earth; (and thereabouts Hevelius, in his Selenography, page 203, doth out of Tycho, eſtimate the proportion; and an exact certainty is not neceſſary in our preſent buſineſs); and the diſtance of the moon's centre from the centre of the earth to be about fifty-ſix ſemi-diameters of the earth, as thereabouts he doth there eſtimate it, in its middle diſtance, and we need not now be very accurate in determining the numbers, wherein aſtronomers are not yet very well agreed; the diſtance of the common centre of gravity of the two bodies, will be from that of the earth, about a two and fortieth part of fifty-ſix ſemi-diameters, that is about $\frac{56}{42}$ or $\frac{4}{3}$ of a ſemi-diameter; that is about $\frac{1}{3}$ of a ſemi-diameter of the earth, above its ſurface in the air, directly between the earth and the moon.

" Now ſuppoſing the earth and moon, as one body jointly carried about by the ſun in the great orb of the annual motion: this motion is to be eſtimated, (according to the laws of ſtatics in other caſes,) by the motion of the common centre of gravity of both bodies. For we uſe in ſtatics to eſtimate a body, or aggregate of bodies, to be moved upwards, downwards, or otherwiſe, ſo much as its common centre of gravity is moved, howſoever the parts may change places amongſt themſelves.

" And accordingly the line of the annual motion (whether circular or eliptical, of which I am not here to diſpute,) will be deſcribed, not to be the centre of the earth (as we commonly eſtimate it, making the earth a primary and the moon a ſecondary planet); nor by the centre of the moon (as they would do who make the moon the primary and the earth the ſecondary planet, againſt which we were before diſputing); but by the common centre of gravity of the bodies, earth and moon, as one aggregate.

" Now ſuppoſing A, B, C, D, E, to be a part of the great orb of the annual motion (ſee Fig. 2 and 3) deſcribed by the common centre of gravity, in ſo long time as from a full moon at A to the next new moon at E, (which though an arch of a circle or elipſe, whoſe centre we ſuppoſe at a due diſtance below it, yet, being but about $\frac{1}{25}$ of the whole, may well enough be here repreſented by a ſtraight line); the centre of the earth at T, and that of the moon at L, muſt each of them (ſuppoſing their common centre of gravity to keep the line at E,) be ſuppoſed to deſcribe a periphery about the common centre, as the moon deſcribes her line of menſtrual motion, of which I have, in this ſcheme, only drawn that of the earth, as being ſufficient for our preſent purpoſe: parallel to which, if need be, we may ſuppoſe one deſcribed by the moon, whoſe diſtance is alſo to be ſuppoſed much greater from T than in the figure is expreſſed, or was neceſſary to expreſs. And in like manner E, T, G, H, I, from that new moon at E, to the next full moon at I.

" From A to E (from full moon to new moon) T, moves (in its own epicycle) upwards from the ſun; and from E to I (from new moon to full moon) it moves downwards, towards the ſun. Again, from C to G, (from laſt quarter to the following firſt quarter) it moves *forwards according* to the annual motion; but from G forward to C (from the firſt quarter to the enſuing laſt quarter) it moves contrary to the annual motion.

" It is manifeſt, therefore, according to this hypotheſis, that from the laſt quarter to the firſt quarter (from C to G, while T is above the line of the annual motion) its menſtrual motion in its epicycle *adds* ſomewhat of acceleration to the annual motion, and moſt of all at E, the new moon: and from the firſt to the laſt quarter (from G forward to C, while T is below the line of the annual motion, and moſt of all at I or A) the full moon.

" So that in purſuance of Galileo's notion, the menſtrual adding to, or detracting from the annual motion, ſhould either leave behind, or caſt forward, the loose waters incumbent on the earth, and thereby cause a tide or accumulation of waters; and most of all at the full moon and new moon, where these accelerations or retardations are greatest.

" Now this menstrual motion, if nothing else were superadded to the annual, would give us two tides in a month, and no more; the one upon the acceleration, the other upon the retardation, at new moon and full moon, and two ebbs at the two quarters; and in the intervals, rising and falling water.

" But the diurnal motion superadded doth the same to this menstrual, which Galileo supposeth it to do to that annual; that is, doth add to, or subtract from, the menstrual acceleration or retardation, and so gives us Tide upon Tide.

" For in whatsoever part of its epicycles (see Fig. 4,) we suppose T to be, yet, because, while by its menstrual motion the centre moves in the circle L, T, N, each point in its surface, by its diurnal motion, moves in the circle L, M, N: whatever effect (accelerative or tardative) the menstrual would give, that effect by the diurnal is increased in the parts of L, M, N, (or rather l, M, n, the semi circle) and most of all at M: but diminished in the parts N, O, L, (or rather n, O, l,) and most of all at O. So that at M and O, (that is where the moon is in the meridian, below or about the horizon) we are to have the diurnal tide or high water, occasioned by the greatest acceleration or retardation which the diurnal arch gives to that of the menstrual, which seems to be the true cause of the daily tides. And with all gives an account, not only why it should be *every day*, but why at such a *time* of the day; and why this time should in a month run through the whole 24 hours, viz. because the moon's coming to the meridian above and below the horizon (or as the seamen call it, the moon's *southing* or *northing*) doth so; as likewise of the spring Tides and neap Tides; for when it so happens, that the menstrual and diurnal accelerations and retardations be coincident (as at new moons and full moons they are) the effect must needs be greater, and though (which is not to be dissembled) this happens but to one of the two Tides; that is, the night Tide at the new moon, (when both motions do most of all accelerate) and the day Tide at full moon, when both do most retard the annual motion; yet this Tide being thus raised by two concurrent causes, though the next Tide have not the same cause also, the impetus contracted will have influence upon the next tide; for a like reason, as a pendulum let fall from a higher arch, will, though there be no new cause to occasion it, make the vibration on the other side, beyond the perpendicular, to be also greater. Or, of water in a broad vessel, if it be so jogged as to be cast forward to a good height above its level, will, upon its recoiling, by its own gravity, (without any additional cause) mount so much the higher on the hinder part.

" But here also we are to take notice, that though all parts of the earth, by its diurnal motion, do turn about its axis, and describe parallel circles, yet not equal circles, but greater near the equinoctial, and lesser near the poles; which may be a cause why the Tides in some parts may be much greater than in others. But this belongs to the *particular* considerations, (of which we are not now giving an account) not to the general hypothesis.

" Having thus endeavoured to give an account of the diurnal and menstrual periods of Tides, it remains that I endeavour the like as to the annual, of which there is at least thus much agreed, that at some times of the year the Tides are noted to be much higher than at other times.

" But here I have a double task; first, to rectify the observation, and then to give an account of it.

" As to the first, it having been observed, grossly, that those high Tides have used to happen about the spring and autumn, it hath been generally taken for granted, without any more nice observation, that the two equinoxes are the proper times, to which these annual high Tides are to be referred; and such causes sought for, as might best suit with such a supposition.

" But it is now the best part of 20 years since I have had frequent occasions to converse with some inhabitants of Rumney Marsh, in Kent, where the sea being kept out with great earthen walls, that it do not at high water overflow the level; and the inhabitants livelihood depending most on grazing or feeding sheep, they are (as you may believe they have reason to be) very vigilant and observant at what times they are most in danger of having their land drowned. And I find them generally agreed, by their constant observations, (and experience dearly bought) that their times of danger are about the beginning of February and November; that is at those spring Tides which happen near those times, to which they give the names of Candlemas stream, and Allhallowed stream; and if they *scape* those spring Tides they apprehend themselves out of danger for the rest of the year.

And as for March and September, (the two equinoxes) they are as little ſolicitous of them as of any other part of the year.

" This, I confeſs, I much wondered at when I firſt heard it, and ſuſpected it to be a miſtake of him that firſt told me, though he were indeed a perſon not likely ſo to be miſtaken in a thing wherein he was ſo much concerned; but I ſoon found that it was not only his, but a general obſervation of others too, both there and elſewhere along the ſea coaſt. And though they did not pretend to know any reaſon of it, nor ſo much as to enquire after it, yet none made doubt of it; but would rather laugh at any that ſhould talk of March and September as being the dangerous times. And ſince that time I have myſelf very frequently obſerved, (both at London and elſewhere, as I have had occaſion) that in thoſe months of February and November, eſpecially November, the Tides have run much higher than at other times, though I confeſs I have not been ſo diligent to ſet down thoſe obſervations as I ſhould have done. Yet this I do particularly very well remember, that in November 1660, (the ſame year that his Majeſty returned) having occaſion to go by coach from the Strand to Weſtminſter, I found the water ſo high in the middle of King-ſtreet, that it came up not only to the *boot*, but into the body of the coach; and the *Palace Yard*, (all ſave a little place near weſt end) overflowed; as likewiſe the Market-place, and many other places; and their Cellars generally filled up with water. And in November laſt, 1665, there were very high Tides, not only on the coaſt of England (where much hurt was done by them) but much more in Holland; where, by reaſon of thoſe inundations, many villages and towns were overflowed. And though I cannot ſo particularly name other years, yet I can very ſafely ſay, that I frequently obſerved Tides ſtrangely high about thoſe times of the year.

" This obſervation did for divers years cauſe me much to wonder, not only becauſe it is ſo contrary to the received opinion of the two equinoxes; but becauſe I could not think of any thing ſignal at thoſe times of the year, as being neither the two equinoxes, nor the two ſolſtices, nor the ſun's apogeum and perigeum: (or earth's aphelium and perihelium;) nor indeed, at contrary times of the year, which at leaſt, would ſeem to be expected. From Allhallow-tide to Candlemas being but three months; and from thence to Allhallow-tide again nine months.

" At length it came into my mind, about four years ſince, that though there do not about theſe times happen any *ſingle* ſignal accident, which might caſt it on theſe times, yet there is compound of two that may do it: which is the inequality of the natural day (I mean that of 24 hours, from noon to noon) ariſing at leaſt from a double cauſe; either of which ſingly, would caſt it upon other times, but both jointly, on theſe.

" It is commonly thought, how unequal ſoever the length be of the artificial days as contra-diſtinguiſhed to nights, yet that the natural day, reckoning from noon to noon, are *equal.* But aſtronomers know well that even theſe days are *unequal.*

" For this natural day is meaſured not only by one entire converſion of the equinoctial, or 24 equinoctial hours, (which is indeed taken to be performed in equal times,) but increaſes by ſo much, as anſwers to that part of the ſun's (or earth's) annual motion as is performed in that time. For when that part of the equinoctial, which (with the ſun) was at the meridian yeſterday at noon, is come thither again to-day, it is not yet noon (becauſe the ſun is not now at the place where yeſterday he was, but is gone forward about one degree, more or leſs), but we muſt ſtay till that place, where the ſun now is, comes to the meridian before it be now noon.

" Now this additament (above the 24 equinoctial hours, or entire converſion of the equinoctial) is upon a double account unequal, firſt, becauſe the ſun, by reaſon of its apogeum and perigeum, doth not at all times of the year diſpatch in one day an equal arch of the ecliptic; but greater arches near the perigeum, which is about the middle of December; and leſſer near the apogeum, which is about the middle of June: as will appear ſufficiently by the tables of the ſun's annual motion. Secondly, though the ſun ſhould in the ecliptic move always at the ſame rate, yet equal arches of the ecliptic do not in all parts of the zodiac, anſwer to equal arches of the equinoctial, by which we are to eſtimate time: becauſe ſome parts of it, as about the two ſolſticial points, lie nearer to a parallel poſition to the equinoctial, than others, as thoſe about the two equinoctial points, where the ecliptic and equinoctial do interſect; whereupon an arch of the ecliptic, near the ſolſticial points, anſwers to a greater arch of the equinoctial, than an arch equal thereunto near the equinoctial points: as doth ſufficiently appear by the tables of the ſun's right aſcenſion.

" According to the firſt of theſe cauſes, we ſhould have the longeſt natural days in December, and the ſhorteſt in June, which if it did operate alone, would give us at theſe times two annual high waters.

"According to the ſecond cauſe, if operating ſingly, we ſhould have the longeſt days at the two ſolſtices in June and December, and the two ſhorteſt at the equinoxes in March and September; which would at thoſe times give occaſion of four annual high waters.

"But the true inequality of the natural days, ariſing from a complication of *thoſe two cauſes*, ſometimes croſſing, and ſometimes promoting each other: though we ſhould find ſome increaſes or decreaſes of the natural days at all thoſe ſeaſons anſwerable to the reſpective cauſes (and perhaps of tides proportionably thereunto:) Yet the longeſt and ſhorteſt natural days abſolutely of the whole year (ariſing from this complication of cauſes) are about thoſe times of Allhallowtide and Candlemas; (or not far from them) about which thoſe annual high tides are found to be: as will appear by the tables of equation of natural days. And therefore I think, we may with very good reaſon caſt this annual period upon that cauſe, or rather complication of cauſes. For, (as we before ſhewed in the menſtrual and diurnal) there will, by this inequality of natural days, ariſe a phyſical acceleration and retardation of the earth's mean motion, and accordingly a caſting of the waters backward or forward; either of which will cauſe an accumulation or high water.

"It is true that theſe longeſt and ſhorteſt days, do (according to the tables, ſome at leaſt) fall rather before, than after Allhallowtide and Candlemas, (to wit, the ends of October and January;) but ſo do alſo (ſometimes) thoſe high tides: and it is not yet ſo well agreed amongſt aſtronomers, what are all the cauſes (and in what degrees) of the inequality of natural days; but that there be diverſities amongſt them, about the *true* time: and whether the introducing of this new motion of the earth in its epicycle about this common centre of gravity, ought not therein alſo to be accounted for, I will not now determine: having already ſaid enough for the explaining of this general hypotheſis, leaving the particularities of it to be adjuſted according to the true meaſures of the motions: if the general hypotheſis be found fit to be admitted.

"Yet this I muſt add, (that I be not miſtaken) that whereas I caſt the time of the daily tides to be at all places, when the moon is there in the meridian; it muſt be underſtood of *open* ſeas, where the water hath ſuch free ſcope for its motions, as if the whole globe of the earth were covered with water. Well knowing, that in bays and inland channels, the poſition of the banks and other like cauſes muſt needs make the times to be much different from what we ſuppoſe in the open ſeas: and likewiſe, that, even in the open ſeas, iſlands, and currents, gulfs and ſhallows may have ſome influence, though not comparable to that of bays and channels. And moreover, though I think, that ſeamen do commonly reckon the time of high water in the open ſeas, to be then, when the moon is there in the meridian (as this hypotheſis would caſt it:) yet I do not take myſelf to be ſo well furniſhed with a hiſtory of tides, as to aſſure myſelf of it: much leſs to accommodate it to particular places and caſes.

" Having thus diſpatched the main of what I had to ſay concerning the ſeas ebbing and flowing, had I not been already too tedious, I ſhould now proceed to give a further reaſon, why I do introduce this conſideration of the *common centre* of *gravity* in reference to *aſtronomical accounts*. For indeed, that which may poſſibly ſeem at firſt to be an object againſt it, is with me one reaſon for it.

" It may be thought, perhaps, that if the earth ſhould thus deſcribe an epicycle about the common centre of gravity, it would (by this its change of place) diſturb the celeſtial motions; and make the apparent places of the planets, eſpecially ſome of them, different from what they would otherwiſe be. For though ſo ſmall removal of the earth, as the epicycle would cauſe (eſpecially if its ſemidiameter ſhould not be above 1¾ of the earth's ſemidiameter) would ſcarce be ſenſible (if at all) to the remoter planets; yet as to the nearer it might.

" Now, though what Galileo anſwers to a like objection in his hypotheſis, (that it is poſſible there may be ſome ſmall difference which aſtronomers have not yet been ſo accurate as to obſerve) might here, perhaps, ſerve the turn; yet my anſwer is much otherwiſe; to wit, that ſuch difference hath been obſerved, and very much puzzled aſtronomers to give an account of. About which you will find Mr. Horrocks (in ſome of his letters, whereof I did formerly, upon the command of the ROYAL SOCIETY, make an extract) was ver y much perplexed; and was fain, for want of other relief, to have recourſe to ſomewhat like *Kepler*'s Amicable *Fibres*, which did, according to the ſeveral poſitions of the moon, accelerate or retard the moon's motion; which Amicable Fibres he had no affection to at all (as there appears) if he could any otherways give an account of thoſe little inequalities; and would much rather (I doubt not) have embraced this notion of the common centre of gravity, to *solve* the phenomenon, had it come to his mind, or been suggested to him. And you find that other astronomers have been seen to bring in (some upon one suspicion, some upon another) some kind of menstrual equation, to solve the inequalities of the moon's motion, according to synodical revolution, or different aspects of new moon, full moon, &c. beside what concerns her own periodical motion.

"For which, this consideration of the common *centre* of *gravity* of the earth and moon, is so proper a remedy (especially if it shall be found precisely to answer those phenomena, which I have not examined, but am very apt to believe) that it is so far from being, with me, an objection against it, that it is one of the reasons, which make me inclinable to introduce it.

"I must before I leave this, add one observation more, that, if we shall, upon these considerations, think it reasonable, that to consider the common centre of gravity of the earth and moon; it may as well be thought reasonable, that the like consideration should be had of Jupiter and his four satellites, which according to the complication of their several motions, will somewhat change the position of Jupiter, as to that common centre of gravity of all these bodies; which yet, because of their smallness, may chance to be so little, as that, at this distance, the change of this apparent place may not be discernible. And what is said of Jupiter, is in the like manner to be understood of Saturn and his satellites, discovered by Hugenius: for all these satellites are to their principals, as so many moons to the earth. And I do very well remember in the letters forecited, Mr. Horrocks expresseth some such little inequalities in Saturn's motion of which he could not imagine what account to give, as if, (to use his expression) this crabbed old Saturn had despised his youth. Which, for ought I know, might well enough have been accounted for, if at that time the satellites of Saturn had been discovered, and that Mr. Horrocks had thought of such a motion as the *common centre* of *gravity* of Saturn and his companion, to be considerable as to the guiding of his motion.

"You have now, in obedience to your commands, an account of my thoughts as to this matter, though yet immature and unpolished: what use you will please to make of them, I shall leave to your prudence, &c."

An Appendix, written by way of Letter to the Publiſher, being an Anſwer to ſome Objections, made by ſeveral Perſons, to the precedent Diſcourſe.

I RECEIVED yours; and am very well contented, that objections be made againſt my hypotheſis concerning Tides; being propoſed but as a conjecture to be examined, and upon that examination, rectified, if there be occaſion; or rejected if it will not hold good.

1. To the firſt objection of thoſe you mention; *that it appears not how two bodies,* that have no *tye, can have one common centre of gravity:* that is (for ſo I underſtand the intendment of the objection) can act or be acted in the ſame manner, as if they were connected: I ſhall only anſwer, that it is harder to ſhew *how* they have than *that* they *have* it. That the load-ſtone and iron have ſomewhat equivalent to a tie, though we ſee it not, yet by the effects we know; and it would be eaſy to ſhew, that two load-ſtones, at once applied in different poſitions to the ſame needle at ſome convenient diſtance, will draw it, not to point directly to either of them but to ſome point between both; which point is, as to thoſe, the *common centre of attraction*; and it is the ſame, as if ſome *one* load-ſtone were in that point. Yet have thoſe two load-ſtones no connection or tie, though a common centre of virtue, according to which they jointly act. And as to the preſent caſe, how the earth and moon are connected, I will not now undertake to ſhew (nor is it neceſſary to my purpoſe:) but, that there is ſomewhat that doth connect them, (as much as what connects the load-ſtone, and the iron, which it draws) is paſt doubt to thoſe, who allow them to be carried about by the ſun, as one aggregate, or body, whoſe parts keep a reſpective poſition to one another: like as Jupiter with his *four ſatellites,* and Saturn with his *one.* Some tie there is, that makes thoſe ſatellites attend their lords, and move in a body; though we do not ſee that tie, nor hear the words of command.

2. And now to the ſecond objection; that at Chatham and in the Thames, the annual ſpring tides happen about the equinoxes; not (as this hypotheſis doth ſuppoſe elſewhere to have been obſerved) about the beginning of February and November If their meaning be, that annual high tides, do then happen, and then only: if this prove true, it will eaſe me of half my work. For it is then eaſily anſwered, that it depends upon the obliquity of the zodiack;

the parts of the equinoctial anſwering to equal parts of the zodiack, being near the ſolſtitial points greateſt, and the equinoctial points leaſt of all. But beſides this *annual viciſſitude* of the *equinoxes*, not to ſay any thing of the four cardinal points (which my hypotheſis doth allow and aſſert;) I believe it will be found, that there is another annual viciſſitude anſwering to the ſun's apogeum and perigeum. And that the greateſt tides of all, will be found to be upon a reſult of theſe two cauſes co-operating: which (as doth the inequality of natural days, depending on theſe ſame cauſes) will light nearer the times I mention. To what is ſaid to be obſerved at Chatham and in the Thames, contrary to that I allege as obſerved in Rumney marſh; I muſt at preſent απεχειν, and refer to a *melius inquirendum*. If thoſe who object this contrary obſervation, ſhall, after this notice, find, upon new obſervations heedfully taken, that the ſpring tides in February and November are not ſo high as thoſe in March and September, I ſhall then think the objection very conſiderable. But I do very well remember, that I have ſeen in November, very high tides at London as well as in Rumney Marſh. And the time is not yet ſo far paſt, but that it may be remembered, (by yourſelf or others then in London) whether in November laſt, when the tides were ſo high at Dover, at Deal, at Margate, and all along the coaſt from thence to Rumney marſh, as to do in ſome of thoſe places much hurt, (and in Holland much more;) whether, I ſay, there were not alſo at the ſame time, at London, (upon the Thames) very high tides. But a good diary of the height and time both of high water, and low water, for a year or two together, even at Chatham or Greenwich, but rather at ſome place in the open ſea, or at the Lands-End in Cornwall, or on the weſt parts of Ireland, or at St. Helen's, or the *Bermudas*, &c. would do more to the reſolving of this point, than any verbal diſcourſe without it.

3. To the third objection, that ſuppoſing the earth and moon to move about a common centre of gravity; if that the higheſt tides be at the new moon, when the moon being neareſt to the ſun, the earth is fartheſt from it, and its compound motion at the ſwifteſt; and that the tides abate as the earth approaches nearer, till it comes into the ſuppoſed circle of her annual motion, it may be demanded why do they not ſtill abate as the earth comes yet nearer to the ſun, and the ſwiftneſs of its compound motion ſtill ſlackens? And ſo, why have we not ſpring tides at the new moon, (when the motion is ſwifteſt) and neap tides at the full moon, (when the motion is ſloweſt) but

ſpring tides at both? The anſwer (if obſerved) is already given in my hypotheſis itſelf. Becauſe the effect is indifferently to follow, either upon a ſudden acceleration, or a ſudden retardation. (Like as a looſe thing lying on a moving body; if the body be thruſt ſuddenly forward, that looſe thing is caſt back, or rather left behind, not having yet obtained an equal *impetus* with that of the body on which it lies; but if ſtopped, or notably retarded, that looſe incumbent is thrown forward by its formerly contracted *impetus*, not yet qualified or accommodated to the ſlowneſs of the body on which it lies.) Now both of theſe happening, the one at the new moon, the other at the full moon, do cauſe high tides at both.

4. To the fourth objection, that the higheſt tides are not at all places about the new moon and full moon; and particularly that in ſome places of the Eaſt Indies, the higheſt tides are at the quadratures: I muſt anſwer in general, that as to the particular varieties of tides in ſeveral parts of the world, I cannot pretend to give a ſatisfactory account, for want of a competent hiſtory of tides, &c. Becauſe, as it is intimated in what I wrote in the general, the various poſitions of channels, bays, promontories, gulfs, ſhallows, currents, trade winds, &c. muſt needs make an innumerable variety of accidents in particular places, of which no ſatisfactory account is to be given from the general hypotheſis though never ſo true) without a due conſideration of all thoſe; which is a taſk too great for me to undertake, being ſo ill furniſhed with materials for it. And then as to the particular inſtance of ſome places in the Eaſt Indies, where the higheſt tides are at the quadratures: I ſuppoſe it may be chiefly intended of thoſe about Cambaia and Pegu, at which places, beſides that they are ſituated at the inmoſt parts of vaſt bays, or gulfs (as they are called) they have alſo vaſt in-draughts of ſome hundred miles within land; which, when the tides are out, do lie (in a manner) quite dry; and may therefore very well be ſuppoſed to participate the effect of the menſtrual tides many days after the cauſe of them happens in the open ſea, upon a like ground, as in ſtraits and narrow channels, the diurnal tides happen ſome hours later than in the ocean: and a like account muſt be given of particular accidents in other places, from the particular ſituation of thoſe places, as bays, channels, currents, &c.

5. To the fifth objection, *that the ſpring tides happen not with us juſt at the full and change, but two or three days after*; I ſhould with more confidence attempt an anſwer, were I certain whether it be ſo in the open ſeas, or only in

our channels: for the anſwers will not be the ſame in both caſes. If *only* in our channels, where the tides find a large in-draught, but not in the open ſeas, we muſt ſeek the reaſon of it from the particular poſition of theſe places. But if it be ſo generally in the wide open ſeas, we muſt ſeek a reaſon of it from the general hypotheſis: and, till I know the matter of fact, I know not well which to offer, leſt, whilſt I attempt to ſolve one, I ſhould fall foul of the other. I know that mariners uſe to ſpeak of ſpring tides at the new and full of the moon, though I have ſtill had a ſuſpicion that it might be ſome days after, as well in the open ſeas, as in our narrower channels; (and therefore I have choſen to ſay in my papers *about* the new and full, rather than *at* the *new* and *full*; and even when I do ſay *at*, I intend it in that laxer ſenſe in which I ſuppoſe the mariners are to be underſtood, for *near* that time); of which ſuſpicion you will find ſome intimations even in my firſt papers: but this though I can admit, yet, becauſe I was not ſure of it, I durſt not build upon it. The truth is, the Flux and Reflux of water in a veſſel, by reaſon of the jogging of it, though it follow thereupon, yet is for the moſt part diſcernible ſome time after; for there muſt upon that jog be ſome time for motion, before the accumulation can have made a tide; and ſo I do not know but that we muſt allow it in all the periods: for as the menſtrual high tide is not (at leaſt with us) till ſome days after the full and change, ſo is the diurnal high water about as many hours after the moon's coming to the ſouth; (I mean at ſea, for in channels it varies to all hours, according as they are nearer or farther from the open ſea): and the annual high tides of November and February, ſomewhat later than (what I conjecjecture to be from the ſame cauſes) the greateſt inequalities of the natural days, happening in January and October. But this, though I can admit, yet (till I am ſure of the matter of fact) I do not build upon: and ſince it hath been hitherto the *cuſtom* to ſpeak with that laxneſs of expreſſion, aſſigning the times of new moon, full moon, and quadratures, with the moon's coming to ſouth, for what is *near* thoſe times, I did not think myſelf obliged in my conjectural hypotheſis (while it is yet but a candidate) to ſpeak more nicely. If the hypotheſis for the *main* of it be found rational, the niceties of it are to be adjuſted in time from particular obſervations.

Having thus given you ſome anſwers to the objections you ſignify to have been made by ſeveral perſons to my hypothſis, and that in the ſame order your Paper preſents them to me: I ſhall next give you ſome account of the two books which you advifed me to confult, fo far as feems neceffary to this bufinefs; which, upon your intimation, I have fince perufed, though before I had not.

And firft, as to that of Ifaac Voffius, De Motu Marium, and Ventorum; though I do not concur with him in his hypothefis, that all the *great motions of the feas*, &c. fhould arife *only* from *fo fmall a warming of the water* as to raife it (where moft of all) not a foot in perpendicular (as in his 12th chapter) or that there is no other *connexion* between the moon's motion and the tides menftrual period, than a *cafual fyncronifm* (which feems to be the doctrine of his 16th and 18th chapters) befides many other things in his philofophy, which I cannot *allow*; yet I am well enough pleafed with what is hiftorical in it, of the matter of fact; efpecially if I may be fecure, that he is therein accurate and candid, not wrefting the phenomena to his own purpofe. But I find nothing in it, which doth induce me to vary from my hypothefis; for, granting his hiftoricals to be all true, the account of the conftant current of the fea weftward, and of the conftant eaftern blafts, &c. within the tropics, is much more plaufibly, and (I fuppofe) truly rendered by Galileo long fince, from the earth's diurnal motion, (which, *near* the equator, defcribing a greater circle than nearer the poles, makes the current to be there more confpicuous and fwift, and confequently the eddy, or recurrent motion nearer the poles, where this is, more remifs) than can eafily be rendered by fo fmall a tumor as he fuppofeth. Not to *add*, that his account of the progreffive motion, which he fancieth to follow upon this tumefaction, and by acceleration to grow to fo great a height near the fhore (as in chap. 13th and 14th) is a notion which feems to me too extravagant to be folved by any laws of ftatics. And that of the moon's motion *only* fyncronizing with the tides cafually, without any phyfical connection, I can very hardly affent to: for it can hardly be imagined, that fuch conftant fyncronifm fhould be in nature; but where either the one is the caufe of the other, or both depend upon the fame *common* caufe; and where we fee fo fair a foundation for a phyfical connection, I am not prone to afcribe it to an independent fyncronifm. In *fome*, his hiftory doth well enough agree with my hypothefis; and I think the phenomena are much better folved by mine than his.

And then as to *Caffendas*, in his Difcourfe de Æftis Maris, I find him, after relating many other opinions concerning the caufe of it, inclining to that of Galileo, afcribing it to the acceleration and retardation of the earth's motion, compounded of the annual and diurnal; and moreover attempting to give an account of the menftrual periods from the earth's carrying the moon about itfelf, as Jupiter doth his fatellites; which, together with them, is *carried* about the fun, as one aggregate; (and that the earth with its moon is to be fuppofed in like manner to be carried about by the fun, as one aggregate, cannot be reafonably doubted by thofe who entertain the Copernican hypothefis, and do allow the fame of Jupiter and his fatellites) but though he would thus have the earth and moon looked upon as two parts of the fame moved aggregate, yet he doth ftill fuppofe (as Galileo hath done before him), that the line of the mean motion of this aggregate (or, as he calls, metus æquabilis et veluti medius) is defcribed by the centre of the earth, about which centre he fuppofeth both its own revolution to be made, and an epicycle defcribed by the moon's motion; not by another point, diftinct from the centres of both, about which as the common centre of gravity, as well that of the earth as that of the moon, are to defcribe feveral epicycles; and for that reafon fails of giving any clear account of this menftrual period. And in like manner, he propofeth the confideration as well of the earth's aphelium and perhelium, as of the equinoctial and folftitial points, in order to the finding a reafon of the annual viciffitudes; but doth not fix upon any thing in which himfelf can acquiefce, and therefore leaves it *in medio* as he found it.

Le Difcernement du Corps et de L'Ame, par M. de Cordemoy.

THIS French Treatife examines the different operations of the foul and body, and the fecret of their union, pretending to difcover to every one what he is, and what is tranfacting within him. This curious work confifts of fix Difcourfes, an abridgment of which may be acceptable.

In the firft the author examines the notions we have in general of bodies and matter, of quantities, qualities, of place, of reft, of motion, of vacuity, of forms; to fhew what is to be underftood by thefe terms, which caufe all the perplexity that is in the ordinary phyfics. He begins with taking notice, that hitherto philofophers have had no diftinct notions of bodies and matter; from the want whereof he conceives, that almoft all the errors in common phyſiology have ſprung. To rectify which, he defines bodies to be *extended ſubſtances*, and *matter* an *aggregate* of bodies: whence he infers, that bodies are indiviſible, and matter diviſible; a body being nothing but *one* and the *ſame* ſubſtance, whoſe different extremities are inſeparable, becauſe they are the extremities of one and the ſame extenſion; and, in a word, of one and the ſame ſubſtance: but matter being nothing but an aſſociation or collection of bodies, it is evident it muſt be diviſible. This doctrine he ſo much inſiſts upon, that he conceives nature cannot ſubſiſt, if a body, in the ſenſe he takes it, be diviſible; and that motion and reſt cannot be explicated without it. As for *quantity*, he makes that to be nothing but more or leſs bodies; not allowing that each body ſhould be a quantity, though it be a part of a quantity no more than an unit is a number, though it make part of a number: ſo that quantity and extenſion are two diſtinct things with him; the *firſt* belonging properly to matter, the *laſt* to a body. Touching vacuity, he conceives that the bodies which compoſe a maſs are not every where ſo near one another, as not to leave ſome interval in ſeveral places. Neither does he think it neceſſary that thoſe intervals ſhould be filled up; nor inconceivable that there ſhould be no body between two bodies, which touch not one another. And when it is ſaid that thoſe intervals cannot be conceived without extenſion, and conſequently that there are bodies that repleniſh them, he frankly pronounces that not to be true, and affirms that though it may be ſaid that between two bodies which touch not one another, other bodies may be placed of ſo many feet, &c. yet ought it not to be inferred that therefore they *are* there, but only that they are thus placed that there *may* be put between them ſo many bodies, as joined together would compoſe an extenſion of ſo many feet; ſo that one conceives only that bodies *may* be placed there, but not that they *are* there: and as we can have an idea of many bodies, though none of them be in being, ſo we can conceive that ſome bodies *may* be put between others, where really there are none. And when it is alleged, that if all bodies that fill a veſſel full were deſtroyed, the ſides of the veſſel would be cloſed together; he profeſſes he underſtands not that ratiocination, nor can conceive that one body does to the ſubſiſtence of another more than to ſuſtain themſelves mutually, when they thruſt by the neighbouring ones; and therefore ſees not why the ſides of the veſſel ſhould cloſe, if nothing ſhould thruſt them together; but underſtands clearly, that two bodies may well ſubſiſt ſo far from one another that one might place a great many bodies between them, or none at all, and yet they neither approach to, nor recoil from one another.

In the ſecond, he examines the changes, which he knows in matter, and makes it his buſineſs to explicate all thoſe that reſpect quantity, qualities, and forms, by local motion, eſteeming that there needs no other.

In the third, he explains the motion of artificial *engines*, and that of natural ones, by one and the ſame cauſe; endeavouring among other things to ſhew, that the body of an animal is moved after the ſame manner as a watch. That cauſe of motion he makes the materia ſubtilis; and the finer or *ſubtiler* that that is, the better and fitter he conceives it to be to preſerve motion.

In the fourth he teaches, that though experience ſeems to evince that the ſoul moves the body, and that one body moves another, yet there is nothing but God that can produce any motion in the world; and all other agents which we believe to be the cauſe of this or that motion, are no more but the occaſion thereof. In doing this he advances certain axioms and concluſions, which are in ſhort, that no ſubſtance has that of itſelf which it can looſe without ceaſing to be what it is: that every body may looſe of its motion till it have no more left, without ceaſing to be a body. That we cannot conceive but two ſorts of ſubſtances, viz. a ſpirit *(or that which thinketh)* and a body, wherefore they muſt be conſidered as the cauſes of all that happens; and what cannot proceed from the one, muſt *neceſſarily* be aſcribed to the other: that to move, or to cauſe motion, is an action: that an action cannot be continued but by the agent who began it.

The concluſions:—that no body hath motion of itſelf: that the firſt mover of bodies is not a body: that it cannot be but a *ſpirit*, that is the firſt mover: that it cannot be but the ſame *ſpirit* who has begun to move bodies that continues to move.

In the fifth, he treats of the union of the body and the ſoul, and the manner how they act one upon the other; and eſteems it not more difficult to conceive the action of ſpirit upon body, and of body upon ſpirit, than to conceive the action of body upon body: the cauſe of the great difficulty in underſtanding the two former, ariſing from thence, that we will conceive the one by the other, not conſidering that every thing acting according to its own nature we ſhall never know the action of one agent, if we will examine it by the notions we have of another, that is of a quite differing nature. Here he notes, that the aɛtion of body upon body is not more known to us than that of ſpirit upon body, or of body upon ſpirit; and yet moſt men admire nothing but this, believing to know the *other*: whereas he judges that all things being well examined, the aɛtion of body upon body is no more conceivable than that of ſpirit upon body. Meanwhile, the opinion of the author touching this ſubjeɛt, is, that the union of ſoul and body conſiſts only in this, that certain motions of the body are followed by certain cogitations of the ſoul, and, on the contrary, that certain thoughts of the ſoul are followed by certain motions of the body. And, having ſuppoſed that bodies are ſaid to aɛt upon one another, when they cauſe ſome change ſuitable to a thought; he infers, that when a body aɛts upon a ſpirit, *that* cannot be by cauſing any change of motion, of figure, or parts, as having none of all theſe, nor when a ſpirit aɛts upon a body, *that* cannot be by producing any change of thought, as having none. But when this body, or its motion, or figure, or other thing depending upon its nature, can be perceived by a ſpirit, ſo as upon that occaſion this ſpirit has thoughts it had not before, it may be ſaid that the body has aɛted upon this ſpirit, for as much as it has cauſed all the change in it whereof it was capable, according to its nature.

In the ſixth, after he hath ſhewn what is to be underſtood by what we call ſoul, and by what we call body, he endeavours to make it appear, that we are much more aſſured of the exiſtence of the ſoul than of that of the body, which he conceives he can prove from hence, *that we cannot doubt* that we *think*, becauſe that even doubting is thinking: but one may doubt whether one has a body, for ſeveral reaſons which he alleges, and thinks ſo cogent, that he concludes, it is not evident to him by the light of reaſon that he has a body. But ſuppoſing there be bodies, he examines what are the operations that belong to the ſoul, and what thoſe that belong to the body. And laſtly, what thoſe that reſult from the union of both; and then explains how all thoſe operations are performed, and particularly, ſenſation; where he ſhews that the nerves, holding at one end to the brain, whereof they are but elongations, and being at the other end extended to the extremities of the body; when an objeɛt comes to touch thoſe exterior ends of the nerves, the interior ones in the brain are preſently ſhaken, and cauſe different ſenſations according to the *diverſity* of nerves, and the different manner in which they are ſhaken. And to ſhew that it is this ſhaking that cauſes ſenſation, he notes, that if any thing ſhakes the interior parts of the nerves, though the object be abſent, the ſoul has preſently the ſame ſenſations as it would have if it were preſent: as if one ſhould knock one's head forcibly againſt a wall, the ſhaking which the blow gives to the brain, moving the interior extremities of the nerve, which cauſes the ſenſation of light, the ſoul has the ſame ſenſation which it would have if it ſaw a thouſand candles: on the contrary, if the interior extremities of the nerves are not ſhaken, though the object be preſent, it cauſes no ſenſation; whence it comes, that if a ſtrong ligature be made upon the middle of the arm, and the hand be then pricked, no pain is felt, becauſe the ſhaking of the nerves that are pricked being ſtopped by the ligature, cannot reach to the extremities of the nerves that are within the brain.

A Relation of a kind of Worms that eat out Stones.—From a letter by M. de la Voye to M. Auzout.

IN a great and very ancient wall of freeſtone in the Benedictines abbey at Caen, in Normandy, facing ſouthward, there are to be found many ſtones ſo eaten by Worms, that one may run his hand into moſt of the cavities; which are variouſly faſhioned, like the ſtones which I have ſeen wrought with ſo much art in the Lovere: in theſe cavities there is abundance of live Worms, their excrement, and of that ſtone-duſt, they eat. Between many of the cavities there remain but leaves, as it were, of ſtone, very thin, which part them. I have taken ſome of theſe living Worms, which I found in the eaten ſtone, and put them into a box with ſeveral bits of the ſtone, leaving them there together for the ſpace of eight *days*; and then opening the box, the ſtone ſeemed to be eaten ſo ſenſibly, that I could no longer doubt of it. I ſend you the box and ſtones in it, together with the living Worms; and to ſatisfy your curioſity, I ſhall relate to you what I have obſerved of them, both with and without a microſcope.

Theſe Worms are incloſed in a ſhell, which is greyiſh, and of the bigneſs of a barley-corn, ſharper at one end than the other. By the means of an excellent microſcope, I have obſerved that it is all overſpread with little ſtones, and little greeniſh eggs; and that there is at the ſharpeſt end a little hole, by which theſe creatures caſt out their excrement, and at the other end a ſomewhat bigger hole, through which they put out their heads, and faſten themſelves to the ſtones they gnaw. They are not ſo ſhut up, but that ſometimes they come out and walk abroad. They are all black, about two lines of an inch long, and three quarters of a line large. The body is *diſtinguiſhed* into ſeveral plyes; and near their heads they have three feet on each ſide, with but two joints, reſembling thoſe of a louſe. When they move, their bodies are commonly upwards, with their mouths againſt the ſtone. They have a big head, ſomewhat and even of the colour of a tortoiſeſhell, *browniſh*, with ſome ſmall white hair. Their mouths are alſo big; where may be ſeen four kinds of jaw-bones, lying *croſſwiſe*, which they move continually, opening and ſhutting them like a pair of compaſſes with four branches. The jaws on both ſides of the mouth are all black; the nether jaw hath a point like the ſting of a bee, but uniform. They draw threads out of their mouths with their four feet, uſing that point to range them, and to form their ſhells of them. They have ten eyes, very black and round, which appear to be bigger than a pin's head. There are five of them on each ſide of the head, ſtanding after this manner:

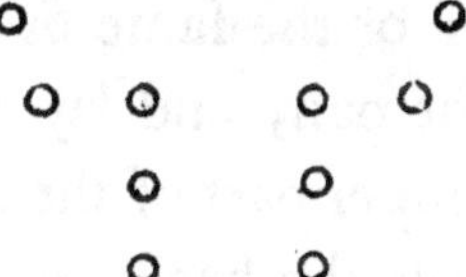

But beſides theſe Worms, I have found that mortar is eaten by an *infinite* number of ſmall creatures, of the bigneſs of cheeſe mites. Theſe have but two eyes, and are blackiſh. They have four feet on each ſide, pretty long. The point of the muzzle is very ſharp, as that of a ſpider. I ſend you but one of them, though I had abundance, but they are dead and loſt. It may be you will find ſome at Paris; ſeeing that in the old mortar betwixt ſtones that is found in walls made with rubbiſh, there is great ſtore of them, together with great plenty of their little eggs. I have not yet examined whether theſe be thoſe that in the ſurfaces of all the ſtones where they are met with, make little round holes, and ſmall traces and impreſſions, which make them look like worm-eaten wood: but it is probable they are ſuch. It ſhould be obſerved whether theſe Worms do not take wings, and all the other appearances of caterpillars; and whether they are not to be found in plaiſter that is full of holes, in bricks, in greety ſtones, and in rocks.

You may obſerve more of them in walls expoſed to the ſouth, than in others; and that the Worms that eat the ſtones live longer than thoſe that eat the mortar, which are not above eight days alive. I have obſerved all their parts with a very good microſcope, without which, and a great deal of attention, it is difficult to ſee them well.

I have ſeen other very old walls altogether eaten; as thoſe of the Temple at Paris, where I could find no Worms, but the cavities were full of ſhells of various kinds, diverſely figured and turned; all of which I believe to be little animals petrified.

The Method obſerved in Transfuſing the Blood out of one Animal into another.

THIS method was firſt practiſed by Doctor Lower in Oxford, and by him communicated to the Hon. Robert Boyle, who imparted it to the ROYAL SOCIETY, as follows:

Firſt, take up the carotidal artery of the dog or other animal, whoſe *blood* is to be transfuſed into another of the ſame or a different kind, and ſeparate it from the nerve of the eight pair, and lay it bare above an inch. Then make a ſtrong ligature on the upper part of the artery, not to be untied again: but an inch below, viz. towards the heart, make another ligature of a running knot, which may be looſened or faſtened as there ſhall be occaſion. Having made theſe two knots, draw two *threads* under the artery between the two ligatures, and then open the artery, and put in a quill, and tie the artery upon the quill very faſt by thoſe two *threads*, and ſtop the quill with a ſtick. After this, make bare the jugular vein in the other dog, about an inch and a half long; and at each end make a ligature with a running knot, and in the ſpace between the two running knots, draw under the vein two *threads*, as in the other: then make an inciſion in the vein and put into it two quills, one into the deſcendant part of the vein, to receive the blood from the other dog, and carry it to the heart; and the other quill put into the other part of the jugular vein, which comes from the head (out of which the ſecond dog's own blood muſt run into the diſhes). Theſe two quills being put in and tied faſt, ſtop them with a ſtick, till there be occaſion to open them.

All things being thus prepared, tie the dogs on their ſides towards one another, ſo conveniently, that the quill may go into each other, (for the dogs' necks cannot be brought ſo near, but that you muſt put two or three ſeveral quills more into the firſt two, to convey the blood from one to another. After that unſtop the quill that goes down into the firſt dog's jugular vein, and the other quill coming out of the dog's artery; and by the help of two or three other quills, put into each other, according as there ſhall be occaſion, inſert them into one another. Then ſlip the running knots, and immediately the *blood* runs through the quills, as through an artery, very impetuouſly. And immediately, as the *blood* runs into the dog, unſtop the other quill, coming out of the upper part of his jugular vein (a ligature being firſt made about his neck, or elſe his other jugular vein, being compreſſed with one's finger;) and let his own blood run out at the ſame time into diſhes; (yet not conſtantly, but according as you perceive him able to bear it) till the other dog begin to cry, and faint, and fall into convulſions, and at laſt *die* by his ſide.

Then take both the quills out of the dog's jugular vein, and tie the running knot faſt, and cut the vein aſunder, (which you may do without any harm to the dog, one jugular vein being ſufficient to convey all the blood from the head and upper parts, by reaſon of a large anaſtomoſis, whereby both the jugular veins meet about the larynx.) This done *ſew* up the ſkin and diſmiſs him, and the dog will leap from the table and ſhake himſelf, and run away as if nothing ailed him.

And this I have tried ſeveral times in the univerſities before ſeveral, but never yet upon more than one dog at a time, for want of leiſure, and convenient ſupplies of ſeveral dogs at once. But when I return, I doubt not but to give a fuller account, not only by bleeding ſeveral dogs into one, but ſeveral other creatures into one another, as you did propoſe to me, before you left Oxford; which will be very *eaſy* to perform, and will afford many pleaſant, and perhaps not unuſeful experiments.

But becauſe there are many circumſtances neceſſary to be obſerved in the performing of this experiment, and that you may better direct any one to do it, without any danger of killing the other dog, that is to receive the other's blood, I will mention two or three:

Firſt, that you faſten the dogs at a convenient diſtance, that the vein nor artery be not ſtretched; for then, being contracted, they will not convey or admit ſo much *blood*.

Secondly, that you conſtantly obſerve the pulſe beyond the quill in the dog's jugular vein (which it acquires from the impulſe of the arterious blood:)

for if that fails, then it is a ſign the quill is ſtopped by ſome congealed blood, ſo that you muſt draw out the arterial quill from the other, and with a probe open the paſſage again in both of them, that the blood may have its free paſſage again in both of them, and that the blood may have its due courſe. For, this muſt be expected, when the dog that bleeds into the other, hath loſt much blood, his heart will beat very faintly, and then the impulſe of the blood being weaker, it will be apt to congeal the ſooner, ſo that at the latter end of the work you muſt draw out the quill often and clear the paſſage; if the dog be faint hearted, as many are, though ſome ſtout fierce dogs will bleed freely and uninterruptedly, till they are convulſed and die. But to prevent this trouble, and make the experiment certain, you muſt bleed a great dog into a little one, or a *maſtiff* into a cur, as I once tried, and the little dog bled out at leaſt, double the quantity of his own blood, and left the *maſtiff* dead upon the table, and after he was untied he ran away, and ſhaked himſelf, as if he had been only thrown into water. Or elſe you may get three or four ſeveral dogs prepared in the ſame manner; and when one begins to fail and leave off bleeding, adminiſter another, and I am confident one dog will receive all their blood, (and perhaps more) as long as it runs freely, till they are left almoſt dead by turns: provided that you let out the blood proportionably, as you let it go into the dog that is to live.

Thirdly, I ſuppoſe the dog that is to bleed out into diſhes will endure it the better, if the dogs that are to be adminiſtered to ſupply his blood, be of *near* an equal age, and fed alike the day before, that both their bloods may be of a *near* ſtrength and temper.

There are many things I have obſerved upon bleeding dogs to death, which I have ſeen ſince your departure from Oxford, whereof I ſhall give you a relation hereafter, in the mean time ſince you were pleaſed to mention it to the ROYAL SOCIETY, with a promiſe to give them an account of this experiment, I could not but take the opportunity to clear you from that obligation, &c.

So far this communication by the Honourable Robert Boyle to the ROYAL SOCIETY; the preſcriptions whereof having been carefully obſerved by thoſe who were employed to make the experiments, have hitherto been attended with good ſucceſs; and that not only upon animals of the ſame ſpecies (as two dogs firſt and then two ſheep), but alſo upon ſome of very differing ſpecies, as a ſheep and a dog; the former *emitting*, the other *receiving*.

It may be proper to obſerve, that inſtead of a quill, a ſmall crooked thin pipe of ſilver or braſs, ſo ſlender, that one end may enter into a quill, and having at the other end that is to enter into the vein and artery a ſmall knob, for the better faſtening them to it with a thread, will be much fitter than a ſtraight pipe or quill, for this operation: for ſo they are much more eaſy to be managed.

It is intended, that theſe trials ſhall be proſecuted to the utmoſt variety the ſubject will *bear:* as by exchanging the blood of old and young, ſick and healthy, hot and cold, fierce and fearful, tame and wild animals, &c. and that not only of the ſame, but alſo differing kinds; for which end, and to improve this noble experiment, either for knowledge or uſe, or both, ſome ingenious men have already propoſed conſiderable trials and enquiries; of which, perhaps, an account will be given hereafter. For the preſent I ſhall only ſubjoin ſome

Conſiderations about this Kind of Experiments.

1ſt. It may be conſidered in them, that the blood of the emittent animal may, after a few minutes of time, by its circulation, mix and run out with that of the recipient. Wherefore to be aſſured of theſe trials, that all the blood of the *recipient* is run out, and none left in him but the adventitious blood of the *emittent,* two or three or more animals (which was alſo hinted in the method above) may be prepared and *adminiſtered,* to bleed them all out in one.

2d. It ſeems not irrational to gueſs aforehand, that the exchange of blood will not alter the nature or diſpoſitions of the animals, upon which it ſhall be practiſed; though it may be thought worth while, for ſatisfaction and certainty, to determine that point by experiments.

The caſe of exchanging the blood of animals ſeems not like that of *grafting,* where the cyons turn the ſap of the ſtock grafted upon, into its nature; the *fibres* of the cyons ſo ſtraining the juice which paſſes from the ſtem to it, as thereby to change it into that of the cyons; whereas in this transfuſion there ſeems to be no ſuch percolation of the blood of animals, whereby that of the one ſhould be changed into that of the other.

3d. The moſt probable uſe of this experiment may be conjectured to be, that one animal may live with the blood of another; and conſequently, that thoſe animals, that want blood, or have corrupt blood, may be *ſupplied* from others with a ſufficient quantity, and of ſuch as is good, provided the transfuſion is often repeated by reaſon of the quick expence that is made of the blood.

An Abridged Account of an ingenious Work, entitled—Pinax Rerum Naturalium Britaniarum continens Vegetabilia, Animalia & Foſſilia, in hæc Inſula reperta, Inchoatus, Anth. Chriſtophoro Merret, M. D. & utriuſque Societatis Regiæ Socio.

THE learned and inquiſitive author of this publication hath, by his laudable example of collecting together what natural things are to be found here in *England*, of all ſorts, (which he has done upon his own expence) given an invitation to the curious in all parts of the world to attempt the like, thereby to eſtabliſh the much deſired and highly uſeful commerce amongſt *Naturaliſts*, and to contribute every where to the compoſing of a *genuine* and full *Hiſtory of Nature*.

In the preface he intimates, that his ſtock does ſtill increaſe daily, and that therefore the reader may expect an appendix to this collection.

In the body of the work, he enumerates all the ſpecies, alphabetically; and, as to Vegetables, he reckons up about 410 ſorts; and gives their Latin and Engliſh names, and the *places* and *times* of their Growth: reducing them afterwards to certain claſſes, hitherto uſed by botanic writers in their hiſtories of plants; adding the etymology of their generic names, and a compendious regiſter of the time when, and how long, the Engliſh plants do ſhoot and flouriſh.

As to Animals, he finds of them about 340 kinds in England, whereof the *four-footed* are about 50; Birds 170; and Fiſhes 120. Inſects are innumerable, which yet he endeavours to enumerate, and to reduce to certain claſſes, into which he alſo brings the three former kinds.

Concerning Foſſils, he firſt takes notice of the metals found in Engliſh mines; ſilver, tin, copper, iron, lead, antimony, and ſome gold extracted out of tin. Next of the ſtones, of which he finds about 70 ſorts; and amongſt them, Briſtol diamonds, agates, hyacinths, emeralds, load-ſtones, toad-ſtones, (which laſt he affirms to be nothing but the grinding teeth of the fiſh lupus) pearls, corals, marble, alabaſter, emery. To which he adds the various kinds of coals, and alſo bitumens, turfs, and jets. And thirdly, of the various kinds of alum, vitriol, nitre, fea-falt, pit-falt. But fourthly, of the various of which he reckons up fifteen peculiar forts, (befides thofe that ferve for hufbandry, which are not eafily numbered,) and amongft them red-lead, black-lead, and fullers-earth.

He concludes all with mentioning the feveral meteors appearing in England; and the hot fprings and medical waters; as alfo the faline, petrifying, and fome more unufual fprings; likewife fubterraneous trees, fubterraneous rivers, ebbings and flowings of wells, &c.

A Relation of the Raining of Afhes in the Archipelago, upon an Eruption of Mount Vefuvius. Communicated from a Letter of Capt. Wm. Badily.

THE 16th of December 1631, being in the gulf of Volo, riding at anchor, about ten of the clock at night it began to rain fand or afhes, and continued till two of the clock the next morning. It was about two inches thick on the deck, fo that we caft it over with fhovels as we did fnow the day before. The quantity of a bufhel we brought home, and prefented to feveral friends*, efpecially to the mafters of the *Trinity Houfe.* There was in our company Capt. John Wild, Commander of the Dragon; and Capt. Anthony Watts, Commander of the Elizabeth and Dorcas. There was no wind ftirring when thefe afhes fell; they did not fall only in the places where we were, but likewife in other parts, as upon fhips coming from St. John D'Acre to our port, they being at that time an hundred leagues from us, we compared the afhes together and found them the fame.

An Extract of a Letter from Rome, rectifying the Relation of Salamanders living in Fire.

THIS came from that expert anatomift M. Steno, to Dr. Croon Videl. That a Knight called Corvini, had affured him, that, having caft a Salamander, brought him out of the Indies, into the fire, the animal thereupon fwelled prefently, and vomited ftore of thick flimy matter, which did put

* Some of thefe Afhes were prefented to the ROYAL SOCIETY.

out the neighbouring coals, to which the Salamander retired immediately putting them out again in the ſame manner, as ſoon as they rekindled, and by this means ſaving himſelf from the force of the fire, for the ſpace of two hours: the Gentleman abovementioned being then unwilling to hazard the creature any further, made no other experiment of that kind. That afterwards it lived nine months. He had kept it eleven months without any other food but what it took by licking the earth on which it moved, and *on which* it had been brought out of the Indies; which at firſt was covered with a thick moiſture, but, being dried afterwards, the urine of the animal ſerved to moiſten the ſame. After eleven months, (the owner having a mind to try how the animal would do upon Italian earth) it died three days after it had changed earth.

Trials propoſed by Mr. Boyle to Dr. Lower, to be made by him, for the Improvement of Transfuſing Blood out of one live Animal into another.

THE following Queries and Trials were read about a month ago before the Royal Society, and do now come forth againſt the Author's intention, at the earneſt deſire of ſome learned perſons, and particularly of the worthy Doctor, to whom they were addreſſed; who think they may excite and aſſiſt others in a matter which, to be well proſecuted, will require many hands. At reading of them the Author declared, that of divers of them he thought he could foreſee the events, but yet judged it fit not to omit them, becauſe the importance of the theories they may give light to, may make the Trials recompenſe the pains, whether the ſucceſs favour the affirmative or the negative of the queſtion, by enabling us to determine the one or the other upon ſurer grounds, than we could otherwiſe do.

The Queries are as follow:

1ſt. Whether by this way of transfuſing blood the diſpoſition of individual animals, of the ſame kind may not be much altered: as, whether a fierce dog, by being often quite new ſtocked with the blood of a cowardly dog, may not become more tame; and *vice verſa*, &c.?

2d. Whether immediately upon the unbinding of a dog, repleniſhed with adventitious blood, he will know, and fawn upon his maſter, and do the like cuſtomary things as before; and whether he will do ſuch things better or worſe at ſome time after the operation?

3d. Whether thoſe dogs, that have peculiarities, will have them either aboliſhed, or at leaſt much impaired by tranfuſion of blood: as, whether the blood of a Maſtiff, being frequently transfuſed into a Blood-Hound or Spaniel, will not prejudice them in point of ſcent?

4th. Whether acquired habits will be deſtroyed or impaired by this experiment: as, whether a dog taught to fetch and carry, or to dive after ducks, or to ſett, will, after frequent and full recruits of the blood of dogs unfit for thoſe exerciſes, be as good at them as before?

5th. Whether any conſiderable change is to be obſerved in the pulſe, urine, and other excrements of the recipient animal, by the operation, or the quantity of his inſenſible tranſpiration?

6th. Whether the emittent dog, being full fed at ſuch a diſtance of time before the operation, that the maſs of blood may be ſuppoſed to abound with chyle, the recipient dog, being before hungry, will loſe his appetite, more than if the emittent dog's blood had not been ſo chylous. And how long, upon a vein being opened of a dog, the admitted blood will be found to retain chyle?

7th. Whether a dog may be kept alive without eating, by the frequent injection of the chyle of another, taken freſhly from the receptacle into the veins of the recipient dog?

8th. Whether a dog, that is ſick of ſome diſeaſe, chiefly imputable to the maſs of blood, may be cured by changing for that of a ſound dog? And Whether a ſound dog may receive ſuch diſeaſes from the blood of a ſick one, as are not otherwiſe of an infectious nature?

9th. What will be the operation of frequently ſtocking (which is feaſible enough) an old and feeble dog with the blood of young ones, as to liveli-neſs, dulneſs, drowſineſs, ſqueamiſhneſs, &c. and *vice verſa?*

10th. Whether a ſmall dog, by being often freſh ſtocked with the blood of a young dog of a larger kind, will grow bigger than the ordinary ſize of of his own kind?

11th. Whether any medicated liquors may be injected together with the blood into the recipient dog? And in caſe they may, whether there will be any conſiderable difference found between the ſeparations made on this occaſion, and thoſe which would be made, in caſe ſuch medicated liquors had been injected with ſome other vehicle, or alone, or taken in at the mouth?

12th. Whether a purging medicine being given to the emittent dog a while before the operation, the recipient dog will be thereby purged, and how? (which experiment may be greatly varied.)

13th. Whether the operation may be ſucceſsfully practiſed, in caſe the injected blood be *that* of another ſpecies, as that of a calf into a dog, &c. and of a cold animal, as of a fiſh, or frog, or tortoiſe, into the veſſels of a hot animal, and *vice verſa?*

14th. Whether the colour of the hair or feathers of the recipient animal, by the frequent repeating of the operation, will be changed into that of the emittent?

15th. Whether by frequently transfuſing into the ſame dog, the blood of ſome animal of another ſpecies, ſomething further, and more tending to ſome degrees of a change of ſpecies, may be effected, at leaſt in animals near of kin, as Spaniels and Setting-dogs, Iriſh Greyhounds, and ordinary Grey-hounds, &c.?

16th. Whether the transfuſion may be practiſed upon pregnant bitches, at leaſt at certain times of their gravidation; and what effect it will have upon the whelps?

There were ſome other Queries propoſed by the ſame Author, as the weighing of the emittent animal before the operation, that (making an abatement for the efluviums, and for the excrements, if it voids any) it may appear how much blood it really loſes. To which were annexed divers others, not fit to be peruſed but by Phyſicians; and therefore here omitted.

A ſhort Account of a conſiderable Loadſtone dug out of the Ground in Devonſhire.

THIS ſtone was lately ſent up out of the ſaid county, and preſented to the Royal Society by the Reverend Archdeacon, Doctor Edward Cotton, with this deſcription, that it weighs ſixty pounds; and that though it take up no great weight, yet it moves a needle about nine feet diſtant.

Some part of it being broken off, he hath ſent up alſo, becauſe being put in its proper place it adds much ſtrength to it, but without that addition it moves not much more than at the diſtance of ſeven feet.

Obſervations concerning Emmets or Ants, their Eggs, Production, Progreſs, coming to Maturity, Uſe, &c. Communicated by Doctor Edmund King, Fellow of the ROYAL SOCIETY.

1ſt, THERE have occurred to my obſervation but three ſorts of Ants, commonly without wings, viz. the very black, the dark brown, and the third ſort of near the colour uſually called philemot.

2d, Each kind inhabit by themſelves in their ſeveral banks, two ſorts being ſeldom or ever found together; and if either of the other two ſorts be put into the black ants bank, it is worth obſerving what enmity there is betwixt theſe little creatures, and with what violence the black ones will ſeize on the red, never leaving to pinch them on the head with their forceps or claws, till they have killed them upon the place: which done, they will carry the dead body out of the field from their bank. But if you put black ants into a bank of the red, the black ſeem to be ſo ſenſible of the ſtrangeneſs of the place they are in, that there they will not meddle with the red, but as if they were frighted, and concerned for nothing but ſelf-preſervation, run away.

3d, Upon opening of theſe banks I obſerve firſt a *white ſubſtance*, which to the bare eye looks like the ſcatterings of fine white ſugar or ſalt, but very ſoft and tender; and if you take a bit of it, as big perhaps as a muſtard ſeed, and lay it on the object plate of a good microſcope, you may, by opening it with the point of a needle, diſcern many pure white and clear appearances in diſtinct membranes, all figured like the leſſer ſort of bird's eggs, and as clear as a fiſhes bladder. This ſame ſubſtance, as it has been now deſcribed, I found in the Ants themſelves, which I take to be the true Ants eggs; it being obvious to obſervation that wherever this is uncovered, they make it their buſineſs to carry it away in their mouths to ſecure it, and will, after you have ſcattered it, lay it on a heap again with what ſpeed they can.

4th, I obſerve they lie in multitudes upon this (if I may ſo call it) ſpawn of theirs; and after a little time every one of theſe ſmall adherences is turned into a little vermicle, as ſmall as a mite, hardly diſcerned to ſtir, but after a few days more you may perceive a feeble motion of flection and extension, and they begin to look yellowish and hairy, ſhaped very like a ſmall maggot; and ſo keeping that ſhape, grow almoſt as big as an Ant, and have every one a black ſpot on them.

5th, Then they get a film over them, whitiſh and of an oval ſhape, for which reaſon I ſuppoſe they are commonly called Ants eggs, which yet (to ſpeak properly) they are not.

6th, I have, to prevent miſtakes, opened many of theſe, vulgarly called Ants eggs, I mean the leſſer ſort, (for there are ſome as big as a wheat-corn, others leſs than a rye-corn) and in ſome I find only a maggot, to appearance juſt ſuch as was deſcribed before. In others I find a maggot beginning to put on the ſhape of an Ant about the head, with two little yellow ſpecks where the eyes are deſigned; in others a further progreſs, and furniſhed with every thing to *complete* the ſhape of an Ant, but wholly tranſparent, the eyes only excepted, which are then as black as black bugles.

7th, But when they have newly put on this ſhape, I could never diſcern the leaſt motion in any one part of this little creature, whereof the reaſon may perhaps be, the weakneſs of their *fibres*; for after a little more time, when they begin to be browniſh, they have ſtrength to ſtir all their parts.

8th, At laſt I met with ſome of theſe reputed eggs, which being carefully opened by me, I took out of ſeveral of them, every way perfect and *complete* Ants, which did immediately creep about amongſt the reſt, no way differing from many other Ants, but by a more feeble motion of their limbs: and this I took for a clear demonſtration of what I deſigned, which was to know, *that* the film does only cover the maggot while ſhe is tranſforming into an Ant, and fitting to ſhift for herſelf.

9th, The black ſpeck that is at one end of every reputed Ants egg, I ſuppoſe to be caſt out of the maggot in her transformation; ſince after it puts on the ſhape of an Ant, the ſpeck is quite gone, and the whole body of the Ant quite pure and clear; ſince alſo this ſpeck at the end of the ſaid egg, lies always cloſe to the anus of the included Ant.

10th, As to the care of their young, (by which I mean all the ſorts and degrees aforeſaid, from the ſpawn to the vulgarly called eggs, in every one of which you will find a young Ant) it is obſervable how upon breaking up of their banks, they make it their buſineſs immediately to carry their young out of ſight again, laying the ſeveral ſorts of them in ſeveral places and heaps; the which, if you mingle again or ſcatter, you ſhall, laying ſome bits of ſlate, or the like, in any place they may come to and get under, after a few hours, ſee all the vermicles, and vulgarly called eggs, laid in their ſeveral and diſtinct parcels, under ſuch pieces of ſlate, &c. provided the place be not ſo cold as to chill their limbs; which if it be, by being brought to the fire they will ſoon recover their ſtrength, and fall to their buſineſs again of ſecuring their little ones.

11th, I have obſerved in ſummer that in the morning they bring up thoſe of their young, that are vulgarly called Ants eggs, towards the top of the banks; ſo that you may from ten in the morning, until five or ſix in the afternoon, find them near the top; eſpecially about one, two or three of the clock, and later, if the weather be hot, when, for the moſt part, they are found on the ſouth ſide of the bank: that towards ſeven or eight at night, if it be cool, or likely to rain, you may dig a foot deep before you can find them.

12th, They know all the ſorts of their young ſo well that you cannot deceive them, though you may with fine ſugar, ſalt, or the crums of very white ſtale bread, ſcattered in the mould where their firſt true eggs are (as I call them) be miſtaken yourſelf, yet the Ants will not, nor touch a bit of what is not their own offspring.

13th, I cannot paſs by the *uſe* of Ants in feeding young pheaſants and partridges, they being the principal food of theſe birds, both wild and tame, for ſeveral reaſons, as is well known to all that are verſed in breeding them up: and a chief reaſon why many find it ſo nice a thing to breed up the ſaid birds, is, that they either give them too ſparingly of this food, or let them faſt too long, not knowing that as ſoon as it is daylight they will ſeek it for their breakfaſts, and if they want it, will in a few hours be faint and weak, and ſoon grow ſo chill for want of that ſupply of nouriſhment, that it is no eaſy matter to recover them.

14th, But though theſe inſects be ſo good a food for theſe birds, whilſt very young; yet, when by ill ordering of thoſe that ſhould keep them ſweet, and often ſhift their water, or by ill diet, as muſty corn, &c. they grow ſick; then Ants will not always recover them, though you give them ever ſo many; and I have been forced to make uſe of other inſects to cure them, to wit, of millepedes and earwigs, either of which will do good, but both together better, given in a good quantity, two or three times at leaſt a day; but then thoſe other things muſt be obſerved too, of keeping their houſe clean, and giving them ſweet corn, and ſhifting their water twice a day, keeping them within till the dew be from the ground, letting them baſk in ſand, partly in the ſun, the place a little ſhaded, and putting them up in a warm houſe before ſun-ſet.

Which particulars I thought not amiſs to add for thoſe who delight in breeding up pheaſants and partridges, myſelf having loſt many of both ſorts till I learned that virtue of thoſe inſects; after which ſeldom any of them, by me intended to be bred up, have died.

From the Hiſtoire Des Joyaux et Des Principals Riccheſſes de l'Orient et de l'Occident. Par le Sr. Chapuzeau.

THIS very inſtructive Hiſtory, (of which a ſhort Extract is given) treats of diamonds, rubies, emerald, pearls, coral, bezoax, yellow amber, ambergris, indigo, &c.

Of diamonds the author ſhews, 1ſt, The places whence they are taken, of which he finds but five in all the Eaſt Indies; whereof two are rivers, *viz.* Saccadan in Borneo, and Nage in the kingdom of Bengala; at the bottom of both which the diamonds are found amongſt the ſand, after the waters that fall as great torrents from the mountains, are run off; and the three others are mines in the kingdoms of Decan, Cuncan, and Golconda. In this relation he obſerves, that the diamonds which are found at the bottoms of thoſe rivers have the beſt water; but thoſe in mines have often flaws, which he imputes to the violent knockings of the rocks, and blebs, aſcribed to the condition of the earth or ſand they are found in, *viz.* when that is not pure, but fattiſh or black. He takes notice alſo that diamonds are the heavieſt of all precious ſtones, as gold is of all metals.

2dly, The manner how they are found and ſeparated; and, 3dly, The price of them, according to the proportion of their weight; for which he gives this rule: take a diamond of 10 carats; this number is to be ſquared (which makes 100); then if the ſtone be clean, each carat, according to its perfection, may be worth from 40 to 60 crowns: if it have no good water, or have a bleb or flaw, the carat will not be worth but from 10 to 30 crowns. So multiplying the ſaid 100 by the number, which each carat of ſuch or ſuch a ſtone may be worth, the product is the price of the ſtone.

For rubies, he mentions the places where they are found, and their price. The *places*, are the kingdom of Pegu, and the Iſle of Ceylon, whence very few are ſuffered to be carried away. The *price* is, that a good ruby, of the weight of one rati (which is $\frac{7}{8}$ of a carat), may be eſteemed at 20 old pagodas in India, each pagoda being about 10 ſhillings Engliſh.

Ratis.			Pagodas.
Of 2	is	valued at	100
Of 3	-	-	250
Of 4	-	-	500
Of 5	-	-	900
Of 6	-	-	1,500
Of 7	-	-	2,300
Of 8	-	-	12,000

Concerning turquois, they are found in Perſia, in the province of Chamaquay, north of Iſpahan, in two mines, called the *Old* and *New* Rock. Thoſe of the *New* are of an ill whitiſh blue; but thoſe of the *Old* are not ſuffered to be digged out, but by the King of Perſia's permiſſion.

Emeralds are affirmed by him never to be found in the Eaſt Indies, but in *Peru*, whence they were carried by that trading people to the Moluccas, even before America was diſcovered by Europeans, and therefore come from the Orient, and are of much leſs value than they were formerly, by reaſon of their commonneſs.

The author notes, that emeralds grow in ſtones, as chryſtals do, forming a vein, in which they are by little and little refined and thickened; and that ſome of them are ſeen half white and half green, others, all white; and others, all green and perfect.

To pearls he aſſigns in the Orient four places where they are fiſhed; to wit, the Iſle of Baharem, in the Perſian Gulf; the Coaſt of Arabia Felix, near the town of Catif, over againſt Baharem; the Iſle of Ceylon, about Manor; and the Iſle of Japan. The *beſt* are at Ceylon, but ſmall; the *biggeſt* at Japan, but uneven. In the Weſt Indies they are fiſhed in the North Sea; in the Iſles of Marguerite, Cubagva, St. Martha; and at

Comana, and Comanagote, near the Continent; and in the South Sea, near Panama; which American ſort, though they are much inferior to the Oriental in luſtre, yet they far excel them in bigneſs, amounting ſometimes to 42 carats.

In this relation it is mentioned, that ſometimes five or ſix pearls are found in one oyſter; that pearl-fiſhers are fed with dry and roaſted meat, to give them better breathing; that the pearl-bearing oyſters are not good to eat, being flat, and hard of digeſtion, &c.

As to the price of good pearls, well faſhioned, he marketh it as follows:

Weight, and Value of Pearls.

Grains.	Crowns.	Carats.	Crowns.
1	1	4¼	289
2	4	4½	324
3	9	4¾	361
Carats.		5	400
1	16	5¼	441
1¼	25	5½	484
1½	36	5¾	529
1¾	49	6	576
2	64	6¼	625
2¼	81	6½	675
2½	100	6¾	729
2¾	121	7	784
3	144	7¼	841
3¼	160	7½	900
3½	196	7¾	960
3¾	225	8	1024
4	256		

On corals he obſerves, that the places where they are fiſhed are eight; three upon the Coaſts of Corſica and Sardinia, viz. at Argueil (where is the beſt), at Baza, and near the Iſle of St. Peter; one upon the Coaſt of Sicily, near Drepanum; two upon the Coaſt of Africa, near the baſtion of Frane, and at Taborca; one more upon the Coaſt of Catalonia, at the Cape of Quiers; and the laſt, about Majorca. Obſerving, that red coral is not found but in the Mediterranean alone, where it is fished from the beginning of April until the end of July, employing generally about 200 boats. The manner of fishing them is with two big beams of wood, laid crosswise, with a large piece of lead on the middle, to make it sink, casting about it coarse hemp, carelessly twisted, and tying this wood to two ropes, whereof one hangs at the stern, the other at the fore part of the boat; and so letting this contrivance fall into the current, along the rocks, where the hemp being turned about, and engaged in the coral, there needs sometimes many boats to draw away the instrument.

The intelligent author further observes, that Bezoor Stone is not only found in Golconda, in the province of *Renquery*, in the maw of the goats, whereof some are at times furnished with a dozen a piece; but also at *Maessar*, in the Isle of Celebes, in the bodies of apes, bigger than those found in Golconda. He mentions that the people in those parts, to find whether a goat hath any of those Bezoor Stones in its body, do beat his belly with their hands, and rub it severely, till all the Stones in the animal come together, and then they feel and tell them, as you would stones in a bag, &c.

An Account of an easier and safer Way of transfusing Blood out of one Animal into another, viz. by the Veins, without opening an Artery of either. (First practised by Doctor Edmund King, and communicated by him to the ROYAL SOCIETY *as follows.)*

1st, I TOOK a calf and a sheep, both of the larger sort, and having prepared a jugular vein in each, I planted my pipes and quills, as is usual, both in the jugular vein of the calf (designed to be the emittent), and in that of the sheep (intended for the recipient). I took out of the sheep 49 ounces of blood, before any other blood was let in; about which time, the company concluding the sheep to be very weak and faint, and finding the blood to run very slowly, I stopped the vein of the sheep, and unstopped the pipe in the calf, letting run out 10 ounces into a porringer, which was done in about 40 seconds of a minute. Then I conveyed pipes from the emittent calf's vein into the recipient sheep's vein, and there run a good free ftream of blood for the fpace of five minutes (though perhaps lefs fwift than the firft 10 ounces). And, not to be deceived in the running, I did often ftrike with my finger the upper part of the emitting vein, and thereby eafily felt every ftroke anfwered on the recipient vein, juft like a pulfe, And now fuppofing that by this time (viz. the lapfe of five minutes) the fheep had received as much, if not more blood than it had loft, we ftopped the current of blood from the calf, and clofed alfo the vein of the fheep; and then having untied her, and fet her down in the room, fhe went about, and appeared to have as much ftrength as fhe had before the lofs of her own blood. Then refolving to bleed the fheep to death, we bound her a fecond time, and opened the emittent part of the vein again; whereupon, having bled about 60 ounces, fhe fell into convulfions; and after the lofs of about five ounces more, fhe died upon the place; and being dreffed by the butcher, there did not, in all the ufual places, appear above three ounces of blood; and the whole fheep looked of a lovely white; and the flefh of it (to the tafte of thofe who eat of it) was very fweet.

The fheep being dead, we refolved likewife to fee the calf bleed to death; but he having bled 10 ounces, and then for the fpace of five minutes more into the fheep, and refted a good while, the blood by that time began to coagulate in the vein, which made open the caroted artery, letting thence run out about 25 ounces of blood of a very vivid colour, vaftly excelling therein the blood of the vein. The calf, when dreffed, had, by the information of the butcher, as little blood as the fheep; and he appeared whiter than they ufually do in the ordinary way of killing.

2d, I took out 45 ounces and better from the jugular vein of a fheep, of lefs fize than the former, by which time the fpectators, as well as myfelf, found her exceeding faint, and fome thought paft recovery, without a fupply of blood. I then conveyed blood from the jugular vein of a calf into that of the fheep, for the fpace of feven minutes, when we did believe, by the continuance of a brifk ftream from the calf, that the fheep had already received more blood than fhe had loft; whereupon we fet her free, and fhe had no fooner got her liberty, but feeing a dog near her (which was a fpaniel, that had formerly fuffered the tranfmiffion of fheep's blood into him), fhe butted with great violence at him three or four times, not appearing at all concerned at what ſhe endured in the experiment. We keep this ſheep alive, ſhe being ſent to graſs again, and ſeeming, hitherto, very ſtrong and luſty.

The calf was much larger than the ſheep. We bled the calf to death, and received from him ſix porringers full of blood after the ſheep had been ſupplied, each porringer containing 11¼ ounces of water. The ſheep loſt four of the ſame meaſures full of blood, which being ſupplied by that of the calf, we reckon that the calf loſt 10 ſuch meaſures in all.

An Account of another Experiment of Transfuſion, viz. that of bleeding a Mangy into a Sound Dog. This was made by Mr. Thomas Coxe, and imparted likewiſe to the ROYAL SOCIETY, *in Manner following.*

I PROCURED an old mongrel cur, all over-run with *mange*, of a middle ſize, and having, ſome hours before, fed him plentifully with cheeſe parings and milk, I prepared the jugular vein, as we uſed to do the *carotidal* artery, of the emittent animal, not deſigning any thing further, than to determine by experiment the infection of the recipient's blood. Then I made as ſtrong a ligature upon the dog's neck as I durſt, for fear of choaking him, to the end that the venal blood, which is much more ſluggiſh in its motion and evacuation than the arterial, might be emitted with the greater advantage of impetus.

Then I took a young land ſpaniel, of about the ſame bigneſs, and prepared his jugular vein, as is uſually done in tbe recipient animal; the heart-ward part of the vein to receive the *mangy* dog's blood, and the head-ward part of it to diſcharge his own into a diſh.

Having thus prepared them both, and placed them in a convenient poſture one to the other, I let ſlip the running knots, and by frequent compreſſion of the neck (beſide the ligature I had made), by reaſon of the tardy running of the venal blood out of the emittent, transfuſed about 14 or 16 ounces of the blood of the infected into the veins of the ſound dog, as near as I could gueſs by the quantity of blood, which ran into a diſh from the recipient, ſuppoſing the recipient animal to loſe about the ſame proportion to what the emittent ſupplies.

The effect of which experiment was no alteration at all, any way, to be obſerved in the ſound dog. But for the *mangy* dog, he was in about ten days or a fortnight's ſpace perfectly cured; which might, with probability enough, I think, have been expected from the conſiderable evacuation he made; (perhaps the quickeſt and ſureſt *remedy* for the cure of that ſort of diſeaſe he was infected with, both in man and beaſt.)

Extract of a Letter of M. Denis, Profeſſor of Philoſophy and Mathematicks, touching the Transfuſion of Blood, which is rendered out of the Eighth Journal des Sçavans of 1667.

SINCE the experiments of which I wrote to you the 9th of March, we have transfuſed the blood of three calves into three dogs, to aſſure ourſelves what the mixture of two ſuch differing ſorts of blood might produce: I ſhall hereafter acquaint you at large with the particulars. At preſent I ſhall only inform you, that the animals into whom the blood hath been tranſmitted, do all of them eat as well as before, and that one of theſe three dogs, from whom the day before ſo much blood had been drawn that he could hardly move, having been ſupplied the next morning with the blood of a calf, recovered inſtantly his ſtrength, and ſhewed a *ſurpriſing vigour.*

We have found new ways of making this transfuſion, with ſo much facility, that M. Emmerez undertakes to perform it *without any ligature,* only by pricking, like that which is uſed in letting of blood.

An Experiment of making Cherry Trees, that have withered Fruit, to bear full and good Fruit; and of recovering the almoſt withered Fruit. Communicated by M. Denis, Profeſſor of Philoſophy and Mathematicks, &c.

ANNO 1665, I made the following experiment with three May Cherry Trees (planted in a rich mould), which lay to a ſouth wall, ſhaded four winter months from the Sun by a high building, ſo that the Sun came not on them till the beginning of March, when being high, and ſhining ſomewhat fiercely upon them, the fruit conſtantly withered for ſome years before. Now this year, the ſeaſon being very hot and dry, I bared the roots of *one* of them, by making a hole about it, and watered it every morning and evening, with about a gallon of water, for about a fortnight before the cherries came to redneſs, and the fruit was full and good. The other *two* trees, left without this ordering, had moſt of their fruit withered, having only ſkin and ſtones. Now to try this experiment farther, I made a hole round about *one* of the other trees, and fed it with water daily, as the former: in a week's time, thoſe that quite withered fell off, and the reſt that were not ſo, grew and increaſed exceedingly. The *other* tree, that was not uſed after this manner, had not any of its fruit come to perfection.

Extract of a Letter written from Paris, containing an Account of ſome Effects of the Transfuſion of Blood, and of Two Monſtrous Births.

I WAS preſent when M. Gayant ſhewed the Transfuſion of the Blood, putting that of a young dog into the veins of an old, who, two hours after, did leap and friſk, whereas he was almoſt blind with age, and could hardly ſtir before.

In the houſe of M. Bourdelot was ſhewn a Monſter in form of an Ape, having all over its ſhoulders, almoſt to his middle, a maſs of fleſh that came from the hinder part of its head, and hung down in the form of a little cloak. The report is, that the woman that brought it forth had ſeen on a ſtage an ape ſo clothed. The moſt remarkable thing was, that the ſaid maſs of fleſh was divided into four parts, correſpondent to the coat the ape did carry. The woman, upon inquiry, was found to have gone five months with child before ſhe had met with the accident of that unhappy ſight. Many queſtions were on this occaſion agitated, viz. about the power of imagination; and whether this creature was endowed with a human ſoul, and if not, what became of the ſoul of the embryo, that was five months old.

A little after, another monſter was produced, which was an infant come to maturity, having, inſtead of a head and brains, a maſs of fleſh like any liver; and was found to move. And this fœtus occasioned a queftion for the Cartefians, how the motion could be performed, and yet the glandula pinealis or conarium be wanting; nor any nerves vifible, which come from the brain? The marrow in the fpine was of the fame fubftance. It lived four days and then died. It was anatomized by M. Emmerez in prefence of the affembly.

There came a letter from Florence, written by M. Steno, which has alfo fomewhat perplexed the followers of Des Cartes. A tortoife had its head cut off, and yet was found to move its foot three days after. Here was no communication with the conarium. As this feems to have given a fore blow to the Cartefian doctrine, fo the difciples thereof are here endeavouring to heal the wound.

Some Obfervations made in Mines and at Sea occafioning a Conjecture about the Origin of Wind. Imparted by Mr. Colepreffe.

ONE John Gill, a man well experienced in mineral affairs, difcourfing with me about the wind and its origin, declared to me his thoughts concerning the fame, as the refult of 20 years experience and obfervations of his own.

Firft, He affirmed, that if in digging deep under ground, the workmen meet with water, they never want air or wind; but if they mifs water (as fometimes it happens even at 12 or 16 fathoms depth) they are deftitute of convenient air, either to breathe in or make their candles burn.

Next, When (as ufual) there happens to be a great quantity of a winter's ftanding water, in a deep mine, they commonly bring, or drive up an adit for drawing away fuch water. But as foon as that part of the level is made, that any of the ftanding water begins to run away, the men muft fecure themfelves as well as they can, from danger of being dafhed in pieces againft the fide of the adits, for the included air or wind in the ftanding water, breaks forth with fuch a terrible noife, as that of a piece of ordnance, and with that violence as to carry all before it, loofening the very rocks, though at fome diftance in the work or adit.

Thirdly, He hath obferved on feveral occafions going to and fro between London and Plymouth by fea, that being in a calm, that way, which the ſea began to loom or move, the next day the wind was ſure to blow from that point of the compaſs, towards which the ſea did loom the day before.

An Advertiſement concerning the Invention of the Transfuſion of Blood.

THE author of this paper returning now to his former exerciſes, which by an extraordinary accident he was neceſſitated to interrupt for ſome months laſt paſt, thought fit to compriſe the tranſactions of all the months omitted in one tract: in the very beginning of which he muſt inform the reader, that if himſelf had publiſhed that letter, which came abroad in July laſt, concerning a new way of curing ſundry diſeaſes by transfuſion of blood, written to Monſieur de Montmor, &c. by J. Denis, Profeſſor of Philoſophy, &c. he ſhould then have taken notice, as he doth now, of what is affirmed in that letter about the time and place of the conception of that transfuſing deſign; and intimated to the curious that how long ſoever that experiment may have been conceived in other parts, (which is needleſs to conteſt) it is notorious that it had its birth firſt of all in England, ſome ingenious perſons of the Royal Society having firſt ſtarted it there, ſeveral years ago, (as appears by their Journal) and that dexterous anatomiſt Dr. Lower reduced it to practice, both by contriving a method for the operation, and by ſucceſsfully executing the ſame, wherein he was ſoon overtaken by ſeveral happy trials of the ſkilful hand of Doctor Edmund King and others encouraged thereunto by the ſaid Society, which being notified to the world in prior numbers of theſe Tranſactions, the experiment was ſoon after that time heard of to have been tried in foreign parts, without hearing any thing then, of its having been *conceived ten years ago.*

An Account of ſome Experiments of Injecting Liquors into the Veins of Animals, lately made in Italy by Signior Fracaſſati, Profeſſor of Anatomy at Piſa.

1. HAVING infuſed into the jugular and crural vein of a dog, ſome aqua fortis diluted, the animal died preſently; and being opened, all the blood in the veſſels was fixed, but that in the guts not ſo well.—It was alſo obſerved that the great veſſels were burſt, perhaps by an effort of nature;

even as in the greateſt part of thoſe that die of an apoplexy, the veſſels of the lungs are found broken. Upon which experiments, the author maketh theſe reflections: Firſt, that an apoplexy being often cauſed by a like coagulation of the blood (as hath been obſerved by the opening made of ſundry perſons, who died of that diſtemper) it might be cured by timely infuſing ſome diſſolvent into the veins. Secondly, that it is likely that uſeful ſecret by which Monſieur de Billy diſſected animals without any effuſion of blood, conſiſts in ſome ſuch infuſion.

2. There was afterwards infuſed into another dog ſome ſpirit of vitriol, which had not ſo preſent an effect; for the animal complained a great while and foamed like epileptics, and had its reſpiration very thick; and obſerving the beating of his breaſt, one might eaſily judge the dog ſuffered much: who dying at laſt, his blood was found fixed in the veins, and grumous, reſembling ſoot.

3. Then there was injected into the dog ſome oil of ſulphur: but he died not of it, though this infuſion was ſeveral times tried upon him. And the wound being cloſed, and the dog let go, he went into all the corners of the room ſearching for meat, and having found ſome bones he fell a gnawing of them, with a ſtrange avidity, as if this liquor had cauſed in him a great appetite.

4. Another dog, into whoſe veins ſome oil of tartar was injected, did not eſcape ſo well, for he complained much, was altogether ſwoln, and then died. Being opened, the ſpectators were ſurpriſed to find his blood not curdled, but on the contrary more thin and fluid than ordinary, which ſeems to hint that a too great fluidity of the blood, as well as its coagulation, may cauſe death.

Some Obſervations communicated by Signior Manfredus Septalius, from Milan, concerning Quickſilver, found at the Roots of Plants, and Shells found upon Inland Mountains.

THIS Italian virtuoſo, famous for his knowledge and curioſity, as well as for his hoſpitality to ingenious ſtrangers, did in a late letter of his to the Publiſher, impart the following particulars.

1. In the valley of Lancey, which runs between the mountains of Turin, grows a plant like the Doronicum (ſo alſo called by the inhabitants and

botanifts), near the roots whereof, you may find pure quickfilver, running in fmall grains like pearls, the juice of which plant being expreffed and expofed to the air of a clear night, there will be found as much mercury as there is loft of juice *.

2. In a voyage he made a few years fince to Genoa, when he was to pafs fome mountains, he met with fome peafants who, digging on the fides of a hill, had found and gathered very many cockle-fhells of divers kinds; which he wondering at, ftopped his intended journey, and went to the very place, where he was fatisfied of the truth of the relation, finding great ftore of different fhells, as the Turbinetts Echini, and fome pearl fhells, whereof one had a fair pearl in it, which, he faith, he put into his repofitory.

An Abridged Account of the Hiftory of the ROYAL SOCIETY *of London, for the Advancement of Experimental Philofophy, &c. &c. By Thomas Sprat.*

IT was indeed highly fuitable, that the hiftory of the ROYAL SOCIETY fhould be dedicated, as the candid author of it hath done, to that King, who was the firft of all kings of Europe, that confirmed this noble and extenfive defign, both by his own example, and by a public eftablifhment.

The difcourfe itfelf, which is modeft and elegant, is divided by the author into thefe three general heads:

The firft gives a fhort view of the ancient and modern philofophy; and of the moft famous attempts that have been made for its advancement, by the Chaldeans, Egyptians, Grecians, Arabians, Romans of old; and then, by feveral new ways of philofophy within the compafs of our memories, and in the age before us; reprefenting what hath been attempted by the *modern dogmatifts*, the *revivers of ancient fects*, the late experimenters, the chemifts, and writers of particular fubjects. All which he deduceth, to the end, that by obferving wherein others have excelled, and wherein they have been thought to fail, he might the better fhew, what was to be expected from thofe new undertakers; and what moved them to enter upon a way of enquiry, different from that on which the former had proceeded.

* This may be compared with thofe relations which acquaint us that in Moravia, Hungary, Peru, and other parts, mineral juices concreted, are found to ftick to the roots of herbs and trees, fome of thofe juices tinging alfo the leaves of vegetables.

The second consists of the narrative itself, in which the historian out of the registers and journals of the ROYAL SOCIETY (which he hath been permitted to peruse,) relates the first occasions of their meetings, the encouragement and patronage they have received; their patent, their statutes *; the whole order and scheme of their design: the qualifications of their members, the largeness of their number; their weekly assemblies; the manner of their inquiries; their way of registering; and their universal correspondency; together with a particular enumeration of the principal subjects, about which they have been employed since they were made a Royal Corporation. And here the historian hopes, that reasonable men will find satisfaction, when they shall consider, first, That, besides that this Society hath passed through the first difficulties of their charter and model, and overcome all oppositions which use to arise against the *beginnings of all great things*; their aim, and the nature of their design, and the extent of their task do admit of no violent and hasty dispatch. Next, that though their work had not been exposed to open view, yet their registers are stored with a great number of particulars they have taken much pains about; as,

1. *Queries* and *directions* they have given abroad.
2. Proposals and recommendations they have made.
3. Relations they have received.
4. Experiments they have tried.
5. Observations they have taken.
6. Instruments they invented or advanced.
7. Theories that have been proposed.
8. Discourses they have written or published.
9. Histories of nature and arts, and works they have collected.

The particulars upon these heads, which the author enumerates are of greater extent, moment and variety, than at this early period of the institution might be easily imagined.

He also adds an account of the library and repository they have obtained by the bounty of two of their members; and gives withal some examples of their experiments; histories both of nature and of art; queries answered; proposals recommended, &c. which done, he concludeth, that if any shall think they have not usefully employed their time, he shall be apt

* For a more particular account of the STATUTES, RULES, REGULATIONS, &c. of the ROYAL SOCIETY, see the Introduction to this volume.

to ſuſpect that they underſtand not what is meant by a diligent and profitable labouring about nature; and that ſuch men ſeem not capable of being ſatisfied, unleſs the Gentlemen of this Society immediately profeſs to have found out the *ſquaring* of *the circle*, or the philoſopher's ſtone, or ſome other ſuch mighty *nothings*; which only argues the extravagance of the expectations of ſuch men. Mean time the author eſteems, that ſince the Society promiſes no miracles, nor endeavours after them; and ſince their progreſs ought to be, as it is, equal and firm, by natural degrees, and through *ſmall* things, as well as *great*, going on leiſurely and warily, it is therefore fit that they alone, and not others, who refuſe to conſider the *nature* of their *work*, and partake of their *burthen*, ſhould be judges by what ſteps and what pace they ought to proceed.

The third part aſſerts both the advantage and innocence of the deſign, in reſpect of all profeſſions, and particularly of Religion, and how proper, above others, it is for the preſent temper of the age wherein we live: and this is done to free it from the cavil of the idle and malicious, and from the jealouſies of private intereſts; all which the author ſhews to have nothing but humour or envy, prejudice or miſtake, to bear themſelves upon.

The promoting of experiments, according to the model of the ROYAL SOCIETY, will be ſo far from injuring education, or being dangerous to the univerſities, that it will both introduce many things of greater concernment and benefit to ſupply the place of what may be laid aſide; and be mainly conducive to recover that divine dignity of human nature, which conſiſts in the knowledge of truth, and the doing of good.

The firſt years of men being ſecured by this new experimental way, it is made out to all profeſſions and practical lives, that they can receive no ill impressions from it, but that it will be the moſt beneficial and proper ſtudy for their preparation and direction; whereas other learning is charged to conſiſt in arguing and diſputing, and to be apt to make our minds lofty and romantic, preſumptuous and obſtinate, averſe from a practical courſe, and unable to bear the difficulties of action; propenſe to things, which are no where in uſe in the world; and careleſs to their own preſent times, by doting on the paſt. This experimental philoſophy will turn men to trials and works; cure their minds of romantic ſwelling, by ſhewing all fit and uſeful things familiarly to them, juſt as large as they are; free them from perverſity, by not permitting them to be too peremptory in their concluſions; accuſtom their hands to things, which have a near reſemblance to the buſineſs of life: and draw away the ſhadows which either enlarge or darken human affairs; and of the crafty, the formal, and the prudent, (the uſual titles by which men of buſineſs are wont to be diſtinguiſhed); our author reſembles the crafty to the empiric in philoſophy; the formal to the mere ſpeculative philoſopher; but the prudent man, to him who proceeds on a conſtant and ſolid courſe of experiments; the one in civil life, rejecting neither the wiſdom of ancient, nor that of modern times; the other in philoſophy, having the ſame reverence for former ages, and regard for the preſent; both raiſing their obſervations unto uſe, not ſuffering them to be idle, but employing them to direct the actions, and ſupply the wants of human life.

And as this *experimental* way will afford much help to our *public duties*, and *civil actions*, ſo it proved to be very uſeful to the cure of men's minds, and the management of their private motions and paſſions, by keeping them from idleness, with full and earneſt employment, and by poſſeſſing them with innocent, various, laſting, and even ſenſible delights.

Hence he proceeds to ſhew that theſe inveſtigations and experiments are a proper ſtudy for the gentlemen of this nation, in which he finds them already well engaged. As alſo, that they will be beneficial to our *wits* and *writers*, who, if truly worthy men, will find in the *works* of *nature* an inexhauſtible treaſure for fancy and invention, which will be diſcloſed proportionably to the increaſe of their knowledge. Fourth, that they are advantageous to the intereſt of the nation, by enlarging the trade and power thereof.

Upon which, and ſeveral other accounts, (not poſſible to be contracted here) our hiſtorian concludes his Diſcourſe with giving us a catalogue of thoſe which at this preſent time compoſe the ROYAL SOCIETY, amounting to near two hundred, whereof the *King's Majeſty* is founder and patron. Amongſt the Fellows are three of the greateſt Princes of Europe, his Royal Highneſs the Duke of York; his Highneſs Prince Rupert, Count Palatine of the Rhine; and his Highneſs Ferdinand Albert, Duke of Brunſwick and Lunenburg; then the two Archbiſhops of England, and four Biſhops. Of Dukes, Marquiſſes, Earls, Viſcounts, and Barons, Engliſh and Scotch, twenty-nine; of Knights, thirty-five; of Doctors and Batchelors of Divinity, fourteen; of Doctors and candidates of Phyſic, twenty-one; of Eſquires, and other Gentlemen and Merchants, ſixty-four; of ſtrangers, ſixteen.

After the enumeration of which, he recommends this undertaking to the *Engliſh nation*; to the *braveſt people* this moſt generous deſign, which at once regards the diſcovering of important ſecrets, and the purifying and repairing all the profitable things of antiquity; and here he repreſents, that if now this enterpriſe ſhould chance to fail for want of *patronage* and revenue, the world would not only be fruſtrated of their preſent expectations, but have juſt ground to deſpair of any future labours toward the increaſe of practical and uſeful knowledge. But he hopes and preſages, that the Engliſh nation will lay hold on this opportunity to deſerve the applauſe of mankind, for having encouraged and ſupported a work, which inſtead of barren *terms* and *notions*, is able to impart to us the uſes of all creatures, and to enrich us with all the benefits of *real knowledge*, true honour, great plenty, and ſolid delight.

Abſtract of further Trials of Transfuſion, accompanied with ſome conſiderations thereon, chiefly in reference to its circumſpect practice on Man; together with a further Vindication of this Invention from Uſurpers.

THIS experiment, as it has raiſed diſputes among the *curious* both here and abroad, ſo it hath put ſome of them upon conſidering ſuch ways, and giving ſuch cautions, as may render the uſe of it ſafe and beneficial. Of the number of theſe ſeems to be that French virtuoſo Gaſper de Gurye de Montpoly, who in a late letter of his to Monſieur Bourdelot, declares to the world that it is a very ingenious invention, and ſuch an one as may prove very uſeful; but withal, that in his opinion it is to be uſed with much caution, as not being likely to be practiſed innoxiouſly, if imprudent men do manage it, and the concourſe of two differing ſorts of blood requiring many trials, and a careful obſervation of many circumſtances to give aſſurance. He ſuppoſes that the blood of every animal is endowed with its peculiar temper, and contains in the aggregate of its parts different natures, principles, figures, and even a different centre. Whence he concludes that two ſubſtances thus differing, and containing plenty of ſpirits, are not reducible to one and the ſame centre, nor to one and the ſame body, without *fermentation*; and that this operation may prove of danger to him that ſhall have admitted into his veins a ſtrange blood (wont to be free in its native veſſels) without paſſing through thoſe degrees that muſt give it impreſſions ſuitable to the temper and functions of the vitals of the recipient: and taking for granted that no conſiderate man will hazard a total transfuſion, he acknowledges that a partial one may be in ſome caſes very uſeful, provided it be practiſed circumſpectly upon a body yet ſtrong enough, and in a moderate quantity, ſo as the ſpirits and blood of the recipient may be able to diſſolve and maſter the transfuſed ſtrange blood, and convert the ſame into its own nature by a gentle ebullition, to obtain by ſuch a commixture a principle of motion that may cauſe a better habit of body: and he believes that this ebullition muſt always happen in bloods of differing parts and qualities; and that very rarely two animals of differing ſpecies, ages and tempers, will be met with, that have blood ſo like each other as not to need a fermentation to make a requiſite mixture. He doubts not that if a ſubſtance could be found ſo reſembling that of our ſpirits, as it would immediately unite itſelf with them, not needing any alteration, the transfuſion of ſuch a ſubſtance would be capable to produce effects little leſs than miraculous, by relieving the proſtrated forces of nature, and by fortifying in us the ſpring of motion and of life: in a word, by exciting that principle of continual motion, which, whilſt it has ſtrength enough, ſtill ſubdues and gathers to itſelf what is proper to entertain it, and rejects what is not ſo. But ſuch an invention as this, he ſees cauſe to eſteem very difficult, in regard that different moulds cannot but characteriſe things differently. Hence he proceeds to the examples wherein transfuſion hath been experimented, even upon men, alleged in that known ingenious letter of Monſieur Denys: and here he intimates how much he was pleaſed to learn, that, according to his conjecture, a moderate intermiſſion of blood had well ſucceeded; and the fermentation, which he foreſaw would be cauſed by the commixture of two bloods, was made with advantage to the patient, which he judges did manifeſtly appear by his bleeding at the noſe (a ſign of ebullition made in the blood); confirmed to him by this, that an expert acquaintance of his transfuſing a great quantity of blood into ſeveral dogs, obſerved always that the receiving dogs paſſed blood.

And as to the other ſucceſsful experiment made upon a healthy and robuſt man, he notes, that he being a luſty fellow, ſtored with blood, and taking the air, and working hard on the ſame day the trial was made upon him, his vigorous blood, ſpirits and conſtitution, and the ſtrong motion of his heart, were able to convert into the ſubſtance of his own blood that of the lamb received, and to impart thereto its own nature, and to mould it into figures ſuitable to the pores where it was to paſs, and proper to the functions it was to perform.

But to theſe reflections he ſubjoins two other inſtances, of an unlike ſucceſs; whereof the one is afforded by a man, the other by a dog. As to the man it ought to be related before hand, to prevent wonder and miſconſtruction, that his inteſtines, when he was opened after death, were found to be gangrened, and conſequently that then he appeared to be a ſubject altogether unfit for this experiment, ſeeing it was naturally impoſſible for him to live with ſuch a putrefaction. But to come to the trial itſelf: this Author ſaith, that Baron Bond, the ſon of the firſt Miniſter of State to the King of Sweden, undergoing the operation twice, appeared the firſt time to find new ſtrength by it; but expired ſoon after the ſecond operation.* The ebullition, it ſeems, of the corrupt blood having maſtered and enervated all the blood he had in his body, which, when opened, no blood at all was found in his heart: probably, as the Author conjectures upon this account, that there being not left in the patient blood enough of his own, nor ſtrength ſufficient to turn a ſtrange blood into a ſubſtance homogeneous to that, he was not capable to admit the blood of the emittent, as conſiſting of parts diſproportionate to his own. But, as has been already obſerved, his entrails were altogether vitiated by gangrene, and he therefore out of the reach of being relieved by this experiment.

Concerning the other inſtance, viz. of the dog, the letter affirms, that that trial was made by Monſieur Gayen, with great exactneſs, after this manner. He drew three great diſhes of blood from the dog that was to receive, and weighed the other dog that was to furniſh; and the operation being performed, he weighed him again, and found him to weigh leſs by two pounds; of which, having abated an ounce more or leſs for the urine made by the dog, and an ounce or two more for the blood ſpilt in the operation, there remained at leaſt one pound and a half of blood that was transfuſed. But the recipient, though well dreſſed, and well fed, died

* It were to be wiſhed the author had expreſſed the interval of time wherein theſe two operations had followed one another; that ſeeming to be a material circumſtance in the caſe.

five days after, the emittent being yet alive. Whence it ſeems evident to this Writer, that the too large intermiſſion of *new* blood was predominant over the *native*, and, as it were, overwhelmed it. Whence he again inculcates the danger of infuſing too much blood at once, in regard that ſuch blood being now ſeparated from that principle of life it had in the emittent, and as yet deſtitute of the ſtamp neceſſary to live the life of the recipient, it could not be moved and aſſimilated by the live blood which remained in the recipient; and the fermentation that was made, paſſed rather to an eagerneſs or ſourneſs, than to ſuch an one as precedes digeſtion. And this kind of eager acidity he *intimates* was *ſeen* by the ſpectators, and *felt* by the receiving animal, which ſwooned, and remained as dead for half a quarter of an hour: and when ſome alleged that the dog died, becauſe he was wounded in the neck, where he could not lick himſelf, which rendered the wound incurable, anſwer was given, that experiments were made wherein not only a vein was opened, but alſo an artery, yea, even the aſpera arteria cut of a dog, that could not lick himſelf, and yet ſurvived.

This whole account concludes with an admonition, that all thoſe, who have conveniency, would make frequent and exact trials of this experiment upon brutes, and carefully obſerve weight and meaſure, and all other circumſtances, before any thing be hazarded that may damnify the public and depreciate the invention.

Abundans cantila non nocet is a maxim very fit to be minded here, though ſeveral ſucceſsful experiments have been made in London, of very plentiful transfuſions; and among others (to mention a ſingle one) that upon a Bitch, which loſt in the operation near 30 ounces of blood, and was recruited accordingly. This animal does not only ſurvive to this very day, but had another more ſevere experiment ſoon after tried upon her, by which her ſpleen was cut out, without tying up the veſſels, whence that viſcus was ſeparated: ſince which time (even before the wound was healed up) ſhe took dog, was with puppy, and brought forth whelps, and remains well and jocund, being kept for a piece of remarkable curioſity in the houſe of a Nobleman, who is as ſevere in examining matters of fact, as he is able in judging of their conſequences.

So that it is not too haſtily to be concluded, that large Transfuſions are dangerous, but rather frequent experiments ſhould be made before any thing be therein determined, with great as well as ſmaller quantities, both upon ſound as well as ſickly beaſts, carefully obſerving how either is endured in either, and what are the effects following thereon.

Before we diſmiſs this ſubject, ſomething is to be ſaid of the *cauſe* why the curious in England make a demur in practiſing this experiment upon men. The abovementioned ingenious Monſ. Denys has acquainted the world how this proceſs was ventured upon at Paris, and what good ſucceſs it there met with: and the Journal des Sçavans glorieth, that the French have advanced this invention ſo far as to try it upon men, before any Engliſh did it, and that with good ſucceſs.

We readily grant *they* were the firſt we know of, that actually thus *improved* the experiment; but then they muſt give us leave to inform them of this *truth*, that the Philoſophers in England had practiſed it long ago upon man, if they had not been ſo tender in hazarding the life of man (which they take ſo much pains to preſerve and relieve) nor ſo ſcrupulous to incur the penalties of the law, which in England is more ſtrict and nice, in caſes of this concernment, than thoſe of many other nations are.

The Publiſher can aſſert, *bona fide*, that ſeveral months ago he ſaw, himſelf, the *inſtruments* ready, and heard the *method* agreed on, thought proper to execute this operation upon man. And, for further proof thereof, he ſhall here inſert the whole way, peculiarly contrived here for this purpoſe, by the ingenious Dr. Edmund King, and by him communicated in a letter; Monſieur Denys not having thought fit to deſcribe the manner they uſed in France for men, nor any body elſe that has come to our knowledge.

The Letter is as follows:—

"SIR,

"THE method of Transfuſing Blood you have ſeen practiſed with facility enough, from beaſt to beaſt; and we have things in readineſs to transfuſe blood from the artery of a lamb, kid, or what other animal may be thought proper, into the vein of a man. We have been ready for this experiment theſe ſix months, and wait for nothing but good opportunities, and the removal of ſome conſiderations of a moral nature. I gave you a view, you may remember, a good while ago, of the inſtruments I think very proper for the experiment, which are only a ſilver tube, with a ſilver ſtopper, ſomewhat blunted at one end, and flatted at the other for conveniency of handling, uſed already upon beaſts with good ſucceſs. The way is in ſhort this: after the artery is prepared in the lamb, kid, &c. let a ligature be made upon the arm, &c. of a man, (hard enough to render the vein turgid) in the place you intend to insert the lesser end of the silver pipe, which is so fitted, that the silver stopper, thrust into the tube, reaches somewhat, by its blunt end, beyond one of the ends of that tube. This done, divide the skin of that part in the same manner that is used in cutting an issue, just over the vein, to be open. Then with a fine lance open the vein; or, if you please, in case the vein lay fair and high (especially if the skin be fine) you may open both together, according to the usual way of letting blood. Which done, let an assistant clap his finger, or a little bolster, prepared before hand, or the like, upon the vein, a little below the orifice, to hinder the blood from ascending. Keeping that position, insert the blunt ended tube upwards into the vein, when it is in, hold it and the skin close together between your finger and thumb; then pull out of the tube the stopper, and insert the pipe, by which the arterial blood is to be infused from the emittent animal; managing the remainder according to the known method of this experiment."

So far *this letter*, which maketh the practicableness of this method look so fair and easy, that nothing seems wanting to encourage the trial but the direction and assistance of discreet and skilful men, taking care not to experiment it upon subjects that have their internal parts vitiated, forasmuch as it seems not reasonable to expect that this transfusion should cure cacochymics, or restore a depraved constitution of the viscera.

I would have said no more of this argument at this time, were it not to remove a mistake found in one of the French Journals, affirming with confidence, that "*it is certain* the French have given the English the first thought or notion of this experiment." And why, because (say they) there are witnesses that a Benedictine Friar, one Don Robert de Gabets, discoursed of it at Monsieur de Monmor's ten years ago. Surely all ingenious men will acknowledge, that the certain way of deciding such controversies as these is a public record, either written or printed, declaring the time and place of an invention first proposed, the contrivance of the method to practise it, and the instances of the success in the execution: all this appears in the field for England.

A Paper of these Transactions, printed in December, 1665, acquaints the world, how many years since Doctor Christopher Wren proposed the experiment of *Infusion* into Veins. And this was hint enough for the ROYAL SOCIETY, ſome while after, to advance *Infuſion* to *Tranſfuſion*; for the trial of which latter, they gave order at their public meeting, in May 1665, as may be ſeen in their Journal, where it was regiſtered by the care of their Secretaries, obliged by oath to fidelity. The trials at that time proving defective, for want of a fit apparatus, and a well contrived method of operation, that learned Phyſician and expert Anatomiſt Doctor Lower ſince found out ſuch a method, which is not only regiſtered in the ſame book, but alſo formerly publiſhed in theſe Tracts, before which time it had been already practiſed by the ſaid Doctor in Oxford, who was followed by ſeveral ingenious men in London, who ſucceſsfully practiſed it by the public order of the aforeſaid Society.

It ſeems ſtrange, that ſo ſurpriſing an invention ſhould have been conceived in *France*, as they will have it, ten years ago, and lain there ſo long in the womb, till the way of midwiving it into the world was ſent thither from London; to ſay nothing of the diſagreement there ſeems to be about the French parent of this fœtus, Monſieur de Gurye, in the letter above mentioned, fathering it upon the Abbot Bourdelot, but the author of the *French Journals* upon a *Benedictine Friar*.

But whoever this parent be, that is not ſo material, as that all who lay claim to this child ſhould join together their endeavours and cares to breed it up for the ſervice and relief of human life, if it be capable of it; and this is the main thing aimed at in this diſcourſe, at the ſame time that it is fit that juſtice ſhould be done to merit.

Obſervations made on a Great Fiſh, and a Lion, diſſected in the King's Library at Paris, on the 24th and 25th of June, 1667.

THIS great fiſh, diſſected by the Pariſian Philoſophers, was a *vulpecula marina* (a ſea fox), in which they obſerved, 1ſt, the length of his tail, equal nearly to the whole length of the reſt of his body (the whole fiſh being eight feet long), and faſhioned after the manner of a ſcythe, bowed, and turned up toward the belly.

2dly, His mouth was armed with two ſorts of teeth, one ſort, in the upper jaw, being pointed, hard and firm, and of one only bone, in the manner of a ſaw; the other ſort, found in the reſt of the upper, and in

5

the whole of the under jaw, were moveable, and faſtened by fleſhy membranes.

3dly, His tongue did altogether adhere to the lower jaw, and his ſkin was hard, and covered with little ſhining points, which rendered it very rough and ſcabrous one way. The points, viewed with a microſcope, appeared tranſparent, like cryſtal.

4thly, His throat was very large, and the œſophagus as large as his maw; concerning which, authors ſay that he hath a dexterity of diſengaging himſelf from the ſwallowed hook, by caſting it up, together with his maw, the inſide of it turned out. They found in his maw the ſea herb varec, five inches long, and the fiſh of the like length, without head, ſcales, ſkin, or guts, all being waſted but the muſcolous fleſh, which remained entire.

5thly, The ſuperior part of his great gut had this peculiarity, that inſtead of the uſual circumvolutions of guts, the cavity of this was divided tranſverſely, by many partitions, conſiſting of the membranes of the gut turned inwards, in the figure of a vice, like ſnail ſhells, or winding ſtairs.

6thly, His ſpleen was double; his liver divided into two lobes; the gall found to have more of bitter than ſour; the heart without a pericordium as big as a hen's egg; the head almoſt nothing but a maſs of fleſh, very little brains in it, and thoſe that were there having very few meanders or windings; the eyes bigger than the noſe of an ox, only half ſpherical, flat before; the ſclarotica formed like a cup, very thin, but very hard; the cornea very tender and ſoft; the cryſtalline perfectly ſpherical; the uvea greyiſh; the choroids of the ſame colour, and pierced, for the production of the retina, by a very large hole; the bottom of the choroids had that luſtre of mother of pearl which is found in terreſtrial animals, but with leſs vivid colours; and the retina was alſo ſtreaked with very apparent ſanguineous veſſels.

The *obſervables* in the *Lion* were,

In general, that for outward ſhape and conſtitution of many parts, as the claws, teeth, eyes, tongue (beſides the likeneſs of the viſcera), a lion reſembles very much a cat. In particular, an admirable ſtructure of his claws; a peculiar ſhape and poſition of his teeth; a very ſtiff neck; a mighty rough and ſharp tongue, having points like claws, both for hardnefs and fhape; eyes very clear and bright, even after death, which, without clofing the eyelids, lions can cover with a thick and blackifh membrane, placed towards the great angle, which by raifing itfelf, and reaching towards the fmall angle, can extend itfelf over the whole cornea, as it is in birds, but efpecially in cats; the reverfe of the anterior uvea, where it lies over the cryftalline, is altogether black; the cryftalline very flat, and its greateft convexity, which is not ufual, in its anterior part, as 'tis in cats; the aqueous humour very plentiful, equalling almoft the fixth part of the vitreous, which plenty was judged to be the caufe of the brightnefs that remains in the eyes after death.

His throat was not above an inch and a half large; the ftomach fix inches large, and 18 inches long; all the guts 25 feet long; the liver divided into feven lobes, as in cats; its cavity under the bladder of gall was full of gall, fhed abroad in the fubftance of the liver, and of the neighbouring parts, which was fufpected by the phyficians adminiftering this operation to have been the caufe of this lion's death; the bladder of gall was feven inches long, and one half inch large, of a peculiar ftructure; the fpleen a foot long, two inches large, and one half inch thick; the kidney weighed fomewhat above feven ounces; the genitals of a peculiar conformation, caufing this animal to caft his urine backwards, and to couple like camels and hares.

His lungs had fix lobes on the right fide, and three on the left; the wind had its annular cartilages entire, excepting two or three; it was above four inches in compafs, being very firm, and by this bignefs and firmnefs enabling a lion ftrongly to thruft air enough through it for his dreadful roaring.

His heart was dry, and without water in the pericardium, much greater in proportion than of any other animal, being fix inches long, and four inches large towards the bafis, and terminating in a fharp point; it had very little flefh, and was all hollow; the ventricles very large; the auricles very fmall; the proportion of the branches which the afcending aorta caft out was fuch, that the carrotides were as big as the left fubclavial branch, and as the reft of the right fubclavial, whence they iffue; which is confiderable, feeing the brain is fo fmall; for the brain was but two inches big of any dimenfion, the reft of the head being very flefhy, and confifting of firm bones.

I

By comparing the little quantity of the lion's brain with the plenty of that of a calf, it was judged that the having but little brain is rather a mark of a fierce and cruel temper, than want of wit; which conjecture was ſtrengthened by the obſervation formerly made in the ſea fox, in whom almoſt no brains were found, though it be thought that his craft and addreſs had occaſioned men to give him that name.

The Hiſtory of Amber, by Juſtus Klobio, Doctor in the Academy of Wittenberg.

THIS author reckons up 18 opinions concerning Ambergris, and having examined every one of them, he embraces that which holds, that it is the dung of a bird (called in the Madagaſcar tongue *Aſchiboluch)*, of which he gives the deſcription out of Odoardus, Barborſa, and others, who affirm it to be of the bigneſs of a gooſe, curiouſly feathered, with a big head, well tufted. Theſe birds being found in great numbers at Madagaſcar, the Maldives, and other parts of the Eaſt Indies, are affirmed by authors to flock together in great numbers, as cranes, and frequenting high cliffs near the ſea, and there voiding their excrement, the ſea waſhes it thence, if it falls not of itſelf into it.

There is another opinion amongſt the ſaid 18, for which the author hath a good inclination, but yet dares not embrace it, viz. that it is the excrement of a certain kind of whales. If this amber were but in thoſe other places, where there is good ſtore of ſuch whales, it ſeems that would make the author relinquiſh the former opinion.

This puts us in mind of a relation in Purchas, which, giving an account of a certain commiſſion of a gentleman to go factor into Greenland for the killing of whales and morſes, takes notice, among other particulars, of a ſort of whales called Trompa, having but one trunk on his head, whereas the Sarda, another kind of whale, hath two. This trompa (ſaith that author) hath teeth of a ſpan long, and as thick as a man's wriſt, but no fins. In his head is the ſpermaceti, and in his entrails the ambergris, being in ſhape and colour like cow's dung. Expreſs order was given in the ſaid commiſſion that the perſon deputed ſhould himſelf be preſent at the opening of this ſort of whale, and cauſe the reſidue of the ſaid entrails to be put into ſmall caſks, and bring them along with him into England.

*An Account of an Experiment * made by Mr. Hook, of preſerving Animals alive by blowing through their Lungs with Bellows.*

I DID heretofore give this illuſtrious Society an account of an experiment I formerly tried of keeping a dog alive after his thorax was all diſplayed by the cutting away of the ribs and diaphragme, and after the pericardium of the heart was alſo taken off. But divers perſons ſeeming to doubt of the certainty of the experiment (by reaſon that ſome trials made of this matter by ſome other perſons failed of ſucceſs), I cauſed at the laſt meeting the ſame experiment to be ſhewn in the preſence of this noble company, and that with the ſame ſucceſs as it had been made by me at firſt; the dog being kept alive by the reciprocal blowing up of his lungs with bellows, and they ſuffered to ſubſide, for the ſpace of an hour or more after his thorax had been ſo diſplayed, and his aſpera arteria cut off juſt below the epiglottis, and bound on upon the noſe of the bellows.

And becauſe ſome eminent phyſicians had affirmed that the motion of the lungs was neceſſary to life, upon the account of the promoting of the circulation of the blood, and that it was conceived the animal would immediately be ſuffocated as ſoon as the lungs ſhould ceaſe to be moved, I did (the better to fortify my own hypotheſis of this matter, and to be the better able to judge of ſeveral others) make the following additional experiment, viz.

The dog having been kept alive (as I have now mentioned) for above an hour, in which time the trial had been often repeated, in ſuffering the dog to fall into convulſive motions by ceaſing to blow the bellows, and permitting the lungs to ſubſide and lie ſtill, and of ſuddenly reviving him again by renewing

* This noble experiment was preſented to the ROYAL SOCIETY Oct. 24, 1667, where it was repeated and improved at their public Meeting, after a former ſucceſsful trial of it by the author.

the blaſt, and conſequently the motion of the lungs; this I ſay having been done, and the judicious ſpectators fully ſatisfied of the reality of the former experiment, I cauſed another pair of bellows to be immediately joined to the firſt by a contrivance I had prepared, and pricking all the outer coat of the lungs with the point of a very ſharp pen-knife, this ſecond pair of bellows was moved very quick, whereby the firſt pair was always kept full and blowing into the lungs, by which the lungs were alſo always kept very full and without any motion, there being a continued blaſt of air forced into the lungs by the firſt pair of bellows, ſupplying it as faſt as it could find its way quite through the coat of the lungs, by the ſmall holes pricked in it, as was ſaid before. This being continued for a little while, the dog, as I expected, lay ſtill, as before, his eyes being all the time very quick, and his heart beating very regularly. But upon ceaſing this blaſt, and ſuffering the lungs to fall and lie ſtill, the dog would immediately fall into dying convulſive fits, but be as ſoon revived again by the renewing the fulneſs of his lungs, with the conſtant blaſt of freſh air.

Towards the latter end of this experiment a piece of the lungs was cut quite off, where 'twas obſervable that the blood did freely circulate, and paſs through the lungs, not only when the lungs were kept thus conſtantly extended, but alſo when they were ſuffered to ſubſide and lie ſtill; which ſeem to be arguments, that as the bare motion of the lungs without freſh air contributes nothing to the life of the animal, he being found to ſurvive as well when they were not moved as when they were; ſo it was not the ſubſiding or moveleſsneſs of the lungs that was the immediate cauſe of death, or the ſtopping the circulation of the blood through the lungs, but the want of a ſufficient ſupply of freſh air.

I ſhall ſhortly further try whether the ſuffering the blood to circulate through a veſſel, ſo as it may be openly expoſed to the freſh air, will not ſuffice for the life of an animal, and make ſome experiments, which I hope will thoroughly diſcover the genuine uſe of reſpiration, and afterwards conſider of what benefit this may be to mankind.

An Account of making a Dog draw his Breath exactly like a Wind broken Horse, as it was devised and experimented by Dr. Richard Lower, with some of his Observations thereon.

THIS Experiment was made before the ROYAL SOCIETY, Oct. 17th 1667, after it had been tried by the Author in private, some while before. The account of it is in his own words, and as follows:—

After I had often considered the manner and way of Respiration, and by many observations been induced to believe that the Diaphragme is the chief organ thereof, I thought there could be no way more probable to try it than by breaking the nerves by which its motion is performed, which may be easily (as it was actually) done after the following manner:—

1st. Pierce the side of the animal between the sixth and seventh rib, in the middle of the thorax, just over against the region of the heart, with a small incision knife, passing the knife but just into the cavity of the breast (which you may justly know by finding no resistance to the point of it); then take it out and put in a director, or a small quill made like it, and thrust it in about an inch, directing the end of it towards the sternum, close to the inside of the breast. Then cut upon it about an inch on the intercostal muscles; by which you may be secured from touching the lungs with the point or edge of your knife. This done, put in your finger, and with your nail separate the nerve, which passeth along the side of the pericardium towards the diaphragme. Then put in a probe a little inverted at the end like a hook, and apprehend the nerve, and pull it to the orifice of the breast and cut it off, and sow the hole up very close. Do the same on the other side, and presently let the dog loose, and you will plainly see him draw his breath exactly like a wind broken horse; which yet you will see plainer, if you run him a little in a string after he is cut. But that any one may perform the experiment the easier, let him first take notice how the nerves of the diaphragme pass along on each side of the pericardium in a dead animal, before the trial be attempted in a living one.

The most obvious observations upon this experiment are,

1st. That the whole manner of respiration is quite altered; for as in a sound animal, in inspiration, the belly swells by the lifting up the bowels by the contraction of the diaphragme, and in expiration the belly falls by the relaxing of the ſame. In a wind broken dog or horſe 'tis quite contrary: for in them it is to be ſeen plainly, that when they draw their breath their belly is drawn in very lank and ſmall, and when they breathe up their belly is relaxed and ſwells again.

2d. It being certain that the lungs do not move of themſelves at all, but wholly depend upon the expanſion of the thorax by the intercoſtal muſcles and the diaphragme: by this experiment it doth appear how much the ſingle motion of either of them doth particularly contribute to reſpiration. For all inſpiration being made by the dilatation of the thorax, and that dilatation being cauſed, partly by the intercoſtal muſcles drawing up the ribs, and partly at the ſame time, the diaphragme by its contraction drawing downwards the lower ſmall ribs to which it is joined, and alſo lifting up the viſcera of the lower belly, by which they do jointly make all the ſpace they can for the air to come in and diſtend the lungs. It muſt hence neceſſarily follow, that the intercoſtal muſcles and the diaphragme being conſtituted for two diſtant employments (though both to the ſame end), and neither being able to perform the others office, where one ceaſeth from its work, the other for the exigence of nature muſt take more pains to ſupply the others defect, which is very evident to be ſeen, for the diaphragme being made uſeleſs by looſing its nerves, the intercoſtal muſcles do dilate the ribs much more than formerly even to the utmoſt diſtance they can, when there is need for it, as when you make the dog run a little after he is cut, or when you gallop a wind broken horſe, doth manifeſtly appear.

3d. The manner of Reſpiration being the ſame in a dog, whoſe diaphragme nerves are cut, and in a wind broken horſe 'tis more than probable that the cauſe may be as nearly the ſame as the ſigns are, and that though there may be other faults found in the lungs of ſuch creatures, yet 'tis very likely that they may be induced from the weakneſs of reſpiration, but that they had their occaſion from the relaxation or rupture of the nerves of the diaphragme at firſt which will ſeem more credible if we remember, that by the ſtraining of the midrif too much (by which the nerves may be quite broken or ſtretched beyond their proper tone), moſt commonly that accident happens.

An Account of the Experiment of Transfusion practised upon a Man in London.

THIS was performed November 23, 1667, upon a Mr. Arthur Coga, at Arundel House, by the management of those two learned Physicians and dexterous Anatomists Dr. Richard Lower, and Dr. Edmund King, the latter of whom communicated the relation of it as followeth :—

The experiment of Transfusion of blood into an human vein was made by us in this manner. Having prepared the caroted artery in a young sheep, we inserted a silver pipe into the quills to let the blood run through it into a porringer, and in the space of almost a minute, about twelve ounces of the sheep's blood ran through the pipe into the porringer, which was somewhat to direct us in the quantity of blood now to be transfused into the man; which done, when we came to prepare the vein in the man's arm, the vein seemed too small for that pipe which we intended to insert into it; so that we employed another, about one third part less, at the little end. Then we made an incision in the vein, after the method formerly published, which method we observed without any other alteration but in the shape of one of our pipes, which we found more convenient for our purpose. And having opened the vein in the man's arm, with as much ease as in the common way of venæ-section, we let thence run out six or seven ounces of blood. Then we planted our silver pipe into the said incision, and inserted quills between the two pipes already advanced in the two subjects, to convey the arterial blood from the sheep into the vein of the man; but this blood was near a minute before it had passed through the pipes and quills into the arm; and then it ran freely into the man's vein for the space of two minutes at least, so that we could feel a pulse in the said vein just beyond the end of the silver pipe, though the patient said he did not feel the blood hot (as was reported of the subject in the French experiment), which may very well be imputed to the length of the pipes through which the blood passed, losing thereby so much of its heat, as to come in a temper very agreeable to the venal blood. And as to the quantity of blood received into the man's vein, we judge there was about nine or ten ounces; for allowing this pipe one third less than that, through which 12 ounces passed in one minute before, we may very well suppose it might in two minutes convey as much blood into the veins, as the other did into the porringer in one minute; granting withal that the blood did not run ſo vigorouſly the ſecond minute as it did the firſt, nor the third as the ſecond, &c. But, that the blood did run all the time of thoſe two minutes, we conclude from thence; firſt, becauſe we felt a pulſe during that time; ſecondly, becauſe when upon the man's ſaying he thought he had enough, we drew the pipe out of the vein, the ſheep's blood ran through with a full ſtream, which it had not done, if there had been any ſtop before, in the ſpace of thoſe two minutes; the blood being very apt to coagulate in the pipes upon the leaſt ſtop, eſpecially the pipes being ſo long as three quills.

The man *after* this operation, as well as *in it*, found himſelf very well, and hath given in his own narrative, under his own hand, enlarging more upon the benefit, he thinks, he hath received by it, than we think fit to own as yet. He urged us to have the experiment repeated upon him within three or four days after this; but it was thought adviſable to put it off ſomewhat longer. And the next time we hope to be more exact, eſpecially in weighing the emittent animal before and after the operation, to have a more juſt account of the quantity of blood it ſhall have loſt.

A Relation of ſome Trials of the ſame Operation lately made in France.

1. MR. Denys, profeſſor of the mathematics and natural philoſophy at Paris, in a letter of his to the publiſher, relateth, that they had lately tranſmitted the blood of four wethers into a horſe of 26 years old, and that this horſe had thence received much ſtrength, and more than an ordinary ſtomach.

2. The ſame perſon was pleaſed to ſend to the ſame hand a printed letter written to the Abbot Bourdelot by M. Gadroys, being an anſwer to a paper of one M. Lamy, and confirming the transfuſion of blood by new experiments. In this anſwer the author is vindicating the transfuſion from objections; where, firſt he takes notice, that whereas the objector undertakes to refute the experiments made by ſimple ratiocination, it ought to be conſidered that the quodlibetical learning of the ſchools is capable enough to find arguments for and againſt all ſorts of opinions, but that there is nothing but experience that is able to give the verdict and laſt deciſion,

eſpecially in matters of natural philoſophy and phyſic: that a hundred years ago there were no arguments wanting to prove that antimony or the vinum emeticum was poiſon, the uſe of it being then forbidden by a decree of the Faculty of Phyſicians, and that at this day there are no arguments wanting to prove the contrary, and to aſſert that it is a purgative of great importance, followed with wonderful effects; the ſame faculty having publiſhed a decree laſt year, by which it permits, and even ordains, the uſe thereof. So that it ought to be ſaid, that ſole experience hath determined this matter; and that the recovery of many perſons, and among them the moſt Chriſtian King himſelf, hath more conduced to convince men of its uſefulneſs, than all the bare ratiocinations that could be employed to defend it. And, ſo it is with all remedies, there being not one that is not approved by ſome phyſician or other, who thinks to have reaſon on his ſide, and diſapproved at the ſame time by others of that profeſſion, who conceive to have it on their's: whereas he is certainly to be eſteemed the moſt rational that in theſe matters is guided by good experience. And ſince the transfuſion of blood is a new thing (unknown for ought we know) to all former ages, ingenious men, and lovers of the increaſe of the ſtock ſerving for the relief and conveniences of human life, do no more in this particular than propoſe and recommend it to the generous and unprejudicate phyſicians to judge of its agreeableneſs to human bodies, and to make trials of it accordingly; themſelves eſteeming, that ſince it concerns the health and life of man, it cannot be examined too ſeverely, and though at the ſame time they conceive that it is unequal to ſtand herein to the verdicts of ſuch arrogant men, who from a ſelf conceit of knowing all things already are very impatient at any thing diſcovered, which they have not thought of themſelves: thoſe men being the beſt adviſed and the moſt to be relied on, who do not precipitate their judgment, but ſtay for many experiments carefully made to conclude themſelves by. For which purpoſe, the author wiſhes that perſons in power would cauſe a good number of experiments of this invention to be made, and examine them either themſelves, or give order to prudent and free ſpirited phyſicians and ſurgeons to do ſo.

Amongſt the objections (which the author finds to be generally grounded upon conſiderations, miſtakes, and ſuppoſitions, as if peremptory affirmations touching the effect of this transfuſion were obtruded, whereas all is left to the ſucceſs of experiments faithfully made) there is one, directed against the effects of that operation which appeared in a young man, who (by M. Denys' relation in his printed letter to Monſieur De Montmor) after he had received the arterial blood of a lamb, was cured of an extraordinary lethargy conſequent to a violent fever, wherein he had been let blood twenty times. And the objection is, that the lively apprehenſion the ſaid young man had of a remedy ſo unuſual, and whereof the ſucceſs could not but appear very dubious to him, and ſo render him exceedingly anxious, did ſo rouſe his ſpirits and put them into ſuch motion, as to diſengage them from that embarraſſment, which rendered their diffuſion; upon which diſentanglement, followed all the other good effects that are imputed to the transfuſion.

To this conceit the anſwer replies, that if the apprehenſion could have cured this young man, the cure would doubtleſs have been effected 24 hours before the transfuſion, becauſe he then happened to have a very great one, by falling down ſtairs, as was alſo obſerved in M. Denys' relation of this experiment. Beſides that this patient was noted to be ſo far from apprehending or fearing this operation, that he did not ſo much as know what the transfuſion was; but thought the lamb was only applied to his arm to ſuck from him his ill blood, as he was made to believe after an ancient and uſual way.

To that objection, wherein ſome put weight, viz. that there is a great difference between the fleſh we eat for food, and the blood that is tranſmitted immediately into the veins; the former undergoing a great alteration which the latter does not; our author replies, that of the three principal digeſtions of the aliment that have been always diſtinguiſhed by authors, the firſt, which is made in the ſtomach, is not conſiderable in compariſon of the two others, which are made of the chyle and the blood in the heart, the liver, and generally in all the parts that receive nutrition: which he illuſtrates by this, that as the concoction which is made of the juices of the earth in the root and heart of the trunk of the tree, does not ſo much ſerve to the production of this or that fruit, as the laſt filtration that is made of thoſe juices in the ſmall fibres of the grafts: ſo alſo all thoſe digeſtions, which are ſuppoſed to be made in the ſtomach and the heart, or the liver of animals, do not ſo much ſerve to give the particles of the aliment thoſe figures which they require to be converted into the ſubſtance of man, as the diverſity of pores that ſtrain them laſt of all, and differ in the bones, flesh, cartilages, and other parts, in which the ancients for this reason did admit as many different assimilating faculties. Now, saith he, though the new blood which is given in the transfusion, undergoeth not the first concoction made in the stomach, yet it suffers the two others in making many circulations together with the native blood, and therefore nothing hinders but it may be fit to be changed into the substance of man without inconvenience.

The rest of the objections here alleged, seeming to be of no moment, though answered by our author, we shall here pass by, and, for a general answer to all, employ the experience and the several successful transfusions he relates, as those of lamb's blood to dogs, which after the space of several months from the time of the operation do not only live, but are very well, and some of them grown fatter than they were before; and of kids blood into a little spaniel bitch of 12 years of age, which, a little while after the operation grew vigorous and active, and even proud in less than eight days; to which he adds a considerable experiment lately made upon a person that had been for three weeks afflicted with the complicated distempers of an hepatic flux, a lientary, and a bilious diarrhœa, accompanied with a very violent fever, and had been attended by four physicians, who had blooded, purged, and clystered him as much as they thought fit, he grew at last so weak that he was unable to stir, lost his speech and senses, and vomited all he took; whereupon they altogether despairing of and abandoning the patient, and declaring that they did so in the presence of divers persons of honour, consented to have the experiment of transfusion made upon the patient, which his relations had proposed as the last refuge; very unwilling to omit any thing that might seem possible to rescue a dying man. M. Denys and M. Emmery were besought to employ this last succour. But they seeing the deplored state of the sick absolutely refused to make the trial, alleging that the transfusion was not the means to restore either the solid parts or to cure a gangrene, which was apparently in his intestines; they should have used it sooner, and at the very time when the great evacuations of blood were made in the patient. But, notwithstanding all this, they were exceedingly pressed to comply with their desires, and not to let their friend die without trying all means possible. They being overcome with this importunity, and having secured their honour and safety by the declaration of the above-mentioned physicians, and by the consent to the trial of this experiment, transfused into his veins a ſmall quantity of calves blood, in a morning; whereupon, although this patient was already in a lethargy and convulſive, and had a very low and creeping pulſe, yet behold, an unexpected change happened to him. His pulſe grew higher in an inſtant and became more vigorous; his convulſions ceaſed, he looked fixedly on the by-ſtanders, ſpoke pertinently, and in divers languages to thoſe that ſpoke to him, and fell into a very quiet ſleep. Awakening three quarters of an hour after, he took ſeveral broths for the reſt of the day, not vomiting at all, not having any ſtool, although for three days before he could take nothing at the mouth, nor had had any intermiſſion of his looſeneſs ſince the very beginning of his ſickneſs. Having thus remained for 24 hours, his forces began to diminiſh again, and his pulſe grew low, and the looſeneſs to return. His friends then urged a ſecond transfuſion, which being at laſt performed the next morning, the patient indeed recovered ſome vigour again, but that was of ſhort duration. For though then alſo he took his broth well without vomiting, yet he voided ſtill by ſtool, and at noon he began to decline, and about five at night he died without the appearance of any convulſions. His body being opened before the phyſicians, the Ilion was found returned into itſelf from the top to the bottom, and below that knot unto the anus, the bowels were all livid, gangrened, and of an inſupportable ſtench. His pancreas was extraordinarily hard, and ſo obſtructed that the pancreatic juice had no liberty to diffuſe itſelf into the guts. His ſpleen was very thick, and his liver thick and in ſome places livid. The heart was very dry, and as it were burnt; and having found the vein by which the transfuſion had been made, there was from the place of the opening of the arm to the heart, almoſt no blood found in it, no more than in the other veins, nor in the ventricles of the heart, for as much as that little he received, had been imbibed by his hot and dry fleſh. All which this author aſſures, can be atteſted both by a dozen perſons of great veracity, who were preſent at this diſſection, and confirmed by the certificates given by the phyſicians themſelves, to be ſent to the parents of the deceaſed ſtranger, who is the very ſame with him of whom a leſs punctual account hasbeen given *.

* See the Paper inſerted at page 95.

Some new experiments of injecting medicated Liquors into Veins, together with the considerable cures performed thereby. This was communicated in a letter from Dantzic, written by Dr. Fabricius, Physician in ordinary, and which it is thought proper to translate.

FORASMUCH as we have a great desire to experiment, what would be the effects of the chirurgery of injecting liquors into human veins, three fit subjects presenting themselves in our hospital, we thought good to make the trial upon them: but seeing little grounds to hope for a manifest operation from only altering medicines, we esteemed the experiment would be more convenient and conspicuous from laxatives, which made us inject by a syphon about two drachms of such a kind of physic into the *median* vein of the right arm. The patients were these: one was a lusty, robust soldier, dangerously infected with the venereal disease, and suffering grievous protuberatings of the bones in his arms. He, when the purgative liquor was infused into him, complained of great pains in his elbows, and the little valves of his arm did swell so visibly, that it was necessary by a gentle compression of the fingers to stroke up that swelling towards the patient's shoulders. Some four hours after, it began to work, not very troublesomely; and so it did the next day, insomuch that the man had five copious stools after it. Without any other remedy those protuberancies were gone, nor are there any traces left of the above-mentioned disease.

The two other trials were made upon the other sex. A married woman of 35, and a serving maid of 20 years of age, had been both of them from their birth very grievously afflicted with epileptic fits, so that little hopes were left to cure them. They both underwent this operation, and there was injected into their veins a laxative rosin, dissolved in an anti-eplileptical spirit. The first of these had gentle stools some hours after the injection, and the next day the fits recurring now and then, but much milder, are since altogether vanished. As to the other, *viz.* the maid, she went the same day to stool four times, and several times the next; but by going into the air and taking cold, and not observing any diet, cast herself away

It is remarkable that it was common to all three to vomit soon after the injection, and that extremely and frequently; the reason whereof we leave to the faculty to assign.

An Extract of a letter written from Bermudas, giving an account of the course of the Tides there; of Wells both salt and fresh dug near the Sea; of the Whale Fishing there practised anew, and of such Whales as have the Spermaceti in them. This letter was written June 18, 1667, by Mr. Richard Norwood.

SIR—I RECEIVED your letter of Oct. 24, 1666, but whereas you mention another formerly sent that never came to hand; neither had I before the receipt of yours the least intelligence of the institution of the ROYAL SOCIETY, founded by the King, but am very glad that God hath put it into the heart of his Majesty to advance such a noble design, and should rejoice were I able to add any mite for the furtherance of it. As to the particulars you recommend to me, I shall answer to them as I can, in the order I find them.

First, *touching the conjunction of Mercury with the Sun,* which you say you gave me notice of in your first, not received, and which happened 25th October 1664; I had also notice of it from Mr. Street, and had provided in some measure to observe it, but the sky was so overcast that the sun could scarce be discerned all day.

Next, *concerning the tides,* I have only taken a general notice of them; as it is high water about seven o'clock of the change day (in some creeks an hour or two later), the water rises but little, as about four feet at high water, but at spring tides it may be a foot more. The tides without are very various in their setting; sometimes the tide of flood sets to the eastward, sometimes to the westward, but in fair calm and settled weather the said tide sets from the south-east, towards the north-west, as they say.

We dug wells of fresh water sometimes within 20 yards of the sea, or less, which rise and fall upon the flood and ebb, as the sea doth; and so do most of the wells in the country, though further up, as I am informed. Wheresoever they dig wells here, they dig till they come almost to a level with the superfices of the sea, and then they find either fresh water or salt. If it be fresh, yet if they dig two or three feet deeper, or often less, they come to salt water. If there be sandy ground, or a sandy crumbling stone that the water ſoaks gently through, they find uſually freſh water; but if there be hard limeſtone rocks, which the water cannot ſoak but paſſeth in chinks or clefts between them, the water is ſalt or brackiſh. Yet, (to mention that by the bye) I never ſaw any ſand in the country ſuch as will grind glaſs or whet knives, &c. as in England, but a ſubſtance like ſand, though much ſofter; neither have we any pebble ſtones or flints.

For the killing of Whales, it hath been formerly attempted in vain; but within theſe two or three years in the ſpring time and fair weather, they take ſometimes one, two, or three in a day. They are leſs I hear than thoſe in Greenland, but more quick and lively, ſo that if they be ſtruck in deep water, they preſently make to the bottom with ſuch violence that the boat is in danger to be hauled down after them, if they cut not the line in time; therefore they uſually ſtrike them in ſhoal water. They have very good boats for that purpoſe, manned with ſix oars, ſuch as they can row forwards or backwards, as occaſion requires. They row up gently to the Whale, and ſo he will ſcarcely ſhun them; and when the harpooner ſtanding ready fitted, ſees his opportunity, ſtrikes his harping iron into the whale about or before the fins, rather than towards the tail. Now the harping irons are like thoſe which are uſual in England in ſtriking porpoiſes, but ſingular good metal that will not break, but wind as they ſay about a man's hand. To the harping iron is made faſt a ſtrong lithe rope, and into the ſocket of that iron is put a ſtaff, which when the Whale is ſtruck comes out of the ſocket; and ſo when the Whale is ſunk and quiet, they haul up to him by the rope, and it may be ſtrike into him another harping iron or lance him with lances and ſtaves, until they have killed them. I hear not that they have found any ſpermaceti in any of theſe whales; but I have heard from credible perſons that there is a kind of ſuch as have the ſperma at Eleutheria, and others of the Bahama Iſlands, (where alſo they find often quantities of *ambergris*) and that thoſe have great teeth which ours have not, and are very ſinewy. One of thoſe at this place (John Parinchief) found one there dead driven upon an iſland, and, though I think ignorant in the buſineſs, yet got a great quantity of ſpermaceti out of it. It ſeems they have not ſo much oil as ours, but this oil I hear is at firſt like ſpermaceti, but they clarify it I think by the fire. When I ſpeak with him (whom I could not meet with at preſent) as now the ſhip is ready to ſet ſail, I ſhall endeavour to be further informed; but at preſent, with the tender of my humble ſervice to the ROYAL SOCIETY, and commending your noble deſign to the bleſſing of the Almighty, I take my leave.

New experiments concerning the relation between Light and Air in ſhining Wood and Fiſh, made by the Honourable Robert Boyle, and by him addreſſed from Oxford to the Publiſher, and ſo communicated to the ROYAL SOCIETY.

SIR—TO perform now the promiſe I made you the other day, I muſt acquaint you with what will perhaps ſomewhat ſurpriſe you, by giving an account of what I tried on Tueſday night laſt (Oct. 29, 1667), and the two or three following nights, about the relation between *Air* and *Light*, as this is to be found in ſome bodies.

The occaſion of theſe trials was this: Having, as you know, long ſince made ſome notes, chiefly hiſtorical, upon particular qualities, and finding light to be (how juſtly I now diſpute not) reckoned by the generality of Philoſophers among qualities, I huddled together what obſervations I had either made myſelf, or received from ſome ingenious travellers (to whom I recommended my inquiries about ſhining bodies; and had alſo prepared ſeveral trials about them, to be made when I ſhould have opportunity and requiſite inſtruments to put them in practice, which as to ſome of theſe deſigned experiments have been long denied me. But having at length got hither one of my little engines, and having alſo procured after much enquiry a few ſmall pieces of ſhining wood, I began on the day above mentioned to try with them an experiment I found in my liſt: and though the main experiment be but one, I intended to ſet down what occurred to me about it, but as ſeveral phenomena of it; yet finding it requiſite to acquaint you with ſome trials that are not ſo properly parts of it, I ſhall for diſtinction ſake propoſe them as ſeveral experiments; the narratives whereof are taken, for the moſt part verbatim, out of the notes I ſet down for my own uſe, when the things to be regiſtered were freſhly done: which advertiſement I give you, both to excuſe the careleſſneſs of the ſtyle, and to induce you not to diſtruſt a narrative that was made only to ſerve my memory, not an hypotheſis.

EXPERIMENT I.

To try whether or no a piece of ſhining wood, being put into a receiver of a pneumatic engine, would, upon the withdrawing and re-admitting of the air, ſuffer ſuch changes as I have often obſerved a live coal placed there to do; having at length procured a piece of ſuch wood, about the bigneſs of a groat or leſs, that gave a vivid light for rotten wood, we put it into a middle ſized receiver, ſo as it was kept from touching the cement, and the pump being ſet at work, we obſerved not during the five or ſix firſt exſuctions of the air, that the ſplendour of the included wood was manifeſtly leſſened (though it never was at all increaſed); but about the ſeventh ſuck it ſeemed to grow a little more dim, and afterwards anſwered our expectation, by loſing of its light more and more, as the air was ſtill further pumped out; till at length, about the tenth exſuction (though by the removal of the candle out of the room, and by black clothes and hats, we made the place as dark as we could) yet we could not perceive any light at all to proceed from the wood.

EXPERIMENT II.

Wherefore we let in the outward air by degrees, and had the pleaſure to ſee the ſeemingly extinguiſhed light revive ſo faſt and perfectly, that it looked to us all almoſt like a little flaſh of lightning, and the ſplendour of the wood ſeemed rather greater than at all leſs than before it was put into the receiver. But partly for greater certainty, and partly to enjoy ſo delightful a ſpectacle, we repeated the experiment with the like ſucceſs as at firſt: wherefore being deſirous to ſee how ſoon theſe changes might be produced, we included the wood in a very ſmall receiver of clear glaſs, and found that in this the light would begin to grow faint at the ſecond, or at leaſt at the third exſuction of the air, and at the ſixth or ſeventh would quite diſappear; and we found by a minute watch that the ſending the candles out of the room, the pumping out the air till the wood would ſhine no more, the re-admitting of the air (upon which it would in a trice recover its light), and the ſending in for the candles to conſult the watch, did in all take up but ſix minutes.

EXPERIMENT III.

The forementioned experiment, without taking notice how long it laſted, being reiterated twice in this new receiver, we had a deſire to ſee whether this luminousness of our wood would more resemble a coal, or the life of a perfect animal, in being totally and finally extinguished, in case the air were kept from it a few minutes; or else the life of insects, which in an exhausted receiver I had observed to lose all appearance of its continuing, and that for a much longer time than a few minutes, and yet afterwards, upon the restitution of air, to recover presently and shew manifest signs of life; wherefore having exhausted the receiver till the wood quite disappeared, we stayed somewhat above a quarter of an hour in the dark, without perceiving that the wood had regained any thing of light, though about the end of this time we made the place about it as dark as we could; and then it being too late at night to protract the experiment, we let in the air, upon whose admission the wood presently recovered light enough to be conspicuous at a distance, though it seemed to me somewhat less vivid than before, which yet may either be a weakness of my sight, or an effect of the steams of the cement, unfriendly perhaps to the luminousness of the wood.

Again, we put in a piece of wood bigger than the former, this being above an inch long, and that shone very vigorously; and having by a few sucks quite deprived it of light, we left it in the exhausted receiver full half an hour, and then coming into the dark room again, we found all had not continued so staunch, but that some small portion of air had insinuated itself into the receiver. This we concluded to be but a small portion of air, because the wood was but visible to the attentive eye, and yet that it was really some air which had got in that caused the little glimmering light, which we perceived, may appear by this, that it did presently (as we expected) vanish at the first or second suck; and then the air being let into the dark receiver, the included wood presently shone again as before; though I suspected that I discerned some little diminution of its brightness, which yet, till farther trials of the like kind, and for a longer time, have been made, I dare not affirm. Before the receiver was sufficiently emptied at the beginning of the experiment made with this greater piece of wood, a small leak accidentally sprung, which letting in a little air, did sooner than we intended recall the almost disappearing light.

Experiment IV.

There is an experiment of affinity with the former, which we thought it not altogether impertinent to try; for having observed on another occasion, that ſometimes the operation which the withdrawing the air hath upon a body included in the receiver, proves more conſiderable ſome *minutes after* we have ceaſed pumping, than *immediately* after the exerciſe is left off, I imagined that even in ſuch caſes, where the light is not made wholly to diſappear (though it be made almoſt quite to do ſo) by emptying of the pneumatical glaſs, the ſuffering the body to remain a while there, though without any pumping (unleſs now and then a very little to remove the air that might have ſtolen in in the mean time) the remaining light of the body might probably be further impaired, if not quite reduced to vaniſh. To examine this conjecture we put in a body that was not wood, which had ſome parts much more luminous than the reſt; and having drawn out the air, all the others diſappeared, and even the formerly brighter ones ſhone but faintly, when the pneumatical glaſs ſeemed to be exhauſted; but keeping the included body a while in that unfriendly place, we perceived the parts that had retained light to grow more and more dim, ſome of them diſappearing, and that which was formerly the moſt conſpicuous, being now but juſt viſible to an attentive eye, and that ſcarce without diſpute; for if we had not known before hand that a ſhining matter had been included in the *receiver*, perhaps we ſhould not have found it out; and he that had the youngeſt eyes in the company could not at all diſcern it (the air being let in, the body began to ſhine again): but this being a ſingle trial, which the lateneſs of the night hindered us from reiterating, is to be further proſecuted, and in differing ſubſtances, before much be built upon it.

Experiment V.

The rarefaction and expanſion of the air having ſo notable an operation upon our ſhining wood, I thought it would not be amiſs to try what the compreſſion of the air would do to it; for which purpoſe we included a piece of it in ſuch a little inſtrument to compreſs, which you may remember to have been deviſed and propoſed by Mr. Hook: but though we impelled the air forcibly enough into the glaſs, yet, by reaſon of the thickneſs requiſite in ſuch glaſſes, and the opacity thence ariſing, we were not able *then* to determine whether or no any change was made in the luminouſneſs of the wood; which I thought the leſs ſtrange, becauſe by ſome experiments purpoſely deviſed (at one of which I remember you were preſent) I had long ſince obſerved that even a great preſſure from a fluid body, which preſſeth more uniformly againſt all the parts it toucheth of the conſiſtent body, does work a far leſs manifeſt change even on ſoft or tender ſubſtances than one would expect from the force wherewith it compreſſeth.

And were it not that one contrary oftentimes minds us of another, I might have forgot that I had divers thoughts about finding ſome good ways of trying whether any ſuch change of texture might be diſcovered to be made in the ſhining wood by the abſence and return of the ambient air, as might with any probability have the loſs or recovery of the wood's ſplendor attributed to it: for I had formerly (if I were not miſtaken) found by ſeveral circumſtances which I ſhall not now ſtay to name, that a ſlight (ſo it be an appropriated) variation of the texture of this wood, and which may ſeem mainly to reſpect the pores (which perhaps ought to be of a determinate ſhape and ſize, and filled with a determinate matter) will have a great operation upon its ſplendour: and I formerly found by other trials that even conſiſtent bodies, if ſoft ones, may have their pores enlarged and vitiated, and their bulk and conſequently their texture (at leaſt as to their pores), manifeſtly enough altered, by having the air withdrawn from about them (whereby the aerial particles within them were enabled to expand themſelves) and let in again, whereby as to ſenſe they ſeemed pretty well reſtored to their former ſtate. But the ſucceſs of my endeavours either with microſcopes (through which a vivid piece of wood will ſhine by its own light) or otherwiſe was not conſiderable enough to deſerve a particular account; eſpecially in this Paper, where I am not to venture at matter of theory.

Experiment VI.

Thinking fit to try whether a ſmall quantity of air, without being ventilated or renewed, might not ſuffice to maintain this cold fire, though it will not that of a live coal or a piece of match, we cauſed a piece of ſhining wood to be hermetically ſealed up in a pipe of clear and thin glaſs: but, though carrying it into the dark, we found it had quite loſt its light, yet imagining that that might proceed from its having been overheated (being ſealed up in a pipe not long enough to afford it a due diſtance from the flame of the lamp we employed to ſeal it) we cauſed two or three pieces of freſh wood, amounting all of them to the length of about two inches, to be ſealed up in a ſlender pipe, between four and five inches in length, which being warily done, the wood retained its light very well, when the operation was over: and afterwards laying it by my bed side when the candles were carried away out of the room, I considered it awhile before I went to sleep, and found it to shine vividly.

The next morning when I awaked, though the sun was risen, yet forbearing to draw open the curtains of my bed, 'till I had looked upon the sealed glass, which I had fenced with a piece of cloth, held between it and the window, my eyes having not yet been exposed to the day-light since the darkness they had been accustomed to, during the night, made me think the wood shined brighter than ever: and this night after 10 of the clock looking on it in a dark place it appeared luminous all its length, though not so much so as in the morning.

The morning after and the night after that, the same wood did likewise manifestly, though not vigorously shine, especially one piece, whose light was much more vivid than the rest. And for ought I know, I might have observed them to shine longer, if one of the sealed ends of this glass had not been accidentally broken.

Experiment VII.

Whilst the former trials were making, I was wishing for a good Bolonian stone to try what effect the withdrawing of the air would have upon it. For though I knew it might be objected that the experiments of light performable in our engine must be made in the night, whereas the Bolonian stone gains its light by being exposed to the sun beams, yet that objection did not hinder my wish, since the better sort of Bolonian stones may be endued with a luminousness by the flame of fire, or of large candles.

I also wished for such a shining diamond as is now in the hands that best deserves such a rarity, our Royal Founder's. For you may remember that in the observations I made of that stone, and annexed to the conclusion of the Book of Colours, I shew how it may several ways be brought to shine; so that by one or other of those ways, especially that of external heat, I thought it very likely I should be able to make the light continue four or five minutes, which would be long enough to try in a very small receiver exhaustible at a suck or two, whether the withdrawing and restoring the air would have any visible operation on it.

I also wished for some of the glow worms with which I formerly made other trials. For, though I forgot not what operation the withdrawing of the air by our engine is wont to have upon living creatures, yet that made me not forbear my wish, not only because of the different effect I have found the engine to have on insects in respect of other animals, but because I am not of the opinion of those modern writers, who will have the light of glow-worms depend altogether upon their life, and end with it. But being not likely by my wishes to procure any new subject to make trials on, I thought fit at least to do what was in my power, and accordingly (to gratify them who I presumed would, if present, propose such a trial) caused a piece of iron to be forged, whose top was of the bigness of a nutmeg, the rest being a stem of an inch or an inch and a half long, for which we provided a little candlestick of tobacco pipe clay, which would not yield any smoke to fill and darken the receiver. Then, having heated the iron red hot and placed it in this clay, so that the round part was clearly protuberant, we conveyed it into a receiver of white glass, which was so placed as to keep the sides at as good a distance as we could from the iron, lest the excessive heat should (as we much feared it would) break the glass. Then, sending away the candles and making the room dark, we hastily pumped out the air, but could not perceive the withdrawing of it had any operation on the glowing iron. And though it continued shining long enough to give us opportunity to pump out and let in the air three several times, yet we could not observe that the air had any manifest operation one way or other. For though upon withdrawing of the air, the iron grew dimmer and dimmer, yet that I attributed to the cooling of it, and the rather, because having (to examine the conjecture) let in two or three times the air when the receiver had been exhausted, there appeared no manifest increase of light upon the sudden admission of it.

Experiment VIII.

Having formerly in our physico-mechanical experiments about the spring of the air, observed that the air is thus far a vehicle of sound, that a body but faintly sounding, being placed in our receiver, gave a yet weaker sound, when the air was withdrawn from about it, than when the receiver was full of air; I presumed some curious persons would, if they had been present, desire to have a trial made, whether or no a small piece of shining wood being so included in the receiver, as that the pumping out of the air should have no injurious operation upon the body of it, its light would upon the withdrawing of the air be manifeftly diminifhed. And this, I was the lefs backward to try becaufe (not to mention the relation which former experiments fhew there may be in fome cafes between light and air) it did not readily occur to my memory that by any manifeft experiment (for I know there are probable reafons to prove it) it appeared that a body more thin than air will or can tranfmit light as well as other diaphonous mediums. And thofe modern atomifts that think there is in our exhaufted receiver, very many times more vacuum than body, would, I prefumed, be glad to be fupplied with an argument againft the peripatetics to fhew that the motion of bodies, viz. the corpufcles of light may be freely made in vacuo and proceed without the affiftance of a vehicle.

Wherefore having hermetically fealed up a fmall piece of fhining wood in a flender pipe, and placed it in a fmall receiver, that was likewife made of clear glafs, we exhaufted it of air and afterwards let in again that which we had excluded. But by neither of the operations could we perceive any fenfible decrement or increafe of the light of the wood, though by that very obfervation it appeared that the glafs had been well fealed, fince otherwife the included air would have got out of the pipe into the receiver, and have left the wood without light.

Experiment IX.

I had alfo a mind to try both what *degree of rarefaction* of the air would deprive the wood of its fplendour in fuch and fuch meafures, and whether or no the felf fame air, which when rarified would not fuffer the wood to fhine, would when reduced to its former denfity allow it to fhine as much as before.

This I propofed to do by putting fome fhining wood into a clear and conveniently fhaped glafs, that the long ftem or pipe being fo far filled with quickfilver, as that there might be about half a fpoonful of air left at the clofed end, where the wood was placed, it might be inverted into a little glafs of ftagnant quickfilver and therewith conveyed into a flender receiver, out of which as the air fhould come to be pumped, that included in the glafs which held the wood might be rarified, and afterwards, upon the admiffion of the outward air (which muft impel up the quickfilver to its former height) might be reftored to its former ftate. But when we came to make a trial of this, we had no receiver conveniently fhaped that was fo clear and thin that we could fee the wood fhine through both the glaffes. And though we would for an expedient have substituted a fine thin bladder wherein the wood was to be put, and a convenient quantity of air strongly tied up with it, yet for want of a bladder fine enough for our turn, that expedient also proved useless to us. But being desirous to make what trial we could by the least unfit means we had in our power, we got an old but thin glass sealed at one end, whose shape was pretty cylindrical, and whose bore was about the bigness of a man's little finger, and whose length was about a foot or more. Into this pipe, near the sealed end, we put a piece of shining wood wedged in with a piece of cork to keep it from falling, and having inverted the nose of it into another slender glass, but not cylindrical, wherein was pretty store of quicksilver, we put them both into a long receiver, shaped almost like a glass churn, and having pumped awhile that the air included in the pipe expanding itself, might depress the quicksilver, and so make escapes into the receiver, as long as we thought fit; we then let in the outward air that the stagnant quicksilver might be impelled into the cavity of the pipe now freed from much of the air, to the height requisite for our purpose.

This done, we plied the pump again, and observed that as the air in the pipe did by its own spring expand itself more and more, and grow thinner and thinner, the shining wood grew dimmer and dimmer, 'till at length it ceased to shine, the internal wood being then got a good way lower than the surface of the external quicksilver: whereupon opening the commerce between the cavity of the receiver and the atmosphere, the quicksilver was driven up again, and consequently the air above it was restored to its former density, upon which the rotten wood also recovered its light. What the greatest expansion of this air was, we could not certainly determine, because the expansion raised the external quicksilver so high as to hinder us to see and measure it. But we guessed that the air reached to about a foot or more from the top of the pipe to the surface of the quicksilver near the bottom of it. But when that rarified air was impelled into its former dimensions, we measured it, and found that the upper part of the tube unpossessed by the quicksilver was about three inches, and the wood being about an inch long, there remained two inches or somewhat better for the air. But this experiment is to be repeated when exacter instruments can be procured.

Experiment X.

Thinking it fit to try, as well, whether ſtinking fiſh that ſhines be of the ſame nature as to luminouſneſs with rotten wood that ſhines too, as, whether the withdrawing of the air will extinguiſh or eclipſe the light of a conſiderable bulk of luminous matter as in the experiments hitherto made we found it would do to a ſmall one: we took a fiſh that we had kept and cauſed to be watched 'till it was almoſt all over luminous, though much more in the belly and ſome parts of the head than elſewhere; and having ſuſpended him in a conveniently ſhaped receiver we found him to give ſo great a light that we ſuſpected before hand that the withdrawing of the air would hardly have its full operation upon a body whoſe bulk was conſiderable, as well as its light very vivid, and which had many luminous parts retired to a pretty diſtance from the air. Accordingly, having exhauſted the receiver as much as we were wont, it appeared indeed, eſpecially toward the latter end of the operation, that the abſence of the air did conſiderably leſſen, and in ſome places eclipſe the light of thoſe parts that ſhone leſs ſtrongly, but the belly appeared not much leſs luminous than before: wherefore, ſuppoſing that upon the turning of the ſtop cock, the air coming in much more haſtily than it could be drawn out, we ſhould have the beſt advantage to diſcern what intereſt it had in the luminouſneſs of the fiſh, we re-admitted it, and upon its ruſhing in perceived the light to be as it were revived and increaſed, thoſe parts of the fiſh that were ſcarce viſible before, or ſhone but dimly, receiving preſently their former ſplendour.

And not to leave unproſecuted the remaining part of the experiment which was to try whether it was the kind of the luminous body or only the greatneſs of bulk and the vividneſs of light, and if I may ſo ſpeak, the tenacity of the ſubſtance it reſided in that made the difference between the fiſh and the wood; we put part of the fiſh of another kind that ſhone much more faintly than that hitherto ſpoken of, and but in ſome places; and by withdrawing the air, we made ſome of the luminous parts diſappear, and the others ſo dim as ſcarce to be diſcerned, and yet both the one and the other acquired their former light on the return of the air.

And to purſue the experiment a little further, we put in ſuch a piece of the firſt fiſh as, though it were bright, was yet but thin and not conſiderably great, and upon pumping out the air we found it according to our expectation quite eclipſed, though it recovered its light upon the air's re-entry.

These, Sir, are the experiments I have lately made about shining bodies in our engine. More I would have tried, notwithstanding the trouble we found in managing the engine in the dark, if rotten wood had not failed us, and if I were not in a place where glass-mens' shops are not near so well furnished as the stationers.

I scarce doubt but that these experiments will occasion among the virtuosi several queries and conjectures according to the different hypotheses and opinions to which men are inclined. And, particularly, 'tis probable that some will make use of this discourse to countenance their opinion, that notwithstanding the coldness (at least as to sense) of fishes and other animals, there may be in the heart and blood a vital kind of fire which needs air, as well as those fires which are sensibly hot, which may lessen the wonder that animals should not be able to live when robbed of air. And, if I had now time, I could possibly furnish you with some other trials that seem much to favour the comparison, though as to the opinion itself of a vital flame, I shall not now tell you my thoughts about it. And though not only the Cartesians will perhaps draw an argument from the past phenomena in favour of their theory of light, but divers others will discourse upon them and propose further questions and, perhaps, inquiries suitable to their several hypotheses, yet I shall content myself at present to have faithfully delivered the historical part of these appearances without making, at least, at this time, any reflections upon them; and the rather indeed because I enjoyed so little health when I was making the experiments, that it was not fit for me to engage in speculations that would much exercise my thoughts, which, I doubt, have been more gratified than my health hath been by the bare trials, which are most seasonably made at hours unseasonable for one that is not well.

Postscript sent by the same Noble Author, from the same place, Dec. 6th, 1667.

MY condition in point of health being not much improved since I wrote to you in October last, when I shall have added that I have not these five or six weeks been able to procure any shining wood, except one single piece, which, though large, was so ill-conditioned that it afforded me but one trial, you will not, I hope, expect that I should add much to the experiments I formerly sent you about the relation betwixt light and air. But, however, since the subject is new and noble, and since your curiosity about other matters has been so welcome and useful to the virtuosi, I shall not decline even on this occasion to comply with it, and the rather because I half promised you some additionals a good while since, and because too, that though what I shall acquaint you with may seem to be but a confirmation of two or three of the former experiments, yet, besides that, it is of them which *most* needed a confirmation, these trials will also afford some circumstances that will not, I think, be unwelcome.

Experiment XI.

To examine then the conjecture mentioned in the last experiment, that the durableness of the light in the shining fish, in spite of the withdrawing the air, might proceed in great part from the vividness of it, and the beauty of the matter it resided in, rather than from the extent of the luminous body in comparison of the small pieces of shining wood I hitherto had made my trials with; I put in the above mentioned piece of wood, whose luminous superficies might be perhaps 10 or 12 times as great as that which the eye saw at once of the surface of such fragments of shining wood as I was wont to employ; and though some parts of this large superficies shined vividly (for the light was usually enough, for rotten wood, inferior to that of our fish) yet this great piece being put into a convenient receiver was, upon the withdrawing of the air, deprived of light, as the smaller ones had been formerly; the returning air restoring its light to the one as it had done to the other.

Experiment XII.

But this is not the chief thing I intended to acquaint you with, *that* being the success of some trials we made in the prosecution of these two neighbouring experiments.

In the *first* of these I told you I had been able to try but for half an hour, or little more, that a shining piece of wood deprived in our engine of light, would yet retain a disposition to be as it were rekindled upon the fresh access of the air. Wherefore, though I could have wished to have made a further trial with the same kind of bodies, yet being able to procure none, I substituted in their room small pieces of rotten fish, that shone some of them more faintly, and some of them more vividly, in reference to one another; but none as strongly as some that I could have employed: and having in a very small and clear receiver so far drawn off the air as to make the included body disappear, we so ordered the matter that we kept out the air for about 24 hours, and then allowing the air to re-enter, and at a dark place and late at night, upon its first admittance the fish regained its light.

Experiment XIII.

This compared with some of my former observations about *putrefaction* put me upon a trial, which, though it miscarried, I shall here make mention of, that in case you who are the better furnished with glasses think it worth while you may get reiterated by the Society's Operator. Considering then how great an interest putrefaction hath in the shining of fishes, and air in the phenomena of putrefaction, I thought it might be somewhat to the purpose to take a fish that was according to the common course I had observed in animals not far from the state at which it would begin to shine; and having cut a piece out of it, I caused the rest to be hung up again in a cellar, and the exsected piece to be put into a small and transparent receiver, that we might observe, if a day or two or more, after the fish in the cellar should begin to shine, that in the exhausted receiver would either also shine, or (because that seemed not likely) would, notwithstanding the check which the absence of the air might be presumed to give the putrefaction, be found to shine too, either immediately upon the admission of the air or not long after it.

But this Experiment, as I lately intimated, was only designed and attempted, not completed; the receiver being so thin that upon the exhaustion of the internal air the weight of the external broke it, and we could ill spare another of that kind from trials we were more concerned to make; notwithstanding which we made one trial more, which succeeded no better than the former, but miscarried upon a quite differing account, viz. because neither the included piece of fish nor the remaining, though it were of the same sort with the fishes I usually employed, would shine at all, though kept a pretty while beyond the usual time at which such fishes were wont to grow luminous.

If this experiment had fucceeded, I had fome others to try in profecution of it, which I fhall not now trouble you with the mention of; but that this paragraph may not be ufelefs to you I'll take this occafion to give you a couple of advertifements that may relate not only to this experiment, but alfo more generally to thofe whether precedent or fubfequent, where fhining fifh are employed.

Advertisement I.

In the firft place then, I will not undertake, that all the experiments you fhall make with rotten fifh fhall have juft the fame fuccefs with thefe I have related; for as I elfewhere obferved (in a difcourfe written purpofely on that fubject) that the event of divers other experiments is not always certain, fo I have had occafion to obferve the like about fhining fifhes. And, befides what I lately took notice of at the clofe of the 10th experiment, I remember that having once defigned to make obfervations about the light of rotten fifhes; and having, in order thereunto, caufed a competent number of them to be bought, not one of them all would fhine, though they were bought by the fame perfon I was wont to employ, and hung up in the fame place I ufed to have them put, and kept them not only till they began to putrefy, but beyond the time that others ufed to continue to fhine, although a parcel of the fame kind of fifhes, bought the week before, and another of the fame kind bought not many days after, fhined according to expectation. What the reafon of this difappointment was I could not determine; only I remember that at the time it happened the weather was variable, and not without fome days of froft and fnow; nor is this the oddeft obfervation I could relate to you about the uncertain fhining of fifhes, if I thought it neceffary to add it in this place.

Advertisement II.

Notice muft alfo be taken in making experiments with fhining fifh, that their luminoufnefs is not wont to continue very many days, which advertifement may be therefore ufeful, becaufe without it we may be apt fometimes to make trials that cannot be foon enough brought to an iffue; and fo we may miftake the lofs of light in the fifh to be a deprivation of it caufed by the experiment, which indeed is but a ceffation according to the ufual courfe of nature.

EXPERIMENT XIV.

I know not whether you will think it worth while to be told of a trial that we made to fave thofe critics a labour that elfe might perhaps demand why it was not made: We put, therefore, a piece of fhining fifh into a wide mouthed glafs, about half filled with fair water, and having placed this glafs in a receiver we exhaufted the air for a good while to obferve whether, when the preffure of the air was removed, and yet (by reafon of the water that did before keep the air from immediately touching the fifh) the exhauftion of the receiver did not deprive the fifh of that contact of air which it had loft before; whether, I fay, in this cafe the abfence of the air would have the fame influence on the fhining body as in the former experiment; and here, as far as the numerous bubbles excited in the water would give us leave to difcern it (for they did, though not unexpectedly, fomewhat difturb the experiment, which inconvenience we might have prevented if we had thought it worth while), we could not perceive that either the abfence or return of the air had any great operation upon the light of the immerfed body, which it did not keep me from intending to make a fomewhat-like trial with fhining wood, (when I can get any) faftened to the lower part of a clear glafs, and covered over, but not very deep, with quickfilver; of which practice I fhall not now ftay to give you the reafons, having elfewhere fully enough expreffed them.

And that this fection may acquaint you with fomething befides the feemingly infignificant experiment related in it, I fhall here inform you (fince I perceive I did not in the firft papers I fent you) that though, when I formerly put together fome notes about luminous bodies, I confined not my obfervations to one or two forts of fifhes, yet the experiments, fent you fince October laft, were all of them (except a collateral one or two) made with Whitings, which among the fifhes I have had occafion to take notice of, is (except one fort that I cannot procure) the fitteft for fuch Trials, and confequently fit to be named to you, to facilitate their future ones, in cafe you think it requifite to make any upon fuch fubjects.

EXPERIMENT XV.

The other of the two neighbouring experiments I lately mentioned (viz. the ninth), I told you, when I fent it you, needed a reiteration to confirm it, ſince we had but once tried it (and that without all the conveniency we deſired), that a ſhining body, which upon the firſt withdrawing the air loſeth *much*, but not all its light, may be deprived of the reſt by continuing in that unfriendly place, though the air be no further exhauſted. To proſecute, therefore, both the experiments in one trial, we took, ſomewhat late at night, a piece of rotten fiſh, which we judged to ſhine too ſtrongly to be quickly deprived of *all* its *light*, and having put it into a ſmall and clear receiver, we found (as we had foreſeen) that the light was much impaired, but nothing near ſuppreſſed by the withdrawing of the air; wherefore, having removed the receiver into a convenient place, I cauſed it to be brought to me about midnight (after I was in bed), and having, by cloſe drawing the curtains, and by other means, made the place pretty dark, I perceived the included body to continue to ſhine more vividly than one would have expected, and again ſaw it ſhining in the morning, whilſt it was yet dark; but the night after, coming to look upon it again, its light appeared no more; notwithſtanding which, I made a ſhift to keep out the air about 24 hours longer, and ſo, after 48 hours in all, we opened the receiver in a dark place, and preſently upon the ingreſs of the air, were pleaſingly ſaluted with ſo vivid an appearance of light, that the included body continued to ſhine when carried into a room where there was both fire and candle, if it were but ſcreened by a hat from their beams.

Being encouraged, as well as pleaſed by this ſucceſs, we forthwith exhauſted the air once more out of the ſame receiver, and having kept it out about four hours longer, we looked upon it again in a dark place, and finding no appearance of light, let the air in upon it, whereby it was made to ſhine again, and that vigorouſly enough, ſo that I cauſed the receiver to be exhauſted once more; but that it being *Sunday* night, I was unwilling to ſcandalize any, by putting my ſervants on a laborious, and not neceſſary work.

The ſuddenneſs with which the included body appeared to be, as it were, rekindled upon the firſt contact of the air, revived in me ſome ſuſpicions I have had about the poſſible cauſes of theſe ſhort-lived apparitions of light (for I ſpeak not now of real lamps found in tombs, for a reaſon to be told you another time), which diſcloſing themſelves upon men's coming in, and conſequently letting freſh air into vaults that had been very long cloſe, did ſoon after vaniſh. Theſe thoughts occurred to me upon what I had before related, by reafon of the fudden operation of the frefh air upon a body that but a minute before difclofed no light. For, though the lights reported to have been feen in caves quickly difappeared, which that of our fifh did not, yet that difference might poffibly proceed from the tenacity, or fome other difpofition of the matter, wherein the luminoufnefs of the fifh refides. For I remembered that I had, more than once, obferved a certain glimmering and fmall light to be produced in certain bodies upon putting them out of their former *reft*, and taking them into the air, which fparks would vanifh of themfelves, fometimes within one minute, fometimes within a few minutes. But as thefe thoughts were but tranfient conjectures, fo I fhall not entertain you any longer about, but rather contenting myfelf with the hint already given, take notice of what may be more certainly deduced from our experiment, which is, that the air may have a much greater intereft in divers odd phænomena of nature than we are hitherto aware of.

And for confirmation of our experiment I fhall add, that, having in another receiver eclipfed a piece of fifh that fhone when it was put in more languidly than divers others that we had tried, I kept it about three days and three nights in a receiver, which, being fomewhat like another, at firft fuggefted to me (when I came to take it), fome fcruple, but afterwards, upon further examination, concluded it to be the fame; wherefore I opened it in the dark, and upon letting in the air on this body, that fhone but faintly at firft, it immediately recovered its long fuppreffed light; and having included another piece, that was yet more faint than this, when it was put into the receiver, I thought it fit to try at once the experiment hitherto confirmed, and the converfe of it; and therefore, having kept this piece alfo three days and three nights in the exhaufted glafs, I let in the air upon it, and notwithftanding the darknefs of the place, nothing of life was thereupon revived; but this being little other than I expected from a body that fhone fo faintly when it was put into the receiver, and had been kept there fo long, I refolved to exercife my patience awhile as well as my curiofity, and try whether the appulfe and contact of the air would have that operation *after fome time* that it had at firft, and accordingly, after having waited awhile, I obferved the fifh to difclofe a light, which, though but dim, was manifeft enough; but having confidered it for fome time, I had not leifure to watch whether it would increafe, or how long it would continue.

I fhall now conclude this paper, as foon as I have added this confirmation, as well of what I laſt related, as of ſomething I obſerved before, that having included in ſmall receivers two pieces of rotten whirings, whereof the one before it was put in ſcarce ſhone ſo vividly as did the other after the receiver was exhauſted; and having ordered the matter ſo that we were able to keep out the air for ſome days, at the end of 48 hours we found that the more ſtrongly ſhining body retained yet a deal of light; but afterwards looking upon them both in a dark place, we could not perceive in either any ſhow of light; wherefore, having let in the air into that receiver whereunto the body that at firſt ſhone the fainteſt had been put, there did not enſue any glimmering of light for a pretty while; nay, upon ruſhing in of the air into the other glaſs (then alſo made acceſſible to the atmoſphere), the body that at firſt ſhone ſo ſtrongly, and that continued to ſhine ſo long, ſhewed no glimmering of light. But being reſolved to expect the iſſue a while longer, our patience was rewarded in leſs than a quarter of an hour with the ſight of a manifeſt light in the body laſt named, and awhile after the other alſo became viſible, but by a light very dim. The more luminous of theſe bodies I obſerved to retain ſome light 24 hours after; and the hitherto recited experiment had this peculiar circumſtance in it, that the two receivers were uninterruptedly kept exhauſted no leſs than four days and as many nights *.

An Obſervation concerning a Blemiſh in Horſes' Eyes, not hitherto diſcovered by any Author; which may be of great uſe in the choice of Horſes to thoſe who are curious. Made by Dr. Richard Lower, at the ROYAL SOCIETY.

AMONGST the many defects and diſtempers in the eyes, the eyes of horſes are peculiarly affected with one, which no animal beſides is troubled withal (neither do I remember any author hitherto to have taken notice of it), and that is a ſpongy excreſcence (commonly of a dark muſk colour), which grows out of the edge of that coat of the eye called the *uvea*; which ſponge, if it grow large or increaſe in number (as it frequently happens), it depraves the ſight very much, or totally intercepts it. But that you may

* The method, which the noble author of theſe experiments uſed in keeping out the air for ſo long a time, was not then generally underſtood.

conceive the manner how it is done, you will recollect that the *uvea* is a musculous part, the use of it being chiefly to contract and dilate itself for the admission of objects with as much light as the eye can conveniently bear, so that the brighter and more refulgent the light is to which the eye is exposed, that membrane contracts itself into a narrower compass; and the more dark the place is, it dilates itself still the more, as you may see in a cat's eye more readily performed than in any other animal I have yet observed; so that if this spongy substance which grows out of the edge of the *uvea* be so great, or the number of them such as that they grow in several places about the pupil of the eye where it contracts itself, the pupil or sight is very much (if not totally) obstructed, and consequently the horse sees very little, or nothing at all; as I have many times taken notice of in some horses, which being brought into the sunshine could not see at all, but suffered me to touch the sight of the eye with my finger without the least winking; which horses being led back into the stable, the *uvea*, in that obscure place, dilating itself, they could see very well again, and would not suffer me to shew my finger near to the eye without frequently closing the eyelids, and tossing their heads. The same horses, I understood by their owners, were very apt to stumble in the day-time, if it were bright and sun-shine, but travelled very well and securely in the evening, and in dark cloudy weather.

What the cause may be of that fungous excrescence, or why horses are peculiarly obnoxious to it, or what kind of horses most, I have not considered. But I cannot think that it comes from straining in great drafts, and races, and hard travel, because I have seen very large sponges (as I may call them) in horses' eyes of two and three years old, before they were backed, which, after they were taken up from the grass, and kept with dry meat, have very much abated, and afterwards being turned to grass to cleanse and cool their bodies, have increased again to the wonted bigness. But whether it were from their moist feeding, or holding down their heads to eat (whereby there might be a greater deflux of humours to that part) I cannot determine. But forasmuch as there are few horses quite free from this evil, and many rendered very inconsiderable by it, I will recount the most remarkable cases which make horses most useless and suspected.

1st, The more and greater those excrescences are, the more the pupil of the eye or the sight is in danger of being quite obstructed; which you may farther examine by turning the horse's eye to the light, and observing how much of the pupil they do obstruct.

2dly, These sponges on the upper edge of the uvea are apt to grow the largest, and hinder the sight most.

3dly, That which grows on the middle of the uvea does more hinder the sight, by distracting the object, than that which grows in either corner or angle of it.

As for the cure, I fear there can be none expected, but from a drying kind of diet; though perhaps outwardly something may be devised to shadow the eyes, and keep them from being nakedly exposed to the sun, whereby the pupil will not be so closely contracted, and consequently the sight not so much obstructed.

An Extract of a Letter from Signior Cassini, Professor of Astronomy in Bononia, to Monsieur Petit at Paris, (translated from the Journal des Sçavans,) concerning several spots, lately discovered there, in the Planet Venus.

TO give you some account of my present studies, I shall acquaint you, that, having been a good while very assiduous and careful in making observations of Venus, to see whether the planet did not turn about its axis, by a motion like to that of Jupiter and Mars, I met at first with many difficulties, but at last considering that I should succeed better in my observations at a time when Venus is at a good distance from the earth, than when she is near thereto; I attentively observed, when she was risen somewhat high above the horizon, and shined brighter, whether I could not discern in her some part remarkable, either by its brightness or obscurity, amongst the rest, especially about the middle of her disk. And this I did not in vain; for I discovered, at last, towards the middle of her body, a part clearer than the rest, by which one might judge of the motion or the rest of this planet.

The first time I saw it was October 14, 1666, h. 5. 45'. P. M., and then this bright part was very near the centre, on the north side. And at the same time I observed, westward, two *obscure* spots, somewhat oblong. But I could not then see that resplendent part long enough to conclude any thing from thence; nor was I able to see any thing well of those parts till

April 28, 1667; on which day, a quarter of an hour before ſun-riſing, I ſaw again a bright part, ſituated near the ſection, and diſtant from the *ſouthern horn* a little more than $\frac{1}{4}$ of its diameter; and near the eaſtern ring I ſaw a dark and ſomewhat oblong ſpot, which was nearer to the northern than the ſouthern horn. At the riſing of the ſun I perceived that this bright part was then no more ſo near the *ſouthern* horn, but diſtant from it $\frac{1}{3}$ of its diameter. This gave me great ſatiſfaction. But I was ſurpriſed at the ſame time to find, that the ſame motion, which was made from ſouth to north in the inferior part of the diſk, was on the contrary made from north to ſouth in the ſuperior part; whence the determination of the motion may be better taken. For we have no example of the *like motion*, except it be in that of the libration of the moon.

The next day, at the riſing of the ſun the ſaid bright part was not far from the ſection, and diſtant from the ſouthern horn $\frac{1}{4}$ of the diameter. When the ſun was four degrees high, the ſame was ſituated near the ſection, and remote from the ſouthern horn $\frac{2}{5}$ of the diameter. The ſun being high 6 deg. 10 min. it ſeemed to have been paſſed the centre, and that the ſection of diſk did cut the ſame. The ſun being 7 deg. high, it appeared yet more advanced northward, together with two *obſcure* ſpots, ſeated between the ſection and the circumference, and equally diſtant from one another, and from each horn on both ſides. The ſky being very clear, I obſerved the motion of the bright part for $1\frac{1}{8}$ hour; which then ſeemed to be exactly made from *ſouth* to *north*, without any ſenſible inclination eaſt or weſtward. Mean time I perceived in the motion of the dark ſpots ſo *great* a variation, that it cannot be aſcribed to *any reaſon* in optics.

May 10 and 13, before ſun riſing, I ſaw ſtill the *bright* part near the centre northward.

Laſtly, June 5 and 6, before the riſing of the ſun, I ſaw the ſame between the northern horn and the centre of this planet, and I noted the ſame irregular variation in the obſcure ſpots. But when Venus began to be farther removed from the earth, it was more difficult to obſerve theſe phenomena.

I ſhall not preſume to declare my ſentiment touching theſe appearances ſo boldly as I did concerning the ſpots formerly diſcovered in Jupiter and Mars. For thoſe ſpots I could very well obſerve for a whole night together, during the oppoſition of thoſe planets to the ſun: I could conſider their motion for the ſpace of ſeveral hours; and at laſt, ſeeing them return regularly to the ſame place, I could judge whether they were the same spots or not, and in how much time they absolved their relation. But it was not so here with the appearances in Venus. For one sees them but for so small a time, that it is far more difficult *certainly* to know when they return to the same place.

Yet I can say, (supposing that this bright part of Venus, which I have observed, especially this year 1667, hath always been the same) that in less than one day it absolves its motion, whether of revolution or libration, so as in near 23 hours it returns about the same hour to the same situation in this planet; which yet happens not without some irregularity. Now, to assirm (supposing it to be always the same bright part) whether this motion is made by an entire revolution, or by a libration, I dare not yet do, in regard that I could not see the continuity of the motion through a great part of the arch, as I did in the other planets. And for this very reason that will always be difficult to determine.

An Extract of a letter written by J. Denis, Doctor of Physic, and Professor of Philosophy and Mathematics at Paris, touching a late cure of an inveterate Frenzy, by the transfusion of Blood.

IT is now almost a twelvemonth since I declared myself publickly in this matter of transfusion, and after I had grounded my conjectures upon divers reasons, and a number of experiments which I made jointly with M. Emmerez, I resolved to expect in the sequel a further confirmation, by carefully observing all that should happen in several trials, I intended to practise.

In this resolution we have let slip no occasion to improve this operation, which hath been followed with good success, and I could here allege some particular relations, the circumstances of which would appear curious enough, if I had not rather chose to refer them to a collection, which possibly I may send you within some time, to have the more to enlarge in this letter on the circumstances of a story, whereof you will be very glad to learn the event.

You have doubtless heard of a *madman* that hath been lately *cured*, and *restored to his wits* by the means of the transfusion. Some spread a rumour that he died soon after the operation; others bore the false report, that he had relapsed into a greater madness than that before, and in short, it hath been ſo diverſely diſcourſed of up and down, and with differing reflections thereon, that I thought myſelf obliged, for the clearing up of thoſe rumours, to give you a faithful and exact account of the condition to which this poor man was reduced before the transfuſion; of what during that operation, and the ſurpriſing effects that have followed upon it hitherto.

The patient is about 34 years of age. His frenzy began to appear ſeven or eight years ago, and as far as can be judged, it was occaſioned by a diſgrace he received a little before, in ſome amours, where he hoped to find a very conſiderable fortune. This firſt fit of extravagance was very violent, and laſted 10 months, without any good interval; but returning afterward by little to his reaſon, and having given all the marks of a ſound underſtanding, he was married to a young gentlewoman, who was perſuaded, that this madneſs of his was the relic of a ſickneſs he had before, and that there was no appearance he would ever relapſe into it. But this was far from proving ſo, as was imagined, and even the very firſt year of his marriage ended not without his returning to his former extravagancies.

Thus then he relapſed and was ſeveral times reſtored theſe ſeven or eight years laſt paſt. But what is here chiefly to be obſerved is, that the fit never laſted with him leſs than eight or ten months without any reſpite, notwithſtanding all the care and means uſed to relieve him. For it is alſo fit to take notice that a perſon of quality having once taken a purpoſe to effect his cure by all manner of ways, cauſed him to be bled in his feet, arms, and head, even 18 times, and made him bathe himſelf 40 times, not to mention innumerable applications to his forehead, and potions. But inſtead of amendment, the diſtemper ſeemed to be provoked by thoſe remedies, and this poor creature fell into that rage, that there was a neceſſity to bind him up from doing miſchief. His madneſs hath been always periodical, and never abated but by little and little, and that abatement hath befallen him rather at ſuch times when nothing was done to him, than when he was tormented with medicines.

The laſt time that he relapſed into his extravagancy was about four months ſince, in a place 12 leagues diſtant from Paris, and his wife hearing of it went immediately to him to relieve him. She ſoon ſhut him up and was even conſtrained to tye him for ſome time, becauſe he was in ſuch an extraordinary rage as to beat her. But for all her care, one time he got looſe, ſtark naked, and ran away ſtraight for Paris, nobody knowing how he could find his way in the dark night. His wife had him fearched for in all the neighbouring villages, whilft he ran here in Paris up and down the ftreets, without finding any place to retire to, in regard that thofe who had the charity of receiving him into their houfes the firft days, knew very well the danger they were in, of having their houfes burnt over their heads.

He was not lefs outrageous in this laft fit, than in the former. He hath fpent three or four months without fleep, and his greateft divertifement during that time was, to tear the cloaths that were given him, to run naked abroad, and to burn, in the houfes where he was, whatever he could meet with.

He moved to compaffion all good people that faw him, and efpecially thofe in the Marais du Temple, where he was known to moft, and where he had been wont to be feen before this diftemper, as well clothed and fafhioned as any one of his condition could be.

Monfieur de Montmor amongft others, was the perfon moft touched with it, and refolved to employ his intereft to procure him a place in one of the hofpitals. But firft he thought on the transfufion, and believed there would be no danger in trying it upon this man, being fo perfuaded by many experiments, we had already made in his prefence. He therefore had been taken up for that end, and having fent for me and M. Emmerez to afk our opinion of the fitnefs of trying the transfufion upon this man; we anfwered, that we could indeed give good affurance for his life, and that this operation was in itfelf, not capable to caufe the death of any one, if difcreetly managed; but as to the cure of fuch an extravagance, as that appeared to us to be, we had not yet experience enough to dare to promife him that; and that our conjectures went no farther than to think, that the blood of a calf, by its mildnefs and frefhnefs, might poffibly allay the heat and ebullition of his blood, being mixed therewith. The matter having been fufficiently examined, we refolved to carry this man into a private houfe; and there we appointed for his guardian the porter, on whom we had already practifed the transfufion eight months ago, both that the thing might not appear fo new to him, as it might do to others, who had never feen the experiment before, and that he might ferve us the more to affure our patient and others, who fhould be prefent at the operation, that there was no danger at all in it.

December 19.—We ufed what art we could to difpofe the fancy of our patient to fuffer the transfufion, which we refolved fhould be tried upon him that night about fix o'clock. Many perfons of quality were prefent, together with several physicians and *chirurgions*, too intelligent to suspect them of being capable of the least surprise. M. Emmerez opened the crural artery of a calf, and did all the necessary preparations in their presence; and after he had drawn from the patient about ten ounces of blood out of a vein of the right arm, we could give him no more again than about five or six ounces of that from the calf, by reason that his constrained posture, and the crowd of the spectators, interrupted very much this operation.

Mean time he found himself, as he said, very hot all along his arm, and under the arm pits; and perceiving that he was falling into a swoon, we presently stopt the blood from running in, and closed up the wound; yet he supped two hours after; and notwithstanding some dulness and sleepiness he was in now and then, he yet passed that night with singing, whistling, and other extravagancies usual with him.

But yet next morning we found him less exorbitant, both in his actions and words; and that induced us to believe, that by reiterating the transfusion once or twice, we might find a more remarkable change in him. We therefore prepared ourselves to repeat it upon him the next Wednesday, at six o'clock in the evening again, in the presence also of several very able physicians. *Bourdelot*, *Lellier*, *Dodar*, *De Bourges*, and *Vaillant*. But in regard that this man appeared very thin, and that it was not at all probable that his blood was peccant in the quantity after three or four months continual watching, and after the hunger and cold he had suffered, in running naked on the streets without finding a harbour at nights, we took but two or three ounces of blood from him, and having put him in a more convenient posture, we made this second transfusion into his left arm more plentiful than the first; for, considering the blood remaining in the calf after the operation, the patient must have received more than one whole pound.

As this second transfusion was larger, so were the effects of it quicker and more considerable. As soon as the blood began to enter into his veins he felt the like heat along his arm, and under his armpits which he had felt before. His pulse rose presently, and soon after we observed a plentiful sweat all over his face. His pulse varied extremely at this instant, and he complained of great pains in his kidnies, and that he was not well in his stomach, and that he was ready to choak, unless they gave him his liberty.

Presently the pipe was taken out that conveyed the blood into his veins, and whilst we were closing the wound, he vomited store of bacon and fat he had eaten half an hour before. He found himſelf urged to urine, and aſked to go to ſtool. He was ſoon made to lie down; and after two good hours ſtrainings, to void divers liquors which diſturbed his ſtomach; he fell aſleep about ten o'clock, and ſlept all that night without awakening till next morning (Thurſday) about eight o'clock. When he awakened he ſhewed a ſurpriſing calmneſs and preſence of mind, in expreſſing all the pains, and a general laſſitude he felt in all his limbs. He made a great glaſs full of urine, of a colour as black as if it had been mixed with the ſoot of chimnies.

Hearing of ſome of the company, that we were in a time of jubilee, he aſked for a confeſſion, to diſpoſe himſelf to be made participant of it; and he confeſſed himſelf accordingly to M. de Vean, with that exactneſs that the Confeſſor gave him the public teſtimony of a ſound underſtanding, and even judged him capable to receive the ſacrament, if he continued in that ſtate and devotion.

He remained ſleepy all the reſt of that day, ſpake little, and prayed thoſe that came to importune with interrogatories, to give him reſt; and he went on to ſleep well alſo the whole night following. Friday morning he filled another urinal with water, almoſt as black as that of the day before. He bled at the noſe very plentifully, and therefore we thought it neceſſary to take two or three ſmall porringers of blood from him.

Saturday morning, the laſt day before Chriſtmas, he deſired again to go to confeſs, and ſo to diſpoſe himſelf for the communion. Then one Mr. Bonnet examined him in hearing him confeſs, and after he had found him to have all the reaſon neceſſary to receive the ſacrament, he preſently gave him the communion. The ſame day his urine cleared up, and after that time it reſumed by little and little its natural colour.

His wife meantime, that had ſought him from town to town, came to Paris, and having found him out, when he ſaw her, he ſoon expreſſed much joy thereat, and related to her with great preſence of mind the ſeveral accidents that had befallen him, running up and down ſtreets, how the watch had ſeized upon him one night, and how calf's blood had been transfuſed into his veins.

This woman confirmed yet more to us the good effects of the transfuſion, by aſſuring us, that at the ſeaſon we were now in, her huſband ſhould be outrageous, and very mad againſt herſelf; and that inſtead of the kindneſs he ſhewed to her at this full of the moon, he uſed to do nothing but ſwear and beat her.

'Tis true, that comparing his calm condition, wherein he now was, with that wherein every body had seen him before the *transfusion*, no man scrupled to say that he was perfectly recovered; yet, to speak the plain truth, I was not so well satisfied as others seemed to be, and I could not persuade myself that he was in so good a temper as to stop there, but I was inclined to believe, by some things I saw, that a third transfusion might be requisite to accomplish what the two former had begun.

Yet in delaying the execution of these thoughts from day to day, we observed so great an amendment in his carriage, and his mind so cleared up by little and little, that his wife and all his friends having assured us that he was restored to the same state he used to be in before his frenzy, we entirely quitted the resolution. I have seen him almost every day since; he hath expressed me all manner of acknowledgement, and has been also with M. de Montmor, thanking him very civilly for his goodness in recovering him out of that miserable condition he was in, by a remedy he should remember as long as he lived. He is at present of a very calm spirit, and performs all his functions very well, and sleeps all night long without interruption, though he saith now and then he hath troublesome dreams. He hath carried himself so discreetly in some visits he made this week, that divers physicians, and other persons of credit, that have seen him, can render an authentic testimony to all the circumstances here advanced by me, who shall not employ against cavils and contradictions any other arguments than the experiment itself.

An exact narrative of an Hermaphrodite now in London.

THIS was communicated by the ingenious Dr. Thomas Allen (now a Fellow of the ROYAL SOCIETY) to a friend of his, in a Latin letter, in which as it was imparted to the said Society, so it was thought fit to publish it here for the view of the learned, viz.

Inter varios insolentesque naturæ lusus, dicam? an errores, quos apud eos, qui de Androgynis egerunt (quorum scripta sedulo deditaque opera perlustravi) in lucem productos adhuc videre mihi contigit, vix alium quenquam notatu digniorem memini occurrere hoc ipso, quem tibi, erudite vir, impræsentiarum exhibeo. Neque emim hunc, quem jam descriptum eo, Hermaphroditum, aut ſpurciſſimis illis fæminis, quæ apud Græcos Τριβάδες audiunt, apud Ægyptios vero frequentiſſime reperiebantur, annumerandum, aut cum deſcriptione quacunque, hactenus quod ſciam evulgata, ullatenus quadrare exiſtimo. Unde nec prorſus indignus mihi videtur, qui nativis depictus coloribus, abſque omni verborum fuco, Illuſtriſſimæ Lectiſſimæque Regiæ Societatis, et tuis oculis uſurpandus veniat.

Nomen ipſi eſt Anna Wilde; natus vero eſt (condonandus enim Hermaphrodito Solæciſmus) menſe Februario ipſo Purificationis Feſto, anno ſalutis 1647, in pago non ignobili agri Hamptonienſis, vulgo Ringwood.—Sexto Ætatis anno inter ſaltandum colluctandumque cum pueris coætaneis (quos omnes viribus facile ſuperabat) Extuberationes duæ, Herniarum Βουβωνοκηλων dictarum, primum emicuere; quibus in ordinem redigendis (id enim illis animi erat) chirugi diu operam luſerunt; Teſticuli enim erant, qui jam prægrande facti, ſcrotis cutaneis, corrugatis, piliſque obſitis incluſi, non alio diſcrimine a virilibus naturaliter ſe habentibus diſtinguuntur, quam quod ſinguli teſtes, ſuo proprio diviſoque ab invicem hic ſcroto guadeant, ita tamen elongato, ut ex utriuſque productione confingantur Labia Vulvæ.

In Sinu Muliebri (ut jam a Mercurio ad Venerem tranſeamus) Nymphæ et Carunculæ myrtiformes, integræ ſe ſatis produnt: quin et Membranula quadam, a Perinæo ſurſum tendente, media pars Vulvæ tegitur.—Clitoris non apparet.—Uterus ejuſque cervix a communi ſequioris ſexus lege ne minimum quidem recedunt. Uſque ad tertium ſupra decimum ætatis annum pro fæmellæ habitus et fæminæo veſtitu indutus, munera illi ſexui deſtinata inter fæminas aſſidue obibat.—Cum forte vero pani ſubigendo ſtrenuam navaret operam, en derepente Priapus, ad id temporis latens, magno cum impetu foras prorupit, accedente non levi ipſius Μεταμορφομενα ſtupore. Erectus penis quatuor circiter pollices æquat.—Locum Virgæ virilis ipſiſſimum occupat; in glandem pariter deſinit, præputio quod illi etiam frænulo, ut in viris fit, annectitur, inſtructum: ſed glans imperforata (ita tamen ut tenuis membranula eam obturans facile pertundi poſſe videatur) ſemini per Urethram, ſeu potius virgæ canaliculum viam affectanti, exitum negat; unde per pudendum muliebre (refluum forte) excernitur.

Cum annorum eſſet ſeptemdecim, Menſtrua periodicè et modo debito fluere cœperunt, atque per biennium perſeverarunt. Quo elapſo, iiſdem non amplius comparentibus pullulavit Barba, et exinde totum Corpus pilofum conſpicitur.—Vox corporiſque habitus virilem æmulantur.—Crinis ſe habet virorum ad inſtar.—Mammæ nullæ exſurgunt; papillæ perquam exiguæ.—Pectus latum eſt.—Iſchia non ita diſſita.—Nates quam ſunt fœminarum contractiores.

Se ad utrumque ſexum comparatum aſſerit ſed fœminis miſceri præeptare; quas etiam cum videt, et concupiſcit, erigitur Penis, qui quoties Virum appetit, flaccidus manet.

Unum hoc, idque nec extra oleas putem, Coronidis loco ſubnectam: quod nempe, cum nocte quadam, quam totam tripudiis, Compotationibus, cæteriſque id genus laſciviæ Incitamentis, cum aliquot ejusdem farinæ congeronnibus inſumpſerat, oculos in virum quendam formæ venuſtioris conjecerat, mox eum adeo deperibat, ut ſequenti die, pro amoris æſtro, in paſſionem hyſtericam incideret, quam revera talem fuiſſe, non ſolum Elevatio Abdominis, Cantus Riſus, Fletus, (notiſſima illius Intemperiei Symptomata) ſed et juvantia, ſatis liquido comprobarunt. Applicato quippe Emplaſtro ex Galbano Regioni Umbilici, exhibitiſque remediis hyſtericis ilico convaluit.

An account of the invention of grinding optic and burning Glaſſes of a figure not Spherical, produced before the ROYAL SOCIETY.

THE ingenious and induſtrious Francis Smethwick, Eſq. Fellow of the ROYAL SOCIETY, having for divers years painfully ſearched after the way of grinding glaſſes not ſpherical, affirms, that at length he hath now found it; for the proof of which he hath (viz. Feb. 27, 1667) produced before the ſaid Society certain ſpecimens of that invention, which were a teleſcope, a reading and two burning glaſſes.

The teleſcope was about four foot long, furniſhed with four glaſſes, whereof three ocular ones, *plano-convexo,* were of this newly invented *not ſpherical* figure, and the fourth a ſpherical object glaſs. This being compared with a common, yet very good teleſcope, longer than it by about four inches, and turned to ſeveral objects, was found by thoſe of the ſaid Society, that looked through them both, to exceed the other in goodneſs, by taking in a greater angle, and reprefenting the objects more exactly in their refpective proportions, and enduring a greater aperture, free from colours.

The reading glafs of the fame figure, being compared with a common fpherical glafs, did far excell it, by magnifying the letters to which it was applied, up to the very edges, and by fhewing them diftinctly from one brim through the centre to the other: which the fpherical glafs came far fhort of. And this effect the new-figured glafs performed only on one of its fides, and not on the other, as being of a different figure from fpherical glaffes, which perform their effects near equally on both fides.

Laftly, The two burning concaves of this new invented figure were one, of fix inches diameter, its focus three inches diftant from the centre thereof; the other of the fame diameter, but lefs concave, and its focus ten inches diftant. Thefe, when approached to a large lighted candle, did fomewhat warm the faces of thofe that were four or five feet diftant at leaft; and when held to the fire did burn gloves and garments at the diftance of about three feet therefrom.

Such were the particulars the ROYAL SOCIETY obferved in thefe glaffes, and gave orders to be regiftered in their books; encouraging the *Inventor* to proceed in his work with all poffible care and diligence, for enabling himfelf to inftruct others in the way of grinding thefe glaffes with facility.

The Inventor having declared his refolution to do fo, added thefe particulars. Firft, that the Lord Bifhop of Salifbury, *Seth Ward*, (who was then abfent from the meeting of the Society) had been by when the deeper of his two concaves turned a piece of wood into flame in the fpace of ten feconds of time; and the fhallower in five feconds at moft, in the feafon of autumn about nine o'clock in the morning, the weather gloomy.* Secondly, that the deeper concave, when held to a lucid body, would caft a light ftrong enough to read by at a confiderable diftance. Thirdly, that by expofing the fame to a northern window, on which the fun fhined not at all, or very little, he had perceived that it would warm the hand fenfibly, by collecting the warmed air in the day time, which it would not do after fun-fet.

* This, the faid judicious Prelate, at another meeting of the ROYAL SOCIETY, attefted to be true.

An account of some observations made by Mr. Samuel Colepresse, at and nigh Plymouth, by way of Answer to some Queries concerning Tides.

1st, OUR diurnal tides, from about the latter end of March till the latter end of September, are about a foot higher (perpendicular, which is always to be understood) in the evening than in the morning; that is, in every tide that happens after 12 in the day, and before 12 at night.

2d, On the contrary, the morning tides from Michaelmas till our Lady Day in March again, are constantly higher, by about a foot, than those that happen in the evening. And this proportion holds in *both*, after the gradual increase of the tides rising from the neap to the highest spring; and the like decrease of its height till neap again is deducted.

3d, The highest menstrual spring tide is always the third tide after the *new* or *full* moon, if a cross wind do not keep the water out, as a north-east or north-west usually doth; whose contrary winds, if strong, commonly make those to be high tides upon our southern coasts which otherwise would be but low.

4th, The highest springs make the lowest ebbs. And,

5th, The water neither flows nor ebbs alike in respect to equal degrees; but its velocity increaseth with the tide till just at mid-water, that is, at half-flow, or at half-flood, at which times the velocity is strongest, and so decreaseth proportionably till high water, or full sea; as may be guessed at by the following scheme, taken from my papers, containing observations, as they were made at several times and places; which I rather set down as a standing proportion of degrees in the general, than to adequate every single flux and reflux so exactly as to half inches or the like, but yet it may bear the odd minutes above six hours well enough. And it is further to be noted, that, although this be restrained to Plymouth Haven, or the like, where the water usually riseth about 16 feet (I say *usually*, because it may vary in this port, from the lowest neap to the highest annual spring, above seven or eight feet), yet it may indifferently serve for other places, where it may rise as many fathom, or not so high, by a perpetual addition or subtraction.

THE SCHEME ITSELF.

Of Flowing.			*Of Ebbing.*		
ho.	f.	in.	ho.	f.	in.
1	1	6	1	1	6
2	2	6	2	2	6
3	4	0	3	4	0
4	4	0	4	4	0
5	2	6	5	2	6
6	1	6	6	1	6

6th, The ufual number of tides, or times of high water, from new moon to new moon, or from full moon to full moon, is 59.

An extract of a printed letter, by M. Jean Denis, Doctor of Phyfic, and Profeffor of Mathematics at Paris, touching the differences arifen about the Transfufion of Blood.

SIR,

YOU have fenfibly obliged me in having affured me, by your letter of April 29, that the Magiftrates of London had not at all concerned themfelves to prohibit the practice of the Transfufion of Blood, and that *that* operation had been hitherto practifed with good fuccefs on brutes, and without any ill confequence upon a man. The enemies of new difcoveries had taken fo great care of publifhing every where this falfe account to decry this experiment, that there needed an authentic teftimony to difabufe the multitude. If one fhould undertake to diffipate all thefe falfe rumours they have fpread touching this matter, one fhould never lay afide the pen; but the beft of it is, that men of difcretion do fo much difdain thefe wild reports, that they hearken no more to them but with difguft. And as to myfelf, I was refolved to write no more of it, until fome new experiments might countenance my firft conjectures. But your laft letters do fo civilly engage me to impart to you the fecret cabal, practifed by fome perfons to embarrafs the hiftory of that madman that was cured fix months ago by the means of the transfufion, that I could not omit fending you the fum of what hath hitherto paffed on that fubject, expecting, mean time, what the Parliament of Paris, who, I believe, will be the judges and arbitrators thereof, shall determine therein.

You already know, that the transfusion of calf's blood did so temper the excessive heat of the blood of the madman, who for four months had ran naked up and down the streets, night and day; that he fell asleep two hours after the operation, and that after ten hours sleep he awaked, being in good sense; and that he remained in that good condition about two months, and until too frequent company with his wife, and his debauches in wine, tobacco, and strong waters, had cast him into a very violent and dangerous fever.

You may also have heard how this operation had effects quite contrary at the same time, and that for one brain cooled thereby it fired many; forasmuch as by curing the madness of one poor wretch, it disturbed the wits of many such as aim at nothing but to signalize themselves by opposing all new discoveries which themselves are not capable to make. It was indeed but three or four days after this man was recovered, that some malicious spirits began to publish that he died under our hands, and that we had put an end to his extravagancies by putting an end to his life. This first story having been convicted of falsity, they mended the tale, and were resolved to make people believe that he was relapsed into his former madness, and even was grown worse than ever. This obliged the first President, and many other persons of quality, to send for him to their houses, to examine the truth themselves; who, after they had entertained him awhile, were satisfied of the good effects of the transfusion, and that those wanted no malice who reported things so contrary to what they saw with their own eyes.

These things you may have learned from our formerly printed letters. But what, perhaps, you know not yet, is, that these envious spirits were not the only ones that were troubled at this cure. The *wife* of the patient was *most* alarmed at it, though she used artifice enough to shew us the contrary, and to persuade us that she thought on nothing else but to relieve him in his distempers. The fact is, that this man having been a lacquey, and since a valet de chambre, had no profession that could bring in a subsistence for his family; a lady of quality, whom he had served, had indeed promised to prefer him, but his deplorable state of health proved an obstacle to the performance of that promise; and indeed the *time* of his madness was not so troublesome to his wife as *that* of his being in his wits;

for whereas she had her freedom to make certain visits, and to live as she listed, when he was not at home, but ran up and down, and even lay at nights in the streets; she was on the contrary in great pain when he came to stay at home, because he observed her narrowly, and could not forbear reproaching her for often having attempted to poison him, now and then expressing also some jealousy he had conceived against her comportment. These are the complaints she herself hath often made to credible persons, who thought themselves obliged to depose the same judicially, thereby to discover the misunderstanding, which, doubtless, hath been the original of the troublesome sequel in this affair.

And, indeed, this poor man falling ill again, his wife urged us beyond measure to try the third transfusion upon him, insomuch that she threatened she would present a petition to the Solicitor General to do what we absosolutely did refuse. At last she came one morning to my house, and not finding me, she left word, that she entreated me to exercise that charity as to come after dinner to her house, where would be a certain meeting. I went, and there met M Emmerez; and finding a calf and every thing ready for a transfusion, we would go away, telling her that her husband was not in a condition for this operation. Then she fell down with tears in her eyes, and by unwearied clamours she engaged us not to go away without giving her the satisfaction of having tried all possible means to recover her husband. Her art was great enough to make us condescend to another trial, to see whether we could give him any relief. M. Emmerez, to content her, passed a pipe into the vein of the patient's arm; and since 'tis necessary to draw away some of the old blood when new is to be infused, he opened a vein in his foot for that end; but a violent fit having seized on him in that instant, together with a trembling of all his limbs, there issued no blood of the foot, nor the arm, which obliged M. Emmerez to take the pipe out of his arm, without opening the artery of the calf, and so without any transfusion.

This poor man dying the night after, and that news being brought us, we went thither the next morning, together with M. Emmerez, and another surgeon; and remembering the complaints the dead man had often made of his wife's attempt to poison him, we would gladly have opened his body, in the presence of seven or eight witnesses, but she did so violently oppose it, that it was not poſſible for us to execute our deſign. We were no ſooner gone, but ſhe beſtirred herſelf exceedingly, as we were informed, to bury her huſband with all ſpeed; but being in an indigent condition, ſhe could not compaſs it that day. Mean time, a famous phyſician of the faculty of Paris happening to be that night at the houſe of a lady, who was ſolicited for charity towards this burial, was of the ſame mind with us, that his body ſhould be opened, and therefore ſent inſtantly for ſurgeons to execute it. But ſhe being reſolved againſt it, uſed lies and other arts to elude this deſign; and when we threatened her that we would return next morning, and do the thing by force, ſhe cauſed her huſband to be buried an hour before day, to prevent our opening him.

As ſoon as his death was bruited abroad, the enemies of the experiment began to triumph, and ſoon after they publiſhed defaming books againſt us. I then reſolved to be ſilent; but that ſilence made our adverſaries but keener; and I was ſurpriſed, when two months after I was informed, that there were three phyſicians that did not budge from the widow, importuning her, by promiſes of a great recompence, only to let them uſe her name to accuſe us before a court of juſtice, for having contributed to the death of her huſband by the transfuſion, and that even they addreſſed themſelves to the neighbours of this woman, to engage them to bear falſe witneſs againſt us. And ſome time after, this woman, raiſed by the hopes given her by thoſe men, came and told us that ſome phyſicians did extremely ſolicit her againſt us, and that ſhe had always refuſed them, knowing her obligations to us for having relieved her huſband freely. But ſhe drawing from hence no profit, as ſhe expected ſhe ſhould, ſhe turned her advertiſements into menaces, and ſent us word, that in the preſent neceſſity to which ſhe was reduced, ſhe was obliged to accept of the offer made her by certain phyſicians, if we would not aſſiſt her. I ſent her this anſwer, that thoſe phyſicians and herſelf ſtood more in need of the transfuſion than ever her huſband had done, and that, for my part, I cared not for her threats. But yet, I *then* thought it time to break ſilence, not only my intereſt being concerned, but the public, to diſcover to the world thoſe perſons that would be engaged in intrigues ſo unworthy of learned men. I complained of it to the Lieutenant in Criminal Cauſes, who preſently allowed me to inform, both againſt the widow and thoſe who ſolicited her. Some witneſſes having been called before juſtices, they depoſed againſt the three phyſicians and the woman, accuſing them to have ſecretly given to her huſband certain powders, which might have contributed to his death.

This information, brought in by five witneſſes, having been preſented in a full court to the ſaid Lieutenant by Mr. Dormeſſon, the King's Advocate, he gave ſentence, that the woman ſhould have a day ſet her to appear in perſon to be examined upon my informations; and that in the mean time new informations ſhould be taken againſt her at the deſire of his Majeſty's attorney. And becauſe he thought there might be danger in permitting indifferently the practice of the transfuſion to all ſorts of perſons, he ordered that for the future it ſhould be uſed but by the preſcript of phyſicians. This is what you will ſee more fully in an extract of the ſentence itſelf, given at the Chaſtelet, by the Lieutenant in Criminal Cauſes at Paris, April 17, 1668, as follows:

1ſt, That the operation of transfuſion was twice performed upon Anthony Mauroy, a madman; and that it was attempted a third time. That it ſucceeded ſo well each time it was performed, that the patient was ſeen for two months after in good ſenſes, and in perfect health.

2d, That from the time of the two firſt operations his wife gave him eggs and broths, and bedded with him *four times*, notwithſtanding the prohibition of thoſe that treated him; and that ſhe carried him to her houſe without ſpeaking to them of it, and with great reluctancy of her huſband.

3d, That ſince that time he went from one cabaret to another, and took tobacco, and falling ill again, his wife ordinarily gave him ſtrong water to drink, and broths, wherein ſhe mixed certain powders; and that Mauroy having complained that ſhe would poiſon him, and gave him arſenic in his broths, ſhe hindered the aſſiſtants to taſte thereof, and making a ſhow of taſting it herſelf, caſt it down upon the ground what ſhe had in a ſpoon.

4th, That Du Mauroy had frequent quarrels with his wife ſince, and that ſhe gave him many ſtrokes, as ſick as he was; but having once received a box on the ear from him, ſhe ſaid he ſhould repent it, though he ſhould die o'nt.

5th, That when the transfuſion was attempted the third time, it was at the inſtant requeſt of his wife; thoſe that were to perform the operation, refuſing to do it without the permiſſion of the Solicitor General: that ſome days after that the operation was begun, but that almoſt no blood iſſuing out of either the foot or the arm of the patient, a pipe was inserted, which made him cry out, though it appeared not any blood of the calf had passed into his veins. That the operation was given over, and that the patient died next night.

6th, That the woman would no way suffer any one to open the body of her husband, saying, for an excuse, he was already in the coffin, when he was not.

7th, That a good while after the decease of the said Du Mauroy, three physicians did solicit the said woman to take money, and to make complaints that the transfusion had killed her husband; that she said, when those persons were gone away from her, that they had been with her on that account; and *that* unless those who had made the operation would give her wherewith to return into her country, she should do what those *others* pressed her to. That a witness deposeth, that she came to pray him that he would advertise those who had made the operation, that unless they would maintain her during her life, she would accept of the offer made her by those physicians. That another witness deposeth, that one was come to him from a physician, and had offered him 12 golden Louis if he would depose that Du Mauroy died in the very act of the transfusion.

That the matter was important enough to enquire into the bottom of it; that there was cause enough to examine this woman, where she had those powders? why she had given them to her husband? and by whose order? why she had hindered the opening of the body by a lie? That he required further information might be taken about it, and she in the mean time put in safe custody.

That as to the three physicians who had solicited her with money to prosecute those who had made the operation, and who had been seen with her, he demanded that a day might be set them to appear in person.

Lastly, That since the transfusion had succeeded well the two first times, and had not been undertaken the third, but at the earnest request of the woman, who otherwise had observed so ill the order of those who had made the operation, and who were suspected to have caused the death of her husband, he demanded that the execution of the decree of prefixing them a day for personal appearance, might surcease.

Whereupon it was decreed the widow of Du Mauroy should on a set day appear personally, and undergo the examination upon the alleged informations; and that more ample informations should be made of the contents in the complaints of M. Denys; and then that for the future no transfusion should be made upon any human body but by the approbation of the physicians of the Parisian faculty.

Since the above sentence was passed, new informations have been given in, considerably stronger than the former; and witnesses have been discovered, to whom the woman had committed it as a trust, that it was arsenic she mingled with her husband's broths; and even that the deceased having given the rest of one of the messes to a cat, the animal died of it a few days after.

As to the transfusion, you see it is not absolutely prohibited by this sentence, there needing no more to practise it, but to have the approbation of some of the physicians of Paris; and at this very time there are seven or eight who have signed the proposition made for one. It is not that I would make use of that licence for the practice of this operation; for the physicians of Montpelier, Rhennes, and other universities of France, who hold at Paris the first places about their Majesties, the Princes, and Princesses of the blood, the chief magistrates, and other persons of quality, find themselves in some manner wounded by this sentence. They do not think they are obliged to stay for the judgment of the doctors of Paris, to enable them to prescribe an operation of this nature; doubtless we shall in a short time have this point determined and regulated by an higher jurisdiction: and I have now before me a paralytic woman, (a neighbour and a friend of her that was cured of the palsy this way) who is resolved to present a petition to the magistrate, and therein to desire that the transfusion may be allowed her.

Meantime, if ever the Parisian physicians meet on this business, I do not believe that they will act with the precipitancy as some fancy; and as to the *Parliament*, I do not see that those who compose it are of a resolution to strike at this operation, unless it should happen that the experiments that may be made before them should not succeed, as those have done that have been made hitherto. It is well known to that court that the faculty made a decree an *hundred years* since against antimony, which was then used by the physicians of Montpelier; and that after they had given it a place amongst poisons, they obtained a sentence prohibiting the use thereof: yet notwithstanding these physicians not having forborne to use it under another name, the effects thereof proved so advantageous, and the recovery of our great

Monarch *thereby* ſo famous, that the faculty of Paris was conſtrained, two years ago, to approve, by a decree, what before it had forbidden; and even demanded another ſentence for permitting the uſe of the ſame.

This example will not let them go ſo faſt for the future upon the like occaſions; beſides, that the time wherein we are ſeems to be much more favourable for new diſcoveries than it was an age ago. His Majeſty, how much ſoever taken up in the government of his kingdom, and in his victories and triumphs, is not wanting to give a very particular encouragement and protection to learned and inquiſitive men: and at a time when his ſaid Majeſty ſends all over the world recompences and gratifications to thoſe that cultivate the ſciences, I cannot believe that in his dominions there will be found magiſtrates reſolved to condemn perſons that have no other crime than that of conſecrating all their intereſt and labour to the progreſs and advancement of knowledge and new diſcoveries.

I ſhall only add that I will not fail to impart to you the iſſue of this affair, which makes ſo much noiſe here and elſewhere.

Account of a controverſy between Stephano de Angelis, Profeſſor of the Mathematics in Padua, and Joh. Baptiſt. Riccioli, Jeſuit; communicated by Mr. Jacob Gregory, a Fellow of the ROYAL SOCIETY. *Tranſlated from the Latin.*

RICCIOLI, in his *Almageſtum Novum*, pretends to have found out ſeveral new demonſtrative arguments againſt the motion of the earth. Steph. de Angelis, conceiving his arguments to be none of the ſtrongeſt, taketh occaſion to let the world ſee that they are not more eſteemed in Italy than in other places. *Manfredi*, in behalf of Riccioli, endeavours to anſwer the objections of Angeli; and this latter replies to Manfredi's anſwer. The ſubſtance of this diſcourſe is as follows:

Although the arguments of Riccioli be many, yet the ſtrength of them conſiſts chiefly in theſe three.

THE FIRST.

All bodies let fall through the air in the plane of the equator, deſcend to the earth with a velocity conſtantly increaſing as they fall. But if the earth were moved by a diurnal motion only about its own axis or centre, no heavy bodies difmiffed through the air in a perpendicular direction would defcend to the earth with a real and notable increafe of velocity, but with an apparent one only. Therefore the earth either does not move at all, or has a diurnal revolution only.

THE SECOND.

If the earth were moved by a diurnal motion, or even by an annual one, the force of a cannon ball would be much more weak difcharged towards the north, or towards the fouth, than from the weft towards the eaft; therefore the confequence is falfe, and likewife the antecedent.

THE THIRD.

If the earth were moved by a diurnal revolution, a ball of baked earth of eight ounces let drop through the ftill air from the height of 24 Roman feet, would fall obliquely towards the earth without real or phyfical increafe of velocity, or certainly not by fo much as is the proportion of the percuffion or found occafioned by the fall from the faid altitude; but the pofterior is abfurd, *ergo et prius*.

In anfwer to the firft of thefe arguments, Angeli denieth the minor, which Riccioli pretends to prove thus:

If the earth is moved by a diurnal motion, any thing heavy difmiffed from the top of a tower C in the plane of the exifting equator, fhould defcribe by its own natural motion a portion of the line C T I, which fhould be to every appearance circular. See Fig. 1.

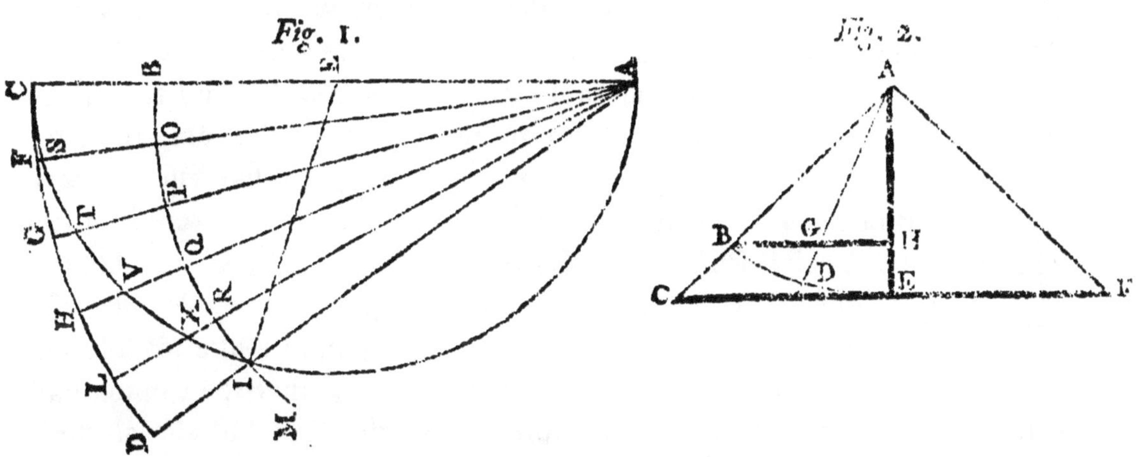

This Angeli denies, shewing by computation that Riccioli's observation proveth no such thing. For, (saith *Angeli*) according to Riccioli, in one second of an hour the weight descends 15 feet; in two seconds, 60 feet; in three seconds, 135 feet; and so continually the spaces from the beginning are in duplicate proportion of the time from the beginning; and, according to the same author, A B (the semi-diameter of the earth) is of 25870000 feet, and B C (the height of the tower of the Asinelli, in *Bononia*) of 240 feet; and therefore A C is 25870240, which hath the same proportion to F S, 15 feet, to wit, the fall in one second, which A C in parts 20000000000 hath to F S 11596 $\frac{54356}{224189}$; but supposing with Riccioli, C S I A a semi-circle, F S is 53 parts, of which A C is 10000000000: hence concludeth Angeli, that C S I A is no ways near to a semi-circle; which is most true, if so be the weight fall not to the centre of the earth precisely in six hours; for, in this case of Riccioli, the weight falls to the centre of the earth in 21 minutes and 53 seconds.

Manfredi, in his answer to Riccioli, affirms, that Angeli understands not the Rule of Three, in giving out F S for 11596 $\frac{54356}{224189}$, of which A C is 20000000000: and Angeli, in his reply, affirms his analogy to be so clear, that there can be nothing said more evident than itself to confirm it; referring in the mean time the further determination to *geometricians*.

Angeli might have answered Riccioli's argument, granting the weight to move equally in a semi-circle, by distinguishing his minor thus:

No heavy bodies descend to the earth with a real and notable increase of velocity, if the velocity be computed within the line of a semi-circle, the minor proposition is true. But not so is the descending motion to be computed: for here the equal motion in the circumference of the semi-circle C I A is compounded out of the equal motion in the quadrant C D; and the accelerated motion in the moveable semi-diameter C A; and this accelerated motion in the semi-diameter is a true and simple descending motion; in which exception the minor proposition is most false, and likewise contrary to the experiments of Riccioli. But it seems that Angeli answereth otherwise, to make Riccioli sensible that C I A is no semi-circle; concerning the nature of which line they debate very much throughout the whole discourse.

The second argument is much insisted on by Angeli, to make his solution clear to vulgar capacities; but the substance of all is, that the cannon ball hath not only that violent motion impressed by the fire, but also all these motions proper to the earth, which were communicated to it by the impulſe received from the earth; for the ball going from weſt to eaſt hath indeed two impulſes, one from the earth, and another from the fire; but this impulſe from the earth is alſo common to the mark, and therefore the ball hits the mark only with that ſimple impulſe received from the fire, as it doth being ſhot towards the north or ſouth; as Angeli doth excellently illuſtrate by familiar examples of motion.

To Riccioli's third argument Angeli anſwereth, deſiring him to prove the ſequel of his major, which Riccioli doth, ſuppoſing the *curve* in which the heavy body deſcends, to be compoſed of many ſmall right lines; and proving that the motion is almoſt always equal in theſe lines; and after ſome debate concerning the equality of motion in theſe right lines, Angeli anſwers, that the equality of motion is not ſufficient to prove the equality of percuſſions and ſound, but that there are neceſſary alſo equal angles of incidence; which in this caſe he proveth to be very unequal. To illuſtrate this more, let us prove, that, other things being alike, the proportion of two percuſſions is compoſed of the direct proportion of their velocities, and of the direct proportions of the ſines of their angles of incidence

Let us ſuppoſe the following axiom, to wit, what percuſſions (other things being alike) may be in direct proportion with the velocities, by which the moveable plane approaches the reſiſtance. Suppoſe a plane C F. See Fig. 2, and that there may be two moveable bodies in every reſpect alike, which approach with an equal motion the plane C F from the point A, in the right lines A D, A F, I ſay the percuſſion towards the point D to the percuſſion towards the point F, to be in the ratio compounded from the ratio of the velocity in the right line A D, to the velocity in A F, and from the ratio of the ſine of the angle A D E, to the ſine of the angle A F E. From the point A to the plane C F, A E by rule may be the right line, and the right line A C equal to the right line A F, A B equal to the right line A D, and the plane B G H parallel to the plane C F. Let us ſuppoſe the moving body, as before mentioned, alike in all reſpects to be moved equally in the right line A C, with the ſame velocity with which the body is moved in the right line A D; becauſe in the plane B G H, C F are parallel; and the motion in the right line A C is equal, therefore the moving body approaches with the ſame velocity the plane B H with which it approaches the plane C F, and thence the percuſſions at the points B C are equal; and the percuſſion at the point D, is to the percuſſion at the point B, as the right line A E to the right line A H, or as the ſine of the angle A D E to the ſine of the angle A B H; as it is evident the moving velocity in the ſtraight line A D, is equal to the velocity of the moving body in the right line A B, wherefore equal to A D. and therefore it is effected in both right lines A D, A B, in the ſame time; and ſo in the ſame time the acceſſions to the reſiſting planes A E, A H, are performed; and therefore the velocities of the acceſſions to the reſiſting planes are in the direct ratio of A E to A H, and likewiſe the percuſſion at the point D is to the percuſſion at the point C in the ratio A E to A H; to wit, the ſine of the angle of incidence A D E to the ſine of the angle of incidence A C E, or A F E. But becauſe the right lines A C, A F, equally incline to the plane C F, the moving bodies in the right lines A C, A F, approach to the plane C F in the ſame proportion in which they are moved in the right lines A C, A F; and therefore the percuſſion at C is to the percuſſion at F, in the ratio of the velocity of the motion at A C, or in A D to the velocity of the motion in A F; but ſince it is demonſtrated that the percuſſion at the point D to the percuſſion at the point C, is in the ratio of the ſine of the angle A D E to the ſine of the angle A F E; and now it is demonſtrated that the ſtroke at the point C, is to the percuſſion at the point F, as the velocity of the motion in A D to the velocity in A F. Therefore the percuſſion at D, is to the percuſſion at F, in the ratio compounded from the ratio of the ſine of the angle of incidence A D E, to the ſine of the angle of incidence A F E, and from the ratio of the velocity in A D to the velocity in A F; which it was incumbent to demonſtrate.

It ſhould not ſurpriſe, becauſe this demonſtration is confined to equal motions in right lines and reſiſting planes, for as much as it is true in every caſe: but ſeeing, when the percuſſions are made in a point in this *right* and *curved* line, equal and unequal, they coincide and agree: but if the percuſſions do not happen in the points, from theſe no geometrical conſiderations can be given, but the defect of the concluſion is to be judged according to the defect of the matter from the requiſite conditions; as it ought always to be, whilſt geometrical demonſtrations are applicable to a phyſical body.

In Angeli's reply to Manfredi, he maketh mention of an experiment, which (as was related to him by a Swediſh gentleman) had been made with all due circumſpection by Carteſius to prove the motion of the earth. The experiment was; he cauſed to be erected a cannon perpendicular to the horizon; which being 24 times diſcharged in that poſture, the ball did fall 22 times towards the weſt, and only twice towards the eaſt.

A curious and exact Relation of a Sand Flood, which overwhelmed a great Tract of Land in the County of Suffolk. Communicated in a Letter by Thomas Wright, Esq.

Sir,—I beg your pardon, that I have not given you an earlier return to your letter, by giving you the account you required of those prodigious *sands*, which I have the unhappiness to be almost buried in; and by which a considerable part of my small fortune is quite swallowed up. But I assure you my silence was not the result of any neglect, but rather of my respects to you, whose employments I know are too great to suffer you often, vacare nugis. The truth is, I suspended giving you any trouble, 'till I was put in some capacity of answering the whole letter, as well concerning those few improvements, this part of the nation has made in agriculture, as those wonderful *sands*, which, although, they inhabit with, and upon me, and have not yet exceeded one century, since they first broke prison, I could not without some difficulty trace to their original. But now I find it to be in a warren in Lakenheath (a town belonging to the Dean and Chapter of Ely, distant not above five miles, and lying south-west and by west of this place) where some great sand-hills (whereof there is still a remainder) having the superficies, or sward of the ground (as we call it) broken by the impetuous south-west winds, blew upon some of the adjacent grounds; which, being much of the same nature, and having nothing but a thin crust of barren earth to secure its good behaviour, was soon routed and dissolved by the other sand, and thereby easily fitted to increase the mass, and to bear it company in this strange progress.

At the first eruption thereof (which does not much exceed the memories of some persons still living) I suppose the whole magazine of sand could not cover above eight or ten acres of ground, which increased into 1000 acres, before the sand had travelled four miles from its first abode. Indeed it met with this advantage, that till it came into this town, all the ground it passed over, was almost of as mutinous a nature as itself, and wanted nothing but such a companion to set it free, and to solicit it to this new invasion. All the opposition it met with in its journey hither, was from one farm house which stood within a mile and a half from its first source. This the owner endeavoured, at first, by force and building of bulwarks against the assaults thereof; but this winged enemy was not to be so opposed: which after some dispute, the owner perceiving, did not only slight the former works, but all his fences, and what else might obstruct the passage of this unwelcome guest, and in four years effected that by compliance, and submission, which could never have been done upon other terms: in which he was so successful, as that there are scarce any footsteps left of this mischievous enemy.

It is between thirty and forty years since it first reached the bounds of this town; where it continued ten or twelve years in the outskirts, without doing any considerable mischief to the same. The reason of which I guess to be, that its current was then *down hill*, which sheltered from those winds that gave it motion. But the valley being once passed, it went above a mile *up hill* in two months time, and over-ran 200 acres of very good corn the same year. It is now got into the body of this little town, where it buried and destroyed divers tenements and other houses, and has enforced us to preserve the remainder at a greater charge than they are worth; which, doubtless, had also perished, had not my affection for this poor dwelling obliged me to preserve it at a greater expence than it was built: where at last I have given it some check, though for four or five years our attacks on both sides were of such various success, that the victory remained very ambiguous. For it had so possessed all our avenues, that there was no passage to us but over two walls of eight or nine feet high, (which encompassed a small grove before my house, now almost buried in the sand;) nay, it was once so near a conquest, as at one end of my house it was possessed of my yard, and had blown up to the eves of most of my out-houses. At the other end it broke down my garden wall, and stopt all passage that way.

But during these hard and various skirmishes, I observed, that that wing of sand that gave me the assault, began to contract into a much less compass. For by stopping of it four or five years (what I could) with furze hedges, set upon one another, as fast as the sand levelled them (which I find to be the best expedient to hinder its passage, and by which I have raised sand-banks near 20 yards high) I brought it into the circuit of about eight or ten acres: and then in one year by laying some hundreds of loads of muck and good earth upon it, I have again reduced it to terra firma; have cleared all my walls, and by the assistance and kindness of my neighbours (who helped me away with above 1500 loads in one month) cut a passage to my house through the main body thereof.

But the other end of the town met with a much worse fate, where divers dwellings are buried or overthrown, and our pastures and meadows (which were very considerable to so small a town, both for quantity and quality) over-run and destroyed: and the branch of the River Ouse, upon which we border, (being better known by the name of Thetford or Brandon River, between which two towns we lie) for three miles together so filled with sand, that now a vessel with two load weight passeth with as much difficulty as before with ten. But had not the stream interposed, to stop its passage into Norfolk, doubtless a good part of that country had ere now been left a desolate trophy of this conquering enemy. For, according to the proportion of its increase in these five miles, which was from 10 acres to 1500 or 2000; in 10 miles more of the same soil it would have been swelled to a great vastness.

And now, Sir, I have given you a history of our sands, I shall out of my respects to your design (which I truly venerate, and should be glad to be subservient to, in the meanest capacity) make this poor essay towards a discovery of a reason and cause of this strange accident. Wherein the first thing observable to me is the quality and situation of the country, in which this troublesome guest first took his rise; which lies east north-east of a part of the great level of the Fens, and is thereby fully exposed to the rage of those impetuous blasts, we yearly receive out of the opposite quarter; which, I suppose, acquire more than ordinary vigour by the winds passing through so long a tract without any check (which, when it has gone so far in triumph, makes its first assaults with the greater fury). The other thing that contributes to it, is the extreme sandiness of the soil, the levity of which, I believe, gave occasion to that land-story of the actions that used to be brought in Norfolk for grounds blown out of the owner's possession. But this county Suffolk is more friendly in that particular, I having possessed hitherto great quantities of this wandering land, without any scruple; which I should yet be glad to be rid of, without any thing for the keeping, if the owners would but do me the kindness to fetch it away.

As to our georgics, they are so little the care and study of any ingenious persons in these parts, that I am ashamed I must be so brief upon a subject so much every bodies concern. The greatest matters that have been done, hath been by marling. For, 50 load of marl to an acre of dry barren lingy heath make (as they say) a very great improvement both for corn, turnips, clover-grass, non-such, and cole-seed. Of the three first, I suppose, I need to say nothing: but of the two last, (which are late experiments) I have received a very good account from some Norfolk gentlemen, one of whom the last year had off seven acres of non-such or hop-clover 70 loads of seed, besides a great crop of good hay; which was twice as much worth as the best crop of wheat in this country. It is sown (as the common clover) with corn, and when it once takes it will hold four times as long in the ground. About a bushel and a half soweth an acre; and the seed is now brought to 12 shillings the comb (or four bushels) which was lately at 40 shillings. The same gentleman had the last year 10 combs per acre of cole-seed upon a very dry heath (only improved by marling) and was this year in expectation of a much greater crop, when I last saw him. I am, Sir, &c. &c.

Downham Armarum in Suffolk,
July 6th, 1668.

An extract of a letter concerning an ingenious and useful Optical Experiment.

I AM to acquaint you with an experiment, if it may deserve that name; the matter of which may be known to many, but unapplied (for ought I know) to such use as it affords; and the use is to myself of *very great* value, and I think it may be equally profitable to many. Thus it is: you know I have mourned for the loss of my eyes. I confess my unmanliness, that I have shed many tears in my study for want of them; but that was quite out of the way of recovering them. I know not whether by standing much before a blazing fire, or by writing often right before a bright window, or what else might be the cause of this decay of my sight, who am not *above* 60 *years* of age. But I seemed always to have a kind of thick smoke or mist about me, and some little black balls to dance in the air about my eyes, and to be in the case as if I came into a room suddenly from a long walk in a great snow. But so it was, I could not distinguish the faces of my acquaintance, nor men from women in rooms that wanted no light. I could not read the great and black English print in the church bibles, nor keep the plain and trodden paths in fields or pastures, except I was led or guided. I received no benefit by any glasses, but was in the case of those, whose decay by age is greater than can be helped by spectacles. The *fairest* prints seemed through spectacles, like *blind* prints, little black remaining.

Being in this sad plight, what trifle can you think hath brought me help, which I value more than a great sum of gold; truly, no other than this: I took spectacles that had the largest circles, close to the semi-circles on the over part, on each side, I cut the bone, then taking out the glasses I put black Spanish leather, taperwise, into the emptied circles, which widened enough, (together with the increasing wideness of the leather) took in my whole eye at the wider end, and presently I saw the benefit through the lesser taper end by reading the smallest prints that are, as if they had been a large and fair character. I caused a glover to sew them with a double drawn stitch, that they might have an agreeable roundness, and exclude all rays of light. So I coloured the leather with ink to take off the glittering, and this was all the trouble I had, besides the practice and patience in using them; only, finding that the smaller the remote orifice was, the fairer and clearer the smallest prints appeared; and the wider that orifice was, the larger object it took in, and so required the less motion of my hand and head in reading, I did therefore cut one of these tapers a little wider and shorter than the other: and this wider I use for ordinary prints, and the longer and smaller for smallest prints. These, without any trouble, as oft as I see need, or find ease in the change, I alter. I can only put the end of my little finger into the orifice of the lesser, but the same finger somewhat deeper, yet not quite up to the first joint, I can insert into the orifice of the wider; sometimes I use one eye, sometimes another, for ease by the change; so you must expect that the visual rays of both eyes will not meet for mutual assistance in reading, when they are thus far divided by tubes of that length.

The lighter the stuff is the less it will cumber. Remember always to black the inside with some black that hath no lustre or glittering. And you should have the tubes so movable that you may draw them longer or shorter, allowing also (as was newly intimated) the orifice wider or narrower as it is found more helpful to them that have need of them. To me it was not necessary, but I conceive it convenient that velvet or some gentle leather should be fastened to the tubulous part next the eyes, to shadow them from all encompassing light.

I have already told you, that I found no benefit at all by any kind of spectacle glasses; but I have not tried what glasses will do, if settled in these tubes; having no need of them I rest as I am. Now I should be heartily glad if any of my friends should receive any aid or ease by such an obvious device (containing nothing but emptiness and darkness) as this is; and probably they may be more proper for some that are *squint-eyed*, whose eyes do interfere, and so make the object as if you would write one line upon another, where, though both should be ever so fairly written, yet neither will be easily legible. Here *squint*-eyes will be kept in peace and at fair law. Certainly it will ease them that cannot well bear the light; and, perchance it will preserve the sight for longer durance.

An extract of another letter from the same, confirming the contents of the former, and adding some further observations about Sight.

THERE is more worth in that slight notice, which I sent you last, than any one who hath not the defect which I have, will easily imagine. And perhaps no man will have the patience to endure to use it, but he that is in a like case of necessity and distress as I am. I praise God for it. I see now by this trifle (*those taper-tubes*) as well as the youngest in my family, and can read through them the smallest and blindest prints, as well as I ever could from my childhood, though my sight be almost lost. And having used these empty holes for spectacles little more than a week, I can now use them without trouble all the day long; and I verily believe, that by this short use of them, my sight already is much amended; for I do now see the greenness of the garden, and pastures in a florid verdure, whereas very lately dark colours, blue and green, had the same hue to my eye.

If you ask me how this device came into my head, I shall tell you all I know. Some years ago I was framing one of Hevelius's polemoscopes: as I was trying the tubes, without the dioptric glasses, I perceived that, though the tube took in very little, and seemed scarce serviceable for any considerable purpose, yet the object appeared to me more distinct and clear through the tube than through the open air. This I recollected, and thereupon made the trial, and found the effect fully to answer to my case, and to be the most proper for characters, as there printed. And then I blamed not a little my own stupidness that I did not sooner apply to myself the hint I might have taken from the ingenious Dr. Lower's observations concerning a blemish in horses' eyes *, though that be nothing to my case, forasmuch as I see very little if the air be gloomy, or the sky clouded; neither have I any resort of humours, or sensible defluxions about my eyes.

And now give me leave to add, that if I had consulted with the learnedest and wisest men living, I make no doubt but I should have been disappointed of all relief; and perhaps I might have lost the crepuscular remains of my sight by adventurous essays upon such a tender organ. Who knoweth how often the wisest of mortals are lost, whilst they trample on the remedy that

* See page 135.

offers itself at hand. We see how many ingenious and laborious artists have long laboured for the *eliptical* or *hyperbolical* section of glasses, hoping thereby to make that brittle body of glass of more worth than the fairest diamonds; yet if this were obtained to perfection I doubt it would not afford me the kindness and relief I gain by these empty and dark tubes. And now I hope that all, who pretend to virtue and philosophy, will use such just scales for the virtue of things, as to estimate every thing, how cheap and contemptible soever it may seem to be, according as 'tis beneficial, and as it brings relief and supply to the distressed.

To conclude, for your trial of tubulous spectacles: the tubes may be of paper, only coloured black, and pasted on, and with the inner folds to be drawn out from one inch to three; some of the folds to be taken out, that the orifice may be wider or narrower as best fits to every degree of defect.

Of the antiquity of the Transfusion of Blood from one Animal to another.

THERE hath been of late some contest about the origin of the *Transfusion*; the *English* first claiming it as a late invention of theirs; the *French* pretending thereupon that it had been proposed among them ten years ago. After which it was affirmed, upon further investigation, by some ingenious persons in England, that *there* it had been known 30 years ago. But it seems that an Italian philosopher, in a certain tract, entitled, Relatione delle Esperience fatte in Inghilterra, Francia et Italia intornola Transfusione del Sangue, lately printed in Rome, (for the notice whereof we are obliged to the author of Journal des Sçavans) undertakes to prove that the transfusion is yet of greater antiquity, as having been known to Libavius above 50 years since.

For which that Roman author alledgeth a place out of the said Libavius (in Defensione Syntagmatis Arcanorum Chimicorum contra Heningum Schneumannum, actione 2, p. 8. edit. Francof. A. 1615.) where the transfusion is so plainly described that one can hardly discourse of it with more clearness than there is done in these words, from Libavius: Adsit juvenis robustus, sanus, sanguine spirituoso plenus: Adstet exhaustus viribus, tenuis, macilentus, vix animam trahens. Magister artis habeat tubulos argenteos inter se congruentes, aperiat arteriam robusti, et tubulum inserat muniatque; mox et groti arteriam findat, et tubulum fæmineum infigat. Jam duos tubulos sibi mutuo applicet, et ex sano sanguis arterialis, calens et spirituosus saliet in ægrotum, unaque vitæ fontum afferet omnemque languorem pellet. This indeed is clear enough, and obliges us to aver a greater antiquity of this operation, than before, we were aware of; though it is true Libavius did not propose it but only to mock at it (which is the *common fate of new inventions* in their cradle), besides that he contrives it with great danger both to the recipient and the emittent, by proposing to open arteries in both, which indeed may be practised upon brutes, but ought by no means upon man.

An extract of a letter written from Dantzick to the Hon. R. Boyle, containing the success of some experiments of infusing Medicines into Human Veins.

MONSIEUR Smith, physician in ordinary in this city, having liberty granted him to try an experiment upon some persons desperately infected with the venereal, then in the public hospital here, adventured the opening a vein, and infusing some medicines into the blood, which was tried upon two persons, whereof the one recovered and the other died. Yet being since further encouraged by corresponding with some of the ROYAL SOCIETY in England, about a month since the said physician, together with Monsieur Schefeler, another ancient practitioner in this city, repeated the experiment, by infusing altering medicines into the veins of the right arms of three persons, the one lame of the gout, the other extremely apoplectical, and the third reduced to extremity by that distemper, the plica polonica. The success of this, as Monsieur Hevelius (who was the only person admitted to be present at the operation) informs me, was, that the gouty man found himself pretty well next day, and shortly after went to work, it being harvest time, and has continued well ever since, leaving the hospital yesterday, and professing himself cured. The apoplectical hath not had one paroxysm since; and the several sores which the plua polonica had occasioned, are healed; and both these persons have been able to work any time these three weeks.—Dated August 18th, 1668.

Extract of a letter concerning the virtue of Antimony.

I MADE an experiment upon a boar, to which I had given an ounce of crude antimony at a time, to try whether he would not be fat a fortnight before another (having no antimony), upon the like feeding. Antimony will recover a pig of the meafles; by which it appears to be a great purifier of the blood. I knew a horfe that was very lean and fcabbed, and could not be fatted by any keeping, to which antimony was given for two months together every morning, and that upon the fame keeping he became exceeding fat. One of my own horfes having had the *fafhions*, and being cured, had notwithftanding extreme running legs, fo that after he had paffed the courfe of farriers twice to be cured, it was not done, but upon my giving him antimony but for one week, he was prefently well.

The manner of ufing it is this: Take one drachm of crude antimony powdered for one horfe, and when you give him his oats in a morning, fhake it out upon them in a little heap in the middle; if he be hungry, and you keep off his head from every other part of the oats, he will fnap it up in his mouth at one bite when his head is freed. Some horfes greatly like it; others refufe it after the firft time of giving. But if he refufe it, cover it with oats thinly, or make it into balls; fo that he takes it, it matters not much after what manner it is given.

An extract of a letter of Mr. R. Norwood, from the Bermudas, concerning the Tides there; as alfo Whales, Spermaceti, ftrange Spiders' Webs, fome rare Vegetables, and the Longevity of the Inhabitants.

AT prefent I fhall inform you, in part of what you require, that the water about our ifland does not flow, by any man's obfervation, above five feet, and that but at one feafon of the year, between Michaelmas and Chriftmas; at other times not above three feet. It is high water when the moon is about an hour high, and the like after her going down. It flows in from the north weft, and runs to the fouth eaft neareft; and in that part of the land which lies moft to the north weft, there it is high water fooneft. But the tide does not always ebb and flow directly that courfe round about our coast; but I suppose the reason is, that some points of land, or *shoals*, may turn its north west and south east course.

We have hereabouts many sorts of fishes. There is amongst them great store of Whales, which in March, April, and May, use our coast. I have myself killed many of them. Their females have abundance of milk, which their young ones suck out of the teats, that grow by their navel. They have no teeth, but feed on moss growing on the rocks at the bottom during these three months, and at no other season of the year. When this is consumed and gone, the whales go away also. These we kill for their oil. But here have been spermaceti whales driven upon the shore, which sperma (as they call it) lies all over the body of those whales. They have divers teeth, which may be about as big as a man's wrist; and I hope, by the next opportunity, to send you one of them. I have been at the Bahama Islands, and there have been found this same sort of Whales dead upon the shore, with sperma all over their bodies. Myself, with about 20 others, have agreed to try whether we can master and kill them, for I could never hear of any of that sort that were killed by any man, such is their fierceness and swiftness. One such whale would be worth many hundred pounds. They are very strong, and inlaid with sinews all over their bodies, which may be drawn out *thirty fathom* long.

There is an island amongst the Bahamas, which some of our people are settled upon, and more are going thither. It is called New Providence, where many rare things might be discovered, if the people were but encouraged; and I am of opinion, there is not a more healthful spot in the world. It is stored with variety of fish and fowl, and with divers sorts of trees, and other plants, whose qualities are not yet known.

As to the age of our inhabitants here, *some* do live to an hundred years, and something upwards; *many* live till they are nigh an hundred; and when they die, it is age and weakness that are the cause, and not any disease that attends them. The general distemper that is yearly amongst us is a cold, and that is most gotten in the hottest weather. The air here is very sweet and pleasant. Our diet is but ordinary, and the people generally poor; and I observe that poor people are the most healthful.

You shall receive by Captain Thomas Morley, the commander of our magazine ship, such things as I could at present procure; among which you shall find of the leaves and berries of that weed you enquire after, which

2

we call poison-weed, growing like your ivy. I have seen a man who was poisoned with it, that the skin peeled off his face, and yet the man never touched it, only looking on it as he passed by. It is not equally hurtful to all.

Here are spiders, that spin their webs betwixt trees standing seven or eight fathoms asunder; and they do their work by spirting their web into the air, where the wind carries it from tree to tree. This web, when finished, will snare a bird as large as a thrush. Yourself may prove it, for I have sent you some.

As to the bark of a tree, with which we are said to cover our houses, that is an error, for it is not the bark, but the leaves of a tree which we put to that use; and it is the palmetto; without which tree we could not live comfortably in this place. The leaves of some of these trees are eight or ten feet long, and nigh as broad. I know of no tree in the world that can equal it in the number of commodities it affords.

It is reported, that in Virginia, and upon the coast of Florida, the Indians live to a very great age, and that some of the people are of gigantic stature, and stronger by far than others.

As to the eclipses of the moon, that you would have observed here, and be informed about, I can say little of them; but I suppose my worthy friend Mr. Norwood will give you an account thereof to your satisfaction: if any thing should cause him to fail, it will be age and weakness. He hath a great desire to serve the ROYAL SOCIETY in every respect; which shall engage me also to serve both them and you to the utmost of my ability, remaining, &c.

Bermuda, July 16, 1668.

An Extract of a Narrative concerning a Voyage from Spain to Mexico, and of the Minerals of that Kingdom.

TO pass by many curious observations touching the vegetable and animal sphere (which I reserve for another occasion), I shall now entertain you only with some of the observables I met with about minerals in the kingdom of Mexico, whither I travelled anno 1664, in the ship that carried thither the new Viceroy of Mexico, remaining in that country almost two years in continual ſtudies and reſearches, eſpecially about minerals, and their generation, ſeparation, &c.

And indeed nature hath ſo prodigally enriched this country with all ſorts of minerals, both perfect, imperfect, and mixed, that ſhe almoſt overwhelms the obſervation of the moſt diligent and moſt curious naturaliſt. I have dealt with the ſkilfulleſt mine-men in thoſe parts, but found them to know of, and care for little in the matter of minerals, but in what related to gold and ſilver. Some of them ſhewed me certain ſtones, gathered in great abundance in the mines of Taſco, which they would have to be amethyſts, by which they ſaid that certain Flemings had got much money.

I was once deſired to viſit a famous cave there, ſome leagues from Mexico, on the north weſt ſide of the city, beyond the lake. This was ſaid to be gilded all over with a kind of leaf gold, which deluded many Spaniards with its promiſing colour, they having been never able to reduce it into a body, neither by quickſilver nor fuſion, though it was reported, that the ancient Indians knew how to make uſe of it, and that the great *Montezuma* had borrowed thence a great part of his treaſure. I rode thither one morning, taking with me one Indian only for my guide, with a tinder-box and candle, and ſome other inſtruments for my deſign. I found it ſituated ſomewhat high, in a place very convenient for the generation of metals, but the mouth ſo barricaded with ſtones, that both my Indian and I had work enough to clear a paſſage for my entrance, which being opened, I went in with my candle lighted, but could not make the Indian follow me, being afraid of ſpirits and hobgoblins. The light of the candle ſoon diſcovered to me on all ſides, but eſpecially above my head, a glittering canopy of the ſaid mineral leaves, at which I greedily ſtretched forth my hand to reach ſome parcels of it, when there fell down preſently ſo great a lump of clotted ſand on my head and ſhoulders, that it not only put out my candle, but my eyes alſo. And calling out with a loud voice to my Indian, who remained at the mouth of the entry, there rebounded within thoſe hollow caverns ſuch thundering and redoubled echoes, that I admired it; and the Indian, imagining by thoſe tumultuous voices that I was wreſtling with ſome infernal ghoſts, ſoon quitted his ſtation, and thereby left a free paſſage for ſome rays of light to enter, and to ſerve me for a better guide. My ſight meanwhile being not a little endangered by the corroſive acrimony of that mineral duſt. Having got my candle lighted again, I proceeded in the cave, and heaped together a quantity of the mineral, mixed with fand, and fcraped alfo from the fuperficies of the earth a quantity of the fame kind of glittering leaves, none of which exceeded the breadth of a man's nail, and which with the leaft handling divide themfelves into many leffer fpangles, and with a little rubbing they leave one's hand all gilded over like gold.

I knew well enough that the ordinary trials made by the Indians, had proved fruitlefs upon the mineral; for it could neither be reduced into a maffy form by the violence of fire, nor feparated from its heterogeneous fubftances by the mild trial of quickfilver, yet on the touchftone it equalized the moft refined gold; fo that there wanted nothing but to reduce it to a fufible and malleable metallic form, which foon would be accomplifhed if it could be made to take quickfilver.

Confidering with myfelf what might be the reafons of its refufing mercury, and being not ignorant that fome of the choiceft mines of filver and gold are almoft of the like nature, till the impediments are removed, which are certain mineral vifcofities, that fometimes by their oleaginous fatnefs, and at other times by a fretting acrimony, hinder the ingrefs of the mercury, I conceived the like might happen in this cafe: whereupon to find a cure for this difeafe, I began firft to make experiment upon the fand, which had been the matrix of the mineral; and there I tried firft the ordinary way ufed in the Indies on fuch occafions, which was to obferve the colour of the fumes yielded from the fpangled fand in a ftrong reverberating fire; but here could little be obferved, by reafon of the aduft drying of the fand, not able to afford any vifible fumes fit for fuch a difcovery. Likewife I proceeded to another way, to boil it in water, and having poured that off, to obferve the alkali left after the water's evaporation. I by this means difcovered that it abounded rather in fulphurous unctuoufnefs than faline acrimony; or elfe I think my eyes in the cave had run a greater hazard. Finding this, I applied firft the quickfilver, mingled with the ordinary magiftrals (as they call them) ufed in that country, to curb and break the force of the fulphurous impediments: but perceiving thefe to be of no effect, I encouraged the quickfilver with the caput mortuum of vitriol and faltpetre (kept as a fecret amongft the chiefeft mine men) but with as little figns of the mercury's operation as before. Then I boiled my mixture over the fire, a way found out in Peru in fuch difficult cafes, but all to no purpofe; fo froward a matter it was, that it could not be brought to receive mercury neither by fair means, nor by foul. Then I devised a way to torment it by a corrosive of ordinary separating water, impregnated with common salt, and it made a dissolution like that of gold. which thus dissolved I shewed it to a mineralist, who had been versed all his life in the separatory art of gold and silver, and he would not believe but that it was true gold. But having steamed away the aquafortis, I found my hopes turned into a dirt, something yellow, out of which, with distilled vinegar, enforced with its own tartarous salt, I extracted a tincture more curious than useful.

The said mineralist would not despair yet, but taking a quantity of the golden dust, he cemented it with the powder of vulgar sulphur, *stratum super stratum*, and this he put into a moderate fire for three days together, hoping that the sulphur would consume all the impediments which kept the mercury from entering: but, (as I told him before hand) it only served to clog the matter with more sulphurous unctuosity than it had before.

I brought for a curiosity some of this mineral from the Indies into Spain, where some of our friends had a view of it; but have not been able hitherto to do any good upon it. What I learnt by these trials was not only caution, but several secrets of extracting metals by quicksilver; in which there is so many cautions and observations, that it require much writing to rehearse them.

I shall only subjoin the grand use of mercury in separating silver in the Indies, when that metal is generated (as commonly it is) in certain rocky stones, abounding with bituminous and corrosive mixtures, so as it is impossible to free it totally from its corrupt matrix by the violent way of melting, whatever auxiliary ingredients may be added, as lead and artificial salts, and the like; because those sulphurous and vitriolic compounds (in the way of fusion) melting together with the silver, sublime part of it away in a volatile fume by their corroding acrimony, calcinating and vitrifying the other part, and robbing the artificer of half his gain. In this case the use of quicksilver is found most advantageous; the practice whereof, because I am of opinion it is not perfectly known, I shall here declare as briefly as possible.

Having reduced the ore into small stones, they calcine it first in a reverberating oven, yet with a moderate fire, for fear of fusion, and driving away into the air part of the treasure, the volatile parts being by nature not perfectly mixed per minima with the fixed, as they afterwards come to be by art and industry. And I have heard some of the more intelligent mineralists say, that they judge their metallic labours and operations not to be so much a reaping of silver ready made, as a kind of artificial compounding and bettering of that which nature had left dispersed and imperfect. The calcination serves chiefly to free the mineral from many infirmities that hinder the operation of the quicksilver, and it serves also to discover, by the colour of the fumes it yields, what corrosive mixture chiefly abounds in it; beside, that it renders the one more tractable and pliant under the mill-stone, which is to reduce it to a small flower before the application of the mercury. This is chiefly observed in those silver veins that are of a hard and dry complexion; yet those that are usually more soft, abounding in oleagenous sulphurs, before burning are first ground into powder, in such mills as I have often seen in glass-houses: and then they receive a gentle calcination, the mineralist mingling therewith ingredients suitable to the peccant humour (if I may so speak) of the ore. As if (*e. g.*) the metal be sulphurous and antimonial, rust and dross of iron are found to be an excellent cure for this distemper; if martial, and abounding in iron, then sulphur and antimony reduced to powder are used as a convenient remedy for that disease. Sulphur hath a particular force, as I have found by experiment, to soften and dissolve iron. But not only in this operation of calcining, but also in applying the quicksilver, there are so many different cases, in which different remedies are to be used, as there are silver veins of several constitutions; of which elsewhere.

The ore being ground, calcined, and curiously sifted, they divide it into several heaps, and then by lesser essays they find out how much silver is contained in every heap, where it is very ordinary to find only six ounces in 100 pounds; sometimes 12, but if it yield 18, it is esteemed a very rich vein: yet sometimes there are great masses found all of pure silver, which is called virgin metal.

Having discovered the quantity of silver contained in each heap, then proportionably they besprinkle them with quicksilver, and that not all at once, but at several times, stirring the ore up and down. Then, according to the diseases already discovered in the vein, by the fumes in the calcination, or according to any new symptoms appearing in the operation of the quicksilver, convenient remedies are applied; if (*e. g.*) the mercury give figns of being *tocado* (as they call it) *i. e.* if it appear mortified, not in fmall and clear fpherical figures, (which is a good prognoftic) but in the form of long worms of a wan, pale, dark, and of a leadifh colour, then the fick mercury is eafily cured of the worms (as they fpeak) by certain magiftrals, fo called, that are diverfely compounded, but have for their bafis or mafter calcined copper mingled with falt. Thefe worms indicate that the mineral abounds with lead and pewter, which overcharging the ftomach (thus they carry on the metaphor) of mercury, hinder his appetite to the filver; in which cafe thofe copper magiftrals, with their vitriolic force, confume and deftroy this impediment.

The heaps of the ore being thus mingled with the quickfilver, they are often ftirred about, the better to incorporate it with the filver. I find they have none but conjectural figns to know when the mercury hath performed its office entirely, in feparating all the filver from thofe heterogeneal fubftances, the uncertainty whereof occafions often very great loffes, efpecially when they work about gold; for in paffing the right time, the greateft part of the gold flies away in a fume, becaufe, to borrow the reafon of chemifts, *fumma volatilis fuperat fummam fixi*; or rather becaufe nature hath not yet accomplifhed the perfect compofition and proportionate mixture of the volatile elements with the fixed; which defect is fupplied by art in this extraction by mercury, in whofe bofom the parts are combined together in fmall atoms, and alfo by gentle fires, fucceeded by violent ones, whofe activity is affifted by ingredients fit for a fuitable and eafy fufion, and fo curbing the volatile parts, that by an exquifite proportion they entertain a perpetual amity with the fixed.

When by the colour of the mercury, coagulated by the filver in clear maffy lumps, they conjecture the work done, they wafh it by means of three veffels, ftanding in order, one under the other, fo that the matter in the firft and higheft veffel being wafhed and ftirred about with a molinet, all the duft of the heterogeneous minerals that embody not with the mercury, is carried away together with the water into the other veffels, and from thence quite thrown out by the current of the water; whereas in the mean while the filver in clotted lumps, called pella's, is by the weight of the mercury depreffed to the bottom of the faid tubs.

This lavatory work being ended, the mercury with the filver is taken out of the veffels, and diligently fqueezed in coarfe and ftrong linen, and even with ſtrokes of a beetle, the quickſilver is ſeparated as much as may be from the ſilver. This maſs is afterwards reduced in moulds of the ſhape of the Indian pine-apple, into a pyramidal or conical figure, which they call *pineas de plata*, thus faſhioned for the eaſier placing them round about the ridges of a great earthen veſſel, of the form of a blind alembeck: round about the tops of which a fire being made, all the reſt of the mercury forthwith abandons the ſilver and falls to the bottom, from whence it is recovered and kept for the like uſe.

Laſtly, the ſilver is melted down with the liga, as it is called, which the King of Spain allows, by which he returns to the people in copper that fifth part which they allow him of all the ſilver.

Having deſcribed this whole operation, you will perhaps expect I ſhould ſomewhat enlarge here upon the generation of metals, and my ſpeculations and theory concerning it. But, though this was indeed one of my chief motives for undertaking this long and tedious voyage, yet conſidering the ſubject to be of ſuch a nature that it requires very many things to be ſuppoſed and premiſed, and more experience than I yet dare pretend to, and I dare not at preſent engulf myſelf in this ocean. I ſhall only ſay this; firſt, that my opinion of this matter is ſomething different from the ordinary, though I will not deny that for the ſubſtance I differ not much from the opinion of the famous Sendivogius, in Libro de 12. Tractatibus. And then that I think it obſervable, that there is very ſtrong offenſive ſmell ranker than that of ſepulchres, which I have obſerved in ſome mines, the workmen telling me that that is one of the chief ſigns of a rich mine.

To conclude, I ſhall preſume to give you ſome of my thoughts reſpecting the ſo much talked of tranſmutation of metals; concerning which I am of opinion that the change is erroneouſly apprehended by many, imagining that the whole imperfect metal is totally transformed into the more perfect by the ſubſtance mixed with it; whereas the mixture added to the melted metal, joins itſelf (as I conceive) to thoſe parts, which being homogeneal, ſymbolize together with the nature of the more perfect, whereby the pure metalline parts are ſeparated from the other heterogeneal impure ſulphurs, which, together with other cauſes, did hinder nature in the mine from concocting that ſubſtance into the perfecter metal.

That which contributed not a little to make me a proſelyte to the art of chemiſtry, was, among others, a very pretty experiment a friend ſhewed me, more curious than gainful: it was a continual budding forth of ſilver in the form of a branch in a glaſs over an indifferent ſtrong fire of coals, which ſprouts being clipped off with ſciſſars, and a ſmall ſupply of crude mercury added to the matter, in a ſmall time there aroſe another branch of true ſilver, which had ſucked and converted into metallic ſprigs a conſiderable portion of the quickſilver. This motion, and the increment of the new ſilver branches ceaſed not, as long as the fire continued, and freſh mercury applied for the due nutriment of this mineral vegetation. This ingenious knack made me reflect on the gold in the Tree of Virgil. 6 Æneid.

——--Primo avulſo non deficit alter
Aureus, et ſimili frondeſcit virga metallo.

The whole complex of ingredients is known to conſiſt only of vulgar aquafortis (abſtracted from two parts of vitriol, and one of ſaltpetre) and quickſilver, and a ſmall quantity of ſilver, far leſs than you may reap in a ſmall time from thoſe ſilver ſprigs; yet gain there is none, there being more expences blown away in ſmoke by continuance of fire in one month, than can be recovered from this ſilver harveſt in a longer time. Though this ſeems but a toy, yet it is very philoſophical, much informing the underſtanding, however it enrich not the purſe; for here we ſee crude mercury manifeſtly turned into ſilver, notwithſtanding it is denied by ſo many.

An Extract out of the Italian Giornale de Litterati, relating to two conſiderable Experiments of the Transfuſion of Blood.

ANNO 1667, May 8. Here was in Banonia, at the houſe of Signior Caſſini, this experiment, viz. There was opened the coroted artery of a lamb, when the blood was let run as long as it could into the right branch of the jugular vein of another lamb, from which there had before been drawn ſo much blood as was judged it could be ſupplied with from a lamb of the like bigneſs, whoſe blood ſhould be let out till it died. After this there were made two ligatures pretty near to one another, in the vein of the lamb that had received the blood; and this vein was quite cut through

4

between the two ligatures, to fee what would happen thereupon. This done the lamb was untied, which without any appearance of feeblenefs, went about, following thofe that had made the operation. It lived a long while after, and its wound being healed up, it grew like other lambs. But the 5th of January 1668 it died, and its ftomach was found full of corrupt food. Its neck being diffected, to fee what had happened to the vein cut through, it was found that it had joined itfelf to the next mufcle by fome fibres, and that the upper part of that vein had communication with the lower, by the means of a little branch, which might in fome manner fupply the defect of the whole trunk.

There was made another experiment the 20th of May laft at Udine, at the houfe of Signior Griffoni, by transfufing the blood of a lamb into the veins of a fpaniel, of a middle fize of that kind, 13 years old, who had been altogether deaf for above three years, fo that whatever noife was made, he gave not any fign of hearing it. He walked very little, and was fo feeble, that being unable to lift up his feet, all he did was to trail his body forward. After the transfufion practifed upon him, he remained for an hour upon the table, where he was yet untied; but leaping down afterwards, he went to find his mafters that were in other chambers. Two days after he went abroad, and ran up and down the ftreets with other dogs, without trailing his feet, as he did before. His ftomach alfo returned to him, and he began to eat more and more greedily than before. But that which was more furprifing is, that from that time he gave figns that he began to hear, returning fometimes at the voice of his mafters. The 13th he was almoft quite cured of his deafnefs, and he appeared without comparifon more jocund than he was before the operation. At length, the 20th of the fame month, he had wholly recovered his hearing, yet thus, that when he was called he turned back, as if he that had called him had been very far off: but that happened not always; in the mean time he heard always when he was called.

Some useful and curious Communications relating to Queries about Vegetation.

THE argument of vegetation is exceeding noble, largely useful, and worthy to be exposed to public consideration, and a general and accurate discussion; to the end that where observations are uncertain, and experiments fickle, or failing, or casual, the various track or operation of nature may be the better discovered by the greater store of confronting trials and observations. It is for this reason that we not only suggest and disperse inquiries upon this important subject, but are also ready to impart such informations as we receive from the curious and inquisitive of what they have experimented and observed therein. At the present we shall insert here what hath been communicated by those two worthy and observing persons Dr. F. Beale, and Dr. Ezerel Tonge.

To the 1st Query. Dr. B.—It will be difficult to enumerate all the vegetables that will grow the wrong end set downwards in the ground. To mention some, besides those mentioned in that query, (viz. Elders and briars) there are Sallies, Willows, the Black Elder, Vines, and most Shrubs; two or three of their joints being covered in the mould, and the stem cut off near the overmost joint, which should be half covered in the mould, and the mould somewhat raised, as it spirts out and grows. Dr. Tonge agrees, saying, that currant trees, and such like, as are of a soft wood, and quick growers, seem most apt to this improvement.

To the 2d, Dr. B.—That the branch of a plant being laid in the ground, whilst yet growing on the tree, and there taking root, being cut off whilst growing, will grow on *both ends* if it be well rooted in the propagation; and the like care had of the last knot or joint, as was before prescribed, Dr. T. saith, that layers of those trees, mentioned in the former query, will grow on both ends, and aptly parted when they have spread roots both ways, make two plants out of each layer.

To the 3d, Dr. B.—In the tapping of trees, the juice certainly ascends from the root, and after it is concocted to partake of the nature of the plant (which feeds as well on the air, as the juice furnished through the root) it descends (as the liquor in a limbeck) to the orifice whence it issues. *Ratray*, the learned Scot, affirms, that he had calculated experimentally that the liquor which may be drawn from the birch in the ſpring time, is equiponderant to the weight of the whole tree, branches, roots, and all together: whence he infers, that it deſerves our diligence fully to enquire into the manifold benefits that may be made by tappings of all ſorts of vegetables; ſome at the roots, ſome in the body, either from the bark, or the timber; ſome under the chief branches (which is noted by V. Helmont to be the proper place for the juice of the birch), ſome from the fruit, kernel, bloſſoms, ſeeds, or huſks containing ſeeds; as Dr. Harvy had a way of filling his ſilver box with a purer ſort of opium, taken from the huſks of poppy ſeeds, being pricked after ſome time of exudation and inſolation. The like whereof may be tried on the male peony, and other plants of greateſt fame and virtue; as well for gums, colours, odours, &c. As for famous juices, *Mr. Evelyn* can acquaint you of a *receipt*, which he had in *Italy*, as a ſpecific againſt fevers, from the tapping of the elm. I hear as much praiſe from the oak for ſtopping the flux of blood by the way of urine, whether it proceeds from the imbecility of nature, or from the defects in the bladder, reins, or other inward paſſages. Some ſay as much of the juice of the alder (though the dwarf alder hath the higheſt praiſe) to cure or ſtop the dropſy. And perhaps this large natural limbeck, where it may be had, may ſometimes prove more effectual than our little, artificial, and more troubleſome diſtillations: and the congeniality of the ſun in his alternative viſits, and the aſſiduous intercourſe of the free air, with the ſpirit of the plant yet living and growing, may have a more effectual influence for a ſpecific virtue than we are apt to imagine. Though we cannot ſee or hear the lungs of vegetables beating, yet we may ſometimes ſmell their breath ſtrong enough both to pleaſe and offend exceedingly; as in ſavin, firs, cypreſs, elder, roſemary, myrtles, and generally in all bloſſomers: and ſome that cannot be ſmelt by us, may yet have a very wholeſome breath. One experiment I will here beſtow on you: when both my hands were manacled for many years (and ſometimes my arms alſo) with deep corroding *teaters*; to the bluſh of my many friendly phyſicians, and in deſpite of many of the beſt medicines and purgations, all was ſuddenly healed, and hath ſo continued theſe 20 years, by the application of the *gum* of *plumb trees* diſſolved in vinegar. I muſt not forget to add that I applied vine leaves, and ſometimes opened raiſins, to draw a moiſture from thoſe teaters ſome few days before I uſed the gum.

Dr. T. is of opinion, that the ſap always riſes, and never properly deſcends, having only a kind of ſubſiding or recidivation, which he ſaith he cannot call a circulation, nor reſemble to the motion of liquors in a pellican, but rather to the ſinking of liquors in an alembick, whilſt the thinner parts are forced over the helm, yet ſomewhat imitating the motion of blood in animals, foraſmuch as it continually ſupplies the want and expence of ſap in the exterior parts from the ſtock of the ſap in the trunk, root, and branches. He underſtands it thus: That the ſap neceſſary to the growth of the leaves, fruit, and upper branches, being diſpenſed and converted into the form neceſſary for thoſe purpoſes, when the tree is fulleſt of ſap, in ſuch manner that the ſap in the innermoſt, feeds the innermoſt, and the ſap of the outward, coats the outward parts, of fruits, &c. that which remains in the body betwixt the ſeveral coats, and betwixt bark and body, begins to condenſe there alſo, firſt into a jelly, and after into wood, bark, roots, &c. according to the ſeveral places to which it hath ſubſided; and becauſe it condenſeth faſter in ſome parts than in others, according as they be higher or lower, (whether it be by heat or cold, or exhalation of thinner parts) the ſap condenſed above or below, filling leſs room, and muſt needs cauſe the ſap, which is not yet condenſed in appearance, to deſcend or ſubſide, and to ſink, as it were, lower and lower in the pores of the timber and bark, *i. e.* to be leſs high, not deſcend from any place to which it was formerly riſen, unleſs (as in blood letting) when ſome lower part is opened, all the ſap above continually flows thither till the tree be emptied, or the continual flux of the ſap (the natural balſam of the tree) heal the wounds, as that of the blood does theſe of the body; and ſo much quicker and eaſier, by how much the air is more favourable, or is better kept out; which he obſerves for their direction, who are curious in inoculation, as the grounds of their ſucceſſes or miſcarriages.

The trees obſerved by the ſame Dr. T. to run are, the vine, and the birch, plentifully at body, branches, and roots; the Walnut-tree at the roots and pruned branches; ſome Willows and Sallies, and ſome ſorts of Maple (ſome call it the Plane) at a gaſh made on the bark of his body, and at the root and branches; the Poplar and Aſp; the Elm and Oak are referred to trial; concerning which laſt, ſome woodmen affirm, that in ſuch of them as are wind-ſhaken, that have large hollowneſſes in their arms and bodies, they have found great quantity of ſap in the cutting of them, whereof having drank they quenched their thirſt without any prejudice. To theſe add the Whitting, or Quicking tree, (Fraxinus Sylveſtris, and by ſome Fraxinus Cambro Britanico) which in its ſeaſon, as ſome affirm, will run plenteouſly, and whence they would have us expect a ſovereign drink againſt ſome ſtubborn diſtempers, eſpecially ſuch as are ſcorbutical and ſplenetic. I have kept, ſaith Dr. T. ſome of the juice of the berries (which being expreſſed, ferments of itſelf) theſe two years in bottles, and it hath now the taſte of auſtere cyder; and I ſuppoſe from its grateful ſmell, that it may be kept till it ripen and becomes a ſtrong vinous liquor. It is the houſehold drink of ſome families in theſe parts about Wales and Herefordſhire, and ſome out of curioſity have brewed ripe berries with ſtrong beer and ale, and kept it till it tranſcended all other beer in goodneſs.

Doctor Tonge's attempt upon the Poplar, Aſp, Elm, Oak, Aſh, Elder, Whitting-berry or Quicking tree, Thorn, Buckthorn, Tile, Nut, Sloe, Briar, Bramble, &c. have not ſucceeded; and he doubts that they, and all Apples and Pears, have ſome degree of gummineſs in their juices, ſo that they will not run.

There are circles obſerved in trees, which are the diſtances of thoſe films or coats, by which the tree receives its yearly increaſe in thickneſs. Through theſe, looking full of circular pores, the ſap ſeems to aſcend in the ſame manner between coat and coat, as between the bark and body; and probably between the two outermoſt of theſe coats, as large a quantity of ſap as between the bark and body. Now the aſcent of ſap is by all parts and pores of the tree, in ſuch ſmall quantities as can hardly be diſcerned, unleſs the tree be quite ſawed off, eſpecially near the root, for then it will appear how it aſcends. In Birches and ſuch like, the ſap iſſues very plentifully in all parts of the body, when they are cut down near the root. And in other trees that have pith, as the Willow, &c. it may be obſerved, when they are ſawed aſunder near the root, whether any ſap iſſues or not, by the pith.

An Extract of the Anatomical Account, written and left by the famous Dr. Harvey, concerning Thomas Parre, who died in London, at the Age of 152 Years and nine Months.

1ſt. THAT Thomas Parre was a poor countryman of Shropſhire, whence he was brought up by the Right Hon. Thomas Earl of Surry and Arundel, and that he died after he had outlived *nine* Princes, in the *tenth* year of the *tenth* of them, at the age of 152 years and nine months.

2d. That being opened after his death (viz. Anno 1635, Nov. 16.) his body was found yet very fleshy, his breast hairy, his genitals *unimpaired*, serving not a little to confirm the report of his having undergone public censures for his incontinency; especially seeing that after that time, viz. at the age of 120 years, he married a widow who owned, *Eum cum ipsa rem habuisse, ut alii mariti solent, et usque ad* 12 *annos retroactos solitum cum ea congressum frequentesse.* Further, that he had a large breast, lungs not fungus, but sticking to his ribs, and distended with much blood, a lividness in his face, as he had a difficulty of breathing a little before his death, and a long lasting warmth in his armpits and breast after it (which sign, together with others, were so evident in his body as they use to be in those that die by suffocation). His heart was great, thick, fibrous and fat. The blood in the heart blackish and dilute. The cartilages of the *sternum* not more bony than in others, but flexible and soft. His viscera very sound and strong, especially the stomach; and it was observed of him that he used to eat often by night and day, though contented with old cheese, milk, coarse bread, small beer, and whey; and which is more remarkable, that he did eat at night a little before he died. His kidneys covered with fat, and pretty sound, only in the interior surface of them there were found some aqueous or serous (as it were) abscesses, whereof one was near the bigness of a hen egg, with a yellowish water in it, having made a roundish cavity, impressed in that kidney; whence some thought it came, that a little before his death a suppression of urine had befallen him, though others were of opinion that urine was suppressed upon the regurgitation of all the serosity into the lungs. Not the least appearance there was of any stony matter either in the kidnies or bladder. His bowels were also sound, a little whitish without; his spleen very little, hardly equalling the bigness of one of his kidnies. In short all his inward parts appeared so healthy that if he had not changed his diet and air, he might perhaps have lived a good while longer.

3d. The cause of his death was imputed chiefly to the change of food and air; forasmuch as coming out of a clear, thin, and free air, he came into the thick air of London, and after a constant, plain, and homely country

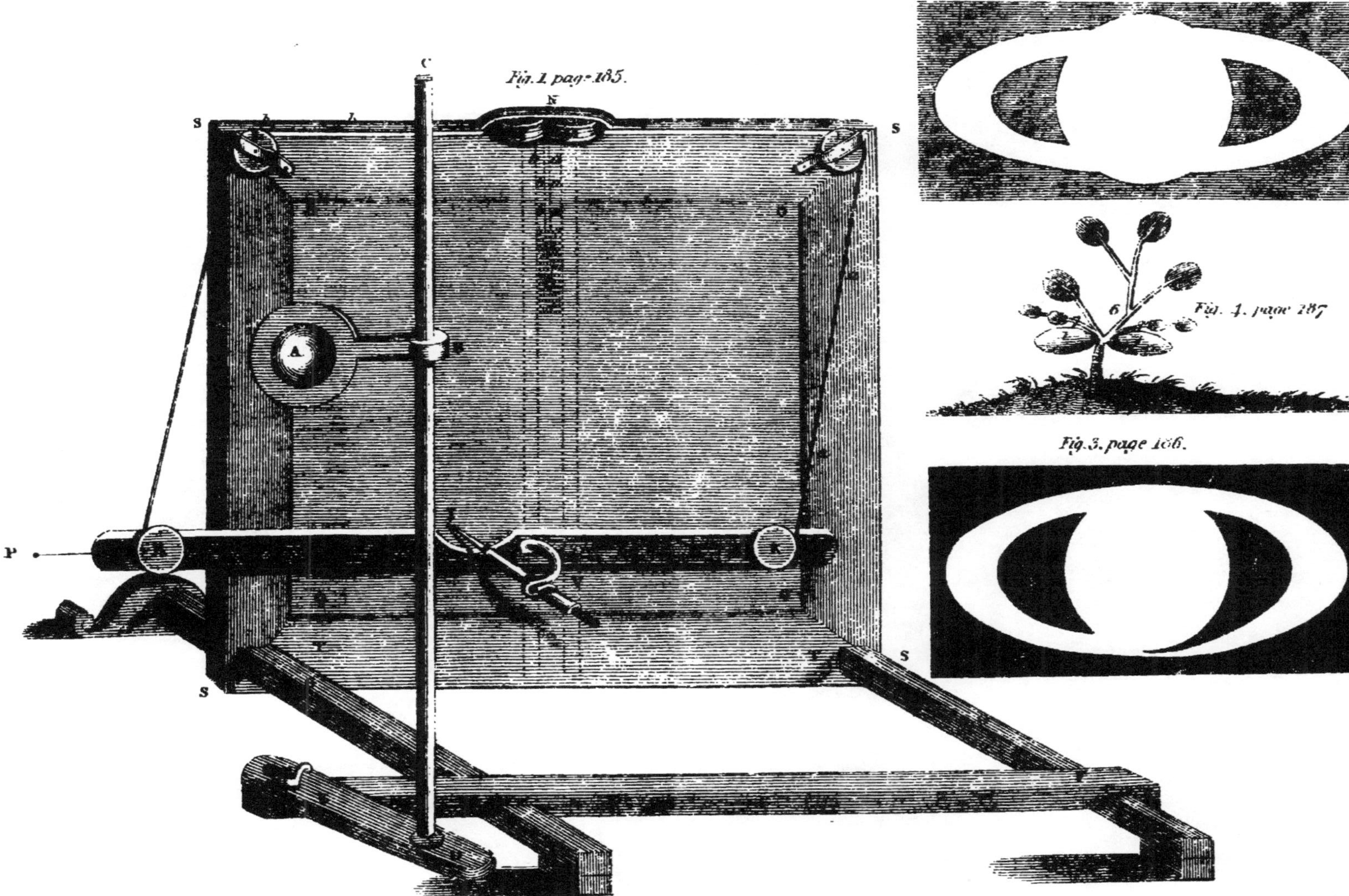

Fig. 1 page 185.

Fig. 2. page 186.

Fig. 4. page 187

Fig. 3. page 186.

diet, he was taken into a ſplendid family where he fed high, and drank plentifully of the beſt wines, whereupon the natural functions of the parts of his body were over charged, his lungs obſtructed, and the habit of the whole body quite diſordered, upon which there could not but ſoon enſue a diſſolution.

His brain was found entire and firm; and though he had not the uſe of his eyes, nor much of his memory, ſeveral years before he died, yet he had his hearing and apprehenſion very well, and was able, even to the hundred and thirtieth year of his age, to do any huſband work, even threſhing of corn.

Deſcription of an Inſtrument invented by Dr. Chriſtopher Wren for drawing the outlines of any object in perſpective.

SEE Fig. 1. (Plate IV.) wherein A is a ſmall ſight with a ſhort arm B which may be turned round about, and moved up and down the ſmall cylinder C D, which is ſcrewed into the piece E D at D. This piece E D moving round about the center E, by which means the ſight may be removed either towards R or F.

E F is a rule faſtened to the two rulers G G, which rulers ſerve both to keep the ſquare frame S S S S perpendicular, and by their ſliding through the ſquare holes T T they ſerve to ſtay the ſight, either farther from, or nearer to the ſaid frame; on which frame is ſtuck on with a little wax the paper O O O O, whereon the picture is to be drawn by the pen I. This pen I is, by a ſmall braſs handle V, ſo fixt to the ruler H H, that the point I, may be kept very firm, ſo as always to touch the paper.

H H is a ruler that is always, by means of the ſmall ſtrings a a a a, b b b b, moved horizontally, or parallel to itſelf; at the end of which is ſtuck a ſmall pin, whoſe head P is the ſight which is to be moved up and down on the outlines of any object.

The contrivance of the ſtrings is this: the two ſtrings a a a, b b b, are exactly of an equal length; two ends of them are faſtened into a ſmall leaden weight Q Q, which is moved in a ſocket on the back ſide of the frame, and ſerves exactly to counterpoiſe the ruler H H, being of equal weight with it: the other two ends of them are faſtened to two ſmall pins H H, after they have been rolled about the fmall pullies N, M M, L L, K K, by means of which pullies, if the pen I, be taken hold of, and moved up and down the paper, the ftrings moving very eafily, the rule, will always remain in an horizontal pofition.

The manner of ufing it is this: fet the inftrument on a table, and fix the fight A at what height above the table, and at what diftance from the frame S S S S you pleafe. Then looking through the fight A, and holding the pen I, in your hand, move the head of the pin P up and down the outlines of the object, and the point I will defcribe on the paper O O O O, the fhape of the object fo traced.

An Obfervation of Saturn, made at Paris, the 17th Auguft, 1668, by M. Hugens and M. Picart.

THE obfervers, employing a telefcope 21 feet long, faw the planet Jupiter as it is reprefented by Fig. 2, the globe in the middle manifeftly appearing, both above and below, beyond the oval of his angles, which was hardly difcernible the laft year.

They meafured divers ways the inclination of the great diameter of the oval to the equator, which inclination was found to be about nine degrees, although, *at that time*, it fhould not be but of four degrees, according to what M. Hugens hath affirmed in his fyftem of Saturn, viz. that the plan of the ring, which environs the globe of this planet, is inclined to the plan of the ecliptic but 23 deg. 30 min. But this laft obfervation, and other like ones of this and the precedent year, being more exact, and made at a time more proper for meafuring that obliquity, than were thofe that had formerly ferved for a foundation to determine it, M. Hugens finds that, inftead of 23 deg. 30 min. the angle of the plane of the ring and of the ecliptic muft be of 31 deg. or thereabout; and that being fo, that not only the fhape which Saturn hath at prefent, but alfo all thofe that have been noted fince the true ones were obferved, do perfectly agree with the hypothefis of the ring; and particularly that of 1664, in the beginning of July, which was obferved and made public by Signior Campani, wherein the great diameter is double to the leffer. See Fig. 3.

As to the round phafis of Saturn, that change of the inclination which was juſt now ſpoken of, cannot alter the time of it but very little, or nothing; ſo that M. Hugens ſtill expects this appearance in 1671 *, when in the ſummer of that year Saturn will begin to loſe his anſes, there being then to remain only the globe in the middle, and will not recover them until about a year after, according to what he hath written of the ſyſtem of Saturn.

An extract of M. De la Quintiny's letter concerning his way of ordering Melons; tranſlated from the French.

I SHALL now anſwer that particular of your letter which concerns melons, as exactly as I can. All the ſeeds I ſent you, produce Melons with a thin and ſomewhat embroidered ſkin, not divided by ribs; ſome of them have their ſkin whitiſh, others of the colour of ſlate. The melons themſelves are not very great; their fleſh very red, dry, and melting upon the tongue; not mealy, but of a high taſte. And theſe are the two only kinds which, after having tried an hundred different ſorts, I make uſe of, and ſend to you, not having obſerved any change in them, after the uſe of 20 years.

As to the manner of cutting them, you know, that the firſt thing appearing of them are two leaves united, here called ears (marked in Fig. 4 by 1. 1.) Out of the midſt of theſe two ears there ſhoots, ſome days after, firſt one leaf, which we call the firſt knot (marked 2.); and out of the ſame place, after ſome days more, ſhoots a ſecond, called the ſecond knot (marked 3.) Out of about the midſt of the ſtalk of this ſecond knot, ſhoots the third knot (marked 4.); and this third knot it is which muſt be cut at the place marked 6, without hurting the branch of the ſecond knot, whence this third came, becauſe from that place will ſpring a branch, which we call the firſt arm; and this arm will ſhoot forth, firſt, one knot, then a ſecond, then a third; and this third it is you are to cut again in the ſame manner as was ſaid before. And you muſt be careful to cut theſe third knots without ſtaying for the ſhooting of the fourth or fifth ones. You ſee out of every

* This hypotheſis was fully verified, the anſæ having nearly diſappeared by the end of the ſummer of that year, November 30th no anſæ to be ſeen, Saturn having retaken his round figure.

knot come forth arms or branches like to the first, spoken of before; and it is at those arms that the Melon will be produced. And they will be good, if the foot or root be well nourished in good earth, and cherished by a good hot-bed and the sun. But let the foot of the melon never pass into the dung, nor the earth be watered but moderately, when you see it grows too dry, so as the shoot may not suffer; which yet you must not delay till it happen, lest the remedy come too late. I water twice or thrice a week in very hot weather, and that about sun-set; and I cover my melons with a straw mat from eleven o'clock in the forenoon, to two in the evening, when the heat of the sun is too violent, or too quickly consuming that little moisture which is necessary for the root. And when it rains I cover also my Melon garden, lest too much wet hurt my fruit. There is some subjection in this; but it is also a pleasure to thrive in working by rule.

If the root produce too many branches or arms, cut away the weakest of them, and leave none but three or four of the strongest and most vigorous, and such as have their knots nearest to one another. When I transplant my melons from the nursery-bed, I put commonly two roots together, except I find one very strong, which I then plant alone, cutting from it neither of the branches that shoot from each side (marked 7. 7.) between the one ear and the leaf before spoken of. But when I join two roots together, I quite cut away both the branches, that shoot from the two ears, standing one over-against the other, to avoid the disordering abundance of branches, which else would wrong the foot.

The Melons being knit, I leave but two of them on each foot, choosing those that are best placed, and next to the first and principal stalk, that is, to the heart of the foot. I also take care to leave none but fair ones, and such as have a short and thick tail. The foot also of your melon must be short, well trussed, and not far distant from the ground. Melons of a long stem, and having the stalk of the leaf too long and slender, are never vigorous, and cannot yield good melons.

It happens sometimes, that at the very first there shoot out from between the two ears, two leaves, though I have spoken but of one, but this occurs but seldom; and when it does, such two leaves must be reckoned but for one knot; and afterwards there will shoot a second, and then a third, &c. and so on to 25 or 30, if you be not careful to cut in time: and it is at the extremity of those branches so distant that Melons will grow; but they cannot be good, becaufe they are fo far from the place, which affords them their nourifhment; and their juice is altered by the length of its paffage through the branches, which the fun fpoileth; whereas the foot of the Melon being fhort, and well truffed, there are always leaves covering the branches, and even the Melons themfelves, until they are near ripe.

Too great heat parches them too much to take nourifhment well, and this you muft take care of. He that is curious, muft every day walk often in his Melon garden, to cut off all the branches, which he fhall obferve to be ufelefs or hurtful; you will find them to fhoot forth almoft to the eye, and they are capable to alter all, if it be not remedied in time.

I muft not forget to tell you, that from the midft between the two ears and the two firft leaves there fhoots out yet one branch more, which ought to be kept, if vigorous; but cut, if weak.

In the Figure I have marked a leaf with 5, fhooting out of the midft of the fourth knot: I might have marked more coming forth fucceffively from one another, as you fee the fourth come from the third, &c.

Inftructions concerning the ufe of Pendulum Watches for finding the Longitude at Sea.

WHEREAS it is generally efteemed that there is no practice for finding the longitude at fea, comparable to that of thofe watches which inftead of a balance-wheel, are regulated by a pendulum, as now they are brought to great perfection, and made to meafure time very equally; and many perhaps here, as well as elfewhere, being not well verfed in the ordering and management of that inftrument, it is thought it may prove acceptable to make known fuch directions as may teach the unexperienced the ufe thereof at fea, by giving a tranflation of thofe inftructions, which fome years fince were made public by the worthy M. Chriftian Hugens, of Zulechem, in the Belgic tongue, as they have been fince altered, or rather enlarged by two other eminent members of the ROYAL SOCIETY.

1ft, Thofe that intend to make ufe of the pendulum watches at fea, muft have two of them at leaft; that, if one of them fhould by mifhap or neglect come to ftop, or (being by length of time become foul) need to be made clean, there may likely always remain one in motion.

2d, The perfon, to whom the care of thefe watches fhall be committed is to inform himfelf from the watch-maker or fome other, fo as to underftand the inward parts of the watches, the manner of winding them up, and how to fet the *indexes*, or hands having the hours, minutes, and feconds, &c.

3d. The watches on fhip-board are to be hung in a clofe place, where they may be freeft from moifture, or duft, and out of danger of being difordered by knocking or touching.

4th, Before the watches be brought on fhip-board, it is convenient they be adjufted to a middle or mean day, the ufe of them being then moft eafy, it being little or no trouble to the watch-makers, when they have one that is fet juft, to fet others accordingly: but yet, if time or conveniency fo to do fhould happen to be wanting, they may notwithftanding be ufed at fea with like certainty, provided you know how much they go too faft or too flow in 24 hours, as directed in the next fection.

5th, To reduce watches to the right meafure of days, or to know how much they go too faft or too flow in 24 hours.—Here take notice that the fun or earth paffeth the 12 figns, or makes an entire revolution in the ecliptic in 365 days, 5 hours, 49 minutes, or thereabouts; and that thofe days, reckoned from noon to noon, are of different lengths, as is known to all that are verfed in aftronomy. Now, between the longest and fhorteft of thofe days, a day may be taken of fuch a length, as 365 fuch days, 5 hours, &c. make up, or are equal to that revolution: and this is called the *equal* or *main day*, according to which the watches are to be fet; and therefore the hour or minute fhewed by the watches, though they be perfectly juft and equal, muft needs differ almoft continually from thofe that are fhewed by the fun, or are reckoned according to its motion. But this difference is regular, and is otherwife called the equation which the following Table explains.

	January. min.	January. sec.	February. min.	February. sec.	March. min.	March. sec.	April. min.	April. sec.	May. min.	May. sec.	June. min.	June. sec.	July. min.	July. sec.	August. min.	August. sec.	September. min.	September. sec.	October. min.	October. sec.	November. min.	November. sec.	December. min.	December. sec.
1	6	10	0	0	4	46	14	23	19	25	16	24	10	45	11	7	19	41	29	16	31	13	21	14
2	5	47	0	2	5	3	14	39	19	28	16	13	10	38	11	16	20	1	29	30	31	3	20	44
3	5	24	0	4	5	21	14	55	19	29	16	1	10	31	11	25	20	22	29	43	30	53	20	14
4	5	2	0	8	5	39	15	10	19	29	15	40	10	25	11	36	20	23	29	56	30	43	19	44
5	4	41	0	12	5	57	15	25	19	29	15	37	10	19	11	48	21	4	30	9	30	32	19	14
6	4	21	0	16	6	15	15	39	19	28	15	24	10	13	12	1	21	25	30	22	30	20	18	44
7	4	2	0	21	6	33	15	53	19	26	15	11	10	7	12	14	21	47	30	34	30	8	18	14
8	3	44	0	26	6	51	16	7	19	24	14	58	10	2	12	28	22	9	30	45	29	55	17	44
9	3	27	0	32	7	9	16	21	19	21	14	45	9	58	12	42	22	31	30	55	29	40	17	14
10	3	11	0	40	7	27	16	34	19	18	14	32	9	54	12	57	22	52	31	4	29	23	16	44
11	2	55	0	48	7	45	16	47	19	15	14	19	9	51	13	12	23	13	31	12	29	6	16	14
12	2	39	0	57	8	3	16	59	19	11	14	6	9	49	13	27	23	33	31	19	28	48	15	44
13	2	23	1	6	8	22	17	11	19	7	13	53	9	47	13	43	23	53	31	26	28	30	15	14
14	2	7	1	16	8	41	17	22	19	2	13	40	9	46	13	59	24	13	31	32	28	11	14	43
15	1	52	1	26	9	1	17	33	18	57	13	27	9	46	14	16	24	33	31	38	27	51	14	12
16	1	38	1	37	9	21	17	43	18	51	13	15	9	46	14	33	24	53	31	43	27	30	13	41
17	1	25	1	49	9	41	17	53	18	45	13	3	9	47	14	50	25	13	31	47	27	8	13	10
18	1	23	2	2	10	1	18	3	18	39	12	52	9	49	15	8	25	33	31	50	26	45	12	40
19	1	2	2	15	10	21	18	13	18	33	12	41	9	52	15	26	25	52	31	53	26	22	12	10
20	0	51	2	28	10	40	18	23	18	26	12	30	9	56	15	45	26	11	31	55	25	58	11	40
21	0	41	2	42	10	59	18	32	18	18	12	19	10	0	16	4	26	30	31	55	25	34	11	10
22	0	32	2	56	11	18	18	39	18	10	12	8	10	4	16	23	26	49	31	55	25	10	10	40
23	0	24	3	11	11	37	18	46	18	1	11	58	10	8	16	42	27	8	31	55	24	45	10	10
24	0	18	3	26	11	56	18	53	17	51	11	48	10	13	17	1	27	26	31	54	24	20	9	41
25	0	13	3	41	12	15	18	59	17	41	11	38	10	18	17	21	27	43	31	52	23	55	9	13
26	0	9	3	56	12	34	19	4	17	30	11	28	10	23	17	41	28	0	31	50	23	30	8	45
27	0	6	4	12	12	53	19	9	17	19	11	18	10	28	18	1	28	16	31	47	23	4	8	17
28	0	3	4	29	13	12	19	14	17	8	11	9	10	34	18	21	28	32	31	43	22	38	7	50
29	0	1			13	31	19	18	16	57	11	0	10	41	18	41	28	47	31	37	22	11	7	23
30	0	0			13	49	19	22	16	46	11	52	10	49	19	1	29	2	31	30	21	43	6	58
31	0	0			14	6			16	35			10	58	19	21			32	22			6	34

By the help of this table you will always know what the hour is by the ſun preciſely, and conſequently, whether the watches have been ſet to the right meaſure of the mean day or no; uſing the table as follows:

When you firſt ſet your watch by the ſun, you are to ſubduct from the time obſerved by the ſun, the equation adjoined to that day of the month in the table, and to ſet the watches to the remaining hours, minutes, and ſeconds, that is, the watches are to be ſet ſo much ſlower than the time of the ſun, as (in the table) is the equation of that day; ſo that the equation of the day, added to the time of the clock, is the true time by the ſun. And when after ſome days, you deſire to know by the watch the time by the ſun, you are to add to the time ſhewed by the watch the equation of that day; and the aggregate ſhall be the time by the ſun, if the watch hath been perfectly well adjuſted after the meaſure of the *mean* days; for the doing of which, this will be a convenient way:—

Draw a meridian line upon a floor (the manner of doing which is ſufficiently known; and note, that the utmoſt exactneſs herein, is not neceſſary:) and then hang two plummets, each by a ſmall thread or wire directly over the ſaid meridian, at the diſtance of ſome two feet, or more, one from the other, as the ſmallneſs of the thread will admit. When the middle of the ſun (the eye being placed ſo as to bring both the threads into one line) appears to be in the ſame line exactly, for the better and more ſecure diſcerning thereof, you muſt be furniſhed with a glaſs of a dark colour, or ſomewhat black with the ſmoke of a candle, you are then immediately to ſet the watch, not preciſely to the hour of 12, but by ſo much leſs, as is the equation of that day by the table, *e. g.* If it were the 12th of March, the equation of that day, being by the table 8 minutes, 3 ſeconds; theſe are to be ſubducted from 12 hours, and the remainder will be 11 hours, 51 minutes, 57 ſeconds; to which hours, minutes, and ſeconds you are to ſet the index of the watch reſpectively: then, after ſome days, you are to obſerve again in the ſame manner, and likewiſe to note the hours, minutes, and ſeconds of the watch, to which you are to add the equation of theſe days, taken out of the table. And if the aggregate do juſt make 12 hours, the watch is ſet adjuſted to the right meaſure; but if it differ, you are to divide the minutes and ſeconds of that difference by the number of the days between both the obſervations, to get the daily difference. Let us ſuppoſe this ſecond obſervation to have been made the 20th of March, viz. eight days after the firſt, and finding, that the middle of the ſun being ſeen in the meridian in the ſame line with the two threads, as before, the watch points - - 11 h. 51 m. 7 ſ.

The equation of the 20th March, by the table, is - 0 10 40

Which being added to the time, ſhewed by the watch, gives 12 1 47

If this had been juſt 12 hours, the watch would have been well adjuſted, but being 1 min. 47 ſec. more than 12, it hath gone ſo much too faſt in eight days. And theſe 1 min. 47 ſec. that is, 107 ſeconds, being divided by eight, there comes $13\frac{3}{8}$ ſeconds for the difference of every 24 hours; which difference being known, if you want time, or have no mind to take the pains to adjuſt the watch to its right meaſure (this being not neceſſary, ſince you may bring it thus on ſhipboard), note only the daily difference, and regulate yourſelf accordingly, as hath been mentioned. But if you will adjuſt it better, you muſt remove the leſs weight of the pendulum a little downwards which will make it go ſlower; and then you muſt begin to obſerve anew by the ſun as before. If it had gone too ſlow, you muſt have removed the above-mentioned weight ſomewhat upwards. And this is of that importance in the finding out of *longitudes*, that, if it be not obſerved, you may ſometimes in the ſpace of three months, miſ-reckon ſeven degrees and more (yet without any fault in the watches;) which, under the tropics, will amount to above 400 miles Engliſh.

Having ſhewed how the watches may be adjuſted at land, or how their daily difference may be known; next ſhall follow, how the ſame may be done when a veſſel rides at anchor, it being hardly feaſible when ſhe is under ſail.

In the morning then, when the ſun is juſt above the horizon, note what hour, minutes, and ſeconds the watch points at, if it be going; if not, ſet it a going, and put the indexes at what hour, minutes, and ſeconds you pleaſe. Let them go till ſun-ſet, and when the body of the ſun is juſt half under the horizon, ſee what hour, minutes, and ſeconds, the indexes of the watch point at, and note them too; and reckon how many hours, &c. are paſſed by the watch between the one and the other, which is done by adding to the evening obſervation the hours, &c. that the morning obſervation wanted of 12 or 24, in caſe the hour-hand hath in the mean time paſſed that hour once or twice; otherwiſe the difference only gives the time. Then take the half of that number, and add it to the hours, &c. of the morning obſervation, and you ſhall have the hours, &c. which the watch did ſhew, when the ſun was in the ſouth; whereunto add the equation in the table belonging to that day, and note the ſum. Then, ſome days being paſſed, (the more the better) you are to do juſt the ſame: and if the hour of this laſt day be the ſame that was noted before, your watch is well adjuſted; but if it be more or leſs, the difference divided by the number elapſed between the two obſervations, will give the daily difference. And if you will, you may let it reſt there, or otherwiſe, removing the leſſer weight of the pendulum, you may adjuſt it better.

	h.	m.	ſ.		h.	m.	ſ.
E. g. Suppoſe March 11th in the morning, when the ſun half appears above the horizon, the watch points at - - -	5	30	10		0	10	3
In the evening when the ſun appears half ſet -	5	20	6		11	59	59
To know by the watch the time elapſed between both, ſubduct the time of the riſing -	5	30	10				
From -	12	0	0				
Reſts -	6	19	50				
Whereunto adding the time of ſetting -	5	20	6				
There comes for the time elapſed between them	11	49	56	diff.	11	49	56
Whereof the half is - -	5	54	58		5	54	58
Which added to the time of the ſun's riſing -	5	30	10		0	10	3
There comes the time of the watch when the ſun was in the ſouth - -	11	25	8		6	5	1
To which adding the equation of the 11th of March	0	7	45		0	7	45
The ſum is -	11	32	53		6	12	46
Seven days after, viz. March 18th, let the riſing of the ſun be obſerved, and the watch point then at	5	19	4		11	58	57
And at his ſetting let the watch point at -	5	25	2		0	4	55
To find the time elapſed between them, ſubduct the time of the riſing - - -	5	19	4		11	58	57
From - -	12	0	0		24	0	0
Reſts - -	6	40	56		12	1	3
To which add the time of the ſetting - -	5	25	2		0	4	55
And you find the time paſſed between them -	12	5	58		12	5	58
Whereof the half is - -	6	2	59		6	2	59

	h.	m.	s.	h.	m.	s.
Which added to the time of the rising -	5	19	4	11	58	57
And you have the time when the sun was in the south	11	22	3	6	1	56
Whereunto adding the equation of March 18 -	0	10	1	0	10	1
The sun is - -	11	32	4	6	11	57
Which sum, if it had agreed with the first, viz. -	11	32	53	6	12	46

then had the watch been set to the right measure; but seeing that the latter is less than the former, the difference being 49 seconds; the watch hath by so much, in seven days, gone too slow; which 49 seconds, divided by the number of days, you have seven seconds for the daily difference; and by so much the watch goes too slow in 24 hours.

You may also, instead of the sun's rising and setting, take two equal altitudes of the sun, before and after noon, and having noted the time given by the watches at the time of both the observations, proceed with it in the same manner, as was just now directed for observing the sun in the horizon. In either of which ways there may be some error, caused by the sun's refraction, which is inconsiderable, and therefore needs not to be taken notice of.

6th, By means of these watches, to find at sea the longitude of the place where you are.

Give to each of the watches a name or mark, as, A, B, C,; and before you set sail, set them to the time observed by the sun in the place where you are, and whence you are departing, allowing for the equation of the day, whereon you make your observation; which day you are to note, if the watch be not well adjusted, otherwise it is not necessary.

Then afterwards, being at sea, and desiring to know the longitude of the place where you are, that is, how many degrees the meridian of that place is more easterly, or westerly, than the meridian of that place where you did set the watches; you must observe by the sun or stars, what time of the day or night it is, as precisely as possible, and note at the same time, to what hour, minutes, and seconds, the watches do point, (which time, if the watches be not set to the right measure, is by the known daily difference to be adjusted,) adding thereto the equation of the present day, which gives you the time of the day, shewed by the sun at the place where the watches were set: and if the time of the day be the same with that observed where you are, then you are under the same meridian with the place where the watches were set by the ſun; but if the time of the day, obſerved where you are, be greater than that ſhewed by the watches, you may be aſſured that you are come under a more eaſterly meridian; and if leſs, you are come under a more weſterly. And counting for every hour of difference of time, 15 degrees of longitude, and for every minute, 15 minutes, or one-fourth of a degree, you ſhall then know, how many degrees, minutes, &c. the ſaid meridians do differ from one another.

E. g. Suppoſe the watches A, B, C, were ſet at the place whence you parted, on the 20th of February, to the time of the day obſerved by the ſun, abating the equation of the 20th of February (viz. 2. min. 28. ſec.) and ſuppoſe that the watch A, be ſet to its right meaſure, but that B goes every ſeven ſeconds too ſlow, and C every day ten ſeconds too faſt. Some days after, ſuppoſe the 5th of May, deſiring to know the longitude of the place where you are at ſea, you

	h.	m.	ſ.
Obſerve the time of the day there to be - -	5	18	10
And you find the watch A to point at - -	2	6	0
But the watch B to point at - - -	1	57	22
Going too ſlow by ſeven ſeconds every day, which make in 74 days, (viz. from the 20th February to the 5th May) -	0	8	38
Which being added to its own time gives the ſame with that of the watch A, viz. - - -	2	6	0
You find alſo the watch C to point at - -	2	20	48
Going 12 ſeconds too faſt every day, which makes in 74 days	0	14	48
Which being ſubducted from its own time gives again -	2	6	0
The time of the day therefore by the watches being -	2	6	0
Add thereto the equation of the 5th of May - -	0	19	29
And ſo you have for the time of the day at the place where the watches were ſet - - -	2	25	29
But the time obſerved being - - -	5	18	10
Exceeds this by - - - -	2	52	41
Wherefore the meridian of the place where you are May 5th, is more eaſterly than the places where the watches were ſet by	2	52	41

Which being reduced to degrees, reckoning 15 degrees for an hour, comes to 43 deg. 10 min. 15 ſec.

It is true, that from the ſame reckoning it may be concluded, that you are 180 degrees more eaſterly, which happens, becauſe the hour index goes round in the ſpace of 12 hours in the watches; but the difference is ſo great, that one cannot be deceived in it; elſe the watch might be ſo made, that the index ſhall go round but once in 24 hours.

7th, To find the time of the day at ſea.

Since for finding the longitude, the time of the day at the place where you are muſt be known (as hath been ſaid above), you muſt have care to obſerve that time as preciſely as poſſible; for every minute of time that you miſ-reckon makes a fourth part of a degree in longitude, which amounts, near the equator, to above 15 Engliſh miles, but leſs elſewhere. Wherefore, to find the time of the day with certainty, you are not to truſt to the obſervation of the ſun's greateſt altitude, thence to conclude that it is juſt noon, or that the ſun is in the ſouth, unleſs being betwixt the tropics, you have it juſt in the zenith. For elſe the ſun being near the meridian, remains for ſome time without any ſenſible alteration of his altitude. Wherefore, though the meridian altitude may ſerve well enough for knowing the latitude or the height of the pole upon occaſion, yet it will not ſerve for finding preciſely the longitude of that place. Much leſs are you to rely upon the ſea-compaſſes, thereby to find the preciſe time of noon. Neither are the aſtronomical rings or other ſorts of ſun-dials, ſure enough for ſhewing the time, to minutes and ſeconds. But it is better to obſerve the ſun's altitude, when it is in the eaſt or weſt, (the nearer the better:) for being there, its altitude changes in a ſhort time more ſenſibly than before or after; and thus from the *height of the pole*, and the *declination of the ſun*, the hour may be calculated; the manner of which is ſufficiently taught by others; yet by reaſon that the calculation is ſomewhat troubleſome, and that alſo there may be ſome errors in taking of the ſun's altitude, here follows an eaſier way.

8th, How by obſerving the riſing and ſetting of the ſun, and the time by the watches, the longitude at ſea may be found.

This way doth neither require the knowledge of the height of the pole, nor of the declination of the ſun, nor the uſe of any aſtronomical inſtruments: neither can the refraction of the ſun or ſtars cauſe any conſiderable error; the refraction of the morning differing little or nothing from that of the evening of one and the ſame day, eſpecially at ſea. Thus then you are to proceed:

At the riſing and ſetting of the ſun, when it is half above the horizon, mark the time of the day, which the watches then ſhew, and though you have in the mean time failed on, it is not confiderable. Then reckon by the watches, what the time is elapfed between them, and add the half thereof to the time of the rifing, and you fhall have the time by the watches, when the fun was at fouth; to which is to be added the equation of the prefent day by the table. And if this together makes 12 hours, then was the fhip at noon under the *fame* meridian, where the watches were fet with the fun. But if the fum be more than 12, then was fhe at noon, under a more wefterly meridian; and if lefs, then under a more eafterly; and that by as many times 15 degrees, as that fum exceeds or comes fhort of hours 12: as the calculation thereof hath been already delivered.

Suppofe, *e. g.* that the watches A B, as before, were fet with the fun at the place whence you parted, the 20th of February; and the indexes fet to the hour, minutes, and feconds, fhewed by the fun, abating the equation of that day, viz. 2 min. and 20 fec.; the watch A being reduced to the right meafure, and B going too flow by feven feconds a day. Afterwards, on the 12th of May, defiring to know the longitude of the place to which

	h.	m.	f.
you are come, you obferve in the morning the fun half above the horizon when the watch points at - -	2	30	10
And in the evening, the fun being half under the horizon, when the fame watch points at - -	3	8	40
To find the time elapfed between them, fubducting the time of the rifing - - - -	2	30	10
From - - - -	12	0	0
There remains -	9	29	50
Adding thereto the time of the fetting - -	3	8	40
You have for the time elapfed between the obfervations -	12	38	30
Whereof the half - - - -	6	19	15
Being added to the time of rifing - - -	2	30	10
You have the time by the watch A, when the fun was in the fouth - - - - -	8	49	25
And after the fame manner you are to feek the time by the watch B, when the fun was in the fouth, which let be	8	38	48
But this watch going feven feconds a day too flow, it is retarded 91 days (from the 20th Feb. to the 22d of May) -	0	10	37
Which therefore added to the faid time, gives -	8	49	25

	h.	m.	s.
That is the same time given by the watch A; now adding to this time of the watches the equation of the 22d of May,	0	18	10
You have - - - - - -	9	7	35
Which is the same time of the day with that of the place where the watches were set when the sun was in the same meridian with the ship, or where the ship was at noon. The difference is, - - - -	2	52	25
Wherefore this last meridian is by so much more easterly than the first, which being reduced to degrees, make -	43	6	15

It is manifest, that by this way you find precisely enough the longitude of the place where you were at noon, or the time of the sun's being in the south, which, although it differs from the longitude of the place where you are when you observe the setting of the sun, yet you may estimate near enough how much you have advanced, or changed the longitude in those few hours, by the log-line, or other ordinary practices of reckoning the ship's way; or (which is the surer way) by the degrees passed in 24 hours by a former day's observation.

You may also, instead of observing the sun's rising and setting, observe the setting first, and then next morning the rising, making at both times the time shewed by the watches; and find thence, after the same manner as before, the longitude of the place where the ship was at midnight.

Finally, you may also, instead of the rising and setting of the sun, observe, before and after noon, two equal altitudes of the sun, noting the time shewn by the watches, and reckoning in the same manner as hath been said of the rising and setting: yet it is to be considered, that the altitudes of the sun are best taken when it is about east and west, as hath been already intimated. But note, that in sailing north and south you make not the observations at the sun's rising and setting, but at its being due east and west.

9th, But you may, especially in such quarters as lie far north and south, yea, and wherever you will, put the rule here prescribed in practice, by taking two equal altitudes of some known star, that riseth high above the horizon. For you shall thence, according to the fore-mentioned rule, know at what time, by the watches, the star hath been in the south, and so the right ascension of that star being known, as also the right ascension of the ſun, you may thence eaſily calculate what time it then was; which being compared with the time of the watches, as before, ſhall give you the longitude of the place where you were when you had the ſtar in the meridian.

10th, If the watches that have gone exactly for a while ſhould come to differ from one another (as in length of time it may well happen that the one or the other fail a minute, more or leſs), in that caſe it will be beſt to reckon by that which goes faſteſt, unleſs you perceive an apparent cauſe why it goes too faſt, ſeeing it is not ſo eaſy for theſe pendulum watches to move faſter than at firſt, as it is to go ſlower. For the wire on which the pendulum hangs may, perhaps, by the violent agitation of the ſhip, come to ſtretch a little, but it cannot grow ſhorter: and the little weight of the pendulum perhaps ſlip downwards, but cannot get up higher.

11th, When you get ſight of any known country, iſland, or coaſt, be ſure to note the longitude thereof as exactly as you can by the help of the rules here preſcribed. Firſt, thereby to correct the ſea maps, after that the longitude of the place ſhall have been found at divers times to be the ſame, ſo that you doubt no more of it; for all maps are very defective as to the ſituation of places in reſpect of eaſt and weſt, chiefly where ſeas are interpoſed. Secondly, to be able always to know, in the proſecution of your journey, how far you have ſailed from any place to the eaſt or weſt. And if by any notable miſchance or careleſsneſs all the watches ſhould come to ſtand ſtill, yet you may at any place, whereof the longitude is certainly known, ſet them a-going again, and adjuſt them there by the ſun, and ſo reckon the longitudes from that ſame meridian. For you are to know, that you are not at all obliged to put *one certain* meridian of any known place as a beginning of the longitude reckoning; this happening only in *maps*, or tables of longitude. As, when you take for that purpoſe the meridian of the Pico in Teneriffe, or that of the iſlands of Corvo and Flores (the moſt weſterly of the Azores), or any others; yet it were very fit that all geographers agreed, and pitched upon one and the ſame firſt meridian, ſo that all places might be known by the ſame degrees as well of longitude as latitude; though in voyaging it is ſufficient to obſerve only the difference of longitudes, beginning to reckon from the meridian of any place you pleaſe, as if it were the firſt.

12th, If it happen, that being at ſea all the watches ſtop, you muſt, as

4

ſpeedily as poſſible, ſet them a moving again, that you may know how much you advance from that place towards the eaſt or weſt; which is of no ſmall importance, ſince, for want of this knowledge, you are ſometimes, by force of *currents*, ſo carried away, that though you ſail *before the wind*, yet you are driven *aſtern*; of which there are many examples.

The Method of a Journal for the Watches.

The watches being diſtinguiſhed by marks, A B or the like, every day about noon, or when moſt conveniently you can, obſerve the time of the day by the ſun, or by the ſtars at night, and ſubduct thence the minutes and ſeconds that are adjoined to that day in the table, and write the remainder down in a paper, wherein nine columns or more are marked, placing them in the *ſecond* column, having placed the day of the month in the firſt; and at the ſame time write down the hours, minutes, and ſeconds of each watch in a diſtinct column, all oppoſite one to another. Then in another column write down the *difference* between the time taken by obſervation and that given by the watches, or one of them: then one column for the latitude; one for the longitude, by the ordinary way of reckoning; another for the longitude taken from the difference between the *time* found by *obſervation* and that given by the watches; and, at laſt, a large column to note the accidents that befal the watches, &c.

An extract of a letter written by Dr. Edward Brown, from Vienna, March 3d, 1669, concerning two Parhelias, or Mock Suns.

I RECEIVED the account of the parhelias, ſeen Jan. 30th laſt, *ſt. n.* about one of the clock in the afternoon, over the city of Caſſovia, in Hungary. It was communicated to me from a learned jeſuit, called Father Michel, who lives at Preſburerg, but is now in this city. There were two parhelias, one on each ſide of the true ſun; and they were ſo reſplendent, that the naked eye could not bear the brightneſs thereof. One of them (the leſſer of the two) began to decay before the other, and then the other grew bigger, and continued well nigh two hours, projecting very long rays from itſelf. They were both, on that part which was towards the ſun, tinged with a pale yellow, the other parts being ſomewhat fuſcous. There were at the ſame time ſeen ſeveral *rainbows*, together with the ſegment of a great white circle, of a long duration, paſſing through the two parhelias and the ſun; and all this at a time when the air was almoſt free from clouds, though here and there were ſcattered ſome very thin ones.

A Relation of the Conferences held at Paris in the ACADEMY ROYAL, *for the Improvement of the Arts of Painting and Sculpture, as it is found in the Journal des Sçavans.*

THESE conferences are held one in a month, by divers able maſters, making reflections and obſervations upon the rareſt pieces in the cabinet of his Moſt Chriſtian Majeſty, the eſtabliſher of that Academy. Monſieur Colbert, who takes a very particular care to make arts flouriſh in France, being pleaſed to viſit thoſe artiſts ſome time ſince, to ſee what progreſs they made, and having received an account of what had been done in their meetings, expreſſed himſelf to this effect: that as it was neceſſary for the teaching of arts, to join examples to precepts, ſo he thought it proper, that from time to time the works of the moſt excellent painters ſhould be examined, and ſuch obſervations made thereon as would inform others wherein the perfection of a picture conſiſts, which hath been ever ſince practiſed amongſt them, as the beſt means to carry the art of painting to its higheſt perfection; ſuch an examine of the beſt pictures diſcloſing many ſecrets of that art, for which there are no rules, and opening a door to debate many important queſtions, hitherto not treated of.

In the particulars which have been made public, of theſe conferences, we may find,

Firſt, a general idea of the art of painting, wherein are conſidered two principal parts, the one belonging to the theory, the other regarding the practice, and the dexterity of the hand; where it is obſerved, that the authors, that have written of painting, have not treated of the former part, how conſiderable ſoever that be, in regard of the deſign and diſpoſition of the pieces.

Next, a relation of ſeven conferences, whereof ſix were made upon as many pieces of Raphael, Titian, Paul Veroneſe, and M. Pouſin, and the ſeventh upon that of Laocoon; where are to be met with many curious remarks, and amongſt many others theſe following:

M. Le Brun conſidering a piece of Raphael, where is repreſented the combat of St. Michael with the Devil, obſerves, that the expreſſion particularly depends from the bodies which environ the figures, affirming, that it is that which ſets out the motion and action in the figure of St. Michael, who ſeems to have life in this piece; for, as if the air were preſſed by the weight of the body deſcending, it cauſeth whatever it meets with as more light to be raiſed, and drives it on high with violence.

In another piece, where Titian repreſents the body of Jeſus Chriſt carried to the grave, M. de Champagne, the elder, obſerves the dexterity of the maſter in ordering the colours and the light. To make the legs of the picture (which firſt preſent themſelves) to ſtand out, he hath wrapped them about with a very white linen ſheet, and hath clothed Nicodemus, who holds them, with a very vivid and very clear *lague*. On the contrary, to ſink the reſt of the body, he hath ſo taken the light of the picture, that the ſhadow of Joſeph of Arimathea, who helps to ſupport the legs, falls on its head and ſhoulders; which alſo contributes to impreſs on the body the image of death. The order of the colours is alſo very remarkable in the cloaths; for betwixt the green habit of Joſeph of Arimathea, and the blue mantle of the bleſſed Virgin, is the yellow habit of Mary Magdalen, wherein what is brown and duſky, is tempered and borrows of the different colours about it, that the eye may paſs by degrees from one of theſe colours to the other: and becauſe the ſleeve of Magdalen, which is of a bright yellow, is near the habit of Nicodemus, which is alſo of a lively colour, the artiſt to hinder that thoſe two vivid colours may not entrench on one another, hath turned up Nicodemus's ſleeve againſt the yellow, ſo that from the ſhadow of one of theſe colours one paſſeth to the ſhadow of the other.

The art of the picture ſpoken of in the fifth conference, is no leſs remarkable. In this piece, done by P. Veroneſe, is ſeen a woman, whoſe carnation colour is ſo freſh and bright, that it dazzleth the eyes. M. Nocret examining what may cauſe this beauty, obſerveth, that it proceeds in part from hence, that the maſter hath ingeniouſly drawn *before* this woman a child clothed in brown; *behind* her a man in black; and on her ſide a negro, who maketh an admirable concert with the great luſtre and ſplendour of that carnation.

The two laſt conferences, treating of two pieces of M. Pouſſin, doth fürniſh amongſt other things, very elegant examples of different characters, ſmiting different perſons. This maſter having to repreſent many perſons gathering manna, gives to them all different poſtures, becoming their humour; on the fore part of the picture there are two youths, who following the genius of their age, fight about the manna. Near them are men gathering manna in the mean time, and eating thereof. A little farther off appears a girl, who unwilling to take the pains of ſtooping, holds out her coat to receive the manna falling down, and looks on it as if the heavens had dropped it down for none but her. Which well expreſſeth (ſaith the obſerver) the ſoftneſs and diſdainful temper of that ſex, which loves not to take pains, and imagines that all muſt come to paſs as they wiſh. In the other piece, which exhibits the recovery of the *two blind* men, to whom our Saviour reſtored their ſight, there is an old man, who comes very near, peeping and looking as if he doubted of the truth of the miracle; in which the artiſt hath well obſerved the genius of aged perſons, who commonly are more incredulous and diffident than others.

Beſides this, there are examined here and there in theſe conferences divers queſtions important in painting; which would be too long to particulariſe in this place.

Experiments concerning the motion of Sap in Trees, made this Spring by Mr. Willughby and Mr. Wray, Fellows of the ROYAL SOCIETY.

1ſt, IN birch trees the sap issues out of the least twigs of branches, and fibres of roots, in proportion to their bigneſs.

2d, In all trees the gravity promotes the bleeding; ſo that from a branch or root that bends downward, there iſſues a great deal more ſap than from another of the ſame bigneſs in a more erect poſture.

3d, Branches and young trees cut quite off whilſt they are full of ſap, and held perpendicularly, will bleed; as we experimented in willow, birch, and ſycamore: and if you cut off their tops, and invert them, they will bleed alſo at the little ends. Hence one may conjecture that the narrowneſs of the pores is not the ſole cauſe of the aſcent of the ſap; for water that hath aſcended in the little glaſs pipes, will not fall out again by its own gravity if the pipes be taken out of the water.

4th, Roots of birch and ſycamore cut aſunder will bleed both ways, that is, from that part remaining to the tree, and from that part ſeparated; but a great deal faſter from that part remaining to the tree. But in a cold ſnowy day the root of one ſycamore we had bared, bled faſter from the part ſeparated, and ten times faſter than it did in warm weather before.

5th, In birches the ſap does not iſſue out of the bark, be it ever ſo thick, but as ſoon as you have cut the bark quite through then it first begins to bleed.

6th, The bark being quite pared off above an hand's breadth round about ſeveral birches, did much abate the bleeding of the trees above the bared places, but did not quite ſtop it.

7th, The ſap doth not only aſcend between bark and tree, and in the pricked circles between the ſeveral coats of the wood, but alſo through the very body of the wood: for ſeveral young birches being nimbly cut off at one blow with a ſharp axe, and white paper immediately held hard upon the top of the remaining trunk, we ſtuck down pins in all the points of the paper as they appeared wet; and at laſt when moſt of the paper became wet, taking it away, but leaving the pins ſticking, we found them without any order, some in the circles, and some in the wood between. And to confirm this further, we cauſed the body of a tree to be cut off aſlope, and then cut the oppoſite ſide aſlope likewiſe, till we brought the top to a narrow edge, ordering the matter ſo that the whole edge conſiſted of a part of a coat of wood, and had nothing of a pricked circle in it, which, notwithſtanding, the ſap aſcended to the very top of this edge, and wetted a paper laid upon it.

8th, To find out the motion of the ſap, whether it aſcended only, or deſcended alſo, we bored a hole in a large birch, out of which a drop fell every fourth or fifth pulſe. Then about a hand's breadth juſt under the hole, we ſawed into the body of the tree, deeper than the hole, whereupon the bleeding diminiſhed about one half; and having ſawed juſt above this hole to the ſame depth, the bleeding from the hole ceaſed quite, and from the ſawed furrow below, decreaſed about half; and it continued bleeding a great while after at both the ſawed furrows the hole in the middle remaining dry. We repeated this with much the like ſucceſs upon the ſycamore.

9th, Some trees of the ſame kind and age bleed a great deal faſter and ſooner than others, but always old trees ſooner and faſter than young.

10th, A wound made before the ſap riſes, will bleed when it doth riſe.

11th, Whilſt we were making theſe experiments, the weather changed from warm to very cold; whereupon the bleeding in the birches, which began to abate before, ceaſed quite. But all the ſycamore and walnut trees we had wounded, bled abundantly; (ſome whereof before bled not at all, and thoſe that did, did ſo but ſlowly) and ſo continued night and day, when it froze ſo hard that the ſap congealed as faſt as it iſſued out. The cold remitting, the birches bled afreſh, the ſycamores abated very much, and the walnuts quite ceased.

12th, We pierced two ſycamores on the north and ſouth ſides, and both of them from equal inciſions bled a great deal faſter from the north ſides than the ſouth, which is conſonant with the preceding experiment.

13th, We ſet ſeveral willows with the wrong ends downward, and cut off ſeveral briars that had taken root at the ſmall ends. This 29th of May the willows have shot out branches near two feet long; and from the top of the ſets, which were a yard high, the briars have alſo grown backwards from that part, which we left remaining to the roots at the lesser ends; they have great leaves, and are ready to flower.

Extract of a letter from Dr. Edward Browne, concerning the damps in the Mines of Hungary, and their effects.

SIR,—HAVING been lately in the copper, ſilver, and gold mines in Hungary, I hope, ere long, to give you a particular account thereof; preſenting this in the mean time concerning damps in theſe mines; whereof I underſtand that they happen in moſt of them that are deep; and that they happen not only in the cuniculi or direct paſſages, where they walk on horizontally (by thoſe mine-men called ſtollen) but alſo in the putic or perpendicular cuts or deſcents (termed ſchachts by the ſame.) They are met with not only in places where the earth is full of clay, or the like ſubſtances, but alſo where it is rocky; and one place they ſhewed me in the copper mine at

Hern-Groundt, where there had been a very pernicious damp, and yet the rock ſo hard, that it could not be broken by their inſtruments; but the deſcent was all made by the means of gunpowder rammed into long round holes in the rock, and ſo blown up. Another place they ſhewed me where there is ſometimes a damp, and ſometimes clear weather: when there is much water in the mine, ſo as to ſtop up the lower part of this paſſage, then the damp becomes diſcoverable, and commonly ſtrong. I procured one to enter it, till his lamp went out four or five times, in the ſame as at Grotto del Cane, in Italy.

Damps are not all of the ſame force, but ſome weaker, ſome ſtronger; ſome ſuffocate in a ſmall ſpace of time, others only render the workmen faint, with no other hurt, except they continue long in a place. The miners, (who think themſelves no workmen if they be not able to cure a damp, or to cure the bad weather, or to *make* the weather, as they term it,) perform it perflation, by letting the air in and out, and cauſing, as it were, a circulation of it. In the mine at Hern-Groundt, they did cure a bad damp by a great pair of bellows, which were blown continually for many days. The ordinary remedy is by long tubes, through which the air continually paſſing, they are able to dig ſtraight on for a long way without impediment in breathing: for ſome cuniculi are 500 fathoms long, which will not ſeem ſtrange to any one that ſhall ſee the map of the copper mine at Hern-Groundt, or the gold mine at Chremnitz; and in the ſilver trinity mine by Schemnitz, I paſſed quite under a great hill, and came out on the other ſide. At Windſcach mine, by Schemnitz, they ſhewed me the place where five men and a gentleman of quality were loſt; for which reaſon they have now placed a tube there, the like they place over all doors, and over all ways where they dig right on for a great ſpace, and have not a paſſage through. At Chremnitz they told me that 28 men had been killed at one time in four cuniculi, ſeven in each; and in the ſinking of Leopold's pit, which is 150 fathoms deep, they were much troubled with damps, which they remedied in this manner:

They fixed a tube to the ſide of the ſhaft or pit from the top to the bottom; and that not proving ſufficient, they forced down a broad flat board which covered or ſtopt the pit, or couched very near the ſides of it, on all ſides but where the tube was, and ſo forced out all the air in the pit through the tube; which work they were forced often to repeat: and now, they having divers other paſſages into it, the air is good and ſufficient, and I was drawn up through it without the leaſt trouble in breathing.

But beſides this miſchief from the poiſonous exhalations, the ſtagnation of the air or water impregnated with mineral ſpirits, they ſometimes periſh by other ways: for there being in theſe mines an incredible maſs of wood to ſupport the pits and the horizontal paſſages, (the putei and cuniculi) in all places but where it is rocky, men are ſometimes deſtroyed by the wood ſet on fire. And in the gold mine at Chremnitz, the wood was once ſet on fire by the careleſsneſs of a boy, and 50 miners ſmothered thereby, who were all taken out but one, that was afterwards found to be diſſolved by the vitriol water, nothing eſcaping either of fleſh or bones, but only ſome of his clothes remained. I am, &c.

Vienna, April 20th, 1669.

A Chronological account of the ſeveral Incendium, or Fires of Mount Ætna.

THE preſent fire of Ætna will make it appear not unreaſonable to reflect upon former ages, and to collect from hiſtory the ſeveral eruptions that happened there, together with the times of them, and ſome obſervations recorded by authors relating thereto.

To paſs by what is related by Baroſus, Orpheus, and other leſs credible authors, about the eruptions of this mountain, both at the time of the ingreſs of the Ionian colonies into Sicily, and that of the Argonauts (which latter was in twelfth before the Chriſtian account), we ſhall firſt take notice of that which happened at the time of the expedition of Æneas, who being terrified by the fire of this then burning mountain, left that iſland; whereof Virgil, L. 3, Æneid, gives this notable deſcription:

"Ignarique viæ, Cyclopum allabimur oris,
Portus ab acceſſu ventorum immotus, et ingens
Ipſe; ſed horrificis juxta tonat Ætna ruinis,
Interdumque atram prorumpit ad æthera nubem,
Turbine fumantem piceo et candente favilla,
Attollitque globos flammarum, et ſidera lambit:
Interdum ſcopulos, avulſaque viſcera montis
Erigit eructans, liquefactaque ſaxa ſub auras
Cum gemitu glomerat fundoque exæſtuat imo."

After this we find, in Thucydides, that in the 76 Olympiad, which was about 476 years before Chriſt, there was another eruption, and about 50 years after that another.

Then in the time of the Roman Conſuls there happened four eruptions of Ætna, recorded by Diodorus Siculus and Polybius.

The next was in the time of Julius Cæſar, related by the ſaid Diodorus to have been ſo fierce, that the ſea about Lipara (an iſland near Sicily), by its fervent heat killed all the fiſhes thereabout.

Another we read of in the reign of Caligula, about 40 years after Chriſt, which was ſo dreadful, that it made that Emperor, then being in Sicily, fly from the iſland.

About the martyrdom of the Romiſh St. Agatha it burned again very fiercely; though ſome ſay, that by the virtue of her interceſſion it was ſtayed from reaching Catania.

Again it burſt out A. C. 812, from which time we hear no more of it till 1160; thence, to 1669, all Sicily was ſhaken with many terrible earthquakes, and the eruptions of the ſame mountain deſtroyed a vaſt tract of inhabited land round about it, and reached as far as Catania, the cathedral of which it deſtroyed, and the religious men living in it.

Particularly in the year 1284 there was a terrible eruption, about the time of the death of Charles, King of Sicily and Arragon.

An. 1329, a continued one until 1333. An. 1400, another. An 1444, another, which laſted till 1447. An. 1536, another, which laſted a year. An. 1633, another, continuing ſeveral years. An. 1650, it burſt on the north eaſt ſide, and vomited ſo much fire, that by the lava iſſuing therefrom in torrents, great devaſtation was made, as Kircher relates in his *Mundus Subterraneus,* whoſe aſſiſtance we have made uſe of in the foregoing chronology, together with that of Philotheus.

The ſame author, having been in Sicily himſelf, obſerveth, that the people of Catania, digging pumice-ſtones, do find, at the depth of 100 palms (which is about 68 feet), ſtreets paved with marble, and many footſteps of antiquity; an argument that towns have ſtood there in former ages, which have been overwhelmed by the matter caſt out of this mountain. They have alſo found ſeveral bridges of pumice-ſtones, doubtleſs made by the flux of the fiery torrents, the earth being very much raiſed ſince.

Now, whether theſe eruptions are cauſed by actual ſubterraneous fires, lighting upon combuſtible matter, or by fire ſtruck of falling and breaking ſtones, whoſe ſparks meet with nitro-ſulphurous, or other inflammable ſubſtances, heaped together in the bowels of the earth, and by the expanſive violence of the fire forced to take more room, and ſo burſting out with the impetuoſity we ſee—may not be worthy of a philoſopher's ſpeculation.

Obſervations concerning ſome curious particulars relating to the Bath Springs, &c.

1. THE country round Bath is very hilly and uneven; but the hills lie in no order; they are generally rocky and ſteep from ſouth-weſt and by weſt, to north and by north. The whole tract of the country, within five and ſeven miles, abounds with coal mines, more or leſs; but there are no other conſiderable mines, that I can hear of, nearer than Mendip, which is 10 miles hence, excepting ſome of lead at Berry, in Glouceſterſhire, which lies on the north of this place, about four or five miles diſtant.

2. The hills for the moſt part afford a free-ſtone, and on the north-weſt of Lanſdown (which hath that ſituation to the town, and is juſt above it) the ſtones digged there are a ſort of hard ſtone, commonly called a Lyas, blue and white, poliſhable.

3. The town and baths are of very great antiquity. Beſides what I find in very ancient chronicles to that purpoſe, one of our great antiquaries (M. P.) aſſerts, that theſe baths were 800 years before Chriſt, which, if ſo, would give occaſion to enquire how, conſiſtent with it, that hypotheſis concerning the cauſe of the heat of theſe waters would be, which makes it to be the fermentation of minerals *in fieri*; and whether it be likely, that the minerals through which theſe waters paſs ſhould be in that ſtate of imperfection ſo many hundred years, and that the whole diſpoſed matter in thoſe places ſhould not be perfectly concreted in ſo great a tract of time. The other conjecture ſuppoſeth the cauſe of this heat to be, that two ſtreams having run through, and imbibed certain ſorts of different minerals, meet at laſt, after they have been deeply impregnated, and mingle their liquors, from which commixture ariſes a great fermentation, that cauſes heat, like

as we ſee it is in vitriol and tartar, which, though ſeparately they are not hot, yet when mingled beget an immenſe heat and ebullition between them. This ſeems to me a probable cauſe of the laſtingneſs of the heat of theſe waters. But it is not my buſineſs to offer hypotheſes, ſo will proceed in my account.

4. It is affirmed here, that the town, for the moſt part, is built upon a quagmire, though the places all about it are very firm ground. Some workmen, that have been employed in digging, have found a mire ten feet deep; without the north gate, the higheſt place of the town, at ſeven. The earth between is a kind of rubbiſh. Sometimes they find *pitching* at a man's depth under ground, and paſſages for the water to paſs. Seven or eight feet down they have met with *oyſter ſhells*.

5. The town and country circumjacent generally abound with cold ſprings; and in ſome places the hot and cold ariſe very near each other; in one place within two yards, and in others within eight or nine of the main baths.

6. The guides of the croſs bath inform me, that when there is a great weſt wind abroad, ſtanding by the ſprings they feel a cold air ariſing from beneath; if the wind be at eaſt, and the morning cloſe, with a little miſtling rain, the croſs bath is ſo hot as ſcarce to be endured, when the King's and hot baths are colder than uſual: in other winds, let the weather be how it will, this bath is temperate. The ſprings that bubble moſt are coldeſt. The croſs bath fills in 16 hours, both in winter and ſummer, without any difference from heat or cold, floods or drought. That of the King's fills in 12 or 14.

7. A man may better (ordinarily) endure four hours bathing in the croſs bath, than one and a half in the others. In the Queen's bath (which hath no ſprings of its own, but all out of the King's) they have found under a flat ſtone, which upon occaſion was taken up, a tunnel, and a yielding mud in and under it, into which they thruſt a pike, but could find no bottom. In the King's bath there is a ſpring ſo hot that it is ſcarce ſufferable, ſo that they are fain to turn much of it away, for fear of inflaming the bath. The hotteſt ſpring will not harden an egg.

8. The Bath water does not paſs through the body like other mineral waters; but if you put in ſalt it purgeth preſently. Upon ſettlement it

affords a black mud, uſeful in aches, applied by way of cataplaſm; to ſome more ſucceſsful than the very waters. The like it depoſits on diſtillation, and no other. Nor hath any more been diſcovered upon all the chemical examinations that have come to our knowledge. One Dr. Aſtendoff found, that the colour of the ſalt drawn from the King's, and hot bath, was yellow; that which was extracted from the croſs bath, white. This doctor concluded that the croſs bath had more of alum and nitre than the hotter baths, which abound more with ſulphur. And yet that bath looſens ſhrunk ſinews, by which it ſhould ſeem it abounds not much with alum. It is harſher to the taſte than the other baths, and ſoaks the hands more.

9. A man cannot drink half the quantity of ſtrong drinks in the bath that he can out of it; but if he hath drank before to exceſs, it allays much, and is a great refreſhment to the body. The bath provoketh urine.

10. They are very uſeful in diſeaſes of the head, palſies, epilepſies, and convulſions; in cuticular diſeaſes, leproſies, itches, and ſcabs; in all obſtructions of the bowels, ſpleen, liver, and meſentery; and the ſcirroſity of thoſe parts. In moſt diſeaſes of women; in the ſcurvy and ſtone; as to which laſt, while I am writing, an alderman of the city aſſures me, that his wife, who had been exceedingly troubled with the ſtone, went into the croſs bath for it, and voided there ſeveral ſtones as big as thoſe of olives, and was never troubled with that diſtemper after. The bath is alſo good in cold gouts, as they call them. The ſame alderman tells me, that it gives him preſent eaſe when he is troubled with the fits of it. He uſes to go in as ſoon as the fit takes him, which then goes off preſently, and returns not in a conſiderable time after: he puts his feet upon the hotteſt ſprings in the King's bath. But it hath contrary effects in hot gouts; and ſome who are troubled with that diſtemper tell me, that the bath puts them into a fit, if they go into it without preparation; or if they have the fit before, it inflames it more, and ſends it about the body, and diſables the joints ſo that there is no treading on it for the preſent. Further, the bath is effectual in the diſeaſes of children, particularly the rickets, removing the humours that proceed from it without fail. It is alſo good for women that are apt to miſcarry, if uſed moderately; the bath guides go in when they are ready to lay down: and other women of the town uſe it ordinarily throughout their

time, and are never known to miſcarry. It facilitates deliverance. Beſides, it is very effectual for the ſtrengthening of broken bones, and good in all cold and moiſt diſtempers, and weakneſs of nerves, ſtupefactions, relaxations, and violent pains; in all which it gives eaſe, except the lues venerea, for in that (except the malignity be overcome by the methods of phyſic) it exaſperates the pain more. It is an excellent remedy to remove the remaining weakneſs from gouts, as hath been remarkably exemplified in old men, even to the age of 83 years.

11. There is no inſtance of cures performed by it in former times, but we have experience of the ſame in ours; yea, and in ſome others, as in dropſies, cachexies, ſpleen, &c. in which caſes they were ſhy, heretofore, of uſing the bath, for fear of confirming thoſe obſtructions, whereas it is now found that their cure is facilitated by it.

12. The bath guides live to a very great age, ſometimes to near 100 years; ordinarily, if they are temperate, to 70. There are two at this time above 80, a man and his wife.

13. In the croſs baths the guides have obſerved a certain black fly, with ſcaled wings, in the form of a lady-cow, but ſomewhat bigger: they ſay it ſhoots quick in the water, and ſometimes bites. It lives under the water, and is never found but in very hot weather. They ſuppoſe it comes up with the ſprings. It is not to be ſeen elſewhere. I had one of theſe inſects ſent me laſt year, which I preſerved till I came to London, but loſt it there, I know not how.

14. The croſs bath eats out ſilver exceedingly; and I am told that a ſhilling, in a week's time, hath been ſo eaten by it that it might be wound about one's finger. The baths agree (as it is vulgarly ſaid) with braſs, but not with iron; for they will eat out a ring of this metal in ſeven years, when braſs rings ſeem to receive no prejudice at all from it.

15. When women have waſhed their hair with the mixture of beaten eggs and oatmeal, this will poiſon the bath ſo as to beget a moſt noiſome ſmell, caſting a ſea-green on the water, which otherwiſe is very pure and limpid. This will taint the very walls, and there is no cleanſing of it but by drawing the bath.

16. The baths purge up a green ſcum on the top, but in winter never; then they leave a yellow on the walls.

17. The walls that keep in the hot ſprings are very deep ſet, and large; 10 feet thick, and 14 deep, from the level of the ſtreet. The cement of the wall is tallow, clay, lime, and beaten bricks. In the year 1659 the hot bath (a bath particularly ſo called, of equal heat with the King's bath) was much impaired by the breaking out of a ſpring, which the workmen at laſt found again, and reſtored. In digging they came to a firm foundation of factitious matter, which had holes in it like a pumice-ſtone, through which the water played; ſo that it is likely the ſprings are brought together by art, which probably was the necromancy the people of ancient times believed and reported to have contrived and made theſe baths; as in a very ancient manuſcript chronicle I find theſe words: "*When* Lud Hidibras *was dead,* Bladud, *his ſon, a great necromancer* (ſo it is there written) *was made King,* and made the wonder of the hot bath *by his nygromany; and he reigned* 21 *years; and after he died, and lies at the New Troy.*" And in another old chronicle it is ſaid, that "King Bladud *ſent for necromancers to Athens to effect this great buſineſs;*" who it is like were no other than cunning artificers, well ſkilled in architecture and mechanics.

18. It hath been obſerved, that leaves, like thoſe of olives, come ſometimes out of the pump of the hot bath.

Extract of a letter written by Mr. Murattus, of Zurich, to M. Haak, Fellow of the ROYAL SOCIETY, *concerning the Icy and Chryſtalline Mountains of Helvetia, called the Gletſcher; tranſlated from the Latin.*

THE higheſt icy mountains of Helvetia, about Valeſia and Auguſta, in the canton of Bern; about Taminium and Tavetſch of the Rhætians, are always ſeen covered with ſnow; which being melted by the heat of the ſummer, other ſnow being fallen, within a little while after is hardened into ice, which by little and little, in a long tract of time, depurating itſelf, turns into a ſtone, not yielding in hardneſs and clearneſs to chryſtal. Such ſtones cloſely joined and compacted together, compoſe a whole mountain, and that a very firm one; though in ſummer time the country people have obſerved it to burſt aſunder, with great cracking, like thunder; which is alſo well known to hunters, to their great coſt, foraſmuch as ſuch cracks and opneings, being by the winds covered with ſnow, are the death of thoſe that would paſs over them.

At the foot of theſe mountains, with great labour, are dug out chryſtals, which are found amongſt other foſſils, of two ſorts of colours; ſome of them are darkiſh and troubled, which by ſome are called the chryſtal-ore, to be plenteouſly found in the aſcent of Mount Gothard; others tranſparent, very pure, and as clear as Venice glaſs, ſexangular, great and ſmall; and in the mountains about Valeſia, and the town called Urſelen, at the foot of the hill Schelenin, they are dug out, and ſold at a good rate. Of this latter kind my parents, four years ago, transmitted a very big and fair one to Milan, for 80 pounds ſterling.

Some obſervations concerning Japan, made by an ingenious traveller, that reſided many years in that country. Communicated from the French, in conſequence of former queries relating to the ſubject matter.

1. THE Japaneſe doubt not at all of their country being an iſland, though it be ſeparated from the continent by ſuch narrow channels that no veſſel of any conſiderable burthen can paſs them.

2. The air is there very ſalubrious, but of another temper on this than on that ſide of the mountains which divide Japan. The plague hath never been heard of there; but the ſmall pox and fluxes are very frequent.

3. Their mountains are fertile almoſt to the very tops.

4. Almoſt all ſorts of European fruits are found there; ſuch as peaches, apricots, cherries, prunes, apples, pears, and particularly pippins, and bon chretien pears. Beſides theſe, there is an infinity of other fruit; but almoſt none but what is found in ſome part or other of India.

5. Silver is there in its higheſt perfection, but not uſed in trade, in which is ſeen nothing but gold, and ſome ſmall coin of braſs, which latter they ſpoil by refining too much. Steel alſo is there very good.

6. The temper of their metals was formerly better than it is now; but yet they make *cutlaſſes*, or ſhort ſwords, exceeding good.

7. The great mountain in Japan is higher than the Pico in Teneriffe, ſince being above 18 leagues diſtant from the ſea ſide, it may be ſeen above 40 leagues off at ſea. There are eight *vulcans* (vulcanos), or fire-ſpitting mountains in Japan; and you cannot go into the champaign but you diſcover one or other of them.

8. There are many medicinal waters and hot ſprings there, which the inhabitants uſe in their diſtempers. They have particular medicines, but they let no blood. They make much uſe of cauſtics, by applying upon ſome nerve or other the powder of artimeſea, or mugwort, and cotton, which they ſet on fire. They always drink their liquors warm.

9. There is ſo great a ſtore of veniſon in Japan, that they care little for cattle, though there be no want of them. They employ moſtly oxen for ploughing; and they make no butter nor cheeſe; nor are they lovers of milk. They have great plenty of corn and rice.

10. The Japaneſe are proper enough of ſtature, and not uncomely in features: they have ſomewhat prominent bellies. They are exceeding active, and want no judgment. They are alſo military and valiant.

11. No arts are to be met with amongſt them that are not known in Europe, except that of making Laca, of which there is ſome ſo fine and curious, that whereas in this country one may buy an ordinary ſmall box for three or four crowns, one of the ſame ſize, when made in Japan, of exquiſite laca, will ſell for more than 1000 crowns. The author of this account has four cabinets of this workmanſhip, which he avers to have coſt him above 40,000 crowns, and which he would not part with for double that ſum.

12. The colours with which they dye their ſtuffs never fade: I have ſeen one of them, which our vermilion and *couleur de feu* come not near to. It is extracted out of a flower like to ſaffron, one pound of which coſts an incredible price. To try whether the colour will not change by lixivium or lye, they apply a hot iron to it, and if there it holds, they aſſure themſelves of the durableneſs of the colour.

13. They have mathematicians amongſt them, and believe judiciary aſtrology; inſomuch that the grandees undertake nothing without pre-conſulting thoſe that make profeſſion of the ſame.

14. Japan yields divers ſorts of good merchantable commodities; but

chiefly all ſorts of ſilken ſtuffs, unwrought ſilk, amber, precious ſtones, muſk, copper, ſteel, lack-work.

15. The country is very well peopled, and exceeding rich, being vaſtly ſtored with gold mines; and I have ſeen ſome of the gold ore, which out of 10 ounces yielded eight of the higheſt fineneſs, and pieces of the weight of 120 marks.

16. Their buildings are very good and commodious: the apartments are all below, on the ground, ſeparated from one another by partitions of carton, painted and gilt, which may be folded and removed like ſcreens. Their floors are covered with mats, and ſometimes with ſilken ſtuffs, embroidered velvet, and cloth of gold. All their buildings are but one ſtory high.

17. They have no other conveniences to defend themſelves from heat and cold, but ſuch as are uſual in Italy and Spain.

18. They uſe the divertiſements of comedies, which are more brave than thoſe of Europe. The ſpectators are about 200 paces diſtant from the theatre, which being covered with a vault, makes the voice of the actors to be underſtood to the very end of the theatre. They love hunting, and gaming, as dice, cards, cheſs, &c. At all times of the day, and in all their viſits, they take *thea* (tea), and tobacco.

19. Their language is altogether different from the Chineſe; but their prieſts and courteſans, that is the learned amongſt them, which bear the offices of the court, underſtanding the tongue of Cochin China, and by this means that of Tonquin, China, Corea, &c. They write neither from the right to the left, nor from the left to the right, but downward.

20. The government is deſpotic: the religion Pagan. The Chriſtian hated upon no other account, but that ſome of thoſe, who there profeſſed it, would perſuade the Japaneſe to acknowledge a ſuperiority above dignity royal, diſpoſing of crown and ſceptres. Their morals are very good, their *faults* being puniſhed as their *crimes*, even *lying* and *detraction*. Their left hand is the more honourable, and they take horſe on that ſide.

An account from Paris concerning a great metaline burning Concave, and ſome of the moſt conſiderable effects of it, communicated by ſeveral perſons upon the plate where trials have been made of it.

IT is true that Monſieur de Vilette of Lyons, who formerly made that burning concave, which was of about 30 inches diameter, (diſpoſed of to the King of Denmark) hath made another, which is larger, now under trial here. It is of 34 inches diameter, and melts all ſorts of metals, and iron itſelf of the thickneſs of a ſilver crown in leſs than a minute of time, and vitrifies brick in the ſame time; and as for wood, whether green or dry, it ſets it on fire in a moment. The King has ſeen it, and the performances of it, with great ſatisfaction; and his Majeſty is likely to make it his, and then to beſtow it on the ROYAL ACADEMY OF PHILOSOPHERS, for making of further experiments therewith.*

An invention for eſtimating the weight of Water in Water, with ordinary balances and weights.

THE author of this invention was the noble Robert Boyle, who was pleaſed to comply with our deſires of communicating it to the curious in England through the medium of the ROYAL SOCIETY. And it will doubtleſs be the more welcome, foraſmuch as nobody we know of hath ſo much as attempted to determine, *how much* water may weigh in water; and poſſibly if ſuch a problem had been propoſed, it would have been judged impracticable.

The method or expedient he made uſe of to perform it may be eaſily learned by the enſuing account of a trial or two he made for that purpoſe, which, amongſt his notes, he cauſed to be regiſtered in the following words:

A glaſs bubble about the bigneſs of a pullets egg was purpoſely blown at

* This kind of concave burning more forcibly than any fire we know of, even beyond that of a wind furnace, would be of great uſe, if they could be ſo contrived as to have a focus of any conſiderable largeneſs ſo as to take in the compaſs of a good quantity of combuſtible matter at once.

the flame of a lamp, with a ſomewhat long ſtem turned up at the end, that it might the more conveniently be broken off. This bubble being well heated to rarify the air, and thereby drive out a good part of it, was nimbly ſealed at the end, and by the help of the figure at the ſtem, was by a convenient weight of lead depreſſed under water, the lead and glaſs being tied by a ſtring to one ſcale of a good balance, in whoſe other there was put ſo much weight as ſufficed to counterpoiſe the bubble as it hung freely in the midſt of the water. Then with a long iron forceps I carefully broke off the ſealed end of the bubble under water, ſo as no bubble of air appeared to emerge or eſcape through the water, when the liquor by the weight of the atmoſphere ſprung into the unreplenished part of the glaſs bubble, and filled the whole cavity about half full; and preſently, as I foretold, the bubble ſubſided, and made the ſcale it was faſtened to preponderate ſo much that there needed four drachms and 38 grains to reduce the balance to an equilibrium. Then taking out the bubble with the water in it, we did, by the help of the flame of a candle, warily applied, drive out the water (which otherwiſe is not eaſily excluded at a very narrow ſtern) into a glaſs counterpoiſed before; and we found it, as we expected, to weigh about four drachms 30 grains, beſides ſome little that remained in the egg, and ſome ſmall matter that may have been rarified into vapours, which added to the piece of glaſs that was broken off under water, and loſt there, might very well amount to ſeven or eight grains; by which it appears, not only that water hath ſome weight in water, but that it weighs very near, or altogether as much in water as the ſelf-ſame portion of liquor would weigh in the air.

The ſame day we repeated the experiment with another ſealed bubble larger than the former (being as big as a great hen-egg); and having broken this under water it grew heavier by ſeven drachms and 34 grains; and having taken out the bubble, and driven out the water into a counterpoiſed glaſs, we found the tranſvaſated liquor to amount to the ſame weight, abating ſix or ſeven grains, which it might well have upon ſuch accounts as have been newly mentioned.

Some obſervations relating to the odd turn of Shell Snails, and the darting of Spiders, tranſmitted by letter to a Member of the ROYAL SOCIETY.

SIR,

AS you wiſh to know of me what I have obſerved concerning the odd turn of ſome ſhell ſnails with us in England, and the darting of ſpiders, I will tell you then of *firſt*, that I have found two ſorts of them, eaſily to be diſtinguiſhed one from the other, and from all beſides, becauſe the turn of the wreaths is from the right hand to the left, contrary to what may be ſeen in common ſnails. They are very ſmall, and might therefore well eſcape, thus long, the more curious naturaliſts, neither of them much exceeding, at leaſt in thickneſs, a large oat-corn.

The firſt I thus deſcribe:—The open of the ſhell is pretty round, the ſecond turn or wreath is very large for the proportion, and the reſt of the wreaths, about the number of ſix, are ſtill leſſened to a point. This turban or conical figure, is well near a quarter of an inch; the colour of the ſhell is duſkiſh, yet when the ſhrunk animal gives leave you may ſee light through it, and then it is of a yellowiſh colour. Theſe ſhells are extremely brittle and tender, ſo that I cannot ſend them in a letter: you may gueſs at the figure, if I tell you they are ſomething like thoſe of Aldrovandus de Teſtaccis, marked page 359, Turbinum lanium.

Of the ſecond ſort I ſend you incloſed at a venture half a dozen, they ſeem to be much ſtronger and thicker ſhelled than the former, they are near half as long again as the other and as ſlender; they have the exact figure of oat-corn, being, as it were, pointed at both ends, and the middle a little ſwelled. The open of the ſhell is not exactly round, there being a peculiar ſinus in the lower part thereof. I think you may number about ten ſpires, having their turn from the right hand to the left. The colour of the ſhell is of a dark and reddiſh brown.

There are two ſorts of this make deſcribed, and with their reſpective cuts, in *Fabius Columna*, but ours agree not with them in any thing more than the odd turn, though 'tis true that the other, the third there deſcribed, and called by him *Cochlea Terreſtris turbinata et ſtreata*, is very frequent in the road between Canterbury and Dover, and likewiſe in ſome woody parts of the Wolds in Lincolnſhire. There are odd differences in this very ſnail, very remarkable, as its having but one pair of horns, as alſo a hard ſhelly cover, its manner of wearing that cover, &c. which I leave to another opportunity and place.

And to return to our two now deſcribed ſnails, they, when they creep, lift up the points of their ſhells towards a perpendicular, and exert with part of their body two pair of horns, as moſt of their kind do.

In March they are ſtill to be found in pairs. Ariſtotle affirms all theſe kind of creatures to be of a ſpontaneous birth, and no more to contribute to the production of one another than trees, and therefore have no diſtinction of ſex. I have no reaſon to ſubſcribe to his authority ſince I have ſeen ſo many of them paired, and in the very act of venery. That they engender then, is moſt certain ; but whether thoſe that are found thus coupled, be one of them male and the other female, or rather as you obſerved and publiſhed at large in the catalogue of plants growing wild about Cambridge, that they are both male and female, and do, in the act of generation, act in both capacities, as will appear evident to any one who ſhall part them at ſuch time.

Moreover, we find in Ariſtotle a circle of other parts, but of this no mention at all. However the Romans knew ſomething extraordinary of theſe kind of animals that made them ſo choice, as to reckon them amongſt their moſt delicate food, and uſe all care and diligence to breed and fat them for their tables, as at large deſcribed to us by Varro.

Of late, comparing Buſſy's Hiſtoire Amoureuſe de Gauli, with Petronius Arbiter, out of whom I was made to believe he had taken two of his letters, word for word, beſide other love intrigues, I found, in running him over, what ſatisfied me not a little in this very ſubject of ſnails, viz. that theſe animals, as well as other odd things in nature, as *truffs*, muſhrooms, and no doubt too the coſſi, or great worms in the oak (another Roman dainty) were made uſe of by the ancients to incite venery. You will there find that the diſtreſſed and feeble lover prepares himſelf with a *ragout* of ſnails' necks (*cervices cochlearum*) and indeed in this part it is, that theſe ſtrange parts of generation are found.

Mr. Hook does as it were, promiſe the anatomy of this inſect. It was ſurely worth his pains, and the learned world would be obliged to him for a piece of this nature; nothing accurately done, of the inward part of any inſect being yet publiſhed*.

Theſe ſnails are to be found frequent enough under the looſe bark of trees, as old willows, and in the ragged clefts of elms and oaks, &c, and in no other place elſe, that I could obſerve.

You tell me that it is generally concluded by philoſophers, that the reaſon of the uſual turn of ſnails from the left to the right, is the like motion of the ſun, and that eſpecially more northward, (there having not been hitherto diſcovered in our parts an inſtance of the contrary) they turn to the ſun's motion. But this is not the only caſe where thoſe are out, who conſult not the ſtores of nature, but their own fancy. What I am further about to tell you concerning ſpiders, is an evident inſtance.

The long threads in the air in ſummer, and eſpecially towards September, have been a ſtrange puzzle to the wiſer world. It would divert you if I here reckoned up the ridiculous opinions concerning them; but I omit them, and proceed to tell you the immediate authors of theſe threads, and how they make them.

I ſay then that all ſpiders that ſpin in a thread, (thoſe that we call ſhepherds, or long-legged ſpiders, never do) are the makers of theſe threads, ſo much wondered at, and in ſuch infinite quantities every where.

I ſent you laſt ſummer a catalogue of thirty ſorts of ſpiders, that I had diſtinguiſhed here with us in England; and I muſt confeſs, I had well near completed that number, with many experiments concerning them, before I diſcovered this ſecret.

I had exactly marked all the ways of weaving, uſed by any ſorts of them, and in thoſe admirable works I had ever noted, that they ſtill let down the thread they made uſe of, and drew it after them. Happily at length, by minutely attending on one that wrought a net, I ſaw him ſuddenly in the midwork, to deſiſt, and turning his tail into the wind, to dart out a thread with the violence and ſtream we ſee water ſpout out of a jet: this thread taken up by wind, was in a moment emitted ſome fathoms long, ſtill iſſuing out of the belly of the animal; and by and by the ſpider leapt into the air, and the thread mounted him up ſwiftly.

After this firſt diſcovery, I made the like obſervation in almoſt all the ſorts of ſpiders I had before diſtinguiſhed; and I found the air filled with young

* When this was written Malpigius de Bombyce was not publiſhed.

and old ſailing on their threads, and undoubtedly ſeizing gnats and other inſects in their paſſage; there being often as manifeſt ſigns of ſlaughter, as legs, wings of flies, &c. on thoſe threads, as in their webs below.

One thing was yet a wonder to me, *viz.* that many of theſe threads that came down from the air, were not ſingle, but ſnarled, and with complicated woolly locks, now more, now leſs; and that on theſe I did not always find ſpiders, though many times I had found two or three upon one of them: whereas when they firſt flew up, the thread was ſtill ſingle, or but little tangled, or it may be, thicker in one place than another. In the end, by good attention, I plainly found what ſatisfied me abundantly, which was this, that I obſerved them to get to the top of a ſtalk or bough, or ſome ſuch like thing, where they exerciſe this darting of threads into the air. And if they had not a mind to ſail, they either ſwiftly drew it up again, winding it up with their fore-feet over their heads into a lock, or break it off ſhort, and let the air carry it away. This they will do many times together, and you may ſee of them that have chains of theſe locks or ſnarled thread before them, and yet not taken flight.

Again, I found, that after the firſt flight, all the time of their ſailing they make locks, ſtill darting forth freſh ſupplies of thread to ſport and ſail by.

It is further to be noted, that theſe complicated threads are much more tender than our houſe-webs.

In winter I have obſerved them buſy in darting, but few of them ſail then, and therefore but ſingle threads only are to be ſeen; and beſides they are but the young ones of laſt autumn's hatch, that are then employed; and it is more than probable that the great ropes of autumn are made only by the great ones, and upon long paſſages in ſummer weather, when great numbers of prey may invite them to ſtay longer up.

But I ceaſe to be tedious: I have many experiments by me to ſatiſfy any doubts that may be made, *viz.* of the infinite number of theſe inſects, and their numberleſs increaſe; and beſides how ſtrangely they are able to furniſh and huſband ſuch great quantities of matter out of ſo ſmall a bulk, &c.

You may expect all from me after another ſummer's leiſure, which I think at leaſt neceſſary to confirm to me theſe, and other things concerning their generation and poiſon. What I have ſaid at preſent, is ſuch as I have certainly obſerved; and you may take the truth of theſe obſervations for excuſe of the ill texture of them.

An anſwer to ſome enquiries concerning the eruptions of Mount Ætna, Ann. 1669. *Communicated by ſome Engliſh Merchants at that time reſiding in Sicily.*

TOUCHING the fore-runners of this fire, there was, for the ſpace of 18 days, before it broke out, a very thick dark ſky in thoſe parts, with thunder and lightning, and frequent concuſſions of the earth, which the people make terrible reports of; and though we never ſaw or heard of any buildings caſt down thereby, ſave a ſmall town or village, called Nicoloſi, about half a mile diſtant from the new mouth, and ſome ſuch other ſlight buildings amongſt thoſe towns, that were afterwards over-run by the fire (*lava*). Beſides it was obſerved that the old top, or mouth of Ætna, did for two or three months before, rage more than uſual; the like of which did Vulcan and Strombolo, two burning iſlands to the weſtward. And the top of Ætna muſt at the ſame time have ſunk down into its old *vorago* or hole, in that it is agreed by all who had ſeen this mountain before, that it was very much lowered: other fore-runners of this fire we have not heard or met with.

It firſt broke out on the 11th of March 1669, about two hours before night, and that on the ſouth-eaſt ſide, or ſkirt of the mountain, about 20 miles below, and 10 miles from Catania. At firſt it was reported to advance three miles in 24 hours; but at our being there, (*viz.* April 5th) when we were come within a ſhort mile of Catania, it ſcarce moved after the rate of a furlong a day; and in this degree of progreſs it continued for 15 or 20 days after, paſſing under the walls of Catania a good way into the ſea; but about the latter end of this month, and the beginning of May (whether it was that the ſea could not receive this matter faſt enough, or rather that the mouth above did caſt forth a larger quantity) it bent all its force againſt the city; and having wrought itſelf up even with the walls thereof, over it paſſed in divers places; but its chief fury fell upon a very ſtately convent, which was that of the Benedictines, having large gardens and other ground betwixt them and the wall; which when it had filled up, it fell with all its force on the convent, where it met with a ſtrong reſiſtance, which made it ſwell, (as it uſually did where it met with any obſtruction) almoſt as high as the higher ſhops in the old London Exchange, this convent being built much after that faſhion, though conſiderably bigger. Some parts of this wall were driven

4

in, whole and entire, almoſt a foot, as appeared by the riſing of the tiles in the midſt of the floor, and bending of the iron bars that went acroſs above. And it is certain, had this torrent fallen in ſome other part of the town, it would have made great havock amongſt their ordinary buildings; but here its fury ceaſed the 4th May, running hence forward in little channels or ſtreams, and that chiefly into the ſea. It had overwhelmed in the upland country 14 towns and villages, whereof ſome were of good note, containing three or four thouſand inhabitants, and ſtanding in a very pleaſant and fruitful country, where the fire had never made any devaſtation before; but now there is not ſo much as any ſign, where ſuch towns have ſtood; only the church and ſteeple of one of them, which ſtood alone upon an high ground, does ſtill appear.

As to the matter which thus run, it was nothing elſe but divers kinds of metals and minerals, rendered liquid by the fierceneſs of the fire in the bowels of the earth, boiling up, and guſhing forth, like as water doth at the head of ſome great river; and having run in a full body, a good ſtone's caſt or more, the extremities thereof began to cruſt or curdle, becoming, when cold, thoſe hard and porous ſtones which the people call ſciarri, having the neareſt reſemblance to huge cakes of ſea coal, full of a fierce fire. They come rolling and tumbling over one another, and where they meet with a bank, would fill up and ſwell over, by their weight bearing down any common building, and burning up what was combuſtible. The chief motion of this matter was forward, but it was alſo dilating itſelf, as a flood of water would do on even ground, thruſting out ſeveral arms or tongues as they call them.

About two or three o'clock in the night we mounted an high tower in Catania, whence we had a full view of the mouth; which was a terrible ſight, being ſo great a maſs or body of mere fire. Next monring we would have gone up to the mouth itſelf, but durſt not come nearer than a furlong off, for fear of being overwhelmed by a ſudden turn of the wind, which carried up into the air ſome of that vaſt pillar of aſhes, which to our apprehenſion exceeded twice the bigneſs of Paul's ſteeple in London, and went up in a ſtraight body to a far greater height than that; the whole air being thereabout all filled with the lighteſt of thoſe aſhes blown off from the top of this pillar: and from the firſt breaking forth of the fire, until its fury ceaſed (being 54 days) neither ſun or ſtar was ſeen in all that part.

From the outſide of this pillar fell off great quantities of ſtones, but none very big, neither could we difcern any fire in them, nor come to fee where that fiery ftuff broke out, there being a great bank or hill of afhes between it and us.

At the mouth, whence iffued the fire or afhes, or both, was a continual noife, like the beating of great waves of the fea againft rocks, or like thunder afar off, which fometimes I have heard here in Meffina, though fituated at the foot of high hills, and 60 miles off. It hath alfo been heard 100 miles northward of this place, in Calabria (as I have been credibly informed), whither the afhes have alfo been carried: and fome of our feamen have alfo reported that their decks were covered therewith at Zant, though it is likely not very thick.

Of thofe burnt ftones of fciarri, I have fome by me of divers qualities, and fhall procure what more I can, to be fent by the firft paffage.

About the middle of May, we made another journey thither, where we found the face of things much altered, the city of Catania being three quarters of it compaffed round with thefe fciarri, as high as the top of the walls, and in many places it had broke over. The firft night of our arrival a new ftream or gutter of fire broke forth among fome fciarri, which we were walking upon an hour or two before, and they were as high as to be even with the top of the wall. It poured itfelf down into the city in a fmall gutter of about three feet broad, and nine feet long, of mere fire, the extremities ftill falling off into thofe fciarri; but this ftream was extinct by the next morning, though it had filled up a great void fpace with its fciarri. The next night there was a much bigger channel difcovered, pouring itfelf over another part of the wall into the caftle-ditch, which continued (as we were informed) fome days after our departure. Divers of thofe fmall rivulets did run, at the fame time into the fea, and it does fo at this time of writing, though faintly.

It was obferved that thofe ftreams of fire never grew broader, nor vifibly longer, nor moved out of the place they were firft feen in; which put us a little more to examine their working, and we concluded, that not only then, but in the fury alfo of its running, it made itfelf certain crufted gutters to run in, to keep itfelf as it were from the air, which, by degrees did cool and fix it, as more plainly appeared above at the mouth, where, the firft time of our going thither, we found fciarri generally thus fuperficially cooled and fixed. And hence alfo it might proceed, that thefe live fciarri, meeting with any bank or high ground, would puff and fwell up, 'till they had overcome it; ſo that in many places, eſpecially under the walls of Catania, were vallies of thoſe ſciarri, where the fire never broke forth, or diſcovered itſelf in thoſe ſtreams, until it had gained its height; for thoſe rivulets ever went declining.

Having ſpent a couple of days about Catania, we again went up to the mouth, where now without any danger of fire or aſhes, we could take a fair view both of the old and new channel of the fire, and of that great mountain of aſhes caſt up. That, which we gueſſed to be the old bed or channel, was a three-cornered plot of about two acres, with a cruſt of ſciarri at the bottom, and upon that a ſmall cruſt or ſurface of brimſtone. It was hedged on each ſide with a great bank or hill of aſhes, and behind that, at the upper end, roſe up that huge mountain of the ſame matter. Between theſe two banks the *fire* ſeems to have had its paſſage. At the upper end, in the nook, upon a little hillock of cruſted ſciarri, was an hole about ten feet wide, whence it is probable the *fire* iſſued; and it might have had ſeveral other ſuch *holes*, ſince, either cruſted over, or covered with aſhes. At the bottom of this hole the *fire* was ſeen to flow along, and below it was a channel of *fire*, beneath that ſurface of ſciarri, which being cleft at top for ſome ſpace, we had an eaſy and leiſurable view of the metal (lava now called) flowing along, the ſuperficies of which might be a yard broad, though, probably it carried a great breadth underneath, the gutter going ſloping. What depth it had, we could not gueſs: it was impenetrable by iron hooks and other inſtruments we had. We were very deſirous to have gotten ſome of this matter at the ſpring head, but we could penetrate no more into it, than with one's finger into the palm of the hand. It is likely that ſome running might have been more yielding than we found this. From this channel, but eſpecially from that *hole* above it, iſſued great ſtore of a ſtrong ſulphurous ſmoke, wherewith ſome of our company were at firſt almoſt ſtifled through inadvertency. About once in a quarter of an hour there would riſe a pillar of ſmoke or aſhes, but nothing comparable to the former; which ſeemed to come from the middle top of that new made mountain. I confeſs it was an omiſſion in us not to go up to this mountain, being ſo near; but becauſe it was troubleſome, and not without danger, the reſt of the company being ſatisfied with what they had already ſeen, would not ſtay to ſee any more.

At this, our laſt being at Catania, we found the people buſy in barricading the ends of ſome ſtreets and paſſages where they thought the fire might break in; and this they did by pulling down the old houſes thereabout, and laying up the looſe ſtones in manner of a wall, which they ſaid would reſiſt the *fire*, as not being mixt with lime; though it was the great weight and force of that fiery matter in preſſing forward, and not its burning, that overthrew the buildings, as plainly appeared in the convent of the benedictines, and in the town walls, where the great deluge of fire did pour itſelf, it not breaking into the city, but pouring itſelf over the walls, as hath been ſaid.

Unto this very time 'tis ſaid to have run a mile into the ſea, and as much in front though it was much leſs when we were there. The ſhore goes gently declining, having at the extremity of the ſciarri about five fathoms, and about half as much they are above the water.

The ſuperficies of the water, for 20 feet or more, over thoſe rivulets of fire, was hotter than to endure one's hand in it, though *deeper* it was *more* temperate, and thoſe live ſciarri ſtill retained their fire under water, as we ſaw when the ſurges of the ſea retreated back in their ordinary reverberations.

The general face of the ſciarri is in ſome reſpect not much unlike, from the beginning to the end, to the river Thames in a great froſt at the top of the ice above bridge, I mean lying after ſuch a rugged manner, in great flakes; but its colour is quite different, being moſtly of a dark duſky blue, and ſome ſtones or rocks of a vaſt bigneſs, cloſe and ſolid.

But notwithſtanding their ruggedneſs, and ſtore of fire which we could ſee glowing in the clifts and cavities, we made ſhift to ramble over a good part of them; and 'tis ſaid alſo, that people would do the ſame in its greateſt violence of burning. For as thoſe live ſciarri, and thoſe rivers of *fire* themſelves were ſo tough and impenetrable as to bear my weight, ſo the ſuperficies of the ſciarri might be touched and handled, the fire being inward, and not to be diſcerned but near at hand, eſpecially in the day time: and it was ſomewhat a ſtrange ſight to ſee ſo great a river come ſo tamely forward; for, as it approached unto any houſe, they not only at good leiſure removed their goods, but alſo the tiles and beams, and what elſe was moveable in their dwellings.

'Tis obſervable that none of thoſe who went to ſee it, when there was little elſe to be ſeen but the cold ſciarri, but declared to have found it a very different thing to what they imagined, though related to them *viva voce* by thoſe who had formerly been there.

I ſhall at preſent only add, that the whole country from the very walls of Catania to twenty miles on this ſide, is full of thoſe old ſciarri which former eruptions have caſt forth, though the people remember none ſo great as this I have been ſpeaking of, or that ever burſt out ſo low. This country is, notwithſtanding, well cultivated and inhabited, for length of time hath either mollified much of thoſe old ſciarri, or new mould or aſhes have overgrown them, though there ſtill remains a conſiderable portion, which it is probable will never become ſerviceable.

What is the perpendicular height of this mountain I cannot learn. It cannot perhaps be rightly taken, being ſo ſubject to alter its height and ſhape. But it is a very goodly mountain to look upon as one paſſes by ſea to the eaſtward, ſtanding alone, and riſing from the very ſhore, and at the ſhorteſt paſſage is reckoned twenty miles up to the top, though from Catania it is thirty miles remote.

A particular account of divers minerals caſt up and burned by the late fire at Mount Ætna, preſented by ſome Engliſh Merchants to the ROYAL SOCIETY.

SINCE it cannot but conſiderably conduce to the rendering a rational account of the cauſe of ſuch fiery eruptions as are frequently made by divers mountains, if the matters by them caſt up, be well examined, in regard that if they are found to be of an eaſily inflammable nature they may quickly be kindled by ſome falling ſtones, which, breaking in pieces, may ſtrike ſparks into, and ſo ſet on fire ſuch combuſtible matter as they may light upon; it was thought it would not be amiſs, by favour of our friends in Sicily, to procure from the lately flaming mountain there what minerals they ſhould be able to get upon the place. And accordingly we received by a ſhip lately arrived from Meſſina:

Firſt, a good quantity of aſhes, taken up in divers parts of and about Ætna, ſome at the top or mouth of the new made mountain, ſome a mile off, ſome four, ſome ten miles, ſome but half a mile diſtant, and others on the ſkirts of the ſaid mountain; whereof the four firſt were found to agree well enough with their diſtances, but the two laſt to differ much, both from the former and from one another; the former four ſorts having been found very dry, like duſt, but the two latter being ſtill very moiſt, though in Sicily (as we are informed) they have *layen* a good while expoſed to the hot ſun; beſides that the two laſt differ from one another, in that one ſort of them conſiſts of ſmall and hard lumps, the other of very ſoft dirty grains, yet both ſoft and of a vitriolic taſte.

Secondly, ſome of the cinders, which the people of Sicily call ſciarri, whereof ſome are coarſer, taken up at a diſtance from the mouth; and of theſe, ſome black with a cruſt of brimſtone, ſome of a red hue, others finer, ſaid to be taken out of the gutters of fire at the very mouth. Both theſe kinds are light; but then there is a third ſort of ſtone, very ſolid and ponderous, which ſeems to be made up of a conflux of divers minerals, melted together.

Thirdly, a piece of ſal-ammoniac and ſeveral pieces of ſandever, beſides thoſe moiſt vitriolic aſhes abovementioned.

All which was accompanied with a map of that part of the country where the fire hath run, in which map the ſcale of a mile was annexed, thereby to ſhow more accurately the extent of the fire, which appears to have ſpread about three miles in breadth, and extended about 17 in length; the ſame being now quite extinct, but that only in the clefts or hollowneſſes of the rocks of ſciarri ſome fire ſtill remains glowing.

An extract of a letter written by Dr. Wm. Durſton, to the Right Hon. Lord Viſcount Brunker, Preſident of the ROYAL SOCIETY.

MY LORD,

IN obedience to the commands of the Right Honourable the Lord Ambaſſador for Barbary I preſent your Lordſhip with a phænomenon and matter of fact in nature, which, for its rarity and prodigiouſneſs, may, with a leſſer check to me from your Lordſhip for the preſumption, and a leſſer regret for the avocation, obtain the favour of your peruſal. The thing is evident, and can be well atteſted by thouſands, but above all the reſt by his Excellency, the ſaid Lord Ambaſſador, who was an eye-witneſs of it, and impoſed this taſk on me of giving your Lordſhip a perfect narrative of the wonder, which is as follows:—

Elizabeth Trevers, 23 or 24 years of age, fair of complexion, brown haired, of an healthy conſtitution, low of ſtature, of honeſt repute, but of mean and poor parentage, near this town (Plymouth) was on Friday, July 3, 1669, in good health, and went well to bed, where ſhe took as good reſt and ſleep as ever before, but in the morning when ſhe awakened and attempted to turn herſelf in her bed, was not able, finding her breaſts ſo ſwelled that ſhe was affrighted to an aſtoniſhment. Then endeavouring to ſit up, the weight of her breaſts faſtened her to her bed, where ſhe hath lain ever ſince, yet without pain or weakneſs, either in her breaſts or in any other part.

This being noiſed abroad, ſeveral Phyſicians and Surgeons reſorted to her: ſome propoſed cutting off her breaſts, which I was wholly againſt, adviſing for the preſent an emollient and temperately warm *fotus*, and one gave her a bolus with ******; upon the taking of which ſhe had ten motions *deorſum*, and the ſwelling ſomewhat abated; but the maid was ſo weakened upon it for two or three days after, that I durſt not attempt any thing of that nature ſince; ſed quia paſſa fuit ſuppreſſionem menſium per ſex retro menſes, diuretica non nulla, et ſanguinis menſtrui prolectamenta præſcripſi, intending alſo phlebotomy.

The tubuli or pipes of the breaſts are all very hard and ſwelled; and, indeed the whole breaſts ſeem to be nothing elſe but thoſe tubuli, and little or nothing of wind or water. As near as we can gueſs, the left breaſt weighs about 25 pounds, but the right ſomewhat leſs; and the ſkin of the back, neck, and belly ſeems to be drawn toward the breaſts to ſerve for the diſtention. The meaſures of the breaſts are theſe :—

	feet.	inches.
The circumference of the right breaſt - - -	2	7
Of the left breaſt - - - - - - -	3	1½
Length of the right breaſt from the collar-bone - -	1	5½
Length of the left breaſt - - - - -	1	7½
The breadth of the right breaſt as it lies - - -	1	1
The breadth of the left - - - - - - -	1	4½

Thus far my Lord the matter of fact faithfully related.

Now what could occaſion thoſe monſtrous tumours of the whole breaſts, and that ſo *ſuddenly* in *one* night, keeps us in great ſuſpenſe.

There occurs nothing in this point ſatisfactory in the writings of Platerus, Rhodericus à Caſtro, Fontanus, Foreſtus, or any of the moderns that I have ſeen writing *De Morbis Mulierum*, ſuitable to what may be offered upon the data of the circulation of the blood, the *Lymphæducts* and the *Vaſa Chylifera Thoracia*, and probably ſome capillary veſſels branching thence (in their progreſs to the ſubclavials) through the intercoſtal muſcles into the breaſts.*

An extract of a letter from William Durſton, M.D. dated Plymouth, November 2, 1669, relating to the Death of the big-breaſted Woman, together with what was thereupon obſerved in her Body.

SIR,

ELIZABETH TREVERS died on Thurſday night, Oct. 21ſt. The next morning I ſent for a Surgeon and ſome others to be preſent at the opening and taking off of her breaſts, though we only took off one, viz. the biggeſt, which was the left, and having weighed it we found it of *ſixty-four* pounds weight. Upon the opening of it (which we made in ſeveral places) we could find neither water nor cancerous humours, nor any thing vitious, more than the prodigious bigneſs; and the tubuli and parenchymus fleſh were purely white and ſolid, and no other than what we ſee in the ſoundeſt breaſts of women, or the beſt udders of other animals. She had loſt her ſtomach and reſt ſeveral weeks before, and made great complaints of her breaſts from their great diſtention; and her whole body was exceedingly emaciated. I have ſent you incloſed one meaſure, which was the breadth of both her breaſts, (as ſhe was laid out on a table, being dead,) I mean from the further end of the one to the other, and which you'll find *three feet two inches* and an *half*; and another meaſure ſhewing the circumference of the breaſts long-wiſe, viz. *four feet* and near *four inches*; and a third giving the circumference of the breadth, viz. three feet four inches and a half.

The right breaſt we took not off, but we gueſs it weighed 40 pounds. I did ſome weeks ſince begin a ſalivation with her, which leſſened her breaſts in circumference ſome inches, but ſhe proving not conformable, I durſt not

* By a ſubſequent letter it appears, that the breaſts of this maiden did yet increaſe in ſize,

proceed to keep up the flux, but was forced to desist. But she was wonderfully revived afterwards for some time. She being weary of that course, I then caused a caustic to be applied, upon which the eschar falling off, yet nothing issued out of the breast. Then I caused an incision knife to be used, and made an incision $2\frac{1}{2}$ inches deep, but it was to no more purpose than the former.

A Letter written by an Englishman from Paris to a Member of the ROYAL SOCIETY *in London, concerning some Transactions there, relating to the Experiment of the Transfusion of Blood.*

SIR,

YOU have such a relation to the ROYAL SOCIETY, that I think myself obliged to impart unto you the honourable mention I heard of that noble Institution in the *Grand Chambre* of the Parliament here, on Thursday last, that Society being then publicly instanced in for the source of *noble experiments*, and having the precedency of those in Germany, Italy, and other places in Europe, in that order wherein the orator thought fit to rank them.

The occasion of mentioning it was: that one Monsieur Denys, a Physician, had been questioned before the Lieutenant Crimenel here for the death of his patient (a man that had been stark mad for several years) who had expired under his hands whilst he was transfusing blood into him, according to the new experiment. The operation had been twice performed with good success; the patient having had thereupon a good interval of two months after the first, and all hopes of a longer, after the second, had it not been for the debauches in wine and brandy that he fell into soon after the operation. He was a Britain by birth, and the original of his madness *love*. That in which Mr. Denys's advocate very much gloried, was, that (besides that the experiment had been practised with good, at least with no ill, success in England, Germany, Italy, Holland, &c. and defended in theses, in almost all the universities of France) there were two persons, a man and a woman, present in the audience, that received a benefit to admiration from the experiment, after they had been abandoned by all Physicians and other helps.

In juſtifying the introduction and uſe of new experiments, he ſaid, that the *moſt precious life to this ſtate* (viz. that of His Moſt Chriſtian Majeſty) had been ſaved by the adminiſtration of a lately invented emetic.

This advocate was the ſon of Monſieur le Premier, Preſident de la Moignon. The ſame was not long ſince in our court, and is, I perceive, well known to it, and infinitely ſatisfied with the civilities he had received from ſeveral perſons there. Though this was his firſt action, yet his performance was a maſter piece, and he had an audience ſuitable, all friends, I ſuppoſe to his family: amongſt them were the Duke of Enguyen, the Dukes of Luynes, Mortimer, Chaulne, and a world of other great perſons.

The pleading for the widow, plaintiff, will be on Thurſday next; but any odds would be laid on the defendants ſide; though ſome partial men are more than ſuſpected to have ſet on the widow.

Paris, Nov. 30, 1669.

An account of an uncommon Lake, called the Zirchnitzer Sea, in Carniola; communicated by Dr. Edward Brown.

HAVING croſſed the river Dravus, and paſſed Mount Luibel, in the Carnick Alps, by that noble paſſage cut through the rocks, and vaulted like that of Panſilipe, near Naples, I had a deſire to take a view of the Lake Zirchnitz, ſo much ſpoken of, and written on by ſo few; and therefore I went into Cruinburg, upon the river Savus, and ſo to Labach, the chief city of Carniola; from whence I continued my journey into Carniola, betwixt the hills and a great marſh, till I came to Brunizza, two leagues from whence and beyond the hills is ſeated the ſaid lake, receiving that name from Zirchnitz, a town of about 300 houſes.

This lake is near two German miles long, and one broad: on the ſouth ſide thereof lies a great foreſt, wherein are many deer, wild boars, wolves, and bears: on the north ſide the country is flat, but the whole valley is encompaſſed with hills at ſome diſtance from it.

This lake is well filled with water for the greateſt part of the year; but in the month of June it ſinketh under ground, not only by percolation, or falling through the pores of the earth, but retireth under ground, through many great holes at the bottom of it: and in the month of September it returns by the ſame, and ſo in a very ſhort time fills up the valley again.

As the time of the water's defcent is fhort, efpecially when the lake grows lower, and hath for a while fhewed fome abatement, fo the afcent and return is fpeedy; for at thefe holes it mounteth with fuch violence that it fprings out of the ground to the height of a pike, and foon covers the tract of earth again.

This piece of ground in the time of the retirement and abfence of the water is not unfruitful; but by a fpeedy and plentiful production of grafs, yieldeth not only fuftenance to the beafts of the field, but a good provifion of hay for the cattle in the winter.

Nor have the inhabitants thereabout only the benefit of the ground commodities, but alfo the recreation and profit by hunting; for at the time of the water's abfence, hares, deer, boars, and other animals, come into it out of the neighbouring foreft and country, and are taken feveral ways by them.

The lake is not only thus filled with water, but every year well ftored with fifh. The Prince of Eckenberg is Lord of it, and of much country thereabout: but on the reftoring of the waters, all have liberty to fifh; and the fifhermen ftanding up to the waift at the holes before mentioned, intercept the paffage of the fifh, and take a very great number of them, which otherwife would be fecure for fome months under the earth, and not fail to return in September.

The fifh of this lake have a clofer habitation than thofe of any other I know; for they pafs fome months under the earth, and a good part of the winter under the ice. I could not learn that there were any others in this lake, (which otherwife muft probably have taken the fame courfe with the fifh); nor that there were any remarkable extraneous fubftances, any vegetables, or unknown fifhes brought up by the water, but thofe that come up are of the fame kind with thofe that defcended.

But befide thefe holes at the bottom of the lake (of which there are many) there are alfo divers caverns and deep places in the country of Carniola, even where there is no water; after the like manner as we have in the *Peak country*, and at Elden-hole, in England.

Half an Englifh mile nearer the lake than the town of Zirchnitz, ftands a village named Seadorf: and nigher to the lake than this, another village called Niderdorf: between thefe two there are corn-fields; yet fometimes thefe lands are alfo drowned, and it is conceived that there are divers fubterraneous caverns under them; for it happens ſometimes at Niderdorf, that the ground ſinks in ſeveral places upon the ſudden retiring of the lake; and the aforeſaid Prince of Eckenberg was once ſo curious as to deſcend into one hole, through which he paſſed under a hill, and came out on the other ſide, as I was informed by Monſieur Andreas Wiſer, the preſent Judge of Zirchnitz; and alſo by Johannes Wiſer, who hath formerly held the ſame place.

The people who are acquainted with the lake, wet and dry, know where they are, and have a particular knowledge of the eminencies, vallies, and inequalities of it; for the bottom of the lake is not even, or near about the ſame depth, but ſometimes two feet, and then ſuddenly twenty yards deep; and becauſe the fiſh haunt the deep places more than the ſhallows, they have given names to the ſeven chiefeſt cavities or vallies in the lake.

I took boat at Niderdorf, and went ſeveral miles on the lake, paſſing over the five firſt vallies. I went alſo to a noted ſtone, commonly called the Fiſhers Stone, which hath ſomewhat of the uſe of the Nileſcope pillar at Grand Cairo; for by a certain appearance of that, they conjecture how ſoon the lake will retire. I alſo paſſed by a noted hill, which when the lake is high becomes a pleaſant iſland; and ſo I returned, &c.

Venice, June 20, 1669.

An extract of another letter from Dr. Durſton, relating to the big breaſted Woman.

IT was deſigned to have examined the viſcera of Elizabeth Trevers, but her aunt, who took care of her, fell into ſuch a paſſion upon the propoſal of opening her, that ſhe ſeemed to be for the time beſide herſelf; and I could not by any art get her out of the chamber where the corpſe was laid out, till ſhe ſaw her nailed up in her coffin. I never ſaw ſuch fondneſs ſhewn to a dead body. I was much diſappointed by the conduct of this tender and extravagant relative: yet I believe if I had examined the entrails, I ſhould have ſeen little or nothing extraordinary; for to the laſt I could perceive no ill ſmell from her breath, nor ſtraitneſs upon the cheſt, or painfulneſs in her breathing; and the *egeſta per urinam*, &c. were well enough.

4

A short extract from a Book just published at Paris, by M. Charas, relating to the bite of Vipers.

THE author of this curious book first takes notice of divers things worthy observation, which he met with in the dissection of Vipers, and amongst them of the salival glands which he discovered in them, as well as in other animals, and those accompanied with lymphatic vessels, passing into a greater vessel, running along and under the said glands, and discharging itself into the vesicle of the gingiva, and carrying with it the salival liquor, which he takes to be the same with that yellow water in the bag, hitherto esteemed venomous, but by him reputed a mere harmless saliva; and having given his sentiments upon these and many anatomical observations relating to this creature, he proceeds to prove,

1st, That the bites of vipers, at least of such as are in France, are indeed venomous, and prove actually mortal; and alledges many experiments made by himself in the presence of several physicians and others, evincing this assertion; in the recitation of which he observeth not a few remarkable phenomena seen in the animals bitten by vipers, both without and also within them when dead and opened; particularly that he found all their vitals and viscera fresh and in a good state, but the blood in all of them that were opened either coagulated already, and blackish, or tending towards coagulation.

2dly, To confute the opinion of those (amongst whom the famous Italian philosopher Redi) who assert that the venom of these animals resides in the yellow liquor contained in the bag about the viper's teeth; whereas this author will have it to be in their vexed and enraged spirits: which he thinks he hath sufficiently proved by wounding several animals with some of the biggest teeth of vipers, pulled out, and letting into wounds thus made that reputed poisonous liquor of the bag; whereupon no ill effects at all have followed: which he confirms by another trial, wherein holding the jaws of a viper, and then thrusting its teeth into the flesh of a living animal, and letting the juice of the bag into the wound, no ill consequence appeared, considering that the angred spirits of the viper in that forced and restrained posture were kept from passing abroad, for the emission of which he supposeth the freedom of the animal is required.

3dly, He recommends, amongſt divers other antidotes to the bite of vipers, the volatile ſalt made of them; the virtues of which he exceedingly praiſes, alledging the example of a perſon, who being bit by a viper, could be ſaved by no other means but by ſeveral doſes of this volatile ſalt, the preparation of which he at large deſcribes.

An account of that great natural curioſity the Stellar Fiſh; preſented with the Fiſh to the ROYAL SOCIETY, *by John Winthrop, Eſq. Governor of Connecticut.*

THE large round box contains a ſtrange kind of fiſh, which was taken by a fiſherman when he was fiſhing for cod-fiſh in that ſea, which is without Maſſachuſett's Bay, in New England. It lived ſome time after being taken, which was by an hook. The name of it we know not, nor can I ſpeak more particularly of it at preſent, becauſe I have not yet ſpoken with the fiſherman who brought it from ſea. It is a rare curioſity: the mouth is in the middle; and they ſay that all the arms you ſee round about were in motion when it was firſt taken.

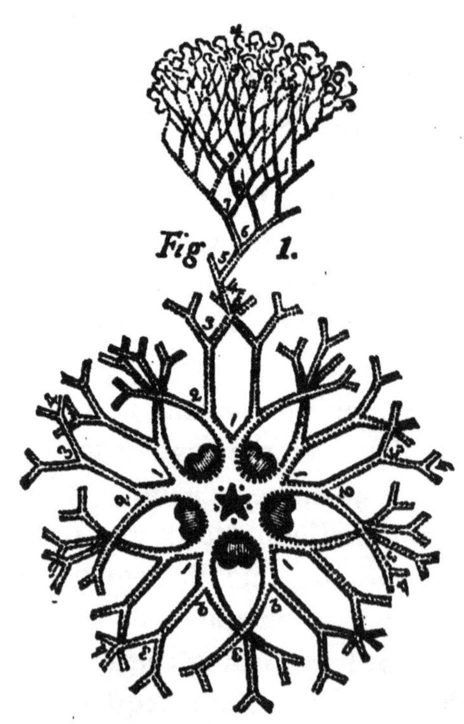

This elaborate piece of nature (See Fig. 1), which, ſince it is yet nameleſs, we may call *piſcis echino-ſtellaris viſciformis*, it's body (as was noted by Mr. Hook) reſembling an echinus, or egg fiſh, the main branches a ſtar, and the dividing of the branch the plant miſletoe. This ſpreads itſelf from a pentagonal root, which encompaſſeth the mouth (being in the middle), into five main *limbs*, or *branches*, each of which, juſt at the iſſuing out from the body, ſubdivides into two (as at 1); and each of thoſe ten branches do again (at 2) divide into two parts, making 20 leſſer branches; each of which again (at 3) divide into two ſmall branches, making in all 40; theſe again (at 4) into 80; and thoſe (at 5) into 160; and they (at 6) into 320; they (at 7) into 640; (at 8) into 1280; (at 9) into 2560; (at 10) into 5120; (at 11) into 10,240; (at 12) into 20,480; (at 13) into 40,960; (at 14) into 81,920; beyond which the further expanding of the fiſh could not be certainly traced, though poſſibly each of thoſe 81,920 ſmall ſprouts or threads, in which the branches of this fiſh ſeemed to terminate, might, if it could have been examined, when living, have been found to ſubdivide yet further. The branches between the joints were not equally of a length, though for the moſt part pretty near: but thoſe branches which were upon that ſide of the joint on which the preceding joint was placed were always about a fourth or fifth part longer than thoſe on the other ſide. Every one of theſe branches ſeemed to have, from the very mouth to the ſmalleſt twigs or threads in which it ended, a double chain or rank of pores, as appears by the figure. The body of the fiſh was on the oppoſite ſide, and ſeemed to have been protuberant, much like an echinus (egg-fiſh, or button-fiſh), and like that divided into five ribs or ridges, and each of theſe ſeemed to be kept out by two ſmall bony ribs.

In the figure is repreſented fully and at length but one of the main branches, whence it is eaſy to imagine the reſt, cut off at the fourth ſubdividing branch, which was done to avoid confuſion *.

* This fiſh is the *ſtella arboreſcens rondeletii*, firſt deſcribed by Mr. Francis Willoughby, and ſince by other naturaliſts.

An extract of a paper, communicated to the ROYAL SOCIETY *by Monsieur de Martell, of Montauban, concerning a way for the prolongation of Human Life, &c.*

ALL I can do at preſent is to make reflections upon ſome experiments, in the doing of which I find I am more particularly engaged in thoſe which regard our health; concerning which I employ much of that time I can redeem from the buſineſs of my voyages, wherein, when I am alone, I frequently entertain myſelf with that ſubject. And in reference to it, I ſhall now declare to you, under the favour of philoſophical liberty, and your friendſhip, a thought of mine, much poſſeſſing my mind, but perhaps one of the moſt extravagant, in the judgment of the vulgar.

After I had often reflected upon the general cauſes of diſeaſes that lead to death, I mean thoſe of the debilitation of nature's ſtrength in the courſe of man's life until its utter extinction, and of the cauſes of a merely natural death, by the failure of that ſtrength in an extreme decrepit age, without the concurrence of any exceſs or external cauſe; I have entertained ſome conjecture, that if we were more intelligent in this matter than we are, we might procure for ourſelves an age of almoſt continual youth, ſetting aſide the ſeveral accidents of Divine Providence, and merely conſidering the forces of nature, not only not hindered, but alſo aſſiſted as much as may be.

A certain philoſopher hath formerly been upon the ſame thing, and Cardan affirms, that being young, this fancy rolled in his head; and the Chineſe ſearch for it with an extreme induſtry: but neither thoſe that have recorded that of the ancient philoſopher, nor Cardan, have ſaid any thing of the ground of their notion, nor of the way which they thought ſhould be obſerved for the attaining the end thereof. *Ne videar inſanire ſine ratione.* I will tell you what it is I have grounded my conjecture upon.

Searching for the true cauſes of old age, and of natural death, I was not ſatisfied with that extinction of natural heat, and deſiccation of the radial humour, aſſigned to be the cauſe thereof, nor with the cauſes of this extinction and deſiccation, that are commonly alleged; it being ſuppoſed that this hot and moiſt principle of life, in its own nature diſſipatible in the courſe of life, not being perfectly repaired by food, is conſiderably diminiſhed, which brings old age, and is at laſt quite conſumed, which cauſeth natural death; where authors make a great difference between the ſeminal heat and moiſture, and that which comes from aliments; ſo that, they ſay, the former cannot be repaired by the latter, as being heterogeneous, which to me ſeems to be true; for doth not this ſeminal moiſture and heat originally proceed from what is ſuperfluous of the third concoction of the aliments? It is therefore of the ſame nature, and nothing hinders, but what is diſſipated thereof may be reſtored by good nouriſhment, well prepared, and taken ſeaſonably, and in due quantity. Whence it may be juſtly concluded, that the defect of repairing this principle of life comes not from its nature, not reparable this way, but from ſomething elſe.

The illuſtrious Bacon finding the weakneſs of this ſuppoſition, did conceive, that this fault came from the unequal reparation of the liquid or ſoft, and the dry and more ſolid parts, which jointly ſerve to maintain and repair themſelves; whence it comes to paſs, that the moſt eaſy to repair, and the moſt neceſſary for life, as the blood, ceaſe at laſt to be ſufficiently repaired by the defect of the others, which are not repaired at all.

Santorius, being almoſt of the ſame ſentiment, holds, that natural death happens, becauſe the fibres do ſo dry up, that they can no more be renewed; he making the maintenance of life to depend from the renovation of the parts; which doth not ſatisfy me, neither, becauſe even the bones themſelves, which are the hardeſt parts, are capable of renovation in old age; in regard that old oxen, which we often eat, have at certain times (I ſay not of the moon, according to the common opinion) their bones of the ſame place altogether dry and marrowleſs, and at other times bedewed with a ſubſtance of the nature of marrow, wherewith they are then filled, which enlargeth their pores, as of a fine ſponge, and ſoftens them; which then eſpecially comes to paſs, after they have fed upon good paſture in the ſpring. We muſt therefore inquire into other more true cauſes of old age and death, which to me ſeem to be the following:

I ſuppoſe that the blood is the principle of life, as far as it is vital, that is, in motion by the hot particles contained therein; ſo that thoſe who expire by age do not die for being deſtitute of blood, which is found abundant and laudible enough in their veſſels, and which hath been ſufficiently repaired till then, but becauſe it ceaſeth to be vital, by reaſon of the too eaſy diſſipation of the igneous particles which make it ſuch; which, in my opinion, comes to paſs as it doth in wine, which evaporates and loſes its ſtrength by the fault of the veſſel, which by ſome opening or other gives paſſage to what gives virtue to the wine. The tunicles and membranes of the veins and arteries which incloſe the blood wear in time away, and wax thin, and their texture gives and breaks in ſeveral places, at which apertures the igneous particles abandon the blood; as in ſtuffs and cloths (whoſe woof is in a manner like that of the tunicles), the threads by wearing do looſen and break, inſomuch that many holes are made in it, as in a ſieve; ſo that, if we had the art to renovate and ſtrengthen anew thoſe coats and membranes, that they might not let ſlip what maketh the blood vital, the life would be preſerved perpetually: for the proof of which this may ſerve for the preſent, that the life of many a dying perſon is maintained, for ſome time, by making them ſwallow ſome hot and ſpirituous liquors, as ſpirit of wine, or ſome eſſence, by which the blood is fortified and quickened for ſome moments; but as this reinforcement of life, conveyed to the heart, and running into the veins, ſoon ſlips out, ſo alſo this new vigour paſſeth away quickly.

As there is no reaſon to deſpair of finding out ſuch medicines or aliments, as are proper to ſtrengthen the coats and membranes of the veſſels ſo as they may at all times retain the fiery and ſpirituous corpuſcles of the blood, as well as in the time of youth, we may alſo hope to be enabled to maintain the blood in a condition always to furniſh alike, as in our vigorous days, for all the functions of life. The engine of our body being not unlike to a chemiſt's furnace, which at firſt well retaining the heat, is very proper for the operations of art, but at laſt chinks and crevices being made therein, it ceaſes to be ſo, the heat getting away through them, what fire ſoever you kindle therein.

I ſhall ſay no more of it, the ſequel of what I have ſaid going very far, if it be true. In the mean time, if you think it not contemptible, I ſhall ſend you ſome further ideas upon it.

An obſervation of M. Adrian Auzout, (a French philoſopher) made in Rome, concerning the declination of the Magnet.

THE declination of the load-ſtone or magnet hath for many years been obſerved not to continue always the *ſame* in the *ſame* places; and the *variation* to be ſuch that it can be no longer imputed to any defect in the obſervations, as it was believed at firſt, when it was not *very* great. It hath been noted, ſome years ſince, that the magnetic needle, which had almoſt every where declined eaſtward to 8, 10, and 12 degrees, (as may be ſeen in P. Kircher and P. Riccioli) after its diminiſhing little by little as far as to the meridian, began to decline weſtward.

M. Adrian Auzout, a great ſearcher of the more conſiderable effects of nature, hath made, here in Rome, the following obſervations about the declination of the load-ſtone on many meridian lines, drawn as exactly as poſſibly he could (in a place where he hath not all the conveniencies for this performance) with a needle three quarters of a palm long; and on all the lines it was ſeen to decline ſomewhat more than two degrees weſtward, and on ſome near two degrees and an half.

That the obſervation might be ſurer, he drew parallel lines in divers places, to ſee whether there were any iron or bricks near the marble, on which he had deſcribed the lines, that might have ſome influence upon the needle; but he always found the ſame quantity of declination weſtward.

But by the obſervations made here formerly, it appears that the needle hath declined eaſtward to eight degrees, and hath afterwards been diminiſhing, until it is come to the other part, where we find it at preſent. The obſervations that may be made hereafter will ſhew how far the declination will advance towards the weſt, and what will happen after its greateſt elongation, it not being probable, it ſhould increaſe always, and make a whole turn.

It ſeems not, that this difference of 10 degrees and more can be attributed to the change of the pole of the earth, as ſome eſteemed, perhaps before they knew it was ſo great; nor (as others would have it) to the magnet, or to the iron, that are found in certain places, becauſe there is but little load-ſtone; and Mr. Auzout affirms, that the mines, which he hath ſeen, make no impreſſion at all on the needle. So that it is difficult to hit the true cauſe of ſuch a variation: yet however, if the direction of the magnet, and of the needle touched by it, depends from the flux of a certain matter, paſſing through the whole earth, or the exterior parts of it, ſtraight along the axis; it may be ſaid, that it proceeds from changes made in the ſaid flux, which, ſuppoſing the inequalities of the earth, and the alterations continually made therein, as well artificial, by excavations and ſuch like other works, as natural, by corroſions cauſed by fire and water, or by the generations of metals and ſtones, (beſides the various changes we cannot think of by reaſon of the little knowledge we have of ſo vaſt a body as the earth) cannot but in progreſs of time change its ſituation. To illuſtrate this with an example taken from rivers; they, although they were running ſtraight, cannot remain long without winding, and changing their courſe, if it happen that the ground, over which they run, be unequal, or of a different nature. So it is probable, that the inequalities of the earth may in time occaſion ſome bending in the current of this magnetic matter, and make it change its bed and channel: whence it comes to paſs, that the needle changeth its direction according as the current changeth, which directs it. And if you will conſider the variety of motions ſeen in rivers becauſe of the higher or lower grounds, which are found in their beds, and cauſe various windings and whirlings in them, poſſibly a reaſon may be rendered of the many differences obſerved in the declination of the needle (*e. g.* why in ſome parts the needle varies much in a little time; why in others it is always turning without any ſtay, as ſome ſay they have obſerved; why the greater alterations are met with at the entering into and going out of iſlands); and of many other things, we for brevity's ſake paſs by; as we alſo omit to deduce from it divers particulars relating to navigation.

Which, if it ſhould be ſo, there would be no hopes of finding a regular hypotheſis for that change, for as much as it would depend from cauſes that have no regularity at all in them, as moſt of the mutations of nature have. You may only take notice, that if there be a proportion between the force of the ſaid current, and the earth, *that* may be able by changing its bed to remove *this* from its proper ſite: which would produce an alteration in the height of the pole, as ſome think they have obſerved, if *that* may not be aſcribed to a defect in the obſervations, of which we may be rendered certain, when more exact ones ſhall have been made. And ſo, where others would impute the various declinations in the magnet to the change of the pole, we ſhould be obliged to attribute the change of the pole to the various declinations of the magnet.

From this obſervation, which it was thought fit to mention here, mathematicians are invited from time to time to make the like in their countries, to ſee whether in this change there be any regularity. If it had been obſerved every year, we ſhould already know the progreſs thereof, and ſee, whether there were an uniformity, and in what time the needle did exactly respect the pole. Wherefore it were very desirable, that for the future, they would use greater care and diligence, in making the most exact meridians, as well for their own observations as for the convenience of those, who in their travels have the curiosity of observing with the needle itself, as M. Auzout designed to do in the cities where he passed, if he had found meridians there, or such as had been unsuspected of the proximity of iron.

It were well to observe, whether the declination, which almost throughout *Europe* hath been eastward, be now every where westward. As also in *America*, where the declination was almost every where westward, it is increased or not proportionably; and so of other parts of the world: noting withal the year, which is not at all minded by some, who relate the observations, without assigning the year, in regard it will be very useful to know the present declination; and it might be put in journals for navigation and for the use of magnetic quadrants.

So far this relation; in pursuance of which, order hath been given by the Royal Society, that precise meridians be made in several places of England, for observing the present declination of the needle from them, in London, and other cities of the kingdom. And that even these meridians, that we made very exactly many years ago, be examined by a carefully describing new ones, to see whether they still hold true, in regard to the suspected alterations in nature.

An extract of an Italian letter, written from Venice by Signor Grandi.

HAVING been honoured with the place of public anatomist of Venice; though I have given as yet but a very slender account of my performances, in comparison of the illustrious examples of Mundinus, Vestingius, Molineta, &c. yet I shall acquaint you with some particulars that have occurred to me.

In my anatomical dissections of the first year, I met with nothing curious, but the *virsungian* channel, manifestly inserting itself in the spleen, and admitting a silver stiletto, which I had never before observed in any subject: and then a liver divided into five lobes, together with a spleen of the figure of a saw, of extraordinary bigness. Last year a person that was drowned of about 35 years of age, had the lacteous vessels so apparent and ſo big, that having ſhewn how they lay in the body, I diſplayed them alſo the day after, in the meſentery taken out and ſhewn upon a table.

Two very odd births likewiſe occurred here; one was of twin females, very handſome, but ſo faſtened together by the breaſt, that there was only diſcerned one trunk of the body; which having their chins united together ſeemed to kiſs one another. I could not diſſect them as I would, becauſe they were delivered to me to embalm, and the indigent father of them, who looked for gain, would not let me have them but for a great ſum of money. Wherefore not to ſpoil them for the purpoſe deſigned, having only opened upwards from the navel which was common to them both, I took out the inteſtines, ſtomach, heart, and lungs. There was but one heart, though greater and rounder than ordinary, ſo that Nature ſeemed to have united the matter of two into one. They had two lungs, and one ſtomach, the pilorus of which did ſtrangely branch itſelf into two ranks in the bowels. There was only one liver, but big; for the reſt, there were two ſpleens, four kidnies, two wombs, full of a white matter, like concreted *ſemen*: two volvas with their diſtinct hymens. In ſhort they were ſo well made in all other members, that the painter who was employed to draw them, affirmed that if they were done in ivory, he would have paid any money for them.

The other monſter was a boy, terrible to behold, born with his breaſt open, the bowels out of the belly, the legs diſtorted, the bladder in the place of the fundament; in the genitals, beſide that the teſticuli were cloſe to the kidnies, there was nothing but a membranous expanſion, wherein the ſpermatic veſſels were loſt. Signor Steno, who honoured me with his viſit, ſaw the adminiſtration of it, which I had before made in the preſence of many noblemen and phyſicians at my houſe.

Venice, January 25, 1670.

An account made by the Philoſophical Academy at Paris, May 12, 1667, *of an Halo or Circle about the Sun; together with a diſcourſe of M. Hugens concerning the Cauſe of theſe Meteors, as alſo that of Parhelions or mock Suns.*

THE diameter of this circle about the ſun was exactly obſerved, and found to be of 44 degrees, and the breadth of the limb thereof about half

ſpectator being ſituated cannot ſee the ſun through that grain, though it may ſee him when poſited elſewhere, as ſomewhere in P.

And to make the company the more diſtinctly underſtand the effect, he drew Fig. 3, in which B is the plan of the eye. B A the axis, which paſſeth from the eye to the ſun; C, M, F, ſome of the icy grains with their kernels, making them half opaque; amongſt which the grain C being in the axis B A, and the lines C K, L H, repreſenting the rays of the ſun neareſt to the axis, the paſſage of which is not hindered by the opacity of the kernel, it is certain, not only that the grain C will not be able to tranſmit any ray of the ſun towards B; but alſo that imagining the ſurface of a cone, whoſe top is in the eye, and its ſides B D, B E, parallel to the rays C K, L H, all the grains M M, which this ſuperficies ſhall compriſe, will likewiſe not ſuffer any ray to paſs to the eye, becauſe it muſt needs be in their cone of obſcurity; but thoſe that ſhall be without this ſuperficies, as the grains F F will let them paſs, becauſe the eye is without their cone of obſcurity. Whence it follows, that the angle of this cone B, D, E, is that which determines the diameter of the halo, which depends from the proportion the opaque grain hath to the tranſparent, in which it is incloſed. For, if this diameter is of 44 degrees, as is obſerved in moſt halos, the bigneſs of the opaque grain will be to the tranſparent as 40 to 19. But, he ſaid, that this proportion was not always the ſame, and that the diverſity of it was becauſe, that ſometimes many halos were ſeen, one about the other, all having the ſun for their centre.

He added, that it was eaſy to know why theſe halos were always of a round figure, whether the ſun be little or much raiſed above the horizon, as alſo to give a reaſon of their colour, which is the ſame with that in the triangular glaſs priſmes, as is evident by the tangents A D, drawn to the grain A, at the points where the ray D A enters or comes out.

Further he took notice, that it was alſo manifeſt why the *red* colour is in the interior circumference of the halo; and why the ſpace which it taketh in and chiefly near the moſt lively coloured parts, appears obſcurer than the air about, viz. becauſe it is there where moſt grains are, which tranſmit no rays of the ſun to our eyes; and ſo do nothing but darken the air, as the drops of water when it raineth.

Moreover he noted, that M. Des Cartes, endeavouring to explain the cauſe of theſe halos, had committed a miſtake, for want of obſervations truly relating to this laſt circumſtance; becauſe he maintains, that the ſpace compriſed within the halo is clearer that the air without; and to render a reaſon of it he ſuppoſeth certain grains, altogether tranſparent, having the form of a lentil; which ſuppoſition cannot therefore be true, becauſe what he deduceth from it, is contrary to what is obſerved, beſides that the roundneſs of the halo in all the elevations of the ſun agreeth not with it, as were eaſy to ſhew.

As to the arch of the circle, which above touched the laſt halo ſeen May 12th, as alſo that the colours were more vivid in this place, and in that below, than in the reſt of the circle; he ſaid that theſe effects did not proceed from the grains he had been ſpeaking of, but from another cauſe, which did alſo ſerve for the production of the parhelions, and the circles which almoſt always accompany them.

Touching which circles and parhelions he obſerved, that beſides the round and half dark grains, there were alſo formed in the air certain little cylinders of the like nature, and of which M. Des Cartes himſelf declared in his Treatiſe of Meteors to have obſerved, ſome not indeed with opaque kernels within, but that the ſame cauſe which produceth them in the round grains could alſo produce them in cylinders; which being ſuppoſed to be ſuch as in Fig. 4, repreſents them, viz. oblong icy grains, and roundiſh at both ends, having the inner kernel of the ſame ſhape, it was found, that from their different diſpoſitions, all the appearances of the parhelions, and their circles did neceſſarily follow.

And firſt, that ſome of theſe cylinders being erect, in the ſituation which probably they ought to have in being formed, there muſt appear in the heavens a great white circle, parallel to the horizon, paſſing through the ſun, and of near the ſame breadth with him, as hath been obſerved in the phenomenon of Rome, Anno 1629, of which Caſſendus and Des Cartes have written, and which is here exhibited in Fig. 5. That this circle L, K, N, M, is cauſed by the reflection of the rays of the ſun upon the ſurface of theſe cylinders, it being eaſy to demonſtrate that there, none but thoſe which are raiſed at the ſame angle above the horizon with that of the height of the ſun, can reflect his rays to our eyes. Whence it manifeſtly follows, that it muſt appear white, and throughout of equal altitude with the ſun itſelf, and by conſequence parallel to the horizon. That conſidering afterwards the tranſparency of theſe perpendicular cylinders, and their opaque kernels, it is eaſily ſeen, that thoſe of the white circle, which are diſtant from the ſun at a certain angle, begin to give paſſage to his rays, to ſtrike our eyes in the ſame manner as hath been ſaid of the round half dark grains. That theſe cylinders are thoſe, which on each ſide of the ſun make us ſee a parhelion in the great white circle, as hath been noted in the obſervation of Rome, (where they are marked with K and N) and in many others. That parhelions have commonly luminous tails, becauſe the cylinders which follow theſe firſt ones that form the parhelions, and which are yet farther diſtant from the ſun, let alſo paſs his rays to our eyes, ſo that theſe tails may be 20 degrees and more in length. That the ſame parhelions are always coloured, becauſe they are made by refraction, as the halo.

That beſides, there are two other images of the ſun, generated by theſe perpendicular cylinders, and ſo diſpoſed in the great white circle, that the ſpectator, turning his face toward the true ſun, hath them behind him, as in the Roman obſervation are the *parhelions* L and M. That theſe are produced by two refractions and one reflection in theſe cylinders, in the ſame manner as the ordinary rainbow in the drops of water, according as M. Des Cartes hath declared; ſo that the opaque kernels do nothing to the production of theſe two ſuns, but that they may be ſometimes ſo big as not to make them appear.

That, according to the altitude of the ſun, more or leſs, theſe two parhelions are more or leſs nigh to one another; of which he promiſeth to give the true meaſures in his Treatiſe of Parhelions.

That they ſhould appear coloured, as the rainbow, and that ſometimes they have been ſeen ſuch; but that when they are faint, they may alſo appear white, even as the halos when they are not very bright.

That theſe ſame perpendicular cylinders can alſo produce an halo about the ſun, by reaſon of the rounding of their two ends; which maketh, that being diſtant from the ſun at a certain angle at what ſide ſoever it be, they begin from thence to give paſſage to the rays, tranſmitting them to the eyes of the ſpectator. And *that* theſe halos are probably what we ſee almoſt always paſs through the two parhelions, that are on the ſide of the true ſun, as the halo G K N I, in the phenomenon of Rome.

That there is yet another ſituation of theſe cylinders very conſiderable, which is of thoſe that are couchant, ſo as their axis are parallel to the *plan* of the horizon, but turned divers ways, ſome one, ſome another, like needles confuſedly thrown on the ground; which horizontal diſpoſition is very natural to thofe cylindric bodies fupported by the vapours which rife from the earth, as may be made out experimentally in bodies thus figured, being let fall into the air.

That it is in thefe cylinders that the *arches*, which touch the halos above or below, are formed; fuch as there were in the phenomenon obferved at Rome, anno 1630, which is defcribed by P. Schenir, in a letter to M. Caffendus, as alfo in all thofe which M. Hevelius hath related at the end of his Mercurius in Sole. And *that* the arch which appeared upon this laft halo at Paris, was of the fame kind. That the figure of thefe arches is different according to the different altitudes of the fun, and the feveral magnitudes of the diameters of the halos. That when the fun is very nigh the horizon, fuch an arch appearing upon an ordinary halo of 44 degrees, muft reprefent, as it were, two horns, as in Fig. 6, A B, A C. But that the fun rifing higher, thofe horns become lower in proportion, and make fuch arches as are reprefented in the fame Fig. 6, where each height of the fun is marked near the arch, which it is to make:—

That the place of the arches, where they touch the halos, being more ftrongly enlightened and coloured than the reft, make us judge that there are parhelions in thofe places.

That the reafon why thefe arches do ordinarily touch a parhelion was, that the fame cylinders couchant which produce the arch, produce alfo that parhelion, by the means of their two round and tranfparent ends, in the fame manner as hath been faid of the perpendicular cylinders. And *that* the parhelion laft feen at Paris hath been formed in thefe couchant cylinders. That *that* was alfo confirmed, by reafon that it was brighter in the fuperior and inferior part, than any where elfe; which neceffarily comes to pafs in a parhelion caufed by cylinders thus difpofed; whereas, when produced by the round grains, it muft appear every where equally ftrong.

That in thefe fame cylinders, parallel to the horizon, there is alfo found the caufe of the *white crofs*, obferved together with the parafelenes or mock-moons, by M. Hevelius, and exhibited at the end of his Mercurius in Sole. The perpendicular fillet of that crofs, coming from the reflection of the rays of the moon upon the furface of thefe cylinders; as the other fillet, parallel to the horizon, is produced by the reflection of the perpendicular cylinders which make the great white circle, of which this fillet is a part. That yet the moon muft not be very high above the horizon, to the end that the couching cylinders may produce this effect; and that it should be well heeded, when the like meteor shall appear, whether the perpendicular *fillet* be not narrower where it passeth through the moon than in other places, and especially upwards, where it must grow larger and disappear.

That besides the perpendicular cylinders, and those that are couched parallel to the horizon, there are often a great many which move to and fro in the air in all sorts of positions; and *that* those, by the same reason that the round grains do, must produce an halo about the sun, and even a more vivid one than that which is caused by the grains, forasmuch as each cylinder sends many more rays to the eye than each of these little spheres. That the little halo D E F, in the Roman phenomenon, Fig. 5, may very well have been caused by such cylinders.

As to those mock-suns, which sometimes show themselves directly opposite to the true sun (such an one as was published by M. Hevelius, and observed Feb. 23, 1661;) that he could find nothing, either in the round grains or in the cylinders, which make those suns necessarily to meet in the great white circle, parallel to the horizon; and that, if *that* should be always verified by future observations, the cause of it must be looked for elsewhere. But that in the mean time he believed that *that* happened not but by chance, which being so, a reason might be given of these suns by the same supposition, which served also for the anthelion, observed by M. Hevelius, Sept. 6, 1661, in which there were two coloured arches of a circle opposite to the sun, which did intersect one another, their intersection being the place of the false sun; which although it be represented in the figure of Hevelius, at the same height with the true sun, yet it was in truth higher by 15 degrees or more, as he hath acknowledged himself afterwards. So that, if there had been a great white circle in this phenomenon, the parhelion was not at all to have been in it.

That for the generation of these suns he did suppose a number of small cylinders with opaque kernels as the precedent, which were carried in the air neither perpendicularly nor couching, but inclined to the *plan* of the horizon at a certain angle, being nearly an half right one; to which were particularly appropriated those cylinders which M. Des Cartes saw fall from the heavens, having stars at both ends, as may be seen experimentally by forming cylinders of that fashion, which is represented in Fig. 7, and letting them descend in the air or in water. *That* in these cylinders was found not only the cause of the anthelia made by the interfection of two arches, as in Fig. 8, but alfo that of fome other extraordinary arches and rods, that are fometimes obferved near the fun; of which, notwithftanding, nothing could be as yet affirmed with certainty, for want of exact and faithful obfervations.

To make all thefe different effects of the cylinders manifeft to the eye, M. Hugens produced one glafs a foot long, of the fhape of that in Fig IV; and for the kernel opaque in the middle a cylinder of wood, and the ambient fpace filled with water inftead of tranfparent ice; which cylinder being expofed to the fun, and the eye put in fuch places as was requifite, there was fucceffively feen all thefe reflections and refractions that have been difcourfed of. Whence it might be concluded that a great number of the like cylinders, although very fmall in comparifon to that, being found in the air, and having the feveral poftures that have been fuppofed, all the appearances of the parhelions, and their circles, mu ftexactly follow.

It was wifhed, for an entire confirmation of the truth of this hypothefis, that fome of thofe fmall cylinders could be obferved to fall to the ground at the time when any parhelions appear, which he fhewed could not eafily be done, becaufe the vapours which then rife from the earth, and which are the caufe of their cylindrical figure, keep them alfo fufpended in the air. He added, that it was not to be thought ftrange that fuch fmall grains of hail were thus kept up in the air by vapours, forafmuch as thefe, by being rarified and dilated upwards, might have motion enough for this effect. That *that* was more eafy to conceive than to imagine how thefe fame vapours could keep fufpended a very great and weighty circle of ice, fuch as M. Des Cartes fuppofeth to explicate the caufe of parhelions, and of the great *white circle* of the Roman phenomenon. In which fuppofition are alfo to be noted the following difficulties, *viz.* *That* therein there appears no reafon why the white circle fhould pafs through the fun, as is always obferved, and that it fhould pafs him according as he changes in height, though the phenomenon doth fometimes laft three or four hours. *That* this fame *white* circle formed of ice, being feen by fpectators diftant enough from one another, could not appear round to all (as it doth) and to traverfe the fun. *That*, when parhelions are obferved, there appears not at all this round cloud encompaffed with the ice circle, which by its thicknefs fhould hide a part of the heavens; but that the weather feems almoſt altogether ſerene, there being none but ſmall clouds which are ſeen to change places, whilſt the great circle and parhelions remain at reſt. That in this hypotheſis it happens not but by chance that the parhelions, which are at the ſide of the ſun, appear in the interſections of an halo and of the great white circle; which is yet obſerved to come to paſs always, and ſhews that the cauſes of theſe halos, and of the parhelions, are very little different againſt the opinion of Des Cartes.

An account of two perſons Deaf and Dumb taught to ſpeak and underſtand a language; by Dr. J. Wallis.

ABOUT the beginning of January 166½ I undertook, ſays Dr. Wallis, to teach a perſon deaf and dumb to ſpeak and underſtand a language; the taſk conſiſts of two very different parts; each of which doth render the other more difficult; for beſide that which appears upon the firſt view to teach a perſon who *cannot hear* to pronounce the *ſound of words*, there is that other of teaching them to *underſtand* a *language*, and know the *ſignification* of thoſe words, whether ſpoken or written, whereby he may both expreſs his own ſenſe, and underſtand the thoughts of others. That each of theſe doth render the other more hard, is obvious. We find by experience that the moſt advantageous way of teaching a child his firſt language, is that of perpetual diſcourſe; not only what is particularly addreſſed to himſelf, as well in pleaſing divertiſements or delightful ſportings (and therefore inſinuate itſelf, without any irkſome or tedious labour) as what is intended for his more ſerious information: but that diſcourſe alſo which paſſeth between others, where without pains or ſtudy he takes notice of what *actions* in the ſpeaker do accompany ſuch words, but theſe helps are wholly obſtructed in our caſe by deafneſs. And as deafneſs makes it the more difficult to teach him a language, ſo on the other hand that want of language makes it more hard to teach him how to ſpeak or pronounce the ſounds: for there being no other way to direct his ſpeech than by teaching him how the tongue, the lips, the palate, and other organs of ſpeech, are to be applied and moved in the forming of ſuch ſounds as are required; to the end that he may by art pronounce thoſe ſounds which others do by cuſtom, they know not how: it may be thought hard enough to expreſs in writing even to one who underſtands it very well, thoſe nice curioſities and delicacies of motion which muſt be obſerved (though we had it not) by him, who, without help of his ear to guide his tongue, ſhall form that variety of ſounds we uſe in ſpeaking: many of which curioſities are ſo nice and delicate, and the difference in forming thoſe ſounds ſo very ſubtile, that moſt of us who pronounce them every day, are not able, without very ſerious conſideration, to give an account by what art or motion we form them, much leſs teach another how it is to be done: and if by writing to one who underſtands a language, it be thus difficult to give inſtruction, how, without help of hearing, he may utter thoſe ſounds, it muſt needs increaſe the difficulty, when there is no other language to expreſs it in but that of dumb ſigns.

Theſe difficulties however did not ſo far diſcourage me from that undertaking, but that I did ſtill conceive it poſſible both parts of this taſk might be effected: as to the firſt of them, though I did not doubt but that the ear doth as much guide the tongue in ſpeaking as the eye doth the hand in writing, or playing on the lute; and therefore thoſe who by accident do wholly loſe their hearing, loſe alſo their ſpeech, and conſequently become dumb as well as deaf, (for it is in a manner the ſame difficulty for one that hears not, to ſpeak well, as for him that is blind to write a fair hand); yet ſince we ſee that it is poſſible for a lady to attain ſo great a dexterity as in the dark to play on a lute, though to that variety of nimble motions the eye's direction, as well as the judgment of the ear, might ſeem neceſſary to guide the hand; I did not think it impoſſible but that the organs of ſpeech might be taught to obſerve their due poſture, though neither the eyes behold their motion, nor the ear diſcern the ſound they make. And as to the other, that of language, might ſeem yet more poſſible; for, ſince that in children, every day, the knowledge of words, with their various conſtructions and ſignifications, is by degrees attained by the ear; ſo that in a few years they arrive to a competent ability of expreſſing themſelves in their firſt language, at leaſt as to the more uſeful parts and notions of it; why ſhould it be thought impoſſible that the eye (though with ſome diſadvantage) might as well apply ſuch complication of letters or other characters, to repreſent the various conceptions of the mind; as the ear, a like complication of ſounds? For though, as things now are, it is very true that letters are with us the immediate characters of ſounds, as thoſe ſounds are of conceptions;

yet is there nothing in the nature of the thing itſelf why letters and characters might not as properly be applied to repreſent immediately, as by the intervention of ſounds, what our conceptions are: which is ſo great a truth, (though not ſo generally taken notice of), that it is practiſed every day, not only by the Chineſe, whoſe whole language is ſaid to be made up of ſuch characters as do repreſent things and notions independent of the ſound of words, and is therefore differently ſpoken by thoſe who differ not in the writing of it: (like as what, in figures, we write 1, 2, 3; for *one*, *two*, *three*; a *Frenchman*, for example, reads *un*, *deux*, *trois*); but in part alſo amongſt ourſelves, as in the numeral figures now mentioned, and many other characters of weights and metals uſed indifferently by divers nations to ſignify the ſame conceptions, to expreſs by different ſounds of words; and more frequently in the practice of ſpacious arithmetic, and operations of algebra, expreſſed in ſuch ſymbols, as ſo little need the intervention of words to make known their meaning, that when different perſons come to expreſs in words the ſenſe of thoſe characters, they will as little agree upon the ſame words, though all expreſs the ſame ſenſe, as two tranſlators of one and the ſame book into another language.

And though I will not diſpute the practical poſſibility of introducing an univerſal character in which all nations, though of different ſpeech, ſhall expreſs their common conceptions; yet that the ſame two or three (or more) perſons may, by conſent, agree upon ſuch characters whereby to expreſs each to the other their ſenſe in writing, without attending to the ſound of words, is ſo far from an impoſſibility, that it muſt needs be allowed to be very feaſible, if not facile. And if it may be done by new invented characters, why not as well by thoſe already in uſe? which though to thoſe that know their common uſe, they may ſignify ſounds, yet to thoſe that know it not, or do not attend to it, may be as immediately applied to ſignify things or notions, as if they ſignified nothing elſe; and conſequently ſo long as it is purely arbitrary by what character to expreſs ſuch a thing or notion, we may as well make uſe of that character or collection of letters to expreſs the thing to the eyes of him that it is deaf; by others expreſs the ſound or name of it to thoſe that hear: ſo that ſhall be to him a real character, which expreſſeth to another a vocal ſound, but ſignifieth to both the ſame conception, which is to underſtand the language.

Theſe were the fundamental grounds of poſſibility in nature; to which

I added the following confiderations, which made me think it morally poffible, that is, not impoffible, to fucceed in practice. I confidered from how few and defpicable principles the whole body of geometry, by continual confequence, is enforced; and if fo fair a pile and curious ftructure may be raifed, and ftand faft upon fo fmall a bottom, I could not think it incredible that we might attain fome confiderable fuccefs in this defign, how little foever we had at firft to begin upon, and, from thofe little actions and geftures, which have a kind of natural fignificancy, we might, if well managed, proceed gradually to the explication of a complete language, and withal, direct to thofe curiofities of motion and pofture in the organs of fpeech requifite to the formation of a found defired, and fo to effect both parts of what we intend. I was further encouraged by the confideration of the perfon, who was very ingenious and comprehenfive, and fo far at leaft a mathematician as to draw pictures, whereby he was already accuftomed to obferve and imitate thofe little niceties in a face, without which it is not poffible to draw a picture well. I fhall add this alfo, that once he could have fpoken, though fo long ago, that (I think) he doth fcarce remember it; but having by accident, when about five years of age, loft his hearing, he confequently loft his fpeech alfo; not all at once, but by degrees, in about half a year's time, which though it confirms what I was faying but now, how needful it is for the ear to guide the tongue in fpeaking, (fince that habit of fpeaking, which was attained by hearing, was alfo loft with it) and might therefore difcourage the undertaking; yet I was thereby very much fecured that his want of fpeech was a confequent of his want of hearing, and did not proceed originally from an indifpofition in the organs of fpeech to form thofe founds.

But though I did believe it poffible for him to learn to fpeak fo as to be underftood, yet I could not promife myfelf that he fpoke fo accurately but that a critical ear might eafily difcern fome failures or little differences from the ordinary tone or pronunciation of other men; becaufe the neglect of it in his younger years, when the organs of fpeech, being yet tender, were more pliable, might now render them lefs capable of that accuratenefs which thofe children attain unto, whereof we have daily experience, it being found very difficult, if not impoffible, to teach a foreigner well in years the accurate pronouncing of that found or language which in his tender years he had not learned. Befides, the ear being fo neceffary to guide and correct the tongue, it is not reafonably to be expected that he who cannot hear, though he may know how to fpeak truly, fhould yet perform it fo accurately as if he had the advantage of his ear alfo.

Nor could I promife, nor indeed hope, that how accurately foever he might learn to fpeak, he fhould be able to make fo great ufe of it as others do; for fince that he cannot hear what others fay to him, as well as exprefs his own thoughts to them, he cannot make ufe of it in difcourfe as others may. And though it may be thought poffible that he may in time difcern, by the motion of the lips vifible to the eye, what is faid to him, yet this cannot be expected till at leaft he be fo perfectly mafter of the language, as that by a few letters known, he may be able to fupply the reft of the word; and by a few words, the reft of the fentence, or at leaft the fenfe of it, by a probable conjecture, (as when we decypher letters written in cypher) for that the eye can actually difcern all the varieties of motion in the organs of fpeech, and fee what founds are made by thofe motions, (of which many are inward, and are not expofed to the eye at all) is not imaginable. But as to the other part of our defign, I fee no reafon at all to doubt but that he might attain a language, and the elegancy of it, as perfectly as thofe that hear.

The way I have taken towards this defign, is in general fufficiently intimated already; as to that of fpeech, I muft firft, by the moft fignificant figns I can, make him to underftand in what pofture and motion I would have him apply his tongue, lips, and other organs of fpeech, to the forming of fuch a found as I direct: which if he hit right, I confirm him in it; if he mifs, I fignify to him in what he differed from my direction, and to what circumftances he muft attend to mend it: and for this work I was fo far prepared beforehand, that I had heretofore upon another occafion, (in my Treatife *De Loquela*, prefixed to my grammar of the Englifh tongue) confidered very exactly (what few attended to) the accurate formation of all founds in fpeaking, (at leaft as to our own language, and thofe I knew) without which it were in vain to fet upon this tafk. As to that of teaching him the language, I begin with that little ftock of fuch actions and geftures, as have a kind of natural fignificancy; and from them, or fome few figns which himfelf had before taken up, to exprefs his thoughts as well as he could, proceed to teach him, what I mean by fomewhat elfe, and fo by fteps to more and more; and this, fo far as well as I can, in method as that what he knows already, may be a ſtep to what he next is to learn.

He hath been already with me ſomewhat more than two months, and the ſucceſs is more than I could expect. There is hardly any word, which (with deliberation) he cannot ſpeak; and he hath already learned a conſiderable part of Engliſh words of moſt frequent uſe. So that I may ſay the greateſt difficulty of both parts of the undertaking is almoſt over; what remains is little more than the work of time and exerciſe.

A further account informs us, that the perſon to whom the foregoing diſcourſe doth refer, is Mr. Damal Whaley, ſon of Mr. Whaley, late of Northampton, and Mayor of that town. He was preſent at the meeting of the ROYAL SOCIETY, May 21, 1662, and did there, to their great ſatiſfaction, pronounce diſtinctly enough ſuch words as by the company were propoſed to him; and though not altogether with the uſual tone or accent, yet ſo as to be eaſily underſtood. About the ſame time alſo (his Majeſty having heard of it, and being willing to ſee him) he did the like ſeveral times at Whitehall, in the preſence of his Majeſty, his Highneſs Prince Rupert, and divers others of the nobility. In the ſpace of a year, which was the whole time of his ſtay with Dr. Wallis, he had read over great part of the Engliſh Bible, and had attained ſo much ſkill as to expreſs himſelf intelligibly in ordinary affairs; to underſtand letters written to him, and write anſwers to them, though not elegantly, yet ſo as to be underſtood; and in the preſence of many foreigners (who out of curioſity have come to ſee him) hath oftentimes not only read Engliſh and Latin to them, but pronounced the moſt difficult words of their languages, (even Poliſh itſelf) which they could propoſe to him.

The ſaid Doctor hath ſince performed the ſame for Mr. Alexander Popham (a young gentleman of very good family, and large eſtate) who did from his birth want his hearing.

An account of the Sal-Gemme Mines in Poland, communicated by a German Gentleman, who deſcended into thoſe Mines to the Depth of two hundred Fathoms.

THE ſal-gemme mines in Poland, a mile diſtant from Cracovia, near the ſmall town of Wilizka, which (the church excepted) are altogether digged, hollow to a vaſt extent, and hath eight deſcents, of which the two chief, being in the town itſelf, are thoſe through which the ſalt is drawn up; the other two ſerve for letting down timber and other neceſſaries. Theſe deſcents or ſhafts are pentagonal, and about five feet diameter, lined throughout with timber. Above is a great wheel with a ſtrong rope of the thickneſs of a luſty arm, drawn about by a horſe as in a horſe-mill. He that would deſcend clean muſt cover himſelf with a frock, and have another man who faſtens another rope to the aforeſaid big rope, and having tied it about himſelf, ſo as to ſit in it, takes a man in his lap and holds him faſt about, whereupon the big rope being let ſomewhat down, another faſtens likewiſe a piece of rope to the other thick rope, and does like the former, ſeating himſelf in it, and taking another man in his lap, and being alſo let down a little way, gives place to others to do the like, in which manner 30 or 40 perſons may be let down all at once, of whom, the firſt having touched the ground, ſteps out and goes aſide, the reſt following him and doing the like; and thus they deſcend to the depth of 100 fathoms. Then they take a lamp and lead you about by ſtrange paſſages and meanders, ſtill more and more deſcending till they come to certain ladders by which they go down an hundred fathoms more, where there are double paſſages and ſhafts one above another in abundance, for the mine-men dig on ſtill, and cut out every where on all ſides, as long as the ſalt-vein laſteth, and ſalt is to be found; but the vein being loſt, and no more ſalt appearing in one place, they ſearch for other veins, whence come ſo many holes and paſſages out of one into another. The great cavities, to ſecure both the town above and the work below from falling in, are very carefully ſupported by ſtrong and well compacted timber, of which there is enough in thoſe works wherewith to build a large town.

Out of theſe mines they dig and cut out three ſorts of ſalt; one is common, coarſe and black; the ſecond ſomewhat finer and whiter; the third very white and clear, and like chryſtal. The coarſe and black ſalt is cut out in great pieces, roundiſh, and three Polonian ells long, and one ell thick, which coſts from 50 to 70 Polonian florins. Meantime the inhabitants of Cracow have a privilege whereby a certain number of pieces is to be delivered to them at eight ſuch florins the piece. The great pieces lie about the ſtreets before the doors of the citizens; alſo in the country, in the ſmall towns and villages, and before the forts and houſes of the nobility; where the cattle paſſing to and fro, lick thoſe ſalt ſtones; which afterwards, by mills and other engines, are ground and beaten ſmall for uſe.

The colour of theſe ſalt ſtones is a darkiſh grey, with ſome mixture of yellow. The inſtruments wherewith they are dug and cut out, have almoſt all German names, with Polonian terminations; for when this ſalt-work was firſt found, (which is now above 500 years ago) the mine men, that firſt began to work in it, were Germans, whence the Poles have retained thoſe names of the tools, but given them Poliſh terminations.

Theſe ſalt-works belong to the King of Poland, who appoints and maintains the officers of them; and are one of his beſt royal revenues, amounting to very conſiderable ſums of money. There is no leſs than 1000 men who are conſtantly employed in theſe mines, and there was then a proviſion of ſalt valued at two millions.

There are in theſe works three horſes that ſtay always below, having their ſtable and other neceſſaries there; they carry the ſalt from the places where it is cut and dug out to thoſe, whence it is by the abovementioned wheel and ropes drawn up by the horſe above ground. The horſes after they have been ſome time below grow blind from the ſharpneſs of the ſalt; and all the three, which then laboured there, were quite blind; and one of them that had been longeſt in thoſe mines had his hoofs grown as long again as they are uſually, ſo that each hoof was nearly a ſpan long.

This ſalt-work hath alſo beneath it certain ſalt ſprings whence the ſalt water is conveyed by channels to ſeveral places where it is boiled to ſalt.

But there is yet another mineral ſalt-work in Poland, viz. at Bochna, but not ſo well ordered as the former. Beſides there are divers other places in Poland, and in Ruſſia alſo, which yield ſalt; as Holitz, Colomeja, Soluns, Pintz, Oſwentz, &c. In the Podolian Deſert, near the river Boriſthenes, is a ſalt-lake, whoſe water is by the heat of the ſun waſted and turned to ſalt, ſo that the people there ride into it with their horſes and waggons, and cut it into pieces like unto ice, and carry it away, as the Poliſh hiſtorian *Cromerus*, at large relateth; who alſo affirms, that in the aforeſaid ſalt-work at Bochna they find a frozen ſubſtance, which by them is called carbuncle, uſed by the people to purge their bodies, by grating and drinking it in a convenient vehicle.

The way of making Vinegar in France, communicated to the ROYAL SOCIETY *by an ingenious Physician of that Nation.*

THEY take two great casks, within each of which they put at the bottom a trevet, which must be one foot high, and as large as the size of the cask permits. Upon this trevet they put vine twigs, whereon they lay a substance called rape, which they fill both vessels within half a foot of the top. This rape is nothing else but the wood or stalks of the clusters of grapes dried and freed from the grapes. The trevet and the vine branches are put at the bottom of the casks, only to keep the rape from settling at the bottom. It is this rape which alone heats and sours the wine. The two vessels being almost quite filled with the rape, one of them is filled up with wine, the other only half full for the time, and every day they draw, by a cock, half the wine that is in the full vessel, therewith quite to fill up the other that is but half full, observing interchangeable turns of filling and unfilling the vessels. Ordinarily, at the end of two or three days, the half filled vessel begins to heat, and this heat augments for several days successively, continuing to do so until the vinegar is perfectly made; and the workmen know that the vinegar is made by the ceasing of the heat. In the summer it is a work of fifteen days; in winter it proceeds more slowly, and *that* according to the degree of cold weather.

When the weather is hottest the wine must be drawn twice a day, to put it out of one vessel into the other. It is only the half filled cask that heats, and as soon as you have done filling up, its heat is choaked and stopped for the time, and the other cask, which is unfilled, begins to heat.

The full vessel is quite open at the top, but a wooden cover is put on the vessel, that is but half full.

The best wine makes the best vinegar, but yet they make good vinegar of wine that is turned.

The wine, in changing, leaves a certain grease, which sticks partly to the sides of the cask, (and *that* they take great care to clean away) partly to the rape; so that if they clean not the rape from it once every year, the wine turns into a whitish liquor, which is neither wine or vinegar.

At the time when they pour the wine out of one vessel into the other, a scum rises on the top of the vessel, which must be carefully taken away.

In the casks which have never served for this purpose the vinegar is made more slowly, than in such that have been used already.

It is further necessary to observe, that when the rape is put into any place to sour before it be cast into the vinegar vessels, that as soon as it is separated from its grapes (which is done immediately after the vintage) it must be carefully put up in barrels, lest it take air; without which it will heat, and be spoiled.

There is no other way of keeping the rape that hath once served already, than by drowning it; that is to say, to fill the vessel wherein it is, with wine or vinegar. Rape will serve a year, more or less, provided that care be taken of cleaning every morning, with a piece of linen, the grease that is on the sides of the vessel, and with a little broom that which swims on the top of the liquor. The rape may be freed from its grease by putting it in water and rubbing it between the hands.

Nobody, that I know, hath hitherto examined what this grease is. When I can get a fit quantity of it I will endeavour to make some experiments about it, especially if I am assisted with suggestions for making proper ones.

I have been lately informed that there have been merchants here who made vinegar with phlegm of wine that remained after the *aqua vitæ* was extracted from it.

Pneumatical Experiments relating to Respiration.*

TITLE I.

Observations upon the duration of Life in Ducks, included in the exhausted Receiver.

NATURE having, as zoologists teach us, furnished ducks and other water fowl with a peculiar structure of some vessels about the heart, to enable them, when they have occasion to dive, to forbear for a considerable time respiring under water, without prejudice; I thought it worth the

* These experiments were made by that indefatigable benefactor to Philosophy, the Hon. Robert Boyle, in order to give more light to the Doctrine of Respiration, and induce others to further researches of the like tendency.

trial, whether *such* birds would much better than *other* animals endure the abſence of the air in our exhauſted receiver. The accounts of trials were, when they were made, regiſtered as follows:—

Experiment I.—We put a full-grown duck into a receiver, whereof ſhe filled, by our gueſs, a third part or ſomewhat more, but was not able to ſtand in any eaſy poſture in it; then pumping out the air, though ſhe ſeemed at firſt to continue well ſomewhat longer than an hen in her condition would have done; yet in the ſhort ſpace of one minute ſhe appeared much diſcompoſed, and between that and the ſecond minute her ſtruggling and convulſive motions increaſed ſo much, that, her head hanging down, ſhe ſeemed to be juſt at the point of death, from which we preſently reſcued her by letting in the air; ſo that this duck being reduced in our receiver to a gaſping ſtate within leſs than two minutes, it did not appear that, (notwithſtanding the peculiar contrivance of nature to enable theſe water birds to continue without reſpiration for ſome time under water,) this duck was able to hold conſiderably longer than a hen, or other bird not aquatic might have done; and to manifeſt that it was not cloſeneſs and narrowneſs of the veſſel, in compariſon to ſo bulky an animal, that in the ſubject of our trial the great and ſudden change above recited, we ſoon after included the ſame bird in the ſame receiver, and ſuffered her to ſtay thus ſhut up with the air for five times as long as formerly without perceiving her to be diſcompoſed; and ſhe would probably have continued longer in the ſame condition, if my patience and leiſure would have held out ſo long, as ſhe could have done in that priſon.

Experiment II.—Having at the ſeaſon of the year procured a duckling that was yet callow, we conveyed it into the ſame receiver wherein the former had been included, and obſerved that, though for a while it appeared not much diſquieted, whilſt the air was pumping out of the glaſs, yet before the firſt minute was quite ended, it gave manifeſt tokens of being much diſordered; and the operation being awhile longer, it grew ſo much worſe, that it fell into ſeveral convulſive motions, before a ſecond minute was expired, which obliged us to let in the air upon it, whereby it quickly recovered.

N. B. I determined not, whether it be proper in this place to add, that when the receiver was pretty well exhauſted the included bird appeared to

4

the ſpectators manifeſtly bigger than before the air was withdrawn, eſpecially about the crop, though that was very turgid before. And to manifeſt that in this duck, as in the former, the convulſions that uſed to be immediately followed by death, proceeded from the *withdrawing* of the ambient air, and not from the cloſing of it, we kept the ſame duckling in the ſame receiver very cloſe, to keep out all external air, and to keep in the excrementitious ſteams of its body for above ſix minutes, without perceiving it to grow ſick upon its impriſonment, which yet laſted above thrice the time that ſufficed to reduce it in the abſence of the air to a gaſping condition.

It not being intended that ducks and other water-fowl ſhould, any more than other birds, live in an exceeding rarified air, but only be able to continue upon occaſion a pretty while under water, it may ſuffice that the contrivance of thoſe parts, which relate to reſpiration, ſo far fitted for the purpoſe, as we ſhall ſee it is when we come to the tenth article.

Title II.

Of the Phænomena afforded by Vipers included in an exhauſted Receiver.

Conſidering that vipers are animals endowed with lungs (though of a differing ſtructure from thoſe of men, dogs, cats, birds, &c.) and that their blood is, as to ſenſe, actually cold; I thought it might upon theſe accounts be very well worth trying what effect the withdrawing and abſence of the air would have upon animals ſo conſtituted. I therefore made divers trials, ſome of which did not diſpleaſe me; but I know not by what misfortune the memorials of them were loſt, except two or three (which were not perfect,) that I ſhall here ſubjoin.

Experiment I.—We included a viper in a ſmall receiver, and, as we drew out the air, ſhe began to ſwell, and afforded us theſe phænomena:

1ſt. It was a good while after we had left off pumping ere the viper began to ſwell ſo much as to be forced to gape, which afterwards ſhe did.

2d. That ſhe continued, by our eſtimate, above 2½ hours in the exhauſted receiver without giving clear proof of her being killed.

3d. That after ſhe was once ſo ſwelled, as to be compelled to open her jaws, ſhe appeared ſlender and lank again, yet very ſoon after appeared ſwelled, and her jaws disjoined as before.

EXPERIMENT II.—We took a viper, and including her in the greater ſort of ſmall receivers, we emptied the glaſs very carefully, and the viper moved up and down within as if it were to ſeek for air, and after a while foamed a little at the mouth, and left the foam ſticking to the inſide of the glaſs: her body ſwelled not conſiderably, and her neck leſs, till a pretty while after we had left pumping; but afterwards the body and neck grew prodigiouſly tumid, and a bliſter appeared upon the back. An hour and an half after the exhauſtion of the receiver, the diſtended viper did give, by motion, manifeſt ſigns of life, but we obſerved none afterwards. The tumour reached to the neck, but did not ſeem to ſwell much the under chap. Both the neck and a great part of the throat, being held between the eye and a candle, were tranſparent enough where the ſcales did not darken them. The jaws remained mightily opened, and ſomewhat diſtorted; the *epiglottis*, with the *rimula laryngis*, (which remained gaping) was protruded almoſt to the further end of the nether chap. As it were from beneath this *epiglottis* came the black tongue, and reached beyond it, but ſeemed by its poſture not to have any life, and the mouth alſo was grown blackiſh within; but the air being admitted after twenty-three hours in all, the viper's mouth was preſently cloſed, though ſoon after it was opened again, and continued long ſo, and ſcratching or pinching the tail made a motion in the whole body, that argued ſome life.

EXPERIMENT III.—To theſe experiments upon vipers, I ſhall add one, made upon an ordinary harmleſs ſnake.

We included ſuch an animal, together with a gauge, in a pretty portable receiver, which being exhauſted and well ſecured againſt the ingreſs of the air, was laid aſide in a quiet place, where it continued from ten or eleven o'clock in the forenoon till about nine the next morning; and then my occaſions calling me abroad, I looked upon the ſnake, which, though he ſeemed to be dead, and gave no ſigns of life upon the ſhaking of the receiver, yet upon holding the glaſs a convenient diſtance from a moderate fire, he did in a ſhort time manifeſt himſelf to be alive by ſeveral tokens, and even by putting forth his forked tongue. In that condition I left him, and by reaſon of ſeveral avocations came not to look upon him again till the next day early in the afternoon; at which time he was paſt recovery, and his jaws, which were formerly ſhut, gaped exceeding wide, as if they had been ſtretched open by ſome external violence.

TITLE III.

Of the phenomena afforded by Frogs in an exhausted receiver.

EXPERIMENT I.—We took a large vigorous frog, and having included her in a small receiver, we drew out the air, and left her not very much swelled, and able to move her throat from time to time, though not so fast as when she breathed before the exsuction of the air. She continued alive about two hours, that we took notice of, sometimes removing from the one side of the receiver to the other; but she swelled more than before, and did not appear by any motion of her throat or thorax to exercise respiration, but her head was not very much swelled, nor her mouth forced open. After she had remained there somewhat above three hours, perceiving no sign of life in her, we let the air in, which the formerly tumid body sunk very much, but seemed not to have any other change wrought in it; and though we took her out of the receiver, yet in the free air itself she continued to appear quite dead. Nevertheless, to see the utmost of the experiment, having caused her to be laid upon the grass in a garden all night, the next morning we found her perfectly alive again.

EXPERIMENT II.—About 11 o'clock in the forenoon we put a frog into a small receiver, containining about $15\frac{1}{4}$ ounces troy weight of water, out of which we had tolerably well drawn the air (so that when we had turned the cock under water, it sucked in about $13\frac{1}{4}$ ounces of water); the frog continued in it (the receiver all the while under water) lively enough till about five o'clock in the afternoon, when it expired. The frog at the first seemed not much altered by the exsuction of the air, but continued breathing both with her throat and lungs.

EXPERIMENT III.—We included in a pretty large receiver a couple of frogs newly taken, the one not above an inch long, and proportionably slender; the other, very large and lusty. Whilst the air was drawing out, the lesser one skipped up and down very lively, and, somewhat to our wonder, clambered up several times to the sides of the receiver, insomuch that he frequently rested himself against the side of the glass. When his body seemed to be perpendicular to the horizon, if not in a reclining posture, he continued to skip up and down a while after the exsuction of the air, but within a quarter of an hour we perceived him lifeless, with his belly upwards. The other frog, that was very large and strong, though he began to swell much upon the withdrawing of the air, and ſeemed to be diſtreſſed, by his frequently leaping up after the air was drawn out, which he did not before; yet being, as we ſaid, very luſty, he held out half an hour, at which time it was remarkable that the receiver, though it had held out againſt the preſſure of the outward air during that ſpace of time, notwithſtanding that a piece of it had been cracked out, and was mended with a cloth dipt in cement, yet at the end of the half hour the weight of the external air beat it in, and thereby brought the impriſoned frog a reprieve, which hindered us from bringing the experiment to an iſſue.

Experiment IV.—We took a ſmall frog, and having conveyed her into a very ſmall portable receiver, we began to pump out the air. At firſt ſhe was lively enough, but when the air began to be conſiderably withdrawn, ſhe appeared to be very much diſquieted (leaping ſometimes after an odd manner, as it were to get out of the uneaſy priſon), but yet not ſo, but that after the operation was ended, and the receiver taken off, the frog was perfectly alive, and continued to appear ſo nearly an hour, though the abdomen was very much, and the throat ſomewhat extended; this latter part having alſo left that wonted panting motion, that is ſuppoſed to argue and accompany the reſpiration of frogs. At the end of about three quarters of an hour the air was let in, whereupon the abdomen, which by that time was ſtrongly ſwelled, did not only ſubſide, but ſeemed to have a great cavity in it, as the throat alſo proportionably had; which cavities continued, the frog being paſt all recovery.

Experiment V.—A large frog was conveyed into a plated receiver, and the air being withdrawn, her body by degrees was diſtended; as appeared very notably, when by a caſual ſpringing of a leak, the air got in again, and made her look much more lank and hollow than ever. The receiver with the gauge were kept under water near ſeven hours, becauſe I was obliged to ſtay long abroad; at which time coming home, I found the receiver ſtaunch, but the frog dead and exceedingly ſwelled: upon letting in of the air ſhe became more hollow and lank than before.

N. B. I have purpoſely, but under this title and ſome others, ſubjoined ſome trials, whoſe events are not altogether ſuch as others recited under the ſame head, which would invite one to expect; but I purpoſely do it, not only to be true to the impartiality I propoſed to myſelf in writing theſe narratives, but to awaken the curious to confider and obferve what variety of phenomena in fuch trials may be attributed to the feafon of the year wherein they are made; and to the ftrength, bulk, age, peculiar conftitutions, &c. that relate to the refpective animals on which the experiments are tried; befides what things may on other accounts be proper to confider.

Title IV.

Of the phenomena afforded by a Kitten not quite a day old, in the exhaufted receiver.

Being defirous to try whether animals that had lately been accuftomed to live either without *any*, or without a full refpiration, would not be more difficultly or flowly killed by the want of air than others which had been longer ufed to a free refpiration, we took the above kitten and put it into a very fmall receiver, (that we gueffed to hold about a pint or lefs) that it might be the fooner exhaufted. As foon as the pump began to play I took notice of the time, and found by a watch that marks minutes and quarter minutes, within one minute or a little more after the air began to be withdrawn, that the little animal, who in the mean time had gafped for life, and had fome violent convulfions, lay apparently dead with its head downwards, and its tongue out; but on letting in the air, it did in a trice fhow figns of life, and being taken out of the receiver, quickly recovered. And to allow it the benefit of its good fortune, we fent for a kitten of the fame age and litter, which being put into the fame receiver, quickly began, like the other, to have convulfions, after which it lay as dead; but obferving very narrowly I perceived fome little motions, which made me conclude it alive, which I foon found I had caufe to do; for though we continued pumping, and could not perceive that the engine leaked more than in the former experiments, the kitten began to ftir again, and after awhile had ftronger and more general convulfions than before; till at the end of fix minutes after the exfuction of the air was begun, the animal feeming quite dead, the air was re-admitted into the receiver, which not reviving it as it had done the other, the kitten was taken out of the veffel, and lay with his mouth open, and his tongue lolling out without any fenfible breathing or pulfation; till having ordered him to be *pinched*, the pain or fome internal motion produced by the external violence done to him, made him immediately give manifeft figns of life, though there was yet no fenfible motion of the heart or the lungs; but afterwards gaſping and fetching his breath in an odd manner, and with much ſtraining, as I have ſeen ſome fœtuſes do when out of the womb, he little by little, in about a quarter of an hour, recovered; wherefore thinking it ſevere to make him undergo the ſame meaſure again, we ſent for another, kittened at the ſame time, and incloſing that alſo in the receiver, obſerved, that divers violent convulſions, as it were gaſping for breath, into which he began to fall at the ſecond or third ſuck, ended in a ſeeming death, within about a minute and a half. But being made more diffident by the late experiments, I cauſed the pump to be plied, and the rather, becauſe I had a mind to obſerve whether when the air was from time to time drawn away, there would not, upon ſtopping of the cock, appear ſome ſudden ſwellings, greater or leſs, of the body of the animal, by the ſpring and expanſion of ſome air (or aërial matter) included in the thorax, or the abdomen. Such an affection (though not great) we thought we obſerved, but till further trial I dare not acquieſce in. A while after, notwithſtanding our continuing to pump, the kitten gave manifeſt ſigns of life, which was not till it had endured divers convulſions, as great as thoſe of the firſt fit, if not greater. When ſeven minutes from the beginning of the exhauſtion were completed, we let in the air; upon which the little creature, that ſeemed quite dead before, made us ſuſpect that he might recover; but though we took him out of the receiver, and put aqua vitæ into his mouth, yet he irrecoverably died in our hands.

Theſe trials may deſerve to be proſecuted with further ones to be made not only with ſuch kittens, but with other very young animals of different kinds; for by what has been related it appears, that thoſe animals continued three times longer in the exhauſted receiver than other animals of that bigneſs would probably have done.

Title V.

Some trials about the air uſually harboured in the pores of water, &c.

It might aſſiſt us to make the more rational conjectures about the phenomena of divers of our experiments, if we knew (ſomething near) what quantity of aërial ſubſtance is uſually found in the liquors we employ about them, eſpecially in that moſt common of them, water. And therefore, though it be very difficult (if at all poſſible) to determine the proportion of

I

the air that lurks in water with any degree of certainty, many circumſtances making it ſubject to vary very much, yet to make the beſt eſtimate, I eaſily could, where none at all that I know of hath been hitherto made by any man, I conſidered that it might afford us ſome light if we diſcovered at leaſt what proportion, as to bulk, the air latitant in a quantity of water would have to the liquor it came from, when the aërial particles ſhould be gathered together into one place: for though about this union, and the ſpring that may be conſonant to it, ſome doubts may be ſuggeſted which I have not now time to diſcuſs, yet I ſuppoſed that at leaſt ſome diſcoveries would by this way be made, though not of the true proportion between the air and the water, yet about two or three particulars, in due time to be taken notice of.

To find inſtruments which would any way accommodate our purpoſe, proved a very difficult work; ſo that amongſt other things that we were feign to do, this was one, that to evince how little the air, latitant in water, did appear to leſſen the bulk of that water, if it were ſuffered to fly away in an open tube; we ſuffered it to eſcape in an exhauſted receiver, without any artifice to catch it; by which trial the water did not part with any thing of its bulk, that made a diminution ſenſible to the eye: wherefore we endeavoured to make this loſs viſible by ſome other trials, of which I can find but a few haſty memorials amongſt my looſe entries.

A chemical pipe, ſealed at one end, and 36 inches, or ſomewhat leſs in length, was filled with water, and inverted into a glaſs veſſel, not two inches in diameter, and but one-fourth of an inch, or a little more, in depth. Theſe glaſſes being conveyed into a fit receiver, and the air being leiſurely pumped out, and ſomewhat ſlowly re-admitted, the numerous bubbles that had aſcended during the operation, conſtituted at the top an aërial aggregate, amounting to $\frac{8}{10}$, wanting about 100th part of an inch.

Preſently after the tube (by me to be deſcribed) was filled again with the ſame water, and inverted, and the water being drawn down to the ſurface of the veſſeled water, and the air let in again, the water was impelled up to the very top within a tenth and half a tenth of an inch.

The tube for meaſuring the air latitant in water was $43\frac{1}{2}$ inches above the ſurface of the ſtagnant water: the air collected out of the bubbles at the top of the water, was the firſt time $\frac{3}{4}$ of an inch, and ſomewhat better; the ſecond time we eſtimated it but $\frac{1}{8}$ and $\frac{1}{16}$. The firſt time the water in the pipe was made to ſubſide full as low as the ſurface of the reſtagnant water: the ſecond time, the loweſt we made it to ſubſide, ſeemed to be four or five inches above the ſurface of the water in the open veſſel.

Matter of fact thus reſiſted would afford divers difficulties worthy to be conſidered, eſpecially the odd thing that happens to the aërial particles of water: for though, whilſt they lay concealed in the water, they took up ſo little room in it, that it was inſenſible, and when they were permitted to eſcape out of the tube, the water was not manifeſtly diminiſhed by their receſs; yet when they were affiated at the top of the tube, their aggregate did ſometimes maintain a place that was conſiderable enough in reference to the capacity of the whole tube; though I muſt here advertiſe that this aggregate did at the top of the tube poſſeſs more room than its bulk did abſolutely require, becauſe it was ſomewhat defended from the preſſure of the atmoſphere by the weight of the ſubjacent cylinder of water, which might be about three or four feet long.

Query. Whether any conſiderable proportion of bubbles will be afforded by the ſame liquor, if it be ſuffered to continue in the glaſs for ſome competent time after it has been once or oftener freed from the bubbles?

Query. How far it may be worthy our conſideration, whether in common water there may not be concealed air enough to be of uſe to ſuch cold animals as fiſhes; and whether it may be ſeparable from the water that ſtrains through their gills?

But though I was at firſt content to make uſe of this way of eſtimating the air concealed in water, yet when I came where I could be a little better accommodated with glaſſes, I bethought myſelf of a ſmall inſtrument that would much better diſcloſe the wonderful plenty of the aërial particles I deſigned to diſcover. The ſtructure and uſe of this glaſs may be eaſily enough underſtood by the recital of the firſt experiment that was made with it, whereof take the following tranſcript.

We provided a clear round glaſs, furniſhed with a pipe or ſtem of about nine inches in length, the globulous part of the glaſs being on the outſide about 3½ inches in diameter; the pipe of this glaſs was within an inch of the top, melted at the flame of a lamp, and drawn out two or three inches, and to about the ſlenderneſs of a crow's quill, that the decrement of the water upon the receſs of the air, harboured in its pores, might, if any ſhould happen, be the more eaſily obſerved and eſtimated. Above the ſlender part of the pipe, the glaſs, as was before intimated, was of the ſame largeneſs (or near it) with the reſt of the pipe, that the aërial bubbles, aſcending through the ſlender part, might there find room to break, and ſo prevent the overflowing or loſs of any part of the water.

This veſſel being not without difficulty and ſome induſtry filled, till the liquor reached to the top of the ſlender part, where not being uniformly drawn out it was ſomewhat broader than elſewhere, we conveyed the glaſs, together with the pedeſtal for it to reſt upon, into a tall receiver, and pumping out the air, there diſcloſed themſelves numerous bubbles, aſcending nimbly to the upper part of the glaſs, where they made a kind of froth or foam; but by reaſon of the above form of the veſſel, they broke at the top of the ſlender part, and ſo never came to overflow.

This done, the pump was ſuffered to reſt a while, to give the aërial particles, lodged in the water, time to ſeparate themſelves and emerge, which when they had done a pretty while, the pump was plied again, for fear ſome air might have ſtolen into ſo large a receiver. Theſe viciſſitudes of pumping and reſting laſted for a conſiderable time, till at length the bubbles began to be very rare, and we were weary of waiting any longer; ſoon after which the external air was let into the receiver, and it appeared ſomewhat ſtrange to the ſpectators, that notwithſtanding ſo great a multitude of bubbles as had eſcaped out of the water, I could not by attentively comparing the place where the ſurface of the water reſted at firſt (to which a mark had been affixed) with that where it now ſtood, I could not, I ſay, diſcern the difference to amount to above, if ſo much, as an hair's breadth; and a principal operator in the experiment profeſſed that, for his part, he could not perceive any difference at all.

Thus far the narrative of the trial made by *water:* but that was not the only liquor, into the aërial particles of which I deſigned by our little inſtrument to enquire; and therefore filling a glaſs of the ſame ſhape, and much of the ſame bigneſs, with claret wine, and placing it upon a convenient pedeſtal in a tall receiver, we cauſed ſome of the air to be pumped out; whereupon in a ſhort time there emerged through the ſlender pipe ſo very great a multitude of bubbles, that were darted as it were upwards, as did not a little both pleaſe and ſurpriſe the beholders: but it forced us to go warily to work, for fear the glaſs ſhould break, or the wine overflow. Wherefore we ſeaſonably left off pumping, before the receiver was any thing near exhausted, and suffered the bubbles to get away as they could, till the present danger was overpassed, and then from time to time we pumped a little more air out of the receiver, till we were weary; the withdrawing a moderate quantity of air at a time sufficing, even at the latter end, to make the bubbles not only copiously, but very swiftly ascend, for above a quarter of an hour together.

Title VI.

Of some phenomena afforded by Shell Fishes.

Experiment I.—An oyster being put into a very small receiver, and kept in long enough to have successively killed three or four birds or beasts, &c. was not thereby killed, nor, for aught we could perceive, considerably disturbed; only at each suck we perceived that the air contained between the two shells broke out at their commissure; as we concluded from the foam which at those times came forth. About 24 hours after, coming to see in what condition this oyster was, I found that both this and another that had been put at the same time into the receiver, were alive; but how long after they continued so I did not observe.

Experiment II.—The same day we put a pretty large craw-fish into a middle sized receiver, and found that though he had been injured by a fall before he was brought thither, yet he seemed not to be much incommoded by being included, till the air was in great measure pumped out, and then its former motion presently ceased, and he lay as if dead; till upon letting a little air into the receiver, he began forthwith to move afresh: and upon withdrawing the air again, he presently, as before, became moveless. Having repeated this trial two or three times, we took him out of the receiver, where he appeared not to have suffered any harm.

Experiment III.—But I thought it not unlikely that there might be some such inequality in, or vivacity of animals, as to such kind of experiments as ours, that it might be well worth while in several cases to repeat our trials. And on this occasion I shall here add, that having put an oyster into a vial full of water, before we included it in the receiver, that through the liquor the motion of the bubbles, expected from the fish, might be the more pleasantly seen and considered, this oyster proved so strong as to keep itself close shut, and repressed the eruption of the bubbles, that in the other it forced open the shells from time to time, and kept in its own air as long as we had occasion to continue the trials.

Experiment IV.—Moreover a craw-fish, that was thought more vigorous, being substituted in the place of the former craw-fish, though once he seemed to lose his motion together with the air, yet afterwards he continued moving in the receiver, in spite of our pumping: whether because there was unperceived leaking, that hindered a sufficient exhausting of the air, or because this particular animal was more strong or vivid than the other, we could not positively determine.

Title VII.

Of the phenomena of a Scale Fish.

The following experiment is far from being the first that was made on a scale fish in our vacuum; but in regard that the receivers, wherein those trials were made, the external air could not be kept out near so long, and so well as in the vessel I am about to mention, I judge it well worth the pains to observe what would happen to a fish in an exhausted vessel, where it should be kept for some hours together from all supply of fresh air: and therefore I made several trials to that purpose; whereof that which I think the most considerable, was registered as follows:

We took a receiver of a roundish shape, containing by estimation near a pint, and the globulous part of it being almost half full of water, we put into it a small gudgeon about three inches long, which when it was in the water swam nimbly up and down therein. Then having drawn out the air so well, that we guessed by a gauge that about nineteen parts in twenty or more might be exhausted, we secured ourselves that the regress of the air should not injure our experiment; about which we observed these particulars.

First, The neck of the glass being very long, though there appeared great store of bubbles all about the fish; yet the rest of the water, notwithstanding the withdrawing of so much air as has been mentioned, emitted no froth, and but few bubbles.

Secondly, The fish both at his mouth and his gills did, for a great while, discharge such a quantity of bubbles as appeared strange, and for about half an hour or more (for much longer I had not opportunity to watch it,) whenever he rested awhile, new bubbles adhered to many parts of his body (as if they were generated there) especially his fins and tail; so that he would appear almoſt beſet with bubbles; and if, being excited to ſwim, he was made to ſhake them off, he would quickly, upon a little reſt, be beſet with new ones as before.

Thirdly, Almoſt all the while he would gape and move his gills, as before he was included; though towards the end of the time that I watched, it often happened that he neither took in nor emitted any aërial particles that I could perceive.

Fourthly, After a while he lay almoſt conſtantly with his belly upwards, and yet would in that poſture ſwim briſkly as before.

Fifthly, Nay, after a while he ſeemed to be more lively than at firſt putting in; whether by reaſon that by diſcharge of ſo many bubbles, which by their diſtention perhaps put him to pain, he found himſelf relieved, or ſome other cauſe, I examined not.

Having occaſion to go abroad, I returned about an hour and an half after he had been ſealed up, and found him almoſt free from bubbles, and with his belly upwards, and ſeeming ſomewhat tumid, but lively as before. But an hour and a quarter after that, when riſing from dinner I went to look upon him again, he ſeemed to be moveleſs and ſomewhat ſtiff; yet upon ſhaking the glaſs, obſerving ſome faint ſigns of life in him by ſome languid motions he attempted to make when excited to them, I opened the receiver under water, to try if that liquor and air would recover him; and the external water ruſhing in till it had filled the vacant part of the ball and the greateſt part of the ſtem too, the fiſh ſunk to the bottom of it, with a greater appearance than ever of being alive; in which ſtate, after he had continued a pretty while, I made a ſhift, by the help of the water he ſwam in, to get him through the pipe into a baſon of water, where he gave more manifeſt ſigns of life; but yet for ſome hours lay on one ſide or other, without being able to ſwim or lie on his belly, which appeared very much ſhrunk in, as if ſomething during the time of its being ſealed up had been broken in his body, or his belly had been exceedingly diſtended, beyond reſtitution to its former tone.

All the while he continued in the baſon of water, though he moved his gills as before he had been ſealed up; yet I could not perceive that he did, even in his new water emit, as formerly, any bubbles, though two or three times I held him by the tail in the air, and put him into the water again;

where at length he grew able to lie conftantly on his belly (which yet retained much of its former lanknefs;) and though it is now about 24 hours fince he was firft included, he continues yet alive.

P. S. He lived in the bafon eight or ten days longer, though divers gudgeons fince taken died there in much fhorter time.

Title VIII.

Of two animals included with large wounds in the abdomen, in the pneumatical receiver.

Experiment I.—A fmall bird, having the abdomen opened almoft from flank to flank, without injuring the guts, was put into a fmall receiver, and the pump being fet to work, continued for fome little time without giving any figns of diftrefs, but at the end of about a minute and an half from the beginning of the exhauftion, fhe began to have convulfive motions in the wings; and though the convulfions were not univerfal, or did appear violent, as is ufual in other birds from whom the air is withdrawn by the engine, yet at the end of two full minutes, letting in the air, and then taking off the receiver, we found the bird irrecoverable; notwithftanding which we did not find any notable alteration in the lungs, and found the heart (or at leaft the auricles of it) to be yet beating, and fo it continued for a while after.

Experiment II.—We took alfo a pretty large frog, and having, without violating the lungs or the guts, made two fuch incifions in the abdomen that two curled bladders or lobes of the lungs came out almoft totally at them, we fufpended the frog by the legs in a fmall receiver, and after we had pumped out a good part of the air, the animal ftruggled very much, and feemed to be much difordered; and when the receiver was well exhaufted fhe lay ftill for a while as if fhe had been dead, the abdomen and thigh very much fwelled, as if fome rarified air vapour forcibly diftended them: but as when the frog was put in one of the lobes it was almoft full, and the other almoft fhrunk up, fo they continued to appear after the receiver had been exhaufted; but upon letting in the air, not only the body ceafed to be tumid, but the plump bladder appeared for a while fhrunk up as the other, and the receiver being removed, the frog prefently revived, and quickly began to fill the lobe again with air.

Title IX.

Of the motion of the separated heart of a cold animal in the exhausted receiver.

Experiment I.—The heart of an eel being taken out and laid upon a plate of tin in a small receiver, when we perceived it to beat there as it had done in the open air, we exhausted the vessel, and saw, that, though the heart grew very tumid, and here and there sent forth little bubbles, yet it continued to beat as manifestly as before, and seemed to do so more swiftly, as we tried by numbering the pulsations it made in a minute, whilst it was in the exhausted receiver, and when we had re-admitted the air, and also when we took it out of the glass, and suffered it to continue its motion in the open air. The heart of another eel being likewise taken out, continued to beat in the emptied receiver, as the other had done.

Experiment II.—The heart of another eel, after having been included in a receiver first exhausted, and then accurately secured from leaking, though it appeared very tumid, continued to beat there an hour, after which looking upon it, and finding its motion very languid, and almost ceased, by breathing a little upon that part of the glass where the heart was, it quickly regained motion, which I observed awhile; and an hour after, perceiving it almost quite gone, I was able to renew it by the application of a little more warmth. At the end of the third hour, coming to look at it once more, a bubble, that appeared to be placed between the auricle and the heart, seemed to have now and then a little trembling motion, but I found it so faint, that I could no more by warmth excite it, so as plainly to perceive the heart to move; wherefore I suffered the outward air to rush in, but could not discern that thereby the heart regained any sensible motion, though assisted with the warmth of my breath and hands.

Title X.

A comparison of the times wherein animals may be killed by drowning, or withdrawing of the air.

TO help myself and others to judge the better of some difficulties concerning respiration, I thought it might be useful that we compared together the times wherein animals may be killed by that *want* of respiration which in those that are drowned is caused by the water that suffocates them, and *that other want* which proceeds from withdrawing the ambient air. Of the latter of these a sufficient number of instances is to be met with amongst our other experiments, and therefore I ſhall now ſubjoin about the former the more trials, becauſe this compariſon hath not, that I know of, been yet thought on by any.

EXPERIMENT I.—A greenfinch, having his legs and wings tied to a weight, was gently let down into a glaſs body filled with water, the time of its total immerſion being marked; at the end of half a minute after the time the ſtrugglings of the bird ſeeming finiſhed, he was nimbly drawn up again, but found quite dead.

EXPERIMENT II.—Whereupon a ſparrow, that was very luſty and quarrelſome, was tied to the ſame weight, and let down after the ſame manner; but though he ſeemed under water to be more vigorous than the other bird, and continued ſtruggling almoſt to the end of half a minute from the time of his being totally immerſed (during which ſtay under water there aſcended, from time to time, pretty large bubbles from his mouth); yet notwithſtanding that, as ſoon as ever the half minute was completed, he was drawn up, we found him, to our wonder, irrecoverably gone.

EXPERIMENT III.—A ſmall mouſe, being held under the water by the tail, emitted from time to time divers aërial bubbles out of his mouth, and at laſt at one of his eyes; and being taken out at the end of half a minute and ſome few ſeconds, retained ſome motions, but they proved but convulſive ones, which at laſt ended in death.

By what is related under the firſt title, it does not appear that water-fowl, or at leaſt that ducks could in our receivers endure the want of air much longer than other birds; but to ſhow that the contrivance of nature is not inſignificant as to the enabling them to continue much longer under water, without freſh air, than the land birds above mentioned, it will not be amiſs to ſubjoin the two following experiments.

EXPERIMENT IV.—We took the duck mentioned in the firſt title, and tied a conſiderable weight of lead to her body, as it did not hinder her reſpiration, and yet would be ſufficient to keep her under water, which we had found that a ſmall weight could not do, by reaſon of her ſtrength, nor yet a great weight, if tied only to her feet, in ſuch a middle-ſized tub as ours was, becauſe of the height of her neck and beak. With the abovementioned clog the duck was put into a tub full of clear water, under the ſurface of which ſhe continued about a minute quietly enough, but afterwards began to appear for a while much diſturbed, which fit being over, our not perceiving any motion in her made us, at the end of the ſecond minute, take her out of the water, to ſee in what condition ſhe was, and finding her in a good one, after we had allowed her ſome breathing time to recruit herſelf with freſh air, we let her down again into the tub, which in the mean time had been filled with freſh water, leſt the other, which had been troubled with the ſteams and foulneſs of the duck's body, might either haſten her death by its being infected with them, or hinder our diſcerning what ſhould happen by its being opakeated by them.

The bird being thus under water, did, after a while, begin, and from time to time continue to emit divers bubbles at her beak. There alſo came out at her noſtrils divers real bubbles from time to time; and when the animal had continued about two minutes or better under water, ſhe began to ſtruggle very much, and to endeavour either to emerge or change poſtures, the latter of which ſhe had liberty to do, but not the former. After four minutes the bubbles came much more ſparingly from her; then alſo ſhe began to gape (which we had not obſerved her to do before), but without emitting bubbles; and ſo ſhe continued gaping till near the end of the ſixth minute, at which time all her motions, ſome of which were judged convulſive, and others that had been excited by our rouſing her with forceps, appeared to ceaſe, and her head to hang down motionleſs, as if ſhe were quite dead. Notwithſtanding which we thought fit, for greater ſecurity, to continue her under water a full minute longer, and then finding no ſigns of life, we took her out and hung her by the heels, and gently preſſing her in convenient places, ſhe was made to void a conſiderable quantity of water, of which, whether any had been received into the lungs themſelves we had not time and opportunity to examine; but all the means that were uſed to recover the bird to life proving ineffectual, we concluded ſhe had been dead a full minute before we removed her out of the water; ſo that, to ſum up the event of our experiment, even this water-bird was not able to live in cold water, without taking in freſh air, above ſix minutes.

EXPERIMENT V.—The duckling mentioned in *Title* I. and *Experiment* II. having a competent weight tied to her legs, was let down into a tub of water which reached not above an inch or two higher than her beak: during the moſt part of her continuance there came out ſtore of bubbles at her noſtrils, but there ſeemed to come out more and greater from a certain place in her head, almoſt equidiſtant from her eyes, but ſomewhat leſs remote from her neck than they. Whilſt ſhe was kept in this condition, ſhe ſeemed frequently to endeavour to dive lower under water, and after much ſtruggling and frequent gaping ſhe had divers convulſive motions, and then let her head fall down backward, with her throat upwards; to which moveleſs poſture ſhe was reduced at the end of the third minute, if not a little ſooner; but awhile after there appeared a manifeſt but tremulous motion in the two parts of her bill which continued for ſome time, but afforded no circumſtances whereby we could be ſure that they were not convulſive motions; but theſe alſo ceaſing at the end of the fourth minute, the bird was taken out, and found irrecoverable.

Experiment VI.—A viper that was kept ſo many hours in an exhauſted receiver, till it was concluded to be quite dead, and to be ſo for a good while, which was nevertheleſs not thrown away till I had tried what could be done by keeping it all night in a glaſs body upon a warm digeſtive furnace. Whereupon this viper was found the next morning not only to have revived, but to be very lively, ſo as to invite me to make with her, without ſeeking for another, the following experiment.

We put her into a tall glaſs body, fitted with a cork to the orifice, and depreſſed with a weight, ſo that ſhe could come at no air. In this ſtate we obſerved her from time to time; and after ſhe lay with very little motion for a conſiderable ſpace of time. At an hour and a quarter's end ſhe often put out her black tongue; at near four hours end ſhe appeared much alive, and, as I remember, about that time alſo put out her tongue, ſwimming all this while, as far as we obſerved, near the bottom of the water. At the end of about ſeven hours more ſhe ſeemed yet to have ſome life in her, her poſture being manifeſtly changed in the glaſs from what it was awhile before, unleſs that might proceed from ſome difference made in her body as to gravity and levity. Not long after ſhe appeared quite dead, her head and tail hanging down motionleſs, and directed towards the bottom of the veſſel, whilſt the middle of the body floated as much as the cork would permit it.

Haſte maketh me omit the mention of divers things ſuggeſted by what hath been delivered upon the preſent title; but it muſt be taken notice of, that though ſome of the above-mentioned animals ſeem, by the relations we have given of them, to have been a little ſooner deſtroyed by drowning than any we have mentioned were by our engine, that is no ſure proof that ſuffocation does kill animals faſter than the deprivation of air they are expoſed to in our engine. For in drowning, *that* which deftroys is applied in its full vigour at the very firft, and all at once; whereas our receivers being made for feveral purpofes, the deprivation of the air that they make cannot be made all at once, but the air muft be pumped out by degrees, fo that till the laft the receiver will be but partly emptied. For confirmation of which I have this to alledge; that having in the prefence of fome virtuofi provided for the nonce a very fmall receiver, wherein yet a moufe could live fome time, if the air were left in it, we were able to evacuate it at one fuck, and by that advantage we were enabled, to the wonder of the beholders, to kill the animal in lefs than half a minute.

Two new Anatomical Difcoveries.

A PROFESSED phyfician hath affured us, that at Montpelier a German hath difcovered the veffels, which convey the chyle to the breafts of nurfing women; and fhewed that they do iffue out of the *ductus* of *Monfieur Pecquet.* This is a difcovery of a thing, the being of which hath been believed long fince, though not made out to general fatisfaction. We are alfo affured, that there is *certainly* another paffage of the urine to the bladder than by the ureters; an experiment having been lately made whereby the ureters of a dog were fo carefully tied up that nothing could pafs that way, and yet the urinary bladder was found full of water.

A narrative of feveral odd effects of a dreadful Thunder-Clap at Sralfund in Pomerania.

AFTER a very hot feafon, from the beginning of this month of June, on the $\frac{18}{28}$ of the fame, early in the morning, a great tempeft was obferved, gathering weft fouth weft, from which there appeared much lightning, with fome thunder at a diftance. On the 19th, being Sunday, after feveral fmall claps, the whole town, and particularly the congregation in St. Nicholas' church (whilft the minifter was preaching) was ftrangely furprifed by a moft terrible flafh of lightning and a fearful thunder-clap, which paffed down through the leffer fteeple upon the body of the church, and through the large round hole in the upper vault within the fame, in the fhape (as fome obferved) of a black fiery ball *directly* upon the *altar*, caufing fuch an hideous crack, fire-flaſh, ſmoke, and damp, as if many fire-balls had been thrown down from the ſaid vault and burſt all at once, begetting a diſmal conſternation amongſt the people, and leaving an ill ſulphurous ſmell behind.

The candle on the ſouth ſide of the altar was put out by the blow, the other remained burning. Two of the chalices there were overthrown, and the wine ſpilt, and the wafers ſcattered about, but the empty chalice ſtood firm. All three were ſomewhat ſmutted at the feet, and one of them a little bent there, and in two places pierced through as if it had been by hail ſhot, and the wafer-boxes were likewiſe a little ſmutted towards the bottom. The church book was flung on the inner paſſage; the covers of the altar were ſinged in divers parts, as by powder, and ſomewhat burnt and ſmutted here and there, and alſo torn in ſome places. A ſtrong piece of wainſcot, with a *picture* upon it, behind the great altar, was ſplit in two. Of the church clock, in the weſt end at the ſame time, both braſs and iron wires of the whole and quarter hours' hammers were partly broken, and the reſt could not be found; and an open poſt fixed in the wall, for the ſupport of the dial, was half torn, and beneath the ſame divers bricks were ſtruck out of the two-head pillars ſupporting the ſteeple. On the top of the ſouthern ſteeple an open gutter and a ſtrong beam and ſupporter were ſhattered, and fell dangerouſly, but that one part of it held faſt yet by a nail.

One of the miniſters, though ſitting near the altar to the ſouth, had no hurt at all. Divers of the people ſeated round about the altar fell down to the ground with the fright. One youth, that ſtood next to the miniſter's pew, not being able to recover his ſenſes, was carried home. On the north ſide of the altar four perſons fell down, and one of the open ſeats being ſplit under him that ſat thereon, that perſon was much hurt by it, and more than any other. Some that ſtood in or by the belfry, near the clock, were ſlightly hurt here and there; and amongſt them a mariner, leaning on a lined open ſeat there, had his right arm bruiſed; and another man, though but ſlightly hurt, yet could not remember how he got home from church.

The ſermon being broke off, and the people making haſte away, ſome obſerved that there iſſued forth a huge damp out of the ſouthern ſteeple, like unto ſmoke which poſſeſſed many with great fears of fire within; but the church carpenter, upon ſearch of the ſaid ſteeple and church roof within, met only with a preſent noiſome and thick damp, which, though it frighted him at firſt into an apprehenſion of fire, yet, getting to the windows and opening them, the damp iſſued with great violence, but there appeared no fire any where, ſave only a little in the ſhattered parts of the ſteeple, which was ſoon quenched.

The church dial was alſo much ſmutted in ſundry parts, ſoiling the *gilt* figures that they could ſcarce be diſcerned. The gilt weather-cocks, upon both the ſteeples, were likewiſe ſmutted on the one ſide of their tails, without any other mark; nor could it be in the leaſt diſcovered, in either of the ſteeples, which way the lightning entered, by all the ſearch that was made.

Amonſt the perſons, that were any way hurt, (who were but eight in all) divers ſingular particulars were obſerved afterwards, viz.

One that ſtood in the belfry had the upper back part of his cloth coat, as alſo his ſhirt and ſkin, ſomewhat torn; but the lining of that coat, which was red frieze, had no hurt at all, between the reſt.

Another ſitting in a pew under the organ, and leaning on the door, whilſt the pew lock (then cloſe to his body) was ſo violently ſtruck out that it hung only by one nail, had no damage at all by it himſelf, nor any other that ſat or ſtood thereby when the ſtroke happened, though they fell all to the ground by the fright, at the inſtant when it was given.

And as for him that had his arm bruiſed, it was remarkable, that afterwards there was found a hole paſſing his coat, waiſtcoat, and ſhirt, without in the leaſt hurting the body, the hole appearing juſt as if ſhot through. And, beſides, notice was taken that the ſaid man's waiſtcoat (being of a red ſarcenet) kept its colour every where but at the place where the arm was hurt; and the waiſtcoat being edged with a ſmall ſilver lace, the lace was ſmutted almoſt every where, and about the neck alſo where the party wore a cravat. The ſame perſon had one half of his ſhoe torn off, the ſole being pierced as with hail ſhot, and a piece of his ſtocking foot ſtruck away, near an hand breadth, without any other hurt to either foot or leg, but for ſome days that foot was benumbed.

Laſtly, one of them that ſat by the altar had his breeches and leather drawers on both ſides pierced through as by hail ſhot, and part of it plainly ſcorched and ſhrunk up, as by fire; and divers ſuch ſmall holes in his ſhirt, yet without any hurt to his body, ſave that he found ſome pain in his foot. One ſide of his ſhoe alſo was half torn, and the ſole ſideways pierced through, as it were, with gun ſhot.

Yet there died not one of all thoſe that were hurt; they recovering either of themſelves, or by the advice and help of others.

A narrative of a Monſtrous Birth.

ONE Grace Battered, the wife of a ſhoemaker, of honeſt repute, and mother of five children, arrived at the full time to be delivered of a ſixth birth; about 12 o'clock at night ſhe began to have travailing pains, and near four o'clock in the morning the head of a child came to the birth; when the midwife, putting her hand to help off this, felt another (by its heat and motion) alive, and therefore made all poſſible ſpeed to deliver her of this. It is obſervable that in three of her former five travails ſhe was ſo quick as that ſhe was delivered before the midwife came; but now ſhe could not ſo ſpeedily effect her deſire, in regard that not only the firſt child was ſuffocated by its ſtay in the birth, but alſo the head of the ſecond turning aſide from the inner orifice of the uterus towards the groin, and the twins being joined together (as afterwards appeared) made it a different birth. But the midwife doing her part exceeding well, and the mother having nimble travail, was delivered of thoſe prodigious twins. I ſend you incloſed an account of what we thought further worth obſervation.

The birth had two heads and two necks, as alſo the eyes, mouths, and ears, ſuitably double. Four arms with hands, and as many legs and feet. There was to both but one trunk, yet two back bones, from the *clavicles* to the *hypogaſtrium*, and from the ſhoulders down to the bottom of the loins they were not diſtinct, but cemented and concorporated after this manner: the right clavicle, or channel bone of the right hand child (being long) joined to the left clavicle of the left hand child. The ribs on the face ſide of both of them, by the cartilages or griſtles were united without any intervening ſternum or breaſt bone, and ſo made a common cheſt to them both; and the ribs of both on the back part were united by the griſtles; and from the clavicle down to the hypogaſtrium or bottom of the belly were ſo conjoined that they made but one common belly, with one navel ſtring to them both; but from the hypogaſtrium downwards they were divided, and became two, each having the perfect parts of females.

Having with ſome difficulty obtained the father's leave to diſſect it, we firſt weighed this birth; the weight whereof was eight pounds and a quarter; the circumference of the left head was about 11 inches, that of the right being half an inch leſs. The circumference of the trunk was about 16 inches and a quarter; and the length of both, from head to foot, was full 18 inches and a half.

We found one navel-vein and one liver, but that was very large, with the bladder of gall ſeated in it's uſual place; but there were two urinary bladders, two wombs, four kidnies, and one ſtomach, *oeſophagus* or *gullet*, perforate and open from the left head; but the oeſophagus from the mouth of the right head deſcended no lower than to half an inch from the midriff, and there it ended. No further could we follow it with the probe, but doubting a failure in that experiment, we made an eſſay with a blow-pipe, and thereby found that the wind would go no further than the place abovementioned, whence it may be concluded that the right hand child muſt have received its nouriſhment by and from the left hand child.

There was but one colon or colick gut, which terminated in two inteſtina recta. So there was but one midriff, and above that we could find little or no appearance of lungs, but only a very large heart, (with two auricles,) the figure of which was not conical, but like a ſoldier's pera knapſack, or the ventricle or ſtomach; and lying near under the clavicles, tranſverſed as the ſtomach lieth under the midriff and liver. We did alſo obſerve two ventricles with the tricuſpid or ſigmoid valves; as alſo the vena cava and aorta dependant, and alſo the aorta aſcending and byfurcate towards each neck, and then byfurcate again.

Theſe twins were exactly like one another; very well featured, having alſo pretty neat and handſome limbs. They had their hair more than ordinarily thick, and about half an inch long, and the nails full grown.

We might have proceeded to further obſervations, but time and the tumultuous concourſe of people, as alſo the night, and alſo the father's importunity to haſten the birth to the grave, hindered us.

The mother is at this time in as good a condition of health as women in child-bed uſe to be.

Obſervations on Inſects lodging themſelves in old Willows, laid before the ROYAL SOCIETY, *by Dr. Edmond King, July* 14, 1670.

YOU may remember, that about the beginning of May laſt, a piece of old willow wood being ſent me from Sir John Bernhard, out of Northamptonſhire, was produced before you, in which were lodged many inſects curiouſly wrapped up in green leaves in ſeveral channels or burrows, each with 12, 14, or 16 leaves round the body, and ſeveral of them with as many little round bits of leaves at each end, to ſtop them up cloſe. Theſe, thus made up, are an inch long, put in one after another into a bore made in the wood, fit for their reception. They are in the manner of cartridges of powder, wherewith piſtols are wont to be charged, or like long ſlugs of lead, they are placed ſo near one another as to touch; in others, at ſome conſiderable diſtance. Theſe inſects obſerve this method in placing themſelves, that ſometimes they make a direct way into the length of the wood, ſometimes they bore out into the ſide and run another way, thoſe channels being not unlike the burrows of rabbits; all which they fill up with theſe round appearances of wrapt leaves, all regularly wrought, in which I find either ſomething alive, or appearances of ſomething that hath died there, and is putrified: in ſome a great number of mites of a dark aſh colour, ſhaped not unlike common mites; in others, I found ſeeming excrements of ſome ſmall inſect, with the decayed parts of the dead inſect; in others, white maggots, ſome of them I took out of their *theca* or bag, and put them in warm places in the ſun, and they thereupon grew ſomething bigger, but changed not ſhape or colour, but died. The reſt I kept cloſe in a box till the 8th of July, preſent; then I took one of them out of the wood, and opened the leaves, and felt ſomething ſtir, hearing alſo a humming noiſe like that of a bee; and as ſoon as I had opened the *theca*, a perfect bee flew out againſt my window, as ſtrongly as a common bee out of a hive, having much of the colour and bigneſs of thoſe when they are new flyers. Then being pleaſed with the ſight, I took five more (all I had left) and put them in a box into my pocket to ſhew them to Lord Brunker, before they were taken out, or had eaten their way out; but his Lordſhip not being at home I brought them back again, and they being diſturbed they all eat themſelves out; and upon opening the box found them all creeping about, but are ſince dead there, as are theſe I here preſent to your view. They have all ſtings as other bees have. I had ſome thoughts at firſt ſight, by the yellowiſh circles under their bellies, that they might be a ſort of waſps; but now am of opinion that they are common bees.

Extract of two letters written by Francis Willoughby, Esq. relating to the foregoing subject.

1st. I HAD the good luck to find a great many of your cartridges in a rotten willow, and by the shape of the maggot was most confident they would produce insects of the bee tribe. And this I should most certainly have foretold you, had I ever received those you sent me; but having only that one you sent me before, I was so fond and choice of it that I durst not open it. I think now I have found out the whole mystery; and if you please to send me Dr. King's account, and one of your bees, because all mine being of a late hatch, and none of them yet turned into nymphæ (which is the word of art for the aurelia of a bee) I fear I shall not see their last metamorphosis this year. In a garden, near a willow, I found where they got their leaves for their cartridges, which are not willow but rose leaves.

2d. At my coming home I found the long expected cartridges, and some of the bees hatched, so that now we want nothing to complete their history. I will trouble you only with those particulars that I find not mentioned in Dr. King's paper, to whom we owe the knowledge of their productions, and whose observations concerning them, our own experience hath since confirmed. Mr. Snell, an ingenious gentleman, brought of them to the Wells at Astrop, who directing me to the place where he got them, I there found great plenty in the trunk of a dead willow. Beginning to unfold some of them, we immediately judged them to be made up of pieces of rose leaves, and called to mind that this very spring a worthy friend of his brought him a rose leaf, out of which he himself saw a bee bite such a piece, and fly away with it in her mouth. Whereupon searching the rose trees thereabouts, we found a great many leaves with such pieces bitten out of them as these cartridges are made up of, some of which I sent you inclosed in my last. The cuniculi, or hole, never crossed the grain of the wood, excepting where the bee comes in, and where they open one into another. From the place of entrance they are wrought both upwards and downwards, so that sometimes the bee maggot lies under her food and sometimes above it. One end of the cartridge, viz. that which is next the entrance is always a little concave; the other end, which is furthest from the entrance, a little convex, and is received into the concave of the next beyond it. The sides of the cartridges are made up of long pieces of leaves, and pasted together; the ends, of round ones, and wherever they do not lie close one to another, the intermediate ſpace is filled up with a multitude of theſe little round pieces laid one upon another.

The cartridges contain a pap or batter, of the conſiſtence of a jelly, or ſomething thicker, of a middle colour, between ſyrup of violets and the conſerve of red roſes, of an acid taſte, and unpleaſant ſmell. In each of theſe, at the concave end, there lies one bee maggot, which feeds upon the forementioned matter till grown to its full bigneſs, and there makes, and incloſeth herſelf in, a *theca* or huſk, of a dark red colour and oval figure, in which ſhe is changed into a bee. The remainder of her food you may find dried into powder at the convex end, and her excrements at the concave without the *theca*.

The bees I found in your box (which are the only ones I have yet ſeen) were of a ſhorter and thicker ſhape than the common honey bee, more hairy, &c. But the ſureſt mark to diſtinguiſh them is, that the forceps or teeth of theſe are bigger, broader, and ſtronger, in ſhape like thoſe of a waſp or hornet; from which ſhe alſo ſufficiently differs in having a tongue like a bee, which they want.

They made their way out along the channel through all the intermediate cartridges, and not through the ſolid wood. Of the corruption of the matter within the caſes, when the bee maggots or nymphæ happen to miſcarry, are bred little hexapods, which produce beetles; two maggots, which produce flies; the mites, &c.

From what hath been obſerved concerning this bee, and by a great many more parallel inſtances, we may anſwer the query of ſome who have written of bees, whether it be the old bee or the bee maggot, that covers the cells before the change? and ſay, that it is the maggot, and not the old one. For here the old bee, when ſhe hath left proviſion enough, with an egg, cloſes up the cartridge, and hath no more to do. The maggot a great while after making the *theca*, which is analogous to the cover of the cells.

Fig. 1 repreſents the leaf, out of which a long piece, as fig. 2, and a round piece, as fig. 3, were bitten. Fig. 4 ſhews the cartridge itſelf; and fig. 5 the *theca*.

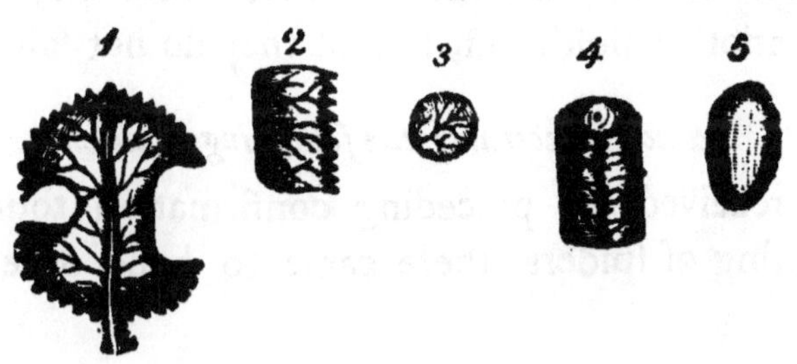

A confirmation of what was formerly given in page 222. Communicated by Mr. John Wray.

CONCERNING the manner of ſpiders projecting their threads, I received the following account from Dr. Hulſe, from whom I muſt acknowlege I had the firſt notice of this particular, which was not long after communicated to me by another ingenious friend, whoſe letter I formerly ſent you to be imparted to the ROYAL SOCIETY. Nor is it any great wonder, that inquiſitive perſons, applying themſelves to obſerve and conſider the ſame ſubjects, ſhould make the ſame diſcoveries.

I have (ſaith he) ſeen them ſhoot their webs three yards long before they began to ſail, and then they will (as it were) fly away incredibly ſwift; which phenomenon doth ſomewhat puzzle me, ſeeing oftentimes the air doth not move a quarter ſo faſt as theſe ſeem to fly. Moſtly they project their threads ſingle, without dividing or forking at all to be ſeen in them: ſometimes they will ſhoot the thread upward, and will mount up with it in a line almoſt perpendicular; and at other times they project it in a line parallel to the plane of the horizon, as you may often ſee by their threads that run from one tree to another, and likewiſe in chambers, from one wall to another. I confeſs, this obſervation firſt made me think, that they could fly, becauſe I could not conceive how a thread could be drawn ſo parallel to the horizon between two walls or trees, unleſs the ſpider flew through the air in a ſtraight line. The way of forking their threads is expreſſed by fig. 6. What reaſon ſhould be given of this dividing I know not, except that the threads being thus winged, become better able to ſuſtain them in the air.

They will often faſten their threads in ſeveral places to the things they creep on. The manner is, by beating their tails againſt them as they creep along; which may be underſtood by fig. 7. By this frequent beating in of their thread amongſt the aſperities of the place where they creep, they either ſecure it againſt the wind, that it may not be eaſily blown away; or elſe, whilſt they hang by it, if one junction breaks, another holds faſt, ſo that they do not fall to the ground.

A note concerning the following relation.

After we had received the preceding confirmation touching the firſt obſerver of the darting of ſpiders, there came to hand a letter from that inquiſitive gentleman, Mr. Martin Liſter, intimating that if we were not yet fully ſatisfied about that matter, he had this further to ſay; that Mr. Wray knew nothing of *his* being acquainted with it, until ſuch time as he occaſionally ſent him a catalogue of our Engliſh ſpiders. Upon which ſubject, in the next letter, Mr. Wray put this amongſt other queſtions to Mr. Liſter, whether he had obſerved the darting of ſpiders? To which he anſwered in the affirmative, relating to him many other circumſtances not obſerved by him before: ſo that he was deſired by Mr. Wray to draw up his notes, and ſuffer him to preſent them to the ROYAL SOCIETY, which he did.

Whence it appears, that this obſervation is as well Mr. Liſter's as Dr. Hulſe's, though it be true alſo, that when it was written and ſent by the former of theſe two gentlemen, it was then a thing altogether unknown to Mr. Wray, but confirmed and enlarged by Mr. Liſter's own obſervations; which it was thought fit to add here that nothing might be detracted from Mr. Liſter for permitting his notes in the lately mentioned tract to be publiſhed as his own, which really they are.

Extract of a letter from Mr. Martindale, of Cheſhire, dated November 12, 1670, *concerning the diſcovery of a rock of Natural Salt in that country.*

A GENTLEMAN of much reputation aſſures us, that in his part of the country there is lately diſcovered a great rarity, viz. a rock of *natural* ſalt, from which iſſues a vigorous, ſharp brine, beyond any of the ſprings made uſe of in our ſalt works; and this not nigh any river or great brook, as all our ſalt ſprings in this country are.

This rock of ſalt, by the relation of the workmen, is between 33 and 34 yards diſtant from the ſurface of the earth, about 30 whereof are already digged; and they hope to be at the flag, which covers the ſalt rock, in about three weeks hence. I doubt it will be ſeveral months before I can accommodate you with a parcel of it, that which the augur brought up being long ſince diſpoſed of, and the workmen not daring to remove the flag till the frame is finiſhed, and well ſettled for the ſecuring of the work. The overſeer hath promiſed to furniſh me with a piece of the rock for your uſe; as alſo to ſignify to me the time when they intend to uncover it, that, if poſſible, we may make ſome experiments. That parcel of natural ſalt which the inſtrument brought up, divers perſons who ſaw it aſſured me was as hard as alum, and as pure; and, when pulverized, became an excellent, fine, and ſharp ſalt. The firſt diſcoverer of it was one John Jackſon, of Halton, as he was ſearching for coals on behalf of the lord of the ſoil, Wm. Marbury, of Marbury, Eſq.

An experiment concerning the progreſs of artificial Conglaciation, and the remarkable accidents therein obſerved, by the Florentine Philoſophers.

THE firſt veſſel we uſed (ſay theſe eminent academiſts) for this experiment, was a globe of chryſtal, whoſe diameter was one-eighth of a *braccio* (which is near three Engliſh inches), with a long ſtraight neck, of about a braccio and an half, graduated into ſmall parts. Having filled it with common water up to the ſixth part of the neck, we put the globular part into ice and ſalt, after the uſual manner of artificial freezing of liquors, and began very attentively to obſerve all the motions of the water, from its level. It was ſufficiently known before, that freezing worketh in all liquors a contraction; as alſo, that in the paſſage which the water maketh from being ſimply cold to the leaving of its fluidity, and taking a conſiſtency and hardneſs by congelation, it not only returns to the bulk it had before it was frozen, but ſwells to a bigger; ſince we ſee, that veſſels, not only of glaſs, but of metal, are forcibly broken thereby; but what might be the limits and periods of thoſe various alterations, which the cold works therein, we as yet did not know; nor is it poſſible to attain that knowledge in opake veſſels. We therefore, that we might not want that inſight, which appeared to be the ſoul of theſe experiments, had recourſe to chryſtal and glaſs, hoping, that by the tranſparency of that body we ſhould be informed of the whole progreſs, in regard that at every motion, which ſhould appear in the water of the neck, we might quickly take the globe out of the ice, and therein obſerve the alterations correſpondent thereto. But the truth is, that we took more pains than we can expreſs before we could find out any thing certain touching the periods of theſe accidents.

And to deliver more diſtinctly the ſucceſs, you are to know, that in the firſt immerſion of the globe, as ſoon as it touched the icy water, there was obſerved in the water of the glaſs's neck a ſmall riſing, but *that* ſufficiently quick; after which, with a motion regular enough, and of middle velocity, it retired back to the globe, till being come to a certain mark, it continued not to defcend any further, but ftopped there for a while, being altogether, as far as we could fee, motionlefs. Afterwards, little by little, it was feen to begin to rife again, but with a very flow motion, which was in appearance even and regular; from whence, without any proportioned acceleration, it fuddenly and furioufly ftarted upwards, in which time it was impoffible to follow it with our eyes, it running with this impetuoufnefs in an inftant, as it were, through feveral tens of the marked degrees. And as this violence began in a moment, fo in a moment it ended; forafmuch as from this very great velocity it fuddenly paffed to another degree of motion, which, though nimble enough, was yet incomparably lefs than the preceding; and going on to rife in this degree, it went to the top of the neck, and at laft run over.

All the while that thefe things happened, there was at times feen on the top of the water fome bubbles, either aërial or of another more fubtile matter, now in a greater, then in a fmaller degree. And this feparation did not begin till the water had become to take a brifk cold, as if the force of fuch a cold had the power of ftraining fuch matter, and fevering it from the water.

Now being defirous to fee whether thofe alterations kept among themfelves any kind of analogy, we began to reiterate the conglaciations, and no fooner was one ice deftroyed but we fet it to freeze anew; and the water went to congeal again in the fame order of alterations, which yet did not every time return to the felf fame points or degrees in the neck, which made us believe that they had no conftant and ftable period, as reafon feemed to perfuade us they had. Meantime it fell out in repeating thefe experiments, that having once unawares let the water of the globe freeze near the neck, the globe burft; whereupon another being taken of a lefs fize, to the end that the cold might more fpeedily and more eafily get into all the water, and the neck of it being two braccios long, that it might not run out; it was filled with water out to the 160th degree, and then put into the ice. Here obferving it with the beft attention we could, we found, *firft*, that all the accidents of fubfiding, rifing, refting, ftarting upwards, running, retarding, did always follow in the fame points of the neck of the globe, that is, when the furface of the water ftood at the fame degrees; provided, that in the act of ſetting it in the ice, care was taken to put it to the very ſame degree where it was when put into the ice the time before, that is to ſay, to the ſame temper of heat and cold; in which caſe the whole veſſel might be conſidered as a very nice thermometer, by reaſon of the great capacity of the globe, and the exceeding ſtraightneſs of the neck. This being provided for, we began to take notice of the preciſe time of congelation, which to find aright we did, after a very little ſpace of time, take up the globe out of the ice; but how frequently ſoever we made ſuch obſervations, we never could ſo hit it as to ſee even the leaſt vein of froſt, but always it was either all fluid or all frozen; whence we conjectured, that the work of congelation was done in a very ſhort time, and that he who ſhould with taking pains have the luck to take the globe out of the ice in that nick of time when the water ſhould receive that ſudden change, would certainly find ſomething very notable thereby. And becauſe by the ſo often taking out and putting the globe into the ice, the whole period of its changes were diſordered, we let it return to juſt the ſame mark as it was at firſt, and then placing it in the ice, we fixed it to that degree in which it was wont to take that very impetuous motion, and half a degree before it arrived thereto we took it out. Then looking conſtantly with a careful eye upon the water in the globe, which by reaſon of the tranſparency of the chryſtal was plainly ſeen to be yet altogether fluid and clear, the water, though now out of the ice, did, by the operation of the introduced cold (after it had attained to its due point with a ſwiftneſs imperceptible to the eye, the tranſparency within the globular part being loſt, and itſelf in an inſtant, as it were, deprived of its motion), totally conglaciate; which experiment we tried over and over again, and found it always ſucceed alike.

A relation of an abundance of Wood found under ground in Lincolnſhire.

THE fenny tract called the Iſle of Axholme, lying part in Lincolnſhire and in Yorkſhire, and extending a conſiderable way, hath anciently been a woody country; witneſs the abundance of oak, fir, and other trees, of late frequently found in the moor, whereof ſome oaks are *five* yards in compaſs, and ſixteen yards long, others ſmaller and longer, with good quantities of acorns near them, lying ſomewhat above three feet in depth, and near their roots, which ſtill do ſtand as they grew, viz. in firm earth below the moor. The firs lying a foot or 18 inches deeper, more in number than oak, and many of them thirty yards long, one of them being, not many years ſince, taken up of *thirty-ſix* yards long beſides the top, lying alſo near the root, having been burnt and not cut down, as the oaks had been alſo. The number of theſe trees is reported to be ſo great, that the inhabitants have, for divers years laſt paſt, taken up vaſt quantities yearly.

As to the firſt time of the overflowing of this woody level, no account is given that I know of, not by the learned and inquiſitive antiquary Mr. Dugdale himſelf. He only ſaith, that the depth of the moor evinceth that it hath been ſo for many hundred years, ſince *that* could not increaſe ſo much in depth in a few ages. Of the cauſe thereof he concludeth, that it hath been due to the muddineſs of the conſtant tides, which flowing up the *Humber* into the *Trent*, left in time ſo much filth as to obſtruct the currents of *Idle*, *Done*, and other rivers, which thence flowed back, and overwhelmed that flat country.

Deſcription of the Stone Quarry near Maeſtrich.

THERE is an excellent quarry within gun-ſhot of Maeſtrich, upon the brink of the river *Maeſe*, lying in a hill, where there are about 25 fathoms of rock and earth overhead; the length of the hill being of ſome miles extent along the river towards *Liege*, ſituated on the ſame river, and near Maeſtrich, in breadth about three quarters of a mile, but ſomething broader further on. This quarry hath one entrance towards the river, where carts can paſs with great eaſe, and unload the ſtones upon the brink of the river, the quarry within lying parallel to the horizon (which is a great advantage), and elevated but very little above the river.

This ſame quarry, which hath well nigh undermined the whole hill, affords one of the moſt ſurpriſing proſpects, when well lighted with many torches, that one can imagine; for there are thouſands of ſquare pillars in large level walks, and thoſe almoſt every where, above twenty, and in ſome places many more feet high, and all wrought with ſo much neatneſs and regularity, that one would think it had been made rather with curious workmanſhip for an under ground palace, than that thoſe pillars and galleries were made quarries, that did it only for getting ſtone to build above ground.

This quarry ſerveth the people that live thereabout for a kind of impregnable retreat when armies march that way; for, being acquainted with all the ways in it, they carry into it whatever they would have ſafe, as well their horſes and cattle as their moveable furniture, till the danger be over, it being ſo vaſtly extenſive that forty thouſand people may ſhelter themſelves in it. And they that would attempt to ſeek them out in this vaſt wilderneſs of walks and pillars, without an expert guide, would not only be in hazard of loſing their way, but of being knocked on the head at the corner of every pillar, where people lurking in the dark with their fire arms would have fair opportunity to ſhoot them by the light of their own torches.

In this vaſt grotto it is remarkable that there is but little rubbiſh, which ſhows both the goodneſs of the ſtone and the carefulneſs of the workmen. And in divers places there are little pools of water, perhaps made on purpoſe for beaſts to drink, and to ſerve for other uſes in time of need; for in no place almoſt are there any droppings to be ſeen; nor are the walks at all wet under foot; only it ſeems, that rain gets in by *air ſhafts*, which, for ſaving of labour, and perhaps, too, to make theſe pools, are let down from ſuch places as where pools are thereabouts, and ſo the rain that falls upon the higher ground doth eaſily find the way thither.

An account of the Tin Mines of Cornwall, and the manner of working them.

IT is ſuppoſed by the miners, that there was a great concuſſion of the waters in that ſeparation of the waters from thoſe at the creation, when the dry land firſt appeared, or at Noah's flood, or at both times, whereby the waters moved and removed the (then) ſurface of the earth; that till then the uppermoſt ſurface of mineral veins, or loads, did in moſt places lie even with the then real, but now imaginary ſurface of the earth, which is now called the ſhelf, or firs country, or ground that was never moved. But at this concuſſion of the waters the ſurface of the earth, together with the uppermoſt of thoſe mineral veins, were looſed, and torn off; and by the deſcending of the waters into the vallies, both the earth, or greut, and thoſe mineral ſtones or fragments ſo torn off from their loads (which are conſtantly termed ſhoads), were, together with, and by the force of the waters, carried beneath their proper places, and from ſome hills, even to the bottoms of the neighbouring vallies, and from thence by land floods many miles down the river.

Traming a load.

1ſt, Where we ſuſpect any mine to be, we diligently ſearch that hill and country, that we may the better know the greut and ſtones, when we meet with them at a diſtance in the neighbouring valley.

2d, Then we obſerve the frets in the banks of rivers that are newly made by any great land flood, which uſually are then very clean, to ſee if happily we can diſcover any metalline ſtones in the ſides and bottoms thereof, together with the caſt of the country (i. e. any earth of a different colour from the reſt of the bank), which is a great help to direct us which ſide or hill to ſearch into. The mineral ſtones are diſcovered either by their ponderoſity, or by their poroſity, for moſt tin-ſtones are porous, not unlike great bones, almoſt thoroughly calcined; yet tin ſometimes lies in the firmeſt ſtones; or by vauning, which is performed by pulverizing the ſtone or clay, or what elſe may be ſuſpected to contain any mineral body, and placing it on a vauning ſhovel, the gravel remains in the hinder part, and the metal at the point of the ſhovel, whereby the kind, nature, and quality of the ore is very nearly gueſſed at.

3d, If no ſhoad be found in theſe frets, we truſt not to any found in the river, it being uncertain from whence the water may have brought them. But we go to the ſides of thoſe hills moſt ſuſpected, where there may be a conveniency of a little ſtream of water, the more the better, and cut a leat, gurt, or trench, about two feet over, and as deep as the ſhelf, into which we turn the water to run two or three days, by which time the water, by waſhing away the filth from the ſtones, and the looſer parts of the earth, will eaſily diſcover what ſhoad is there. If we find any, we may have a certainty of a load in the upper part of the hill, or at leaſt a ſquat.

4th, Sometimes ſhoad may be found upon the open ſurface of the ground, but then it is brought thither by ſome accident, for the corruption of vegetables, &c. having ſince the deluge begotten a new ſurface, heightened in ſome places a foot or more above the ſhelf; and this is demonſtrable to the eye in every tin work.

5th, At the foot or bottom of the hill we ſink an eſſay hatch, or a hole about ſix feet long, and four feet broad, and always as deep as the ſhelf. If we find no ſhoad before, or when we come to the ſhelf, there is none to be expected; yet ſometimes the ſhoad is waſhed away clean when we come within two or three feet of the load, which then lies ſo much farther up in the hill. If we find ſhoad, we are almoſt at a certainty: and this is held as an infallible rule, that the nigher the ſhoad lies to the ſhelf, the nigher the load is at hand, and *vice verſa*.

6th, If we find no ſhoad in this firſt hatch, we aſcend commonly about 12 fathoms, and ſink a ſecond hatch, as the former; and in caſe none appear in this, we go then as many fathoms on each hand at the ſame height, and ſink there as before; and ſo aſcend proportionably with three or four hatches, if the ſpace of ground requires, as it were in breaſt, till we come to the top of the hill; and if we find none in any of theſe hatches, then farewell to that hill.

7th, But if we find any ſhoad in any of theſe hatches, we keep our aſcending hatches in a direct line; and as we draw near the load, we leſſen our firſt proportion of 12 fathoms to ſix, or leſs, as our conjecture guides us.

8th, If finding ſhoad lying near the ſhelf in one hatch, and none in the next aſcending, we conclude that we have certainly over-ſhot the load, and we ſink nigher that hatch wherein we laſt found ſhoad.

9th, Sometimes we find different ſhoad in the ſame hatch at different depths, and then we have a certainty of another load above the former; and it may be, in training up to the ſecond, we meet with the ſhoad of a third. Some tinners affirm, that ſeven load may lie parallel to each other in the ſame hill, but yet only one maſter-load, the other ſix, three on each ſide, being the leſſer concomitants. So may five lie in like manner; three are common.

10th, Every load has, as it were, a peculiar coloured earth or greut about it, which is found likewiſe with the ſhoad in a greater quantity, the nearer the ſhoad lies to the load, and ſo leſſened by degrees to about a quarter of a mile diſtance, further than which that peculiar greut is never found with the ſhoad.

11th, A valley may ſo lie as at the feet of three ſeveral hills; and then we may find three ſeveral deads, i. e. common earth, or that looſe earth which was moved with the ſhoad in the concuſſion, but not contiguous to the load in its firſt poſition, which is alſo termed by us the run of the country, with as many different ſhoads in the midſt of each. And here the knowledge of the caſt of the country, or each hill, in reſpect of its greut, will be very neceſſary for the ſurer training of them one after another, as they lie in order, according to the foregoing rules of eſſay hatches, for the uppermoſt will direct you with which hill to begin firſt.

12th, It may be, that after we have trained up the hill, inſtead of a load, we find nought but a bonny, or ſquat, which likewiſe have their ſhoad, whoſe form is about two or three fathoms long, and half as broad, few larger, moſt leſs, which communicates with no other load or vein, neither doth it ſend forth any of its own, but is entire of itſelf, and may go down into the ſhelf five or ſix fathoms deep, and there terminate.

Manner of digging the Ore.

When we have found the load, the laſt eſſay hatch is then called a tin ſhaft, or tin hatch, which we ſink down about a fathom, and leave a little long ſquare place, termed a ſhamble, and ſo continue ſinking from caſt to caſt, *i. e.* as high as a man can conveniently throw up the ore with a ſhovel, till we find either the load grow ſmall, or degenerate into ſome ſort of weed, which are divers, as *mundick*, or *maxy*, corrupted from marchaſite, white, yellow, and green; *daze*, which is a kind of glittering ſtone enduring the fire, of different colours, white, black, and yellow; *iron-mould*, black and ruſty, *caaul*, red, (differing both from mundick and ſparr,) enduring the fire, which marchaſite will not; *gliſter*, blood red, and black.

We then begin to make a drift three feet wide, and ſeven high; and if the load be not broad enough of itſelf, as ſome are ſcarce half a foot, then we uſually break down the deads, or that part of the ſhelf which contains the metal, but encloſeth the load, as a wall, between two rocks; and then we begin to rip the load itſelf.

The inſtruments we make uſe of are, 1ſt, a beele, or Corniſh tubbar, *i. e.* double points of eight or ten pounds weight, ſharped at both ends, well ſteeled and holed in the middle; it may laſt in a hard country half a year, but new pointed every fortnight at leaſt: 2d, a ſledge, flat headed, from 10 to 20 pounds weight; it will laſt about ſeven years, new ordered once a quarter: 3d, three gadds or wedges, of two pounds weight, four ſquare, well ſteeled at the point; they will laſt a week, then ſharped: four ladders, five wheelbarrows, to carry the deads and ore out of the drifts or adits to the ſhambles.

There are two ſhovel men, and three beele men, which are as many as one drift can contain, without being a hindrance to each other. The beele men rip the deads and ore, the ſhovel men carry it off, and land it, by caſting it up with ſhovels from one ſhamble to another, unleſs it be where we have a winder with two reebles or buckets, one of which comes up as the other goes down.

It is generally obſerved, that moſt of our tin loads run from weſt to eaſt, and then they *conſtantly* dip towards the north; ſometimes they underlie, that is, ſlope down towards the north, three feet in height perpendicular: yet in the higher mountains of Dartmoor there are ſome conſiderable loads, which run north and ſouth, and theſe underlie towards the eaſt.

Four or five loads may run parallel to each other in the ſame hill, and yet, which is rare, meet altogether in one hatch, as it were in a knot, which well tins the place, and ſo ſeparate again, and keep their former diſtances: ſuch a knot hath been obſerved and wrought in Hingſton, a known mineral down or common in Cornwall.

The breadth of maſter loads may generally be from three to ſeven feet, ſeldom larger, unleſs where ſeveral loads may chance to make a knot, or ſend forth ſtrings or veins. Neither retain they their uſual breadth in all parts; for they may be ſix feet at one part, and not two at another, nay, ſometimes ſcarce half an inch over; but that is to be underſtood of ſtrings, and the narroweſt places of the concomitant loads. The load is commonly in a hard rocky country, made up of metals, ſpars, and other weeds, as it were all along a continued rock; but it hath many veins and joints, as we ſpeak; but in ſome ſofter countries, the tin may lay in a ſofter conſiſtence, as that of clay, in a manner petrified.

In moſt places we meet with water at ſome feet deep from the loady ſurface, in others not as many fathoms deep. It runs continually through the heart of the load. When it begins to be troubleſome, we begin at the foot of the hill a drift or adit, ſcarce half ſo big as that of the load, and work it on a level, till we come up to the load. But if we have not this conveniency of an adit, or if we paſs that level, we are forced to draw it with winders and keebles, or with pumps. Some, but very few, works may prove dry.

We obſerve, that if we have water, we never want air ſufficient for reſpiration, and our candles to burn in; yet ſometimes, in a ſoft clayey country, our air is ſo much condenſed that it becomes in a manner a damp, and requires an air ſhaft for vent; which damps are ſometimes enlarged by working of the mundick with the ore.

If the country be not ſtrong enough, we underprop our drifts with ſtemples and wall-plates, placed much like a carpenter's ſquare, on the one ſide and over head.

To know which way the load inclines, or to bring an adit, or to ſink an air ſhaft to the deſired place, the uſe of the dial is needful, which we term plumming and dialling, and is thus performed. A ſkilful perſon firſt faſtens the end of a long line at a known place, and then exactly obſerves the point at which the needle of his dial or compaſs reſts; and at the next flexure he makes a mark on the line, and again notes the point at which the needle ſtands at this ſecond ſtation; and ſo proceeds from turning to turning, ſtill marking the points, and his line, till he comes to the intended place. He then repeats above ground what he had done below, and his dial and line lead him, 'till he comes exactly over the place where he ended in the mine.

Manner of dreſſing the Tin.

When the ore is landed, and the greater ſtones broken at the top of the mint by the ſhovel men, it is brought on horſes to the ſtamping and knocking mills, and unloaded at the head of the paſs (*i. e.* two or three bottom-boards with two ſide-boards ſlopingwiſe) in which the ore ſlides down into the coffer. But that it may not tumble down all at once, there is placed a hatch near the lower end of the paſs (*i. e.* a thwart-board to keep up the ore); beneath that comes in the cock-water in a trough cut in a long pole, which, with the ore, falls down into the coffer (*i. e.* a long ſquare box of the firmeſt timber, 3 feet long, and half over, wherein the three uſual lifters, placed between two ſtrong broad lones, having two braces, or thwart pieces, on each ſide to keep them ſteady as a frame, with ſtamper-heads, weighing about 30 or 40 pounds a-piece, of iron, which ſerve to break the ore in the ſaid coffer. Theſe lifters, about eight feet long, and half foot ſquare, of heart-oak, and having as many in-timbers, or guiders, between them, are lifted up in order by double the number of tapples, faſtened to as many arms paſſing diametrically through a great beam, turned by an over-ſhot water-wheel, on two boulſters, which exactly, but eaſily meet with the tongues ſo placed in the lifters, as that they quickly ſlide from each other, ſuffering the lifters to fall with great force on the ore, thereby breaking it into ſmall ſand, which is waſhed out by the cock-water, through a braſs gate, holed very thick, and placed within two iron bars at one end of the coffer into the launder, *i. e.* a trench, cut out in the floor, eight feet long and ten feet over, ſtopped at the other end with a turf, ſo that the water runs away, and the ore ſinks to the bottom; which, when full, is taken up and emptied with a ſhovel.

The ſtamping-mill is thus contrived to go two hours, or more, after we give over our attendance on it. We have a tiller, *i. e* a long pole, faſtened without at one end to the ſlew, or ponder, *i. e.* that looſe and laſt part of the trough that conveys the ſtream to the mill-wheel; and at the lower end is tied a ſhort rope, with a tranſverſe ſtick at the end of it, curiouſly, but trapwiſe hitched at both ends under two little pins, faſtened in the lones for that purpoſe. There is another pin ſet in one of the lifters, at ſuch an exact height, as that if there be no ore in the coffer to keep that lifter high enough, the purpoſed pin, in deſcending, knocks out the water, carrying it quite over the mill-wheel; ſo that when the coffer is emptied, the mill reſts of its own accord.

The launder is divided into three parts, the forehead, the middle, and the tail. That ore which lies in the forehead, within a foot and half of the grate, is the beſt tin, and is taken up in a heap a-part. The middle and tails in another, accounted the worſt.

The latter heap is thrown out by the trambling buddle, *i. e.* a long ſquare tie of boards or ſlates, about four feet deep, ſix long, and three over; wherein ſtands a man bare footed, with a trambling ſhovel in his hand, to caſt up the ore, about an inch thick, on a long ſquare board juſt before him, as high as his middle, which is termed the Buddehead; who dexterouſly, with one edge of his ſhovel, cuts and divides it longwiſe, in reſpect of himſelf, about half an inch aſunder; in which little cuts the water coming gently from the edge of an upper plain board, carries away the filth and lighter parts of the prepared ore firſt, and then the tin immediately after; all falling down into the buddle, where, with his bare feet, he ſtrokes and ſmooths it tranſverſely, to make the ſurface the plainer, that water and all heterogeneous matter, may, without let, paſs away the quicker.

When this buddle grows full we take it up, here diſtinguiſhing again the forehead from the middle and tails, which are trambled over again: but the forehead of this, with the forehead of the launder, are trambled in a ſecond buddle, but not different from the firſt, in like manner. The forehead of this being likewiſe ſeparated from the two other parts, is carried to a third, both drawing buddle, whoſe difference from the reſt is only this, that it hath no tie, but only a plain ſloping board, whereon it is once more waſhed with the trambling ſhovel, and ſo it new names the ore, black-tin, *i. e.* ſuch as is completely ready for the *blowing-houſe.*

We have another more curious way termed ſizing, that is, inſtead of a drawing-buddle, we have an hair ſieve, through which we ſift, caſting back the remainder in the ſieve into the tails, and then new tramble that ore. After the ſecond trambling, we take that forehead in the ſecond buddle, and dilve it, that is putting it into a canvas ſieve, in a large tub of water, luſtily ſhaking it, ſo that the filth gets over the rim of the ſieve, leaving the black tin behind, which is put into hogſheads, covered and locked, till the next blowing.

The tails of both buddles, after two or three tramblings, are caſt out into the firſt ſtrake or tie, which is a pit purpoſely made to receive them, and what over-ſmall tin elſe may waſh away in the trambling. There are commonly three or four of them ſucceſſively, which contain two ſorts of tin; the one which is too ſmall, the other which is too great. The latter is new ground in a craze-mill, in all reſpects like a griſt-mill, with two ſtones, the upper and the nether, and after that trambled in order; the former, by reaſon of its exceeding ſmallneſs, is dreſſed on a reck, provided for that purpoſe, that is, a frame made of boards about three feet and an half broad, and ſix long, which turns upon two iron pegs faſtened in both ends, and the whole placed on two poſts, ſo that it hangs in an equilibrium, and may, like a cradle, be eaſily removed either way, with the ſhovel and water.

The manner of blowing the tin.

When we perceive much mundick in our tin, which makes it britly hard, we are neceſſitated to burn away the weed in a tin kiln; this kiln is ſquare, and at the top a large moor-ſtone, about ſix feet long, and four broad; in the middle thereof is a hole made about half a foot diameter. About a foot beneath this ſtone is placed another, not ſo long by half a foot, becauſe it muſt not reach the innermoſt or back part of the wall, which is the open place through which the flame aſcends from the leſſer place below that where a very ſtrong fire of furze is conſtantly kept. The fore part is like a common oven; but near the back on one ſide there is another little ſquare hole. When the kiln is thoroughly heated, the black tin that is to be burned, is laid on the top ſtone, and as much of it caſt down at the ſquare hole upon the ſecond or bottom ſtone, as will cover it all over about three or four inches thick; then the hole at the top is immediately covered with green turf, that the flame may reverberate the ſtronger, and a rake-man with an iron coal-rake, conſtantly ſpreads and moves the tin, that all parts of the mundick may get uppermoſt of the tin, and ſo be burnt away; which we certainly know by this, that then the flame will become yellow, (as uſual) and the ſtench leſſened; for whilſt the mundick behind burns, the flame is exceeding blue, then with the rake he thruſts it down, at the open place into the open fire, and receives a new ſupply of tin from above. Now, when the place beneath where the fire is made, grows full of tin, coals, and aſhes, with his rake he draws it forth with the coals, at the little ſquare hole on one ſide, near the back, where the ore (fiery hot and red) lies in the open air to cool, which will ſcarce be in three days, becauſe of the coals that lie hid in it: but in caſe we cannot ſtay ſo long, then we quench it with water, and it becomes like mortar. Whether it cools of itſelf, or is cooled by water, we muſt new tramble it, or waſh it, before we put it into the furnace which is no other than an *alman* furnace. Moor tin, ſuch as is digged up in the moors, we find runs or melts beſt with moor coal, charked: but our tin, which lies in the country, runs beſt with an equal proportion of charcoal and peat, *i. e.* moor coals, for the firſt running; but when we come to re-melt our ſlags, then we uſe charcoal. When all is melted down, and re-melted, there ſometimes remains a different ſlag in the bottom of the float, which we term mount egg, and that is moſtly an iron body, though of a tin colour; as I accidentally aſſured myſelf by applying one of the poles of a loadſtone to it, which quickly attracted it, yet not to ſuch a degree, by far, as that of perfect iron.

The Corniſh diamonds, ſo called, lie intermixed with the ore, and ſometimes on heaps. They are hard enough to cut glaſs, and ſome of them are of a tranſparent red, and have the luſtre of a deep ruby. Theſe diamonds ſeem to me to be but a finer, purer, and harder ſort of ſpar.

Concerning the Flux of the Euripus, communicated by the learned Jeſuit Bertet.

ALTHOUGH the Euripus be a ſymbol of inconſtancy, yet hath it this advantage, that whereas the great things which the antients have recorded of the cities and rivers of Greece, are, or appear no more in being, the Euripus ſtill remains what it hath been. It is true that the town of Chalcis is deſtroyed, but in the place thereof we may ſee that of Negropont in Eubæa, which is ſevered from Bœtia only by an arm of the ſea, where this Euripus is found; over which is built two bridges, one of ſtone, the other of wood; in the middle whereof is a rock, on which the Venetians formerly built a caſtle, which on its gates doth yet ſhew the *lions*, the arms of the city.

I have not contented myſelf with reading what antient writers have left us of this *phenomenon*, who did either not ſee it, or not conſider it with that carefulneſs and attention I have done, having made upon the place long obſervations, which were found conformable to thoſe intelligent natives of whom I made enquiry, eſpecially of the Turks, who have the care of the mills of the *Euripus*, and know all the times when the wings and wheels of them are to be moved and turned according as the water of the ſtrait by its flux and reflux changes its courſe.

The Euripus then is a ſtrait of the Ægean ſea, ſo narrow that a galley can ſcarce paſs through it, under a bridge built between the citadel and the Donjon of Negropont. But not only this place where the bridge is, is called the *Euripus*, but alſo ten or twelve leagues on each ſide of it, where the channel being larger, the inconſtant courſe is not ſo ſenſible as at the foot of the caſtle: for three or four leagues on each ſide there are found ſix or ſeven gulphs, wherein this water ſhuts itſelf up, to iſſue thence as often as it enters there; and the ſituation of theſe gulphs contributes to the oddneſs of this flux and reflux, of which the moon ſeems to be the principal cauſe.

There are twenty days of each moon, in which the courſe of the Euripus is regular, and ten in which it is irregular; that is to ſay, five days before and five days after the new and full moon, the courſe of it is regular and ſtrong; and then you ſee there the like phenomena with thoſe of the ocean at *Bourdeaux*. The ſea hath two fluxes and refluxes in twenty-four hours, and every day it retardeth almoſt an hour. But there are nine or ten changes of the courſe of the water during the remaining ten days of inequality, unleſs it blow hard, for then the courſe changeth not above ſix or ſeven times. I once ſtayed on the mill, (which is under the bridge) an hour and a half, and ſaw the courſe of the water change thrice, though the wind was pretty high; and the wheels of the mill turned as often divers ways. Monſieur de la Hogue, a Pariſian gentleman, being curious, ſtaid there almoſt a whole day with a Janiſſary; and the moon being near the full, he obſerved the ſame thing that happens in the ocean. But though he deſigned to ſtay there full 24 hours during the irregular days, he was diſſuaded from it for fear of the Turks, who might take him for a ſpy, and do him ſome miſchief.

I ſaid that for twenty days the flux and reflux is as in the ocean, or as at *Venice*; but with this difference, that the water of the ocean riſes many feet high; but in the Euripus it riſeth not much above a foot: beſides, in the ocean it is obſerved, that the water in its riſing flows into the *ports* and *towards* the land, and in its *fall* runs into the *Main:* but in the Euripus, when the water riſeth, it runs then into the ſea; and when it ſinks, it flows into the Channel, going towards Conſtantinople.

The ſmall gulphs that are on the left ſide of the port of Negropont, are filled when the water riſeth, and emptied, running toward Theſſalonica or Conſtantinople, when it deſcends. I wrote to *F. Vabois,* deſiring him to obſerve, and he took notice of the ſame at Conſtantinople, viz. that the waters of the Black ſea that come from Conſtantinople, drive the Euripus in its riſing towards the main ſea, and that thereafter the waters retire towards the ſame place again, whence they came.

I cauſed the ſame perſon to make another obſervation, which was, that the ſwelling of the Euripus, which is irregular, laſted not above a quarter of an hour, and the ſinking thereof three good quarters, though then the water ran with more rapidity, and ſeemed to him to come away in thrice as great plenty as when he ſaw it riſe. I know not whether this proceeded from the wind, not being able to aſſure you that this effect is ordinary, till I have oftener obſerved it.

Between the aſcent and deſcent there is a little interval, wherein the water ſeems to be at reſt and ſtagnating, ſo that if there be no wind ſtirring it, bits of wood and ſtraw lie ſtill upon the water without motion.

From what I have ſaid it is not difficult to reconcile the authors who have written ſo differently of the Euripus: for thoſe who have ſaid that there is nothing in it but what is ſeen in the ocean, that is, *two* fluxes and refluxes in twenty-four hours, have only obſerved it in thoſe twenty days of its regularity. And the antients have not delivered a falſehood when they ſay, that there are ſeven reciprocations in one day, becauſe that happens when the winds trouble and retard the courſe of the waters: and I do aſſure, by often reiterated obſervations, that when it is ſtill weather, the flux and reflux are made even to nine or ten times in a natural day.

An account of two remarkable Hurricanes.

OCTOBER 30th, 1669. Between five and ſix o'clock in the evening, the wind being weſterly, at Aſhly, in Northamptonſhire, there happened a formidable hurricane, ſcarce bearing ſixty yards in its breadth, and ſpending itſelf in about ſeven minutes of time. Its firſt diſcerned aſſault was upon a milk-maid, without the leaſt regard to *decency*, and at the ſame time depriving her both of hat and milk pail, beyond recovery. Next it ſtormed the yard of a farmer, dwelling in Weſtthorp, where it blew a waggon body off the axle-trees, daſhing them to pieces, and blowing three of the wheels ſo ſhattered, over a wall. Another waggon without horſes was ſet a going with great velocity, running right againſt the houſe of its owner, to the aſtoniſhment of the inhabitants. A branch of an aſh tree of that bigneſs that two luſty men could ſcarce lift it, was blown over a Mr. Saliſbury's houſe without hurting it, and yet this branch was torn from a tree an hundred yards diſtant from that houſe. A ſlate was forced upon the houſe of Samuel Templer, Eſq. which very much bent an iron bar in it, and yet it is certain that the place the ſlate was at firſt forced from was two hundred yards diſtant. On ſome houſes its effects were dreadful, forcing in the doors, burſting out the windows, overſetting every thing, and carrying the roofs of ſome clean away, amongſt which was the parſonage houſe, whoſe roof it more than decimated. Some perſons were violently forced into houſes, others out. A large pea-ſtack was carried from one place and ſet down in another, without other injury: a gate poſt was torn from the ground, in which it was ſet 2½ feet deep, and carried into the fields to a conſiderable diſtance.

In this caſe the ſcite of that part of Aſhley, moleſted by the wind, is conſiderable with the poſition of the field to the point of the compaſs wherein the wind ſtood. About half a mile diſtant from the town is a ſmall wood on the top of a hill, and partly deſcending into a vale, encompaſſed by northerly and ſoutherly hills; ſo that the wind ſeemed confined to the vale as a channel before it aſſaulted the town, and thereby enforced to ſpend itſelf only in that direction.

But I am inclined to think that ſome flatus from the deſcending wood-ground might contribute to this accident, becauſe the wind continued, ſo far as men could judge, as high in the field afterwards, and the ſcite of the town did expoſe (by reaſon of thoſe vallies) a far greater part of the town to this damage than was aſſailed by it, the valley being above four or five times the breadth of that part of the town that was concerned in it.

The other inſtance was October 13, 1670, at Braybrook; likewiſe in Northamptonſhire, about eleven o'clock, when the wind in a ſtrange ſtorm aſſaulted a peas-rick in the field, uncovering the thatch of it, and leaving another within 20 yards of it unmoleſted. Thence it proceeded alſo to the parſonage, where it carried ſcarce eight yards in breadth, blowing up the end of a barley-rick, and therewith ſome ſtakes in it of near five feet long; yet left a wheat hovel, within ſix yards of the barley rick, untouched, no part of the thatch of the hovel being ſo much as furled, though void of all ſhelter. Neverthelеſs it beat down a jackdaw from the rick with ſuch violence as forced the guts out of the body, and made it vomit blood at the mouth; this I ſaw, and took the daw up immediately after. Thence it went to the parſonage houſe in a right line, took off the roof of all the houſe in its compaſs: from thence it paſſed over the town without any damage, the reſt of the town being low in ſituation, and went on to a place called Fort-hill, where it uncloathed ſo much of a malt-houſe as lay within its current, yet the malt on the floor was undiſturbed.

Here it may be noted that Braybrook ſtands in a valley, environed by hills on three ſides, at three quarters of a mile diſtant from it. But (what I would chiefly obſerve) there is a hill, called by the name of Clack-hill, within a mile of it, and exactly in that point of the compaſs in which the wind then ſtood; no hill in the way till it had paſſed over all the places it had damaged: and which is remarkable, there have been two earthquakes in this town within theſe ten years, when the then gentle zephyr only vibrated upon that point of the compaſs.

A narrative of two Petrifactions in human bodies; communicated by Dr. Kirby, in a letter from Dantzick.

A WOMAN of 56 years of age, unmarried, whoſe whole courſe of life had been extremely ſedentary, was troubled ſome years before her death with great pains in her back, eſpecially towards the right ſide, and a continual inclination to vomiting; her urine for ſome time before was turbid, and as it were mingled with blood, yet totally void of ſalſuginous matter. She was under the hands of the beſt doctors in this place, who adjudged that ſymptom of bloody water to have proceeded *ex præmatura ceſſatione menſium* (which left her in the 40th year of her age); thereby perhaps deceived, becauſe there was never ſtone or gravel voided by her. Her laſt doctor adjudged it to proceed *ab affectu nephritico & quidem graviſſimo.* This perſon, when dead of theſe diſtempers, was opened by her laſt phyſician, and among many other common phenomena, he found the left kidney filled with large ſtones, but the right wholly petrified, covered with the ordinary ſkin, without any fleſh; the half of which (the other being broken by injurious diſſection) repreſenting ſtill the kidney, I have ſeen, which was both maſſy and ponderous, ſo concreted by the cloſer coalition of minute ſand, which might be rubbed off by your finger.

The other was a lad about 19 years old, who from his cradle was diſpoſed to conſumption, attended with continual coughing, great emaciation, and conſtant heat, ſo that he was reduced to a ſkeleton, and labouring under this diſtemper died. Being opened, a great quantity of watery matter run out at the abdomen, of a chilous conſiſtence; almoſt all the glanduls of the meſentery, through which paſs the *venæ lacteæ*, were very large, and hardened beyond that of a ſkirrhus. The breaſt being opened, the lungs we found grown to it round about, almoſt inſeparable, full of purulent ulcers, but more eſpecially the left ſide obſtructed and filled with much gravel and ſmall ſtones; whole pieces of the lungs, eſpecially the extremities, about the thickneſs of a finger and more, were hardened into a ſtony matter.

An account of a curious Subſtance found in great quantities in ſome mines of Italy. From the Venetian Journal de Litterati.

SIGNOR Marco Antonio Caſtagno, ſuperintendant of ſome mines in Italy, diſcovered in one of them a great quantity of that lanuginous ſtone called amianthus, which he knows ſo to prepare, as to render it ſo tractable and ſoft that it reſembles well enough a very fine lambſkin dreſſed white. He thickens and thins it to what degree he pleaſeth, and thereby maketh it like to either a very white ſkin, or to a very white paper; both which reſiſt the moſt violent fire, as hath been experimented ſeveral times. Firſt, the ſkin was covered with kindled coals, whence it took flame, but being taken out after it had been left there a while, the fiery colour preſently diſappeared, and it became cold and white again as before; the fire it ſeems paſſing only through, without waſting or altering any thing of it; whereas ſome of the hardeſt and ſolideſt metals, as iron and copper, reduced to very thin plates, and kept as long in the fire as this ſubſtance was, would caſt ſcales. Again, this ſkin being made as thin as paper, doth not only yield that ancient and ſo much admired amianthus, but is alſo more perfect than that which comes from Cyprus, and not inferior to that which ſometimes, though but ſeldom, comes out of China. This *paper* was alſo tried in the fire, and there it remained likewiſe without any viſible detriment, or the leaſt change of its firſt whiteneſs, fineneſs, or ſoftneſs. Of the ſame material this artiſt hath wrought a wick never to be conſumed as long as it is fed, nor altering its quality after the aliment is waſted away: and if that famous incombuſtible oil were found out again, (which oil we have heard ſo much of) this matter would yield the wick for that everlaſting light, ſo much celebrated by the ancients.

Some experiments by Signor Carolo Rinaldini, philoſopher and mathematician in the univerſity of Padua, ſhewing the difference of ice made without *air*, *from* that *which is produced* with *air*.

THERE was taken a glaſs cane, about 1½ of a Florentine *braccia* or ell, open at one end, of which above an ell and a quarter was filled with quickſilver, the reſt with common water. This open end was ſhut with a finger, and inverted into a veſſel with ſtagnant mercury; then removing the finger, the mercury began to fall out, ſo that the aggregate of the quickſilver and water falling, the water remained in the upper part of the inverted cane, now free from air. This being done, the cane was thus expoſed to the open air in the month of January, in froſty weather, and in one night the water in it was congealed into ice of a very good conſiſtence. Afterwards Signor Rinaldini having compared this ice with that which was produced in the open air, found that the ice in the cane was in ſubſtance altogether like that of hail, that is, an opake and whitiſh body; whereas *that* which was made in the air, was tranſparent like chryſtal. Beſides he obſerved that the ice made in the cane, was heavier in *ſpecie* than that in the ambient air; which he diſcovered by putting it into a fluid, which was in *ſpecie* lighter than water, but heavier than ice made in the open air; whereby he found, that whereas the ice made in the cane ſunk, that in the air floated therein.

Which experiment ſeems not to favour thoſe who eſteem that ice made in the common air is produced by the extruſion of air latitant in the water, and by the reſolution of the more ſubtile parts, receiving in their ſtead the mixture of terreſtrial exhalations; conſidering that by the above experiment it appears that in the production of the ice made in the open air, the very air is mixt with the water.

A letter from York, dated 10th Jan. 1670, concerning a kind of Fly that is viviparous; together with a ſet of curious inquiries about Spiders; by Mr. Martin Liſter.

I HAVE ſent you the viviparous fly, and the ſet of inquiries you deſire of me. The fly is one, if not the very biggeſt, of the harmleſs tribe that I have met with in England. I call them *harmleſs*, becauſe that they are without that hard tongue or ſting in the mouth, with which the æſtrum kind, or gad-flies, trouble and offend both man and beaſt. This fly is ſtriped upon the ſhoulders grey and black, and as it were checkered on the tail with the ſame two colours: the female may be known by a redneſs on the very point of the tail. The very latter end of May 1666, I opened ſeveral of them, and found two bags of live white worms of a long and round ſhape, with black heads; they moved both in my hand and in the unopened veſicles, backwards and forwards, and being all diſpoſed in their cells lengthways, the body of the female like a ſheaf.

Some ſuch thing is hinted by Aldrovandus, lib. 1. de Inſect.

This is the only fly I have obſerved with live and moving worms in the belly of it; yet I think we may venture to ſuſpect all this tribe to be in ſome meaſure viviparous.

With theſe flies I have ſent a paper incloſing ſome of thoſe odd turned ſnails, mentioned in my former letter, which perhaps you may think worthy a place in the repository amongst the rarities of the ROYAL SOCIETY.

Some general enquiries concerning Spiders.

1. What sorts * of spiders are to be found with us in England, and what is the best method to distinguish them and reduce them into classes?

2. Whether spiders come not of spiders, that is of creatures of their own kind; and whether of spiders are bred grasshoppers?

3. Whether spiders are not male and female; and whether female spiders growing bigger than the male, be sufficient to distinguish sexes?

4. Whether all kinds of spiders be alike, as to the place and number of *penis's*, and whether all the thread-yielding kinds are not furnished with a double *penis*; that is, if the cornicula, or certain knobbed horns, by which all males are best distinguished, be not each a penis, and used in the coit alternately?

5. Whether eggs in spiders be not formed, and very large before the time of the coit?

6. What spiders breed in spring, and what in autumn? What spiders are content with one brood in the year, and lay all their eggs at a time? What seem to breed every summer month, at least to have many subordinate broods; and whether the eggs be accordingly distinguishable in several matrices or cells in the body of the female?

7. Whether spiders do not take their form and perfection in the egg, and are not thence hatched necessarily at a stated and set time, (that is, after a certain number of days, as 21) coming forth complete animals of the parent kind? and whether the presence of the female be necessary in order to the hatching of the eggs, at least for three days, as the ancients seem to affirm.

8. Whether the perfectly round eggs of spiders ought to be called and esteemed worms, as Aristotle and Pliny will have them; that is, in Swammerdam's phrase and doctrine? whether they be puppets in the egg, and undergo all the alterations accordingly, before they be thence hatched perfect spiders?

9. What different colours are observable in the eggs of spiders, as well of pulps as shells, as white, yellow, orange, purple, greenish; and what respective tincture they will give, or be made to strike with in the several families of salts?

* The *different sorts* of English spiders amount to 33.

10. Whether there be not eggs of fome forts of fpiders, which the worms of certain flender wafps delight to feed on? and whether the fable of Vefpæ Ichneumones, told us by the ancients, be not made out by the fame obfervation of thefe wafp-worms feeding on the eggs, and perfected into wafps in the very webs of fpiders?

11. After what manner do fpiders feed; whether in fucking they devour not alfo a part of their prey? How long can they live without food, fince they ftore up none for winter?

12. Whether fpiders feed only of their own kind of creatures, as of infects; that is, of flies, beetles, bees, fcolopendræ, and even of one another? or whether they kill fnakes too, as the ancients affirm, for food or delight?

13. Whether fome of them choofe not to feed on one fort of fly or other infect only; and what properties fuch have?

14. When and how often in the year they caft their fkins, and the manner of their cafting them? What variety of colours immediately after fhifting the hackle in one and the fame fpecies of fpiders, that may, if not well heeded, make the hiftory of them more confufed?

15. What mean the ancients by fpiders cafting their threads, which Ariftotle compares to a porcupine's darting her quills, or bark ftarting from a tree; and Democritus to animals voiding their excrements?

16. Whether the thread be formed in the body of the animal fuch as it comes from it; I mean whether it be, as it were, unwound off a ftock or clew, as I may fay, and which indeed to me feems to have been Ariftotle's meaning; or whether it be drawn off a liquid mafs, as in fpinning of glafs or melted wax, which feems to have been the meaning of Democritus?

17. Whether the fpider's thread being glutinous, every thing fticking to it upon the lighteft touch, be not fo much the reafon of the fpider's taking her prey, as the figure of the net?

18. Whether the net be flamable; and whether it can be diffolved, and in what menftruum?

19. What difference betwixt the thread of fpiders, and that of the filk-worm or caterpillars? What ftrength a fpider's web is of, and what proportion it bears with the like twift of filk? Whether there be no ftronger thread from fome fort of fpiders than from others, as there are threads from them of very different colours, as white, greenifh, blueifh, dark hair co-

lour, &c.? Whether the ſtrength of the Bermuda nets to hold a thruſh, as mentioned in one of the Tranſactions *, conſiſts in the thickneſs only, or much alſo in the nature of the thread?

20. Whether its being to be eaſily drawn out at any time, and at what length one pleaſes, and many threads together in ſpite of the animal, be not as advantageous to the working of it up and twiſting, &c. as the unravelling the cods of ſilk-worms.

21. Whether either the viſcous ſubſtance of their bodies or webs be healing to green wounds, &c. as the ancients have taught us, and we vulgarly believe? and whether ſome one kind of them be not preferable for the purpoſe, before others?

22. What uſe may be made of thoſe animals which devour ſpiders for their daily food, as wrens, red-breaſts, &c.? Whether ſpiders be a cure for ſick poultry, as the good wives ſeem to experiment?

23. Whether the reaſon why ſpiders ſail not in the air until autumn, be not becauſe they are buſily employed the ſummer months in breeding, or what other reaſons may be aſſigned?

The firſt article of enquiry I have in part anſwered, by ſending you encloſed a ſcheme, which, after ſome years obſervation, I have corrected and enlarged to what it is: yet I muſt acquaint you that ſuch draughts will be ever liable to change and improvement, according to the meaſure of knowledge a continued obſervation may bring us. However, it is the firſt that I know of that will be extant on this ſubject, and it may be acceptable to the curious.

A Table of Spiders found in England.

Tranſlated from the Latin.

Of the Spiders that ſhoot forth their threads and weave them in an orbicular form for the purpoſe of catching their prey, there are nine.

1. *Araneus ſubflavus*, or the ſpider inclining to yellow, the bunch or paunch a little pointed and bent.

2. *Araneus rufus*, having a ſaffron tinge, and the ſuperior part of the bunch ſtudded with little prominences.

3. *Araneus cinereus*, or aſh-coloured; the alvum divided by five lines, and thoſe very much diſtended.

* See page 220.

4. *Araneus flavus*, or the yellow ſpider; the form foliated, with white ſpots on the hips.

5. *Araneus nigricans*, the ſpider of a blackiſh hue; the buttocks reſembling an oak leaf.

6. *Araneus ex viridi inauratus*, or of a ſhining green; the alvum or bunch long and ſlender.

7. *Araneus cinereus*, the duſky ſpider of the woods; the paunch curiouſly pointed, and ſomewhat triangular.

8. *Araneus viridis*, or greeniſh ſpider; the ſuperior part of the tail marked with black ſpots, the vent yellow.

9. *Araneus pullus cruciger*, or of a dark yellow; full bunch, with roundiſh ſtripes: there are *four*.

1. *Araneus variegatus*, or the variegated ſpider; the alvum orbicular.

2. *Araneus rufus*, the reddiſh ſpider; roundiſh behind, and radiated like a ſtar.

3. *Araneus pullus domeſticus*, the dark, or blackiſh domeſtic ſpider.

4. *Araneus cinereus*, or aſh coloured; adorned with a few black ſpots on the upper part of the hips.

Of thoſe that weave their webs like linen cloth there are *eight*.

1. The domeſtic hairy ſpider; a little yellow, with long feet.

2. The black (houſe) ſpider; very large, and ſpotted on the upper part of the hips, and obliquely ſtriped in other parts.

3. The duſky coloured ſpider, beautifully marked, the tail divided.

4. The yellowiſh ſpider, marked on the hips with a chain of quadrangular black ſpots; likewiſe on the ſides with beautiful yellow ſtripes, running obliquely.

5. The great aſh coloured ſpider; the tail forked.

6. The cheſnut coloured ſpider, without hair; the hips ſingularly beautiful.

7. The duſty coloured ſpider, gentle; the paunch obliquely ſtriped, with black and red ſpots on the ſides.

8. The livid coloured ſpider, or *araneus plerumque lividus*, without any pointed figure on the paunch: this ſpider makes no web (ſhooting out the thread whereby it flies or travels) unleſs for the purpoſe of preſerving its young, or for a retreat in winter; yet it is hoſtile to flies; and of this *ſort* there are *five*; thoſe are called *lupi*, having eight diſtinct eyes.

1. *Araneus ſubrufus*, or reddiſh ſpider; ſmall, but very nimble.

2. *Araneus cancriformis*; crab-like, with eyes of a purple or violet colour, ſlow in its motion.

3. *Araneus cinereus*, aſh-coloured; the paunch undulated, or waved and pointed: this ſpider is remarkably tall.

4. *Araneus fuſcus*; the brown ſpider, obliquely ſtriped behind.

5. *Araneus niger ſylvicola*, or black ſpider; an inhabitant of the woods.

Of the kind called phalangia, which aſſail by leaping on their prey, there are *three* ſorts. Thoſe have ſix eyes only.

1. *Araneus cinereus*, variegated with black and ſilver.

2. *Araneus ſubflavus*, a yellowiſh ſpider, with eyes like emeralds.

3. *Araneus ſubrufus*, or reddiſh ſpider, reſiding in heath and rocks.

Of the ſpiders that ſhoot forth no threads, there are *four* kinds; which for the moſt part have long ſlender feet, and two eyes only.

1. *Araneus rufus*, or red ſpider, not tufted; they live in companies.

2. *Araneus cinereus*, or aſh-coloured *tufted* ſpider, having a ſort of creſt.

3. The ſpider diverſified with black and white; a very little animal, an inhabitant of the woods.

4. *Araneus coccineus*, commonly called the crimſon ſpider.

Further obſervations by Doctor M. Liſter, relating to an Inſect feeding upon Henbarie.

THERE is a *cimex* of the largeſt ſize, of a red colour ſpotted black, and which is to be found very plentifully and frequently, at leaſt in its ſeaſon, upon henbarie: I therefore in my private notes entitle it *cimex ruber, maculis nigris diſtinctis, ſuper folia hyoſcyami frequens*. This inſect doth in all probability feed upon this plant (on which only we have yet obſerved it) if not upon the leaves, by ſtriking its *trunk* (the note of diſtinction of this kind of inſect from the reſt of the beetle kinds) into them, and ſucking thence much of its ſubſtance, like as other ſorts of cimices will upon the body of man, &c. Yet upon the unctious and greaſy matter with which the leaves ſeem to the touch to abound, it is further obſervable that that horrid and ſtrong ſmell with which the leaves of this plant do affect our noſtrils, is very much qualified in this *inſect*, and in ſome meaſure aromatic and agreeable;

and therefore we may expect that that dreadful *narcosis*, so eminent in this plant, may likewise be usefully tempered in this insect.

About the latter end of May, and sooner, you may find adhering to the upper sides of the leaves of this plant, certain oblong, orange coloured eggs, which are the eggs of this insect. These eggs, yet in the belly of the female, are white, and are so some time after they are laid: but as the young ones grow near the time of their being hatched, they acquire a deeper colour, and are hatched cimices, and not in the disguise of worms. If the riper eggs be crushed upon white paper, they stain it of themselves, without any addition of salt, with as lively a vermilion, or colour de feu, as any thing I know in nature; cochineal scarce excepted, when assisted with oil of vitriol.

Some observations concerning Glow-worms; by Mr. John Templer.

MAY 27th. I put a glow-worm into a small thin box (such as pills are sent in) between 11 and 12 at night I saw her shine through the box very clearly on one side, the box shut; putting white paper into the box, and the worm into the paper, it shined through the paper and box both.

May 28th. In the morning, about eight o'clock, she seemed dead, and holding her in a very dark place, I could perceive very little light, and that only when she was turned upon her back, and by consequence put into some little voluntary motion. After sun-set that night she walked briskly up and down in her box, shining as clearly as the night before, and that when there was so much day light that I could read without a candle.

May 29th. In the morning she seemed dead again, at night recovered herself, and shined as well as ever through the box; and upon opening the box, and holding a large candle in my hand, the light of it did not sensibly diminish that of the glow-worm.

May 30th. At ten in the evening I set the box with the worm in it about four yards from me, in a window, where I perceived it shine through the box for almost an hour. At four o'clock in the morning I found it shining, and observed it in plain day light for above half an hour.

May 31. The worm shined pretty clearly in a very lightsome room at five o'clock in the evening, at which time the sun shined gloriously into the same room.

Give me leave to add, that I never ſaw her ſhine without ſome ſenſible motion either in her body or legs. In her cleareſt ſhining ſhe extends her body a third part beyond its uſual length; and if my ſenſes fail me not, ſhe emits a ſenſible heat in her clear ſhining.

Even now looking into my box the glow-worm ſhined little, having contracted her body into a bending poſture, the light ſcarcely ſo big as a great pin's head: upon touching of her ſhe extended herſelf, walked in her box, and at firſt extent ſhined as glorioully as ever.

Extract from a work lately publiſhed upon the uſefulneſs of experimental *natural philoſophy; by the Hon. Robert Boyle, Fellow of the* ROYAL SOCIETY. *Oxford* 1671, *in 4to.*

THIS illuſtrious author, in purſuance of his deſign, which is to manifeſt that experimental philoſophy is conducive to improve the underſtanding, and to increaſe the power of man, proceeds to deliver ſix very uſeful and inſtructive eſſays.

The *firſt* of which contains ſome general conſiderations about the means, whereby experimental philoſophy may become advantageous to *human life*; not only by bringing improvements to the *trades* that miniſter to the neceſſities of mankind, and to thoſe that ſerve for man's accommodation and delight; but alſo by introducing *new* ones, partly ſuch as are altogether newly invented, and partly ſuch as are *unknown* in the place where the naturaliſt brings them into requeſt. And not only ſo, but it ſhews further that there is not any one profeſſion or condition of men (perhaps not any ſingle perſon of mankind) that may not ſome way or other be benefited or accommodated, if all the truths diſcoverable by natural philoſophy, and the applications that might be made of them, were known to the perſons concerned in them: intimating withal the cauſes of barrenneſs that have hitherto kept phyſics from being conſiderably uſeful; ſuch as are many falſe and fruitleſs doctrines of the ſchools; the prejudices by which men have been hitherto impoſed on about *ſubſtantial forms*, and the eſſential difference between natural and artificial things, &c. A too plauſible deſpondency; a want of belief that phyſics much concerned men's intereſt; want of encouragement, of curioſity, of a method of enquiring and experimenting; of mathematics and mechanics; of aſſociated endeavours, and the like.

The *ſecond* Eſſay treats of the uſefulneſs of mathematics to natural philoſophy; ſhewing that the empire of man may be conſiderably promoted by the naturaliſt's ſkill in *thoſe* ſciences, as well pure as mixt.

The *third* proveth the uſefulneſs of mechanical diſciplines to natural philoſophy, ſhewing that the power of man may be much increaſed by the naturaliſts ſkill in *mechanics*; for as much as nature does play the mechanician, not only in plants and animals, and their parts, but in many other curiouſly contrived bodies.

The *fourth* manifeſts that the good of mankind may be much increaſed by the naturaliſts inſight into *trades*; for making out of which, the noble author endeavours to ſhew two things; the one, that an inſight into *trades* may improve the naturaliſts knowledge; the other, that the natural philoſopher, as well by the ſkill thus obtained as by the other parts of his knowledge, may be able to improve trades; and this partly by increaſing the number of them, and adding new ones; *partly* by uniting the obſervations and practices of different trades into one body of collections; partly by ſuggeſting improvements in ſome kind or other of the particular trades. And here we cannot but obſerve, that our noble author taketh particular care in the Preface to this ingenious work, very fully to anſwer the objections, clamorouſly preſſed by ſome, as if tradeſmen were injured by diſcovering thoſe things which are called the myſteries of their arts.

The *fifth* ſheweth, that that may be done by *phyſical* knowledge, which is wont to require *manual ſkill*; or, that the knowledge of peculiar qualities, or uſes of phyſical things, may enable a man to perform thoſe things phyſically, that ſeem to require tools and dexterity of hand, proper to artificers.

The *ſixth* and laſt repreſents men's great ignorance of the uſes of natural things; or, that there is ſcarce any one thing in nature, whereof the uſes to human life are yet thoroughly underſtood; which is proved, both to rouſe up the curioſity of men by ſhewing how much it hath been defective, and to encourage it alſo by pointing out how much of nature there remains yet undiſcovered to recompence as well as to exerciſe our induſtry.

From the whole it will be found, *Firſt*, that it may afford many materials for the hiſtory of nature; which that it might the more copiouſly do, the author hath on ſeveral occaſions added a greater number of inſtances than were abfolutely neceffary for the making out what he intended to prove. *Secondly*, it may afford fome inftructions and intimations for promoting the practical or operative part of natural philofophy in divers particulars, wherein men have been either not able, or not folicitous to affift the curious. *Thirdly*, it may enable gentlemen and fcholars to converfe with tradefmen, and benefit themfelves, and the tradefmen too by that converfation; or at leaft it will qualify them to afk queftions of men who converfe with things; and fometimes to exchange experiments with them. Fourthly, it may ferve to beget a confederacy and union between parts of learning, whofe poffeffors have hitherto kept their refpective fkills ftrangers to each other; and by that means bring great variety of obfervations and experiments of different kinds into the notice of one man, or of the fame perfons; a thing that may prove very advantageous towards the increafe of knowledge. *Fifthly*, it may contribute to the refcuing of natural philofophy from that unhappy imputation of barrennefs, which it hath fo long lain under. And *laftly*, and principally, it may ferve, by pofitive confiderations, to awaken the generality of thofe that are any thing inquifitive, and both forcibly excite and affift the curiofity of mankind; from which alone may be expected a greater progrefs in ufeful learning, and confequently greater advantages to men, than in the prefent ftate of human affairs will be eafily imagined.

Enchiridion Metaphyficum, five de rebus incorporeis differtatio. Per H. M. Cantabrigienfem Londini 1671, *4to.*

A SHORT extract from this refined Treatife cannot be rejected, it being fo complicated with what philofophers look upon as the very principles of the effects of nature, matter, and motion. The learned author worthily defigning to evince the *exiftence* of *incorporeal beings*, and to explain the *nature* of them, thinks fit, for the compaffing of that defign, to confider and examine divers of the chief phenomena of the world, which have been by *Defcartes*, and other noted philofophers, referred to mere mechanical caufes; and upon examination to reprefent that they are in vain and falfely afcribed to fuch principles, and confequently *immaterial* beings muft needs be the acknowledged caufes of them.

Paſſing by that part of this diſſertation which is merely metaphyſical, we ſhall obſerve, Firſt, that our author chargeth the famed Deſcartes to have delivered a precarious and very unphiloſophical definition of *motion*, ſuch an one as is repugnant to ſenſe, and all the rational faculties, and to have introduced ſuch principles, whereby he might aſſert a *neceſſity* of *exiſtence* in *matter*.

Next, he makes it his buſineſs to demonſtrate that there is ſome *extended immoveable*, not *imaginary*, but *real* being, diſtinct from *moveable matter*; which *thing* he maketh *ſpiritual* and *immaterial*, pervading the whole univerſe, and penetrating *all* matter, and that which hath ever been and will be for ever *ſomething* divine. Where it may be obſerved, that whereas *Deſcartes* will have that ſpace which is called *vacuum*, to be that *corporeal ſubſtance* called *matter*, he (our author) profeſſes to ſhew that that ſpace, or *internal place*, is really diſtinct from *matter*, and an incorporated ſpirit; affirming thereupon, that by the ſame door by which the *Carteſian philoſophy* hath endeavoured to *exclude* God out of the *univerſe*, he hath again introduced him; and attributing the ſame titles to this *internal place*, that are aſcribed to God, and making the exiſtence of this ſpace as eternal and neceſſary as that of a Deity.

From this extended *immoveable ſubſtance* he deduceth that all ſpirit, contradiſtinct to *matter*, is *extended*, or hath an *amplitude*, yet not *phyſically*, though *mentally*, diviſible into parts; and would have us conſider this immenſe and *immaterial ſpace* and *ſubſtance* as ſome repreſentation of the Divine eſſence, yet with a preciſion from the life and operations of the ſame.

Then proceeding to the *firſt matter*, as it is in itſelf, he defineth it to be an homogeneal congeries of phyſical monads or minute particles, that are not any more diviſible, and that are impenetrable, and incapable to cohere and move of themſelves, though capable to be united and moved; whence he eſteems, that the *exiſtence* of an *incorporeal ſubſtance* can be ſufficiently demonſtrated; foraſmuch as thoſe minute particles cannot coaleſce or move of themſelves.

Another argument to demonſtrate the exiſtence of incorporeal beings, he deduceth from the ſucceſſive duration of the world: and then paſſeth on to prove the ſame from divers phenomena of nature, by him conceived not explicable by mere *mechanical* cauſes; as from thoſe of gravity, from ſome experiments performed in the *Machino Boyliano*, as that of the ſuckers afcent with a great weight hung to it, and that of the firm cohefion of the two marbles; as alfo thofe hydroftatical experiments, concerning the gravitation of water upon water; and concerning ponderous bodies not finking at a competent depth, and the body of a diver not fenfible of pain: to which he adds thofe proofs, which he thinks may be taken for the fame purpofe, from the flux and reflux of the fea; from magnetifm; from the bignefs and figure of the fun and ftars; from the immenfe celerity of globuls in the upper part of the vortex, and the motion of comets; from the nature of light and colours; from the generation of the clouds and the roundnefs of rain-drops, and the rainbow; from the winds, thunder, and lightning; from the ftructure of plants and animals; from the operations of the foul; and from all thofe *phenomena* that are above and befides nature. After all which, he giveth us his definition of a fpirit in general, together with its explication; where he undertaketh to make it evident why an *extended fpirit* is more capable of *perception* than extended *matter:* and to fhew how a fpirit fo *fubtle* and *penetrative,* that it feems not capable of adhering to matter, may yet be conceived able to move and impel *matter:* and that the cohefion of a *fpirit* with *matter* is as intelligible as the union of one part of matter with another.

Compreffion of air under water.

SOME members of the ROYAL SOCIETY did, with two different forts of inftruments, make divers experiments for finding the proportions of the compreffion of the air under water, in the month of July inftant, at Sheernefs, in the mouth of the river Medway, at the time of high water, where the depth was then about 19 fathoms, and the proportion of the weight of the falt water to that of the fame quantity of frefh water taken out of the river Thames, was as 41 to 42.

One of the inftruments was a glafs bottle that held a quart of water, having a brafs ring faftened to the mouth of it, with a valve or flap that opened inward, fo well fitted, that the bottle being filled more or lefs with water, none dropped out though forcibly fhaken. This let down thirty-three feet into the water, the mouth downwards, and after a little ftay drawn up, was found to be fo very near half full of water at feveral trials, that it was thought fit to ſtate the compreſſion of air at that depth to that meaſure.

The quantity of compreſſion was known by weighing the bottle with the water in it, after that a forcible depreſſion of the flap had made way for the eruption of the compreſſed air (which kept it up, even when the bottle was placed with the mouth upwards,) and then filling the bottle full of the ſame water, and weighing it again; and laſtly, by weighing the bottle after the water was all let forth; the weight whereof being deducted, the firſt quantity of water weighed juſt half as much as the ſecond, or ſo near it, that the fraction was not conſiderable. Whence it was concluded that the quantity of the air that filled the bottle before it was immerſed in the water, was, at the depth of thirty-three feet, compreſſed into half the ſpace it took up before, and ſo comparatively at other depths.

Of a certain Inſect, hatched of the Engliſh kermes. By Dr. Liſter.

JANUARY 10, 1671. I found ſeveral *patellæ kermiformes* hatched in a box, where I had purpoſely put them; they prove a ſort of bees, but certainly the leaſt I ever ſaw of that tribe, as not much exceeding in their whole bulk the half of a piſmire. They are very compact and thick for their bigneſs, and of a coal black colour. There is a remarkable ſpot on the back, white or ſtraw colour, large and round. The upper pair of their wings are ſhaded, or dark ſpotted, the undermoſt pair are clear.

It is to be further obſerved, 1ſt, That thoſe that look the blackeſt yield the deepeſt and beſt purple.

2d, That as the bees come to maturity, the dye ſeems to be ſpent, and the huſks grow dry.

3d, That the young ones make their way out at ſeveral ſmall holes, the hole in the ſhop kermes being accidental only, and ever on the bottom part, cleaving to the branch; and the time of gathering them for colour is without doubt before they are pierced, and whilſt the animal is yet in vermiculo, and conſequently the huſk entire.

We compared theſe purple kermes with the ſcarlet kermes or grains of the ſhops, and found them in every point to agree, ſave in the colour of their juices; and particularly (finding in ſome parcels of the ſhops many yet ſticking to little twigs of the ilex) we confidently affirm, that thoſe, as well as ours, are only contiguous to the ilex branches, and are not excreſcences of the tree, much leſs fruit or berries, by which abuſive names they have been too long known, but that they are the artifice and ſole work of the mother bee, in order to the more convenient thriving and nouriſhment of her young.

Theſe things are alſo certain, viz. 1ſt, That we have ſeen the very gum of the apricot and cherry trees tranſudated, at leaſt ſtanding in a chryſtal drop upon ſome (though very rarely) of the tops of theſe kermes.

2d, That they change colour, from a yellow to a *dark brown*, and that they ſeem to be diſtended, and to wax greater, and from ſoft to become brittle.

3d, That they are filled with a ſort of mites, concerning which I am pretty well aſſured by my own, and alſo by Doctor Johnſon of Pomfret's more accurate *microſcopical obſervations*.

4th, That the bee grubs actually feed on mites, there being no other food for them.

5th, That there are other ſpecies of bees or waſps beſide thoſe by me deſcribed, which are ſometimes found to make theſe mites their food, Doctor Johnſon having opened one huſk with only one large maggot in it.

6th, That there are probably different ſorts of mites in theſe huſks, making poſſibly different ſpecies of kermes; for ſome I have found to hold *carnation coloured mites*, encloſed in a fine white cotton, the whole huſk ſtarting from the twig, ſhrivelling up, and ſerving only for a cap or cover to that company of mites. Other mites I have ſeen white, and, which is moſt uſual, the huſks continuing entire, and not coming away from the twig they adhere to, and but little cotton at the bottom.

7th, That the ſhrivelled cap to be found upon the mites incloſed in the cotton, as alſo to the whole huſk itſelf, if taken early in April, while ſoft, will (dried in the ſun) ſhrink into the very figure of *cochineal*; whence we gueſs that *cochineal* may be a ſort of kermes, taken thus early and ſun-dried.

I conceive that the ſmall *ſcarlet powder*, mentioned by Mr. Verney, is to be underſtood of thoſe mites, and that they are to be diſtinguiſhed from the bee grubs, which are changed into the ſkipping fly, that is, the bee, for kind at leaſt, here deſcribed by us.

Doctor Lister further adds, The account I have given of the purple kermes, both affords a clear light to the discovery of the nature of the scarlet kermes, a thing wholly unknown to the *ancients*, and also is an evident instance, that some things confidently believed to be vegetable excrescences are no such matter, but artificial things, merely contiguous to the plant, and which have no other relation to it than the patella shell fish to the rock it cleaves to.

2d, Generally, insects eggs laid upon the leaves of plants, their respective worms feeding on them, do not occasion or raise excrescences.

Thus, for example, the eggs of the common red butterfly, laid upon the nettle, are thereon hatched without blistering the plant into an excrescence; and the stiff-haired, or prickly caterpillars, hatched from those eggs, feed upon the leaves without any ill impression, save that they make clean work, and eat all before them.

3d, Some *insect* eggs laid upon the leaves, or other part of plants, do, as soon as hatched, pierce and enter within the plant to feed. I had a convincing proof of the certainty of *this*.

Observations of the new Star near the beak of the Swan. From the French Journal des Sçavans, Paris, 22d June, 1671.

THE new star, which Don Anthelme, a Carthusian of Dijon, hath lately discovered, is one of the rarest appearances observed for a considerable time. As this person contemplated the heavens at night, June the 20th of the last year, desirous to discover that admirable star which hath appeared and disappeared twice since the beginning of this century, in the constellation of the Swan, he perceived near the same constellation a star of the *third magnitude*, which he had never yet observed. He presently signified it to the company which assembled in the library of the King, and divers of that assembly having inspected the starry regions, about the end of June and the beginning of July, took notice that there was indeed about the *beak* of the *Swan* a *new* star of the third magnitude, not to be met with in any catalogue of astronomers, although many other neighbouring stars, that are much ſmaller, be exactly marked by them. It was ſituated as appears in the following figure.

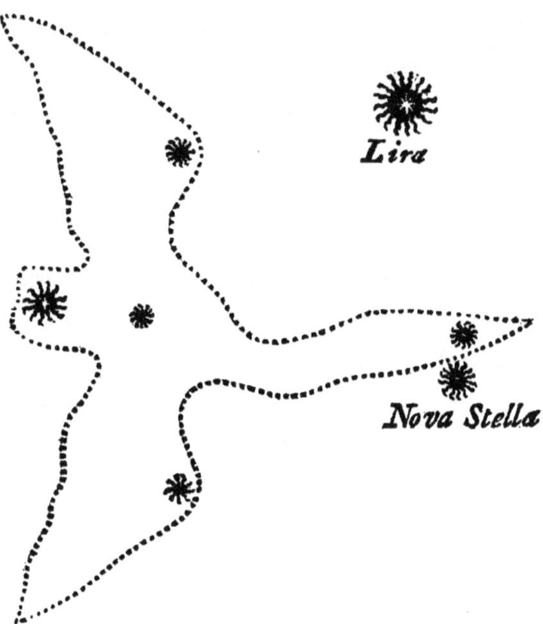

The obliquity of the ecliptic ſuppoſed to be 23½ degrees; the longitude of this ſtar, according to the obſervation of Mr. Picard, was,

	min.	deg.	ſec.	
	1	55	0	of Aquarius.
The right aſcenſion, - -	293	33	0	
The boreal latitude, - -	47	28	0	
And the declination, - -	26	33	0	
It came to the meridian after the ſtar in the beak of the Swan, - -	16	44	0	
And before the lucid ſtar of the Eagle,	0	27	0	
It was diſtant from the great ſtar of the conſtellation of Lira, -	18	39	40	
From the beak of the Swan, - -	3	47	30	
And from the tail of the Swan, -	20	54	30	

But it is further remarkable, that in the beginning of July this ſtar was obſerved to decreaſe. In the night of July 3, it appeared yet of the *third magnitude*, but her light was ſenſibly fainter. In the night of the 11th of the ſaid month ſhe ſcarce appeared of the *fourth magnitude*. In the night of

Auguſt the 10th ſhe was but of the *fifth*. And ſhe hath ever ſince decreaſed, ſo that at laſt ſhe became ſo ſmall that ſhe was ſeen no more.

And ſo ſhe hath remained for ſix months without once ſhowing herſelf, as we could not diſcover her again till the night of March 17th laſt, when Don Anthelme ſpied her in the very ſame place where ſhe was the year before, and found that ſhe was of the *fourth magnitude*.

The aſſembly that meets in the king's library having notice thereof, ſeveral of them obſerved the ſtar in the night of the 2d of April laſt, finding her preciſely in the ſame place where they had ſeen her the preceding year. The 3d of the ſame month, *M. Caſſini* found her greater than the two ſtars of the *third magnitude* that are below in the conſtellation of Lira, but a little ſmaller than that in the beak of Cygnus.

The 4th of the ſame month, ſhe appeared to him almoſt as great, and much more radiant than *that* in the beak of the Swan.

The 9th of the ſame he found her a little diminiſhed, yet almoſt equal to the greateſt of the two ſtars that are below in Lira.

The 12th ſhe was equal to the leaſt of theſe two ſtars.

The 15th he perceived that ſhe increaſed, and he found her equal, the ſecond time, to the greateſt of theſe two ſtars.

From the 16th to the 17th ſhe appeared of different magnitudes, being ſometimes equal to the biggeſt of theſe two ſtars, ſometimes equal to the leaſt, and now and then between both.

But the 27th and 28th ſhe was become as big as the ſtar in the *Swan's beak*. The 30th ſhe became a little clearer. And the firſt ſix days in May ſhe was greater.

The 15th May ſhe was ſeen ſmaller than the ſame ſtar. The 3d ſhe was in bigneſs between the two ſtars that are below in Lira: and ever ſince ſhe hath diminiſhed.

Thus this ſtar hath been ſeen twice in her greateſt ſplendour, firſt on the 4th of April, and the ſecond time in the beginning of May, which we know not to have *ever* happened to any other ſtar.

As far as can be judged from the obſervations of this ſtar, it is likely ſhe is returning in about *ten* months to the ſame appearance, whereas that in the Whale's neck maketh its revolution in eleven months. As to the ſtar in the *Swan's breaſt*, we have as yet no certain knowledge of the period of her revolution; yet one may aſſure that ſhe taketh no leſs than *fourteen* years to finiſh it.

The diſcoveries that have been made in the Heavens this laſt age do evince that changes are not ſo rare there as formerly believed. If that be true which *Pliny* ſaith, that Hipparchus, on the occaſion of a *new* ſtar he perceived, made an enumeration of all thoſe which appeared at that time, there would not be any one conſtellation in which ſome change were not found ſince that time, in regard there are few wherein there are not found more ſtars now than that aſtronomer hath noted.

But as we have no great aſſurance of the exactneſs of Hipparchus's catalogue, there is cauſe to believe that many ſtars, which were not in that catalogue, were yet in the heavens; ſo we may well grant, that ſome of thoſe that have been obſerved ſince have not appeared always; for, not to ſpeak of the ſtars that have been ſeen in the conſtellation of *Caſſiopea*, in the neck of the *Whale*, in the breaſt of the *Swan*, and in *Serpentarius*, Monſieur *Caſſini* hath diſcovered many other little ones, which may very well be preſumed to be new. For example, he hath obſerved one of the *fourth* magnitude, and two of the fifth, in Caſſiopea, where it is certain they were not ſeen before, many aſtronomers having exactly reckoned up the very ſmalleſt ſtars of that conſtellation, and yet not *one* of *them* mentioned thoſe *three*. He hath diſcovered *two* others, towards the beginning of the conſtellation of *Eridanus*, *where* we were ſure they were not yet about the end of the year 1664, conſidering that this place of the Heavens, where the then appearing comet paſſed, was diligently beheld by many, who perceived divers other ſmall ſtars, without obſerving thoſe *two*. He hath alſo obſerved, towards the arctic pole, four of the fifth or ſixth magnitude, which aſtronomers, who have always their eyes upon that place, would not have failed to note, if they had there appeared before.

Nor are we to wonder at it, that we ſee now more ſtars in the Heavens than appeared formerly; yet we are not preſently to ſay that the ſtars which have been lately diſcovered were not in the Heavens before, although they were not ſeen there. For as we know that there are ſtars which appear and diſappear from time to time, ſo we have cauſe to ſuſpect that moſt of the ſtars that were not ſeen formerly, or that are ſeen no more now, or are found diminiſhed, are of the ſame nature of the ſtar in the Whale's neck, and do not ceafe to be in the Heavens, though there they appear not.

It is alfo probable, that thefe new ftars not only were in the Heavens, but even appeared there, before they were taken notice of as *new* ones. And it is very likely, that it is with moft ftars as with that in the neck of the Whale, which was not obferved at firft, nor until it was already of the *third* magnitude, although it hath been fince found, that it is not really fo great when it begins to appear, but that, being very fmall in the beginning, it increafes infenfibly until it comes to that greatnefs.

However, thefe phenomena deferve always to be carefully obferved by all aftronomers.

Spots obferved in the Sun. By the Hon. Mr. Boyle.

AN. 1660, April 27, about eight of the clock in the morning, there appeared a fpot in the lower limb of the Sun, a little towards the fouth of its equator, which was entered about $\frac{1}{70}$ of the diameter of the Sun itfelf, being about $\frac{1}{160}$ in its fhorteft diameter of that of the Sun, its longeft about $\frac{1}{70}$ of the fame. It difappeared upon Wednefday morning, May 9th, though we faw it the day before, about 10 in the morning, to be near about the fame diftance from the weftward limb, a little fouth alfo of its equator, that it firft appeared to be from the eaftward limb, a little fouth alfo of its equator. It feemed to move fafter in the middle of the fun than towards the limb. It was a very dark fpot, almoft of a quadrangular form, and was inclofed round with a dufkifh cloud.

We firft obferved this very fame fpot, both for figure, colour, and bulk, to be re-entered the Sun May 25th, when it appeared to be in a part of the fame line it had formerly traced, and was entered about $\frac{4}{31}$ of its diameter about feven o'clock in the afternoon. At the fame time there appeared another fpot, which was juft entered, and appeared to be entered not above $\frac{1}{111}$ part of the Sun's diameter. It appeared to be longeft towards the north and fouth, and fhorteft towards the eaft and weft. There feemed to be difperfed about it divers fmall clouds here and there.

An. 1671, M. Picard, at fea near the Texel, obferved a fpot in the Sun from Auguft 3, St. N. to the 19th. It appeared at firft like the tail of a fcorpion, but on the 19th day refembling a melon-feed.

On Spontaneous Generation. By Mr. John Ray.

WHETHER there may be any ſpontaneous or anomalous generation of animals, as hath been the conſtant opinion of naturaliſts heretofore, I think there is good reaſon to queſtion. It ſeems to me at preſent moſt probable, that there is no ſuch thing; but that even all inſects are the natural iſſue of parents of the ſame ſpecies with themſelves. *F. Redi* hath gone a good way in proving this, having cleared the point concerning generation *ex materia putrida.* But ſtill there remain two great difficulties: the firſt is to give a ſatisfactory account of the productions of inſects bred in the by-fruits and excreſcences of vegetables, which the ſaid Redi doubts not to aſcribe to the vegetative ſoul of the plant that yields thoſe excreſcences; but for this I refer you to Mr. Liſter: the *ſecond,* to render an account of inſects bred in the bodies of other animals. I hope ſhortly to be able to give you an account of the generation of ſome of thoſe inſects which have been thought to be ſpontaneous, and which ſeem as unlikely as any to be after the ordinary and uſual way.

Of ſuch an inſect as you mention, feeding on ranunculus, which when dried yields a muſky ſcent, I have no knowledge. I can at preſent call to mind but two ſorts of inſects that I have ſeen which ſmell of muſk. The one is like the common capricornus, or goat-chaffer, which is mentioned by all naturaliſts that write of inſects, and ſmells ſo ſtrong of that perfume, that you may ſcent it at a good diſtance, as it flies by, or ſits near you. The other is a ſmall ſort of bee, which in the ſouth and eaſt parts of England is frequently to be met with in gardens amongſt flowers in ſpring time.

Of the hatching of a kind of Bee, lodged in old Willows. By Francis Willoughby, Eſq.

THE cartridges that I got at Aſtrop, near a twelvemonth ago*, do now, almoſt every day, afford me a bee; and I can hear them gnawing out their way before I ſee them; ſo that there is nothing irregular in the way of breeding of theſe bees, but the contrivance of God and Nature in it is very

* See page 288.

admirable. Having ſhut their young ones in thoſe cells with ſufficient proviſion, they all, as well the uppermoſt as lowermoſt, before winter, come to their full growth, or are turned into nymphas, in which condition they are deſigned to lie all winter, as moſt inſects do. The next ſummer thoſe muſt neceſſarily be firſt excited out of their torpor, and changed into fliers, by the external heat and air that lie next thereto. If any be laid ſo late that they have not time enough to come to the ſtate of nymphas before winter, they will moſt certainly die, and then it is no loſs or inconvenience, though their cells be perforated.

An account of the Stellar Fiſh.

THIS account was communicated by the ſame gentleman, who imparted the former *, in a letter from Boſton in New England, October 26th, 1670, as follows:—Since my former I found out the fiſherman who brought *that* ſtellar fiſh from ſea. I aſked all the queſtions I could think needful concerning it. I underſtood from him, that he never ſaw or heard of any but thoſe few that were taken by himſelf, which were not above ſix or ſeven in all, and thoſe at ſeveral times, not far from the ſhoals of Nantucket (which is an iſland upon the coaſt of New England), when he was fiſhing for cod, &c. This ſtellar fiſh, when it was alive, and firſt pulled out of the water, was like a baſket, and had gathered itſelf round in that form, having taken faſt hold of the bait on the hook, which he had ſunk down to the bottom to catch other fiſh, and having held *that* within the ſurrounding *brachia*, would not let it go, though drawn up into the veſſel, until by lying a while on the deck, it felt the want of its natural element, and then extended itſelf into the flat round form, in which it appeared when preſented to your view.

What motion theſe fiſhes had in the water, could not be known to him, for the water was deep, and they could not be ſeen in any other form than ſo gathered up together to hold faſt the bait. The only uſe that could be diſcerned of all that curious compoſure wherewith nature had adorned it, ſeems to be to make it as a purſe-net to catch ſome other fiſh, or any other thing fit for its food, and as a baſket of ſtore to keep ſome of it for future ſupply, or as a receptacle to preſerve and defend the young ones of the ſame kind from fiſh of prey: if not to feed on them alſo (which appears probable the one or

* See page 238.

the other); for that ſometimes there were found pieces of mackerel within that concave: and he told me, that once he caught one which had within the hollow of its embracements a very ſmall fiſh of the ſame kind, together with pieces of another fiſh, which were judged to be of a mackerel. And that ſmall one (it is like) was kept either for its preſervation, or for food for the greater; but being alive, it ſeems moſt likely it was there lodged for ſafety.

An extract concerning the formation of Fœtusses, &c. from the Italian.

THE author, Signor Gieron Borbato, firſt delivers the chief ſentiments of the ancients and moderns concerning the formative ſoul; ſhewing that from variety of thoſe opinions there reſults nothing but darkneſs. He alſo mentions ſome others touching the uſe of the teſticles, which he modeſtly refutes, animadverting upon ſome errors both of old and new anatomiſts: and beginning with the *vaſa pampiniformia,* he affirms, that they are made up of a great many arteries, and of one only vein, and that this vein, being conſiderably big, is circularly ſituate, that ſo it may the more conveniently unite itſelf by a curiouſly contrived *anaſtomoſis,* to thoſe many arteries. Then he deſcribes the uſe of theſe pampiniform veſſels, informing us, that the ſaid arteries are not directly inſerted into the ſubſtance of the teſticles (as moſt anatomiſts have believed); but that they form, on the ſide, another membrane, hitherto unobſerved, (altogether different from the *albugenea* and the two others called the *elytroides,*) which being made of veſſels, reſembles the meninges of the brain, and is by him eſteemed to have the like uſe with it. And thereupon he ſhews, that from the arteries of that membrane do proceed ſome ſmall arteries, for the moſt part double in their origin, but afterwards becoming one, and ſo paſſing into the ſubſtance of the teſticles; but when they are come to the centre of them returning to the above ſaid membrane, without being accompanied by the veins: where he renders a reaſon why in the ſubſtance of the teſticles there are no veins, and ſhews, that in the return of the ſaid arteries there appear ſome other ſmall veſſels, which contain no aliment, but only ſeminal matter; and that theſe do frame in the midſt of the teſticles another whitiſh ſmall membrane, very like the *ſeptum lucidum*; which membrane, receiving veſſels from all the parts of the teſticles, except from the back part, does therefore grow crooked there, and thereby hath deceived that famous anatomiſt Dr. *Higmore*, perſuading himſelf that it is a round and pervious veſſel. Moreover he ſaith, that the curvature of the ſaid little membrane ſerves for a kind of ventricle, to purge away an aqueous moiſture, ſeparated by means of the medullar ſubſtance of the teſticles from the ſeminal matter contained in the veſſels. He obſerveth further, that the ſmall membrane reſtrains itſelf towards the upper part, and it being ſuch a one as conſiſts of minute veſſels, there remain yet in that place ſome of them, though very ſmall ones, which may be obſerved by a microſcope to be diſſeminated in that little coat, which paſſeth into the *albigunia* near the pampiniform, and is inſerted into the *epididymis*; whence paſſing through a glandul above the *epididymis*, it there depoſeth a wateriſh humidity, like that which the double membrane brings with it from the centre of the *teſticles*, and which through the lymphatic veſſels is conveyed towards the urethra, and comes away before the ejaculation of the *ſemen prolificum*. And the ſaid little veſſels, afterwards multiplying themſelves exceedingly, and being divided into ſmall cells, do with a wonderful and curious conformation frame the *epididymis*, where he detects the error of him, who believed the *epididymis* could be ſevered from the teſticles without laceration, aſſigning withal the uſe of that part differently from all other anatomiſts. Thence he paſſeth to the *paraſtatæ varici-formes*, which emulating the *epididymis*, appear alſo to be full of pretty big veſſels, ſituate after a curiouſly contrived manner, and make a nobler ſhew than that of the *epididymis* itſelf, it having the reſemblance of an heart. And declaring the uſe of the *paraſtatæ*, he ſaith, that they do not terminate in a *nervous body*, but plainly in a nerve, by him called the *vas deferens*, which, he eſteems, carries nothing elſe but ſtore of animal ſpirits, which yet, according to him, are not generated in the brain, (nor tranſported by the nerves into the teſticles,) but in the ſmall veſſels, which make up the medullar ſubſtance of the teſticles themſelves; which being at laſt obliterated in the *paraſtatæ*, are changed into a thick membrane, of which is formed the *vas deferens*, ſenſibly pervious; that ſo, by the abolition of the lately mentioned ſmall veſſels, it may receive abundance of ſeminal ſpirits, called *animal*; they being produced from one and the ſame matter, and in one and the ſame manner. And that they are ſo, he further proveth from this obſervation, that the two little nerves, taken notice of by anatomiſts, are inſerted only in the external part of the teſticles, receiving their internal ſenſe and motion from the ſaid ſpirits, generated as above. And here he maintains, that theſe ſpirits are the *ſenſitive* and *moving ſoul,* and conſequently the *anima formatrix,* and that there is no other proximate inſtrument, ſave the *intellective ſoul, quæ deſeris venit et divina eſt.*

Beſides he endeavours to prove that opinion to be falſe, which holds the ſeed to be an excrement of the laſt aliment, and maketh it appear, that a ſmall quantity of ſeed excerned, enfeebles more than the loſs of ſo much blood. He refuteth thoſe that have taught the origin of the ſeed from the brain; as alſo thoſe, that have believed it to proceed from the whole body. He aſſigneth the manner, how the ſpirit is corporified and incraſſated, and why it is ſo; proveth experimentally, that being ſubtilized by the warmth of the *uterus*, it becomes a very fine ſpirit; refuting, on this principle, the opinion of Galen, importing, *that* from the corpulency of the *ſemen virile* the ſpermatic parts are generated, and aſſerting on the contrary, *that* theſe are formed *de ſero utili ſanguinis menſtrui.* By the ſame experiment he undertakes to evince, that Dr. Harvey was miſtaken, believing the *uterus* to be immaterially made fecund, when he found nothing of a ſeminal body in the wombs of all thoſe animals opened by him. Beſides, he teacheth how the ſemen is mixed *cum menſtruis*; and how it is moved ſuitably to the diverſity of kinds. He examines how the ſolid parts are generated, and, refuting all other opinions about this point, he maintains that they are produced all at once, though they be diſcerned at different times, according to the greater or leſs neceſſity of thoſe parts. He ſhews how they become ſenſitive, and begin to have life, contending that they are not nouriſhed till they are ſenſible. He explains, from what cauſe and from what end the heart is moved; what thing the *punctum ſaliens* is, and upon what account it hath been reputed to be the heart. And having attempted to reſolve many difficulties, he ſeems to have determined many other curious and conſiderable particulars by experimented principles.

Experiment upon a Jaſper. By Joh. Joachimi Becheri Spirenſis, M.D.

THE doctor obſerves that having a mind, for a certain end, to melt a jaſper, he put it into a crucible, and actually melted it by an intenſe fire, and ſome other requiſites neceſſary to the operation. But to the end that no coals might fall into the paſte, he covered and luted the crucible, which was about half filled with jaſper ſtone; which being melted, he opened the crucible when cool, and, to his great wonder, found at bottom the jaſper melted together into one maſs, as hard as before, but milk-white and half opaque, reſembling a natural white agate; but the cover, at the upper parts of the crucible, that were unfilled, and could not be touched by the jaſper in the melting, were tinged with the natural colour of the jaſper; inſomuch, that if there had been the hardneſs of the jaſper, and the colour not ſuperficial only, the fragments of the crucible might have been ſold for the beſt and moſt poliſhed jaſper, having here and there greeniſh ſtreaks and ſpecks, the reſt being red and yellowiſh; all ſo beautiful, that a good painter would ſcarce have been able to imitate thoſe various colours. Of this the doctor ſaith, he keepeth ſtill the pieces in his laboratory at Munchen in Bavaria, as a very extraordinary treaſure, eſteeming that thoſe upper parts were tinged by the *anima* of the jaſper, driven up by the force of the fire from its inferior part, and adhering to the body of the crucible.

Further obſervations of Spots in the Sun, made at the Royal Academy of Paris, the 11th, 12th, and 13th of Auguſt 1671. Tranſlated from the French.

IT is now eleven years ſince * aſtronomers have ſeen any conſiderable ſpots in the ſun, though before that time, (ſince the invention of teleſcopes) they have occaſionally obſerved them. The ſun appeared all that while with an entire brightneſs, and ſo Signor Caſſini ſaw it on the 9th of this Month Auguſt.

But the 11th of the ſame month, about ſix o'clock at night, being furniſhed only with a three foot glaſs, he remarked in the ſun's diſk, *two ſpots* very dark, diſtant from his apparent centre about the third part of his ſemidiameter. And that he might the more exactly note their ſituation, in reſpect of the ſeveral parts of the world, he made uſe of two very fine threads, cutting each other at right angles in the common focus of the two glaſſes, and in the axis of the teleſcope: and having directed it towards the ſun, he ſo turned it, that letting it afterwards reſt, one might ſee the ſun's centre, according to one of theſe threads, advance weſtward, this ſame thread marking in the ſun a circle parallel to the equator; and the other

* See page 329.

thread marking the circle of declination, or the horary circle of the ſun. See fig. 1.

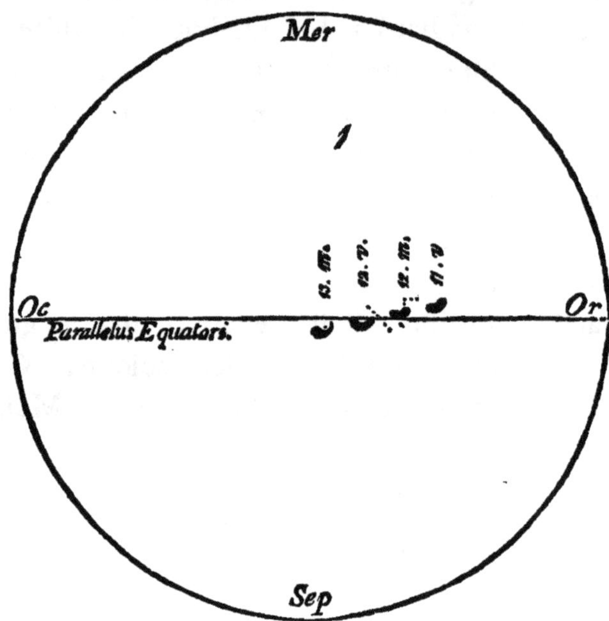

Then he obſerved that the *ſpots* were in the ſouthern part of the ſun; that their elongation from this parallel, paſſing through his centre, could be no more than about the ſixtieth part of his diameter; and that they were ſituated on the eaſtern ſide in reſpect of the ſaid centre of the ſun. He alſo meaſured ſeveral times, from ſix o'clock at night till ſeven, the time which lapſed between the paſſage of the ſun's centre, and that of the firſt of theſe ſpots through the ſaid horary circle, which ſometimes he found to be 23, ſometimes 22 ſeconds, the ſemi-diameter of the ſun then paſſing in 66 ſeconds.

The firſt of theſe ſpots, being looked upon with a teleſcope 17 feet long, appeared of a ſomewhat oval figure; the other was oblong and a little curved, like the Hebrew letter jad; and both together were ſurrounded by a corolla or coronet made up of little dark points, which conformed itſelf to the figure of the ſpots, conſidered as they joined together: which coronet was more exactly obſerved the days following.

The 12th of Auguſt he obſerved them from the time of ſun-riſing, and perceived that now they were nearer his centre. The time between the paſſage of the ſun's centre, and that of the interior edge of the coronet which encompaſſed them both, was then of 16 ſeconds. At ſeven o'clock it was but of 15, and the ſouthern limb of the coronet touched the parallel paſſing through the ſun's centre.

He continued exactly to observe them with a great telescope, from six o'clock in the morning to seven, and found them to be there, as they are represented in fig. 2. The first was composed of two others almost round and conjoined. The second represented the shape of a scorpion The third was rather round. And they were all three environed with a coronet, which was composed, as was said above, of abundance of little obscure pricks. This coronet appeared to be *clearer* than the rest of the sun when looked upon with the short glass, and *darker* when seen with the long. Without it there were other points which were very black, *viz.* five near the round spot on the south side, and another near the scorpion's tail on the north side.

2

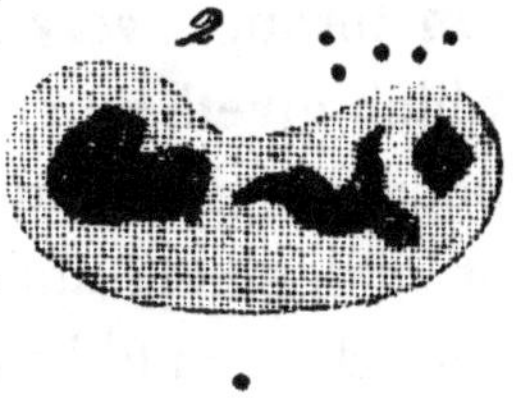

At 48 minutes past eight o'clock, the figure of the scorpion was seen divided into several pieces, as if his tail and arms had been cut off, represented by fig. 3. The northern point appeared no more, there remaining none but those on the south side; and the length of the enclosure of all the spots, comprehended between the extremities, was of 1 minute and 15 seconds, and the breadth of 30 seconds.

3

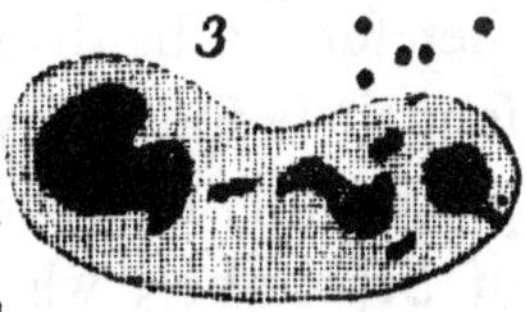

The same 12th day, at six in the evening, he found no great change in the first spot. The other two were severed into five distinct ones, compassed about with a coronet as appears in fig. 4, together with five black points, which stood in a straight row, and after another manner than they did in the morning. From six at night unto seven, the time between the passage of the sun's centre, and that of the coronet's limb, was found to be at one time of *eight* seconds, and another time of *seven seconds* and an *half*. The distance of the spots unto the parallel, passing through the sun's centre, was near the same on the north side with what it had been observed to be in the morning on the south side.

4

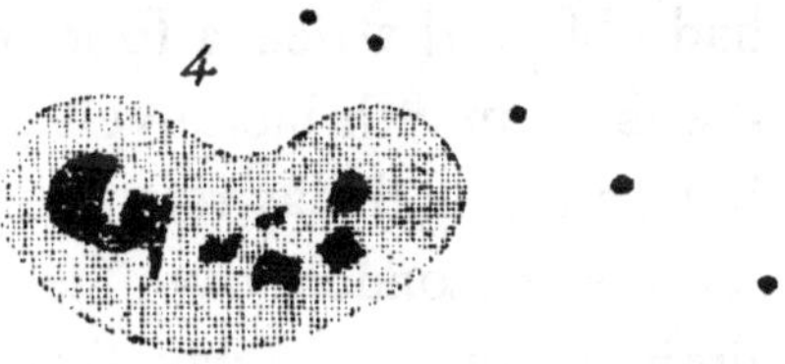

The 13th of August, between the rising of the sun and half an hour past six in the morning, the spots stood as is seen in fig. 5, the edge of the coronet, being turned to a point on the south side, was distant from the *equator* on the north side, half a minute; and there was but a second of time from the passage of the sun's centre into the passage of the same anterior edge of the coronet.

5

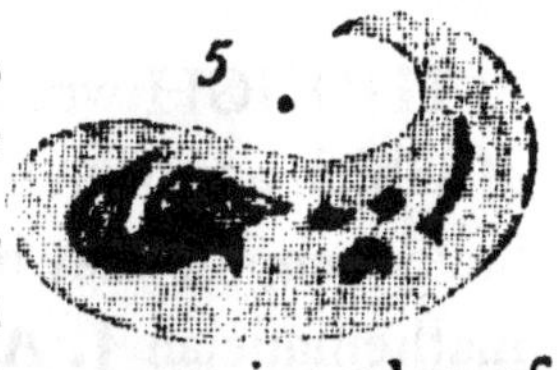

At 30 minutes after eight o'clock, the fore edge was in the ſame *horary circle* with the centre of the ſun: ſo that in one day and a half theſe ſpots have run through very near the third part of the ſun's apparent ſemi-diameter, which giveth an arc of 19 degrees and a half of the circumference of the ſun's body; and conſequently their diurnal motion about the ſun's axe hath been of 13 degrees; and the time of their periodical revolution, as far as we could conjecture in ſo little time, muſt be about 27 days and a half: which yet will be more exactly determined by obſervations of a longer time. Meanwhile, thoſe that have been made, give us hopes to ſee them yet ſix or ſeven days longer, if they diſappear not before they arrive to the ſun's limb.

We thought it not amiſs to advertiſe thoſe, who are addicted to celeſtial obſervations, of the diſcovery of theſe phenomena, that they may alſo obſerve the ſame; and if they be not furniſhed with great teleſcopes, they ought not therefore to be diverted from it, ſince we have found, that by a glaſs of one foot theſe ſpots may be ſeen, at leaſt as making but one ſpot. But it will be particularly neceſſary, to obſerve with care from about the 4th unto the 18th of September, whether theſe ſpots, after they have paſſed over the upper hemiſphere of the ſun which is hid from us, will return not, and be ſeen again in his apparent diſk.

So far the French academiſts. To which we now add: 1ſt, that Mr. *Picard* had obſerved at ſea a ſpot in the ſun from the 3d of Auguſt to the 19th of the ſame month incluſively; and ſeen it the firſt like the tail of a ſcorpion; but on the 19th day reſembling a melon-ſeed. 2dly, That ſeveral curious obſervers at London have ſeen one of thoſe ſpots recurred to the ſun's eaſtern limb, on the ſame day that Signor Caſſini predicted in the relation above, that they ſhould return, if they continued: the particulars of whoſe obſervations will be mentioned hereafter.

A ſhort extract from the Meteorological Hiſtory of the eruption of Mount Etna, An. 1669. By Joh. Alph. Borelli.

THOUGH we have ſeen many accounts of this extraordinary eruption, one of which has been before inſerted *; yet it will be eaſily allowed by thoſe who have ſeen, or may hereafter ſee, that publiſhed by the famed philoſopher and mathematician J. Alph. Borelli, that all others, who have hitherto written on

2

* See page 208.

the ſubject, muſt give the pre-eminence to him in reſpect of method, fullneſs, and philoſophical reflections; to the performance of which he avers to have been induced by his Eminence the Cardinal de Medicis, and the Engliſh Royal Society.

After having given a ſhort topography of this mountain, he proceeds to a diſtinct relation both of the old and later eruptions, and particularly this laſt of Etna, alledging its perpendicular height, ſhewing it not to exceed *three Italian miles*; obſerving that Kepler aſſigned two ſuch miles for the height of the atmoſphere, and thence concluding the top of Etna to be conſiderably raiſed above that region of the common air; confirming the ſame by a known experience, whereby thoſe that are on the ſaid top at a clear break of day, may plainly ſee the whole iſland of Sicily, and all the towns thereof, as it were, elevated and hanging in the air, near the eye, upon that principle of refraction, *that*, ſtones lying at the bottom of a pond appear near the ſurface of the water.

After diſcuſſing many other matters, he comes to treat of the eruption itſelf, which he informs us happened on the 8th of March 1669, accompanied with earthquakes, and a rent of the ground 12 miles long, and five or ſix feet wide, as alſo with a terrible noiſe, roaring and cracking; *vaſt* globes of ſmoke firſt riſing into the air, and abundance of fiery melted ſtones being ejected ſoon after, which firſt ran like a flood of fire, and overwhelmed in a ſhort ſpace of time *thirteen towns*, beſides a part of the city of Catania itſelf, and afterwards were by the air, hardened into vaſt heaps of black and pumice-like ſtones, there called *ſciarra*; waſting and ſpoiling abundance of vines, olives, and other plants.

The caſting out of the aſhes and ſand continued for three whole months without ceaſing, and filled all the neighbouring country, and covered all the towns thereof for 15 miles about; the ſmalleſt duſt flying even over the ſea into Calabria by a ſouth wind, and into the moſt ſouthern parts of Sicily by a north wind.

But on the 25th of March, by a new earthquake, the top or turret of the mountain fell in, whereby was made an opening or cauldron of three miles in compaſs, and vaſt quantities of new matter caſt out, and amongſt it, abundance of fiery ſand, falling down with a yet burning heat at eight miles diſtance from the cauldron; whereupon the ſame by particular view and obſervation was found widened to the circumference of ſix miles. Meanwhile all confidering men there, were amazed at the force that threw out to fo great an height fuch huge ftones, whereof one was meafured to be 60 palms (or about 40 feet) long, which had fallen down a mile from the cauldron with fuch violence, that it was ftruck 30 palms into the ground.

When this fiery torrent affaulted Catania itfelf, and had already by its impetuofity forced from its place a whole mount, planted with vines, belonging to the Jefuits, and carried them floating, together with the foil bearing them, till it fo fwelled as to cover and *fink* them all: at this time there appeared fome gallant perfons, who by their ingenuity and extraordinary diligence, with fit inftruments, and raifing vaft ftrong walls, diverted the courfe of the fiery torrent from that city, but chiefly by boring through the ftony heaps, and thereby making paffage for that current another way, and turning part into the fea, wherein it made a promontory of a mile's compafs before the town.

It ceafed by the 11th of July of the fame year it began: and in May 1670 our author himfelf could handle without hurt, the inner parts of the cauldron and the former torrent, and faw not fo much as any fmoke remaining in the higheft part of that opening; where yet he obferves, that notwithftanding this entire ceafing in the faid places, there were yet found in feveral parts of this newly ejected *fciarra*, hot and ftrong fmelling fumes arifing on high, efpecially near the walls of the fouth fide of *Catania*, where wells had been digged for watering their garden grounds.

He next comments upon the *form*, *confiftence*, *bulk*, and *motion* of the ejected *matter*; taking particular notice of the great abundance of *fal-ammoniac* that was found in all the holes and vents of the ground, and in the clefts of the ftones; and obferving that in three months time the fiery flood (*lava*) ran out 12 miles in length, and taking the medium at one mile and two thirds in breadth, ftopping at laft by the ceafing of new matter.

He eftimates the quantity of the newly ejected matter, and finds it to be nearly equal to a 14,000th part of the bulk of the whole mountain.

He is of opinion that Mount Etna hath no fuch vaftly deep caverns, as fome imagine to be within its bowels, but that *there* it is filled up with folid and ftony matter, the huge weight of the fuperincumbent hill rather compreffing it, than fuffering any confiderable hollownefs to continue therein. And rejecting the imperfect meteorology delivered by the ancients of this mountain, he treats of fubterraneous heat, and deduces the caufe of it from fome concrete oleaginous and fatty ſubſtances, as ſulphur, bitumen, and oil, eaſily reducible to flame; examining the origin of ſuch ſulphureous and bituminous matter, and the cauſe of ſuch matter taking flame; which he conceives to be moſt probably as quick lime is heated by the affuſion of water, whereupon he ſhews how earthquakes, eruptions, and conflagrations do enſue.

He next examines the origin and production of the fluid matter that was thrown out, and vitrified; and aſſerts, upon experimental reaſoning, that it was not any ignated or melted ſulphur or brimſtone, or any metalline bodies that were converted into thoſe vaſt ſtony and black maſſes, which they call ſciarras, but rather earth and ſand, together with ſome alcaline ſalts, burnt by the fervent heat of the Ætnean furnaces, and ſo turned into a vitrious *fluor*, and afterwards, upon being cooled by the air, into hard ſubſtances; ſhewing how the aſperity and opacity of theſe ſtones are conſiſtent with this ſentiment.

After deſcribing the burning down and falling in of the higheſt top of Ætna, he enquires into the generation of thoſe ſands above-mentioned, and accounts *why* in the new opening of the mountain there were heard ſuch terrible and perpetual thundering noiſes, and by what cauſe and force thoſe ſands, &c. were thrown out; ſhewing that they were really ſands and not aſhes, and ſolving the objections alledged againſt it.

He concludes, that ſince by his calculation, the upper part of Mount Ætna hath been juſt ſo much depreſſed, as the maſs of ſands and ſtones ejected amounts to, this maſs was furniſhed by the mountain itſelf, and by the earth and ſands thereof produced and vitrified: and with great ingenuity explains, how all that prodigious quantity of matter thrown out now and in former ages, and ſeeming far to exceed the bulk of the whole mountain, could be furniſhed by Ætna alone, and yet be not quite levelled with the ground; the ſame he conſiders of Mount Veſuvius.

He rejects the opinions of thoſe that maintain that the Ætnean fires have been perpetual and never extinguiſhed, aſſerting the frequent ceſſation of them, and aſſigning the cauſe of that ceſſation, as well as of their renovation, &c.

Some curious obſervations upon that kind of Waſps called Veſpæ Ichneumones. By Francis Willoughby, Eſq.

I REMEMBER M. Liſter's opinion to be, that the muſcæ ichneumones lay their eggs in the bodies of caterpillars, to which opinion I freely ſubſcribe, though I cannot yet abſolutely demonſtrate the fact, as I hoped to have done before this. Theſe ichneumones have four wings, antumæ like bees; the body hanging to the breaſt by a ſlender ligament, as in waſps; moſt, if not all, having ſtings, and are produced of a maggot, that ſpins herſelf a theca before ſhe turns into a nympha. There is great variety of them; ſome breed as bees do, laying an egg, which turns to a maggot, which they feed till it comes to its full growth. Others thruſt their eggs into plants, the bodies of living caterpillars, maggots, &c. Thence it is very ſurpriſing to obſerve, that a great caterpillar, inſtead of being changed into a butterfly, (according to the uſual courſe of nature) ſhould produce ſometimes one, ſometimes two or three, and often a whole ſwarm of ichneumones. I have obſerved this anomalous production in a great many ſorts of caterpillars, both hairy and ſmooth; in ſeveral ſorts of maggots, and, which is moſt ſtrange, in one water inſect. When there come many of theſe ichneumon maggots out of the body of the ſame caterpillar, they wave all their thecas together into one bunch, which is ſometimes round with web about it like a bag of ſpider's eggs; but I dare venture to anſwer M. Liſter's *tenth query* [ſee page 313.] negatively, that none of them *feed* on ſpider's eggs, but it is the ſimilitude of thoſe thecas, conglobated together, to the eggs of ſpiders, that hath occaſioned the conjecture.

One of the green caterpillars, common in the heaths in the north, went ſo far on to her natural change, that ſhe made herſelf up into a great brown *theca,* almoſt of the ſhape of a bottle, which was filled with a ſwarm of ichneumones. And I have obſerved in one or two other ſorts, that from the very aurelia itſelf hath come an ichneumon; which is very odd, that the caterpillar, ſtung and impregnated by the ichneumon, ſhould be yet ſo far unhurt, and unconcerned, as to make herſelf a theca, and become an *aurelia.*

I have often ſeen a great *ichneumon (waſp)* dragging a caterpillar for its intended purpoſe. M. Wray, lately in company with an ingenious neighbour, obſerved *one* dragging a large green caterpillar much bigger than herſelf, which after ſhe had drawn the length of a perch, ſhe laid down, and then took out a little pellet of earth, with which ſhe had ſtopped the mouth of a ſmall hole, like a worm-hole, in the ground, then went down into it, and ſtaying a very ſhort time, came up again, and drew the *eruca* down with her into the hole, and there left her; and afterwards not only ſtopped but filled up the hole, ſometimes carrying little clods, and ſometimes ſcraping duſt with her feet, and throwing backwards into the hole, went down after to ram it cloſe. Once or twice ſhe flew up into a pine tree, which grew juſt over her hole, perhaps to fetch cement; when the hole was full, and even with the ſuperficies of the ground about it, ſhe dragged two pine tree leaves, and laid them near the mouth of the hole, then flew away. Not taking notice that ſhe came any more in three or four days, we dug for the caterpillar, and found it pretty deep. I put it into a box, expecting it would have produced an ichneumon, but it dried away, and nothing came of it. We lately obſerved a ſort of ichneumones, or rather veſpæ, which prey on ſeveral ſorts of flies; when they fly with them they hold them by the heads, and carry them under their bellies. Theſe make holes a great depth in the ground, in which they lay their young, and feed them with the flies they catch, creeping backwards into the ground, and drawing the flies after them. I ſuſpect they may at firſt lay their eggs in the very body of a fly, but one fly being not enough to nouriſh the young one to its full growth, they feed it with more: their thecas are at laſt covered over with the wings, legs, and other fragments of flies.

Obſervations by Mr. Liſter relating to the foregoing paper, the Muſk-ſcented Inſect, and Petrified Shells.

I HAVE obſerved the two inſects that Mr. Ray ſaith ſmell of muſk *, which indeed they do in an high degree. The ſmall bees are very frequent in the wolds in Lincolnſhire, and about the latter end of April are to be found in paſtures and meadows, upon the early blown flowers of a ſort of ranunculas, as was formerly mentioned. But it is ſomething improper to ſay that bees feed on flowers: the ſame bees are no leſs frequently on the flowers of the dens leonis, &c. The ſweet beetle is a very large inſect, and well known about Cambridge. All the trials I have made to preſerve them, with their ſcent, have proved ineffectual; for both of theſe inſects will of themſelves, in a very few weeks, become almoſt quite ſcentleſs. To theſe I ſhall add another ſweet-ſmelling inſect, which is a hexapode worm, feeding on gallium luteum.

* See page 330.

The obſervation of the *veſpæ ichneumones*, as it hath relation to ſpiders, I willingly reſerve for other papers; yet I may tell you in general, that this kind of inſect is one of the greateſt puzzles in nature, there being few excreſcences of plants, and very many births of inſects, wherein theſe ſlender waſps, after divers ſtrange ways, are not concerned. But I leave this for the preſent, and proceed to a remark of my own, relating to petrified ſhells; I mean ſuch ſhells as I have obſerved in our Engliſh ſtone quarries. Firſt, then, we will eaſily believe that in ſome countries, and particularly along the ſhores of the Mediterranean ſea, there may be found all manner of ſea-ſhells *promiſcuouſly* included in rocks or earth, and at good diſtances too from the ſea. But for our Engliſh inland *quarries*, which alſo abound with infinite numbers and great varieties of ſhells, I am apt to think there is no ſuch matter as petrifying of ſhells in the buſineſs, but that theſe cockle-like ſtones ever were as they are at preſent, *lapides ſui generis*, and never any part of an animal. That they are ſo at preſent is in effect confeſſed by *Steno*; and it is moſt certain, that our Engliſh quarry ſhells (to continue that abuſive name) have no part of a different texture from the rock or quarry in which they are lodged; that is, that there is no ſuch thing as *ſhell* in theſe reſemblances of ſhells, but that iron-ſtone cockles, are all iron-ſtone, lime or marble, all lime-ſtone or marble, ſpar or chryſtalline ſhells all ſpar, &c.; and that they never were any part of an animal. My reaſon is, that quarries of different ſtone yield us quite different ſorts of ſpecies of what are called ſhells, not only one from another, as thoſe cockle-ſtones of the iron-ſtone quarry of Alderton, in Yorkſhire, differ from thoſe found in the lead-mines of the nighbouring mountains; and both theſe from that cockle-quarry of Wansford-bridge, in Northamptonſhire; and all theſe from what are to be found in the quarries about Gunthrop and Beavour Caſtle, &c.), but, I dare boldly ſay, from any thing in nature beſides, that either the land, ſalt, or freſh water doth yield us. It is true that I have picked out of that one quarry of *Wansford* very great reſemblances of *murices*, *telinæ*, turbines, cochleæ, &c. and yet I am not convinced, when I particularly examined ſome of our Engliſh ſhores for ſhells, alſo the freſh waters and the fields, that I did not meet with any one of *thoſe ſpecies* of ſhells any where elſe but in their reſpective quarries, whence I conclude them *lapides ſui generis*, and that they were not caſt in any *animal mould*, whoſe ſpecies is yet to be found in being at this day.

This argument, perhaps, will not ſo readily take place with thoſe perſons who think it not worth the while exactly and minutely to distinguish the several species of the things of nature, but are content to acquiesce in *figure*, *resemblance*, *kind*, and such general notions; but when they shall please to condescend to be heedful to accurate descriptions, they will, I doubt not, be of that opinion, which an attentive view of these things led me into some years ago. Though I make no doubt but the repository of the ROYAL SOCIETY is amply furnished with things of this nature, yet, if you shall command them, I will send you up two or three sorts of our English cockle-stones, of different quarries, which I think will speak for themselves, upon examination.

A paper from Mr. Lister, enlarging his former communications relating to Ichneumon Worms, &c.

IN my last paper about vegetable excrescences, I was wholly silent on the opinion which Mr. Willoughby is pleased to favour; and because that worthy gentleman hath so far made it probable, that now it seems only to depend upon the good fortune of some lucky observer, I am willing to resume my former thoughts, that all these odd observations we have made of the *births* of ichneumons do but beget in me a strong belief that they have a way unheeded, whereby they do as boldly as subtilely convey their eggs within the bodies of insects and parts of vegetables.

It has been observed that the substance of many vegetable excrescences seemed not to be the food of the worms found in them. My meaning was, that the substance of the vegetable excrescences in which those ichneumon worms were to be found, was rather augmented, than diminished or worm-eaten. And the like conformity of their feeding *within insects* is well observed by Mr. Willoughby, that the impregnated caterpillars seem not to be concerned, though their bodies are full of insects of a quite different kind, but go on as far as they may towards the achievement of the perfection of their own species. Thus I have seen a *poppy-head* swoln to a monstrous bulk, and yet all the cells were not receptacles of *ichneumons*, but some had good and ripe seed in them. I shall not refuse Mr. Willoughby the satisfaction of an answer to my 10th query, by him resolved negatively: It is true, the swarms of ichneumons coming out of the sides of caterpillars do immediately make themſelves up into bunches, and each particular *theca* (from the cabbage-caterpillar for example) is wrought about with yellow ſilk, as thoſe from the black and *yellow jacobæa* caterpillar with white; but as for webs to cover thoſe branches of thecas, I never obſerved but in the green caterpillar, ſo common in our Lincolnſhire heaths, which are affixed to bents and other plants. Theſe in truth never deceived but my expectation, for I verily thought I had found, when I firſt obſerved them, a caterpillar equivalent to the Indian ſilk-worm; but having cut them aſunder, and expected to have found a caterpillar's chryſalis in the middle, there preſented themſelves a ſwarm of ichneumons; theſe are as large, many of them, as my thumb, that is, at leaſt four times bigger than the *folliculus*, or egg-bag of any Engliſh ſpider I ever yet have ſeen. By good fortune I have not thrown away the boxes wherein I made the obſervation concerning ichneumons feeding upon the eggs of certain ſpiders. I have had them in ſeveral boxes, ſome eight, ſome ten, ſome twelve days *in vermiculo*, feeding upon the very cakes of ſpiders' eggs, before they wrought themſelves thecas for further change; and they ſeldom exceeded the number of five to one cake of eggs, &c. ſo that Mr. Willoughby may be aſſured this is no conjecture, but a real obſervation, accompanied with more circumſtances than I am willing at preſent to relate.

*Obſervations made by Mr. Hook, of ſome Spots in the Sun, returned after they had paſſed over the upper hemiſphere of the Sun, which is hid from us; according to what was predicted**.

AUGUST 30, 1671, I ſaw a large ſpot in the centre of the ſun's face, about noon, but had not time then to make any more exact obſervation thereof.

September 1ſt, at three o'clock, I ſaw the ſame ſpot moved about a quarter of the diameter of the ſun weſtward, and it appeared of this form exactly, that is, it conſiſted of one greater and two leſſer black ſpots with a duſky cloud encompaſſing them. The diameter of the whole phenomenon was about $\frac{1}{72}$ of the diameter of the ſun, and it was diſtant from the next adjoining limb $\frac{18}{72}$ (that is, exactly one quarter) of the diameter of the ſun. This I examined and meaſured ſeveral times, and found very exact.

* See page 335.

An account of a very curious and inſtructive publication on Naval Architecture, &c. by N. Witſon, printed at Amſterdam, 1671, folio.

THE ingenious and induſtrious author of this work having conſidered with himſelf that his countrymen, though ſo flouriſhing in navigation and naval architecture, had yet publiſhed nothing of that ſubject, except what De Heer Tjaſſens had written of the politie of ſhipping, did reſolve to break that ſilence, and communicate to the world a hiſtory both of the *ancient* and *modern* way of *building*, *equipping*, and *governing* ſhips; which deſign having been by him put in execution in this work, he therein largely treateth not only of the manner of naval architecture uſed by the *Greeks* and *Romans*, together with their naval exerciſes, battles, diſcipline, laws, and cuſtoms, but alſo the method and way uſed at that time both in his own country, England, France, and the Indies, together with the difference between the manner of building ſhips practiſed by others from that of the *Dutch*, and particularly of the Indian way of equipping their ſhips, and the manner of building gallies; all enriched with an ample ſeaman's dictionary, and a great number of illuſtrative diagrams.

The whole work is divided into two main parts; the firſt contains 19 chapters, whereof the

1ſt, Gives an account of the earlieſt builders of ſhips, and in general of the building of the ancients, both before and after the deluge; where the author particularly diſcourſes of Noah's ark, of divers ſhips found deep *under ground*, of the ſtructure of the ſhip *Argo*, of the navigation of the *Phœnicians*, *Rhodians*, *Corinthians*, *Egyptians*, *Tyrians*, *Cretians*, *&c.*

2d, Explains the manner of the naval architecture of the *Greeks* and *Romans*, both for war and commerce, together with the mode of equipping their ſhips worked by oars, both of ſingle and manyfold ranks, and the ſitting of the rowers; where he treats of the *biremis piſtrix*, the *biremis vallata oneraria cerealis ciracuſia*, the *biremis* and *triremis turrita*, the triremis vallata, &c.

3d, Of ſeveral ſorts of the ancient ſtructure of ſhips, and chiefly of the great veſſels built by *Philopater* and *Hiero*, the pompous make of both which is repreſented, as alſo of the numbers and launching of their ſhips.

4th, Enumerates divers uncommon obſervables in ſhips, both of ancient and latter times, as in Noah's *ark*, the ſhips of *Argo*, *Theoris*, *Paralon*, *Salamine*, *Magellan*, *Drake*, &c.; to which he adds that noble frigate built in England, anno 1637, called the *Soverain*, of 1637 tons, having a keel that required 28 oxen and four horſes to draw it; as alſo a deſcription of the Spaniſh *armada* of anno 1588, called the *Invincible*, the *Bucentoro* of the *Venetians*, and the *Magaleza* of the *Swedes*, a man of war appearing at ſea about the year 1560, and having ſides of that thickneſs that no bullet could penetrate. In this chapter is inſerted a relation of a ſhip found in the time of Pius II. in the *Numidian Sea*, 12 fathoms under water, 30 feet long, and of a proportionate breadth, built of *cyprus* and *larix* wood, and reduced to that hardneſs that it would not burn, and was alſo very hard to cut; no ſigns of rottenneſs in it any where; its deck covered with paper, linen, and leaden plates, faſtened with gilt nails, as alſo were the boards; the whole ſhip ſo cloſe, that not a drop of water was found ſoaked through into any cloſe room. The author concludes it to have lain there about 1400 years.

5th, Relates what great fleets were anciently fitted out, and what diſtant voyages undertaken; where he makes particular mention of the expedition of the *Argonauts*, of *Xerxes*, of *Alexander*, of *Rome*, *Carthage*, the *Saxons*, *Britons*, &c.

6th, In which he treats of what the ancients obſerved in building their ſhips, and how they cloſed, rigged, and beautified them: where occur ſeveral relations of divers ways of cementing, caulking, pitching, and defending ſhips from rottenneſs and worms, of which I ſhall only mention what he occaſionally ſays of a certain cement uſed by the Indians, made of finely beaten reeds, chalk, and oil, with which their ſhips are *over-laid* to keep them from rotting.

7th, He rehearſes the ſtate of naval architecture after the ruin of the Roman Empire, eſpecially amongſt the *Scythians* and *Saracens*, invading Italy, Spain, France, &c. together with the endeavours of the *Romans*, under Juſtinian and others, to defend themſelves againſt thoſe barbarians, not omitting what was done by the *Danes*, *Huns*, *Engliſh*, *Saxons*, and particularly by that brave and vigilant king Edgar, who maintained a fleet of 3600 ſail, which he divided into three ſquadrons, called the eaſtern, weſtern, and northern, ſailing in them himſelf every year round the iſland; to this he annexes at what time ſhipping was at the loweſt ebb, and how it began to be reſtored by ſome kings of *Portugal,* the *Friezelanders,* and *his* countrymen in general, about the year 1470.

8th, Gives an ample and very particular account of the preſent way of building ſhips, both for war and trade, in Holland; wherein are repreſented not only the parts of a ſhip in their ſeveral figures, together with their names and uſes, but alſo an whole ſhip perfectly rigged, and on its parts marked, with reference to the annexed diſcourſe, wherein they are deſcribed.

9th, Contains all the proportions of the parts of a Dutch ſhip, and the meaſures of ſome peculiar ſorts of veſſels of that country; where he inſtances in ſeveral ſhips of different lengths, and aſſigns the meaſures and proportions of the reſpective parts thereof.

10th, He deſcribes the fit make and weight of all ſorts of anchors, and the bigneſs and weight of cables in general, and in particular of certain ſhips built there, as alſo the meaſures and proportions of maſts and ſails of divers veſſels, and how ſails may be beſt ordered to take in moſt wind, mathematically ſhewn; where occaſion is taken to inſert conſiderable remarks about the ſeveral ſorts of hemp, and the beſt way of working cables, and the care to be had in the manner of tarring them, and in the degree of heating the tar for that purpoſe, &c.

11th, Shews the method of conjoining the parts of a ſhip one after another, uſed by the *Dutch* ſhipwrights, together with a repreſentation of a ſhip upon the ſtocks, and the manner of launching, adding the way of redreſſing a ſhip laying on her ſide, and alſo of laying her on her ſide for the repairing or cleanſing; and intimating, that amongſt them a ſhip of 180 or 185 feet long, can be conveniently built up by 50 men in five months, and that the charges of building a ſhip 165 feet long, 43 feet broad, and 31 feet high, of the beſt timber, amounts to 74,152 guilders, beſides its iron-work, which, together with its rigging, comes to 19,483 guilders more, without the warlike equipage; judging withal, that ſuch a ſhip well built, and *kept* with *care,* may laſt 20, 30, 40, or to 50 years; mentioning alſo that he had ſeen a certain Engliſh veſſel of 70 years old, and not yet altogether uſeleſs.

12th, Treats of the meaſures and proportions of ſeveral other ſea-veſſels, that are of a ſtructure and uſe different from that of the former, ſuch as flutes, Greenland veſſels for whale-fiſhing, advice-yachts, boyars, galliots, fire-ſhips, pinks, buſſes, &c.

2

13th, Of other ſorts of veſſels, as coaſters, ſhallops, lighters, boats, ſkiffs, double-bottomed veſſels, and ſuch as move under water, or againſt the ſtream, and eſpecially of a veſſel uſed at *Amſterdam*, whereby in one day may be fetched up 50 or 60 boats of mud, performed by the means of a big wheel and large ſpoons. In the ſame chapter, inſtructions are given concerning the choice of ſhip-timber; where are to be found many neceſſary and very uſeful obſervations and directions relating to the purpoſe in hand, and a particular commendation of the Engliſh and Iriſh oak for ſhips; to all which is added, an enumeration of all ſorts of tools and engines requiſite for this kind of building.

14th and 15th, Conſiders the ſtructure of galleys and galleaſſes, and the proportions obſerved by the *Engliſh* and *French* in the building of their reſpective ſhips; where he takes particular notice of four frigates of four diſtinct rates, exhibiting and deſcribing them as they are to be found in the Duke of Northumberland, *Robert Dudley*, his *Arcana de' Mare*, printed at *Florence*; concluding the 15th chapter with a deſcription of the frigate called the Royal Charles (ſome years ſince fallen into *Dutch* hands), and an encomium of the Engliſh orders at ſea.

16th, He narrates the Indian way of framing ſhips; where firſt occur the canoes, and their ſtructure out of one only tree, hollowed by burning; next the Chineſe *yonks* of *Nankin* (a ſort of flat-bottomed boats), and other veſſels of the ſame country, amongſt which, thoſe are deſcribed that are as big as little iſlands, and hold many houſes and families, floating upon the waters, going up and down through all the parts of *China* that have the conveniency of navigable rivers, to which is added, a deſcription of a Royal *Chineſe* boat, of a ſerpentine ſhape, ſent to receive the *Dutch* Ambaſſadors in thoſe parts; next, the ſhips of *Malabar*, *Ternate*, *Sumatra*, *Japan*, and *Terra del Fuego* (in which laſt are made very artificial boats of the corks of the thickeſt trees, as in Malabar ſome are made of large canes, called bamboo); moreover of *Borneo*, and *Calecut*. After this the author returns to *China*, and relates that ſhips are found there, which upon rollers ſail over land; and gives a large account of the vaſt number of ſhips, both warlike and mercantile, maintained in that Empire; together with the old architecture of the ſame, and the ſkill of that people in navigation; as alſo an intimation out of Martinius touching the antiquity of the *Chineſe* ſhipping, their colonies found ſettled in Madagaſcar, and their ſailing in old times even as far as the *Red*

Sea. He concludes this chapter with defcribing the fhips of *Madagafcar, Bengala, Macaffar, Siam, Pegu, Maldivus, Ormus, Congo, Ruffia, Lapland, Virginia,* &c.

17th, He demonftrates how much weight of water there lies againft a fhip moving at fea, having firft laid down certain propofitions made out by *Stevinus* in his hydroftatics, which writer's footfteps our author acknowledges to have followed herein; befides, he examines alfo the centre of gravity of a fhip, which being known, it may be certainly concluded how a fhip is to lie upon the water, and how heavy fhe is when floating, laden or unladen. Laftly, he imparts the way of the excellent *Hudde,* of calculating exactly what burthen a fhip can carry either in falt or fweet water; where he alfo examines the weight of the water in which a fhip is floating, for which purpofe he caufed to be made a *cube* of copper-plates, of half an Amfterdam foot afide, fitted after a certain manner, too particular to be here related, whereby he found, that upon the 15th of March a foot of *rain water* weighed 49lb. 14½ oz. and Y-water 46lb. 2⅛ oz.; and Texel water 46lb. 9 oz.; to all which he adds the way of meafuring the quantity of a fhip's burthen, that hath been agreed upon between the King of Denmark and the States of the United Provinces, and alfo feveral ways of doing the fame, ufed by other nations, particularly the *Englifh* and *French.*

18th, Explains and gives reafons for the feveral fizes and fhapes of the various parts of a fhip; as, why the mafts ought to be precifely of fuch dimenfions; why fome of them muft incline backwards, fome ftand upright; why a fmall rudder can turn a great fhip, and a little anchor ftay it; what maketh fhips not feel the rudder; why veffels too broad are weak, and prove inconvenient in high winds; why long and moderately narrow veffels endure the fea better than fhort and broad ones; how the keel ought to be placed; why gallions and the parts of them are framed as they are; why a fhip is to be broader before than abaft; that frigates built long, narrow, and low, fail beft; what hinders well failing; why Turkifh veffels are excellent failers; and many queftions more, *confidered* and *refolved* by this *fcientific* author.

19th, Reckons up the particulars of the loofe apparatus neceffary in a moderately long voyage for an hundred men, in a fhip 134 feet long, both for conduct and defence, and the food of the mariners, &c. &c.

The ſecond part comprehends the equipping and conduct of ſhips and navies, as well by the ancients as moderns, couched in four chapters.

1ſt, Of the ordering and equipping of ſhips and ſeamen, practiſed by the *Greeks* and *Romans*, as alſo of the *old* rights and laws of mariners, their victuals, encouragements, puniſhments, and arms, together with their manner of fighting, and triumphing upon a victory obtained; where are related ſeveral ſea battles and their events, as alſo divers famous pirates, recorded in the Roman Hiſtory.

2d, Treats of the *then* conduct and government of the States General of the United Provinces in their warlike fleets, together with their orders for convoy-ſhips; where are inſerted the particular commands and inſtructions given by the States in the war at that time between England and that Republic, as alſo their placart concerning prizes; to all which is ſubjoined, the ſhip-maſter's and ſteer-man's way of diſciplining the ſeamen, and the manner and form of commanding them to perform the various parts of their duty at ſea; which chapter is concluded with ſeveral remarks concerning the *laadſtone* and ſea compaſs, and eſpecially with what care the needle for the compaſs is to be touched by the magnet.

3d, Obſerves the ordering of merchant ſhips, and the conduct of Admiralties; as alſo how they man and arm their trade ſhips in general, and in particular thoſe that navigate northward, and their herring buſſes, as alſo thoſe that ſail to the Mediterranean. Further, how things are managed amongſt them on ſhip-board, in reference to the ſeamen, officers, ſoldiers, &c. in their navigation to the Eaſt and Weſt Indies, Greenland, &c. In this chapter it is alſo repreſented what benefits redound to a country by ſhipping, as to the increaſe both of its power and wealth.

4th, Contains a ſea dictionary, explaining the names of the parts of a ſhip, and the words and phraſes uſed among ſeamen for all ſorts of naval concerns.

Relating to Vipers. By Monſieur Bourdelot.

THIS ſmall diſcourſe is an anſwer to a letter which the excellently learned author had received from Signior Redi, firſt phyſician to the great Duke of

Florence. In this Monſieur *Bourdelot* declares, that though Signior Redi's letter doth not fully decide the matter in queſtion, yet it is very uſeful to the further knowledge of the nature of vipers, by the particularities by him recited; the controverſy being, whether the yellow liquor about the long and crooked teeth of vipers is, even when they are not irritated, venomous (which is affirmed by Signior *Redi*), or whether it be a ſimple innoxious ſaliva or ſpittle, as is maintained by Monſieur *Charas*. This author obſerves, that *that* liquor is not yellow in French vipers, as it is in thoſe of Italy; which remark he makes uſe of to the advantage of the often mentioned *Redi*, who would reconcile theſe two opinions, by ſuggeſting, that the vipers of Italy and France are differently diſpoſed, countenancing this obſervation with what he hath taken notice of, that venom of the *lues venerea* is much more malign in hotter than in colder climates; and alſo with what is conſtantly related by voyagers, viz. that animals are more venomous in Africa than elſewhere. But that notwithſtanding this, the objection made by M. Charas ſeems not cogent, when he ſpeaks of a viper's teeth, whoſe bite proved mortal, although the teeth had been rubbed and perfectly dried with bread crumbs; whereby he would ſupport that experiment, in which he cauſed to be bitten and killed ſeven or eight animals one after another, of which the laſt bitten died firſt; it ſeeming impoſſible to him that there ſhould be remaining any of that ſalival juice about his teeth after ſo many bitings; and that therefore to give a cauſe of that death, recourſe muſt be had to the fierceneſs of the ſpirits tranſmitted to the crooked teeth, to be revenged of thoſe againſt whom theſe animals are provoked; which angry ſpirits being thruſt into the fleſh and veins, do infect the ſpirits and blood of thoſe who are bitten. To which our author anſwers, that it is hard to maintain that the vindictive ſpirits can paſs through a body ſo ſolid as teeth are, eſpecially ſince the *little teeth* have been found by experience to cauſe as dangerous effects as the *great ones*, after that theſe had been broken out: and that therefore it may be juſtly doubted whether by the ſaid bread crumbs all the ſalival liquor about the teeth of the animal alive could be taken away; as it may be truly affirmed that the viper's teeth are inceſſantly plunged into their ſheaths, and do there continually fill themſelves with the ſaid juice.

But he eſteems withal that in hot countries this liquor may work alone, when conveyed into our fleſh by the teeth of a dead viper, or even with an ear-pick, into a wound; as it comes to paſs in Italy, and hot countries; but in France, and in colder parts, eſpecially ſuch vipers being uſed as are kept in tuns, and brought from afar off, the ſaid juice not being ſtrong enough alone, needs to be made keen by the bilious breath of the angered viper.

And here the author expatiates his diſcourſe, that without recurring to a vindictive ſpirit, paſſing through a ſharp tooth as through a needle, the choleric breath of an incenſed viper may exceedingly invigorate that liquor, and prove a ferment to the ſame, like ſome *afflatus malignus & halitus teter:* where, amongſt other particulars, he ſpeaks of a gardener, who upon the grafting of his trees never found more than half the grafts to thrive, of which at laſt the cauſe was diſcovered, in that he ſtill took two grafts together to inoculate, of which he firſt grafted that which he held in his hand, and then the other which he had held in his mouth, which, having rotten teeth, did taint the ſweetneſs of the vegetative juice in the ſecond graft, which was always found withered away. To which he adds, how certain breaths of wind corrupt meat, eſpecially when it thunders and lightens; how the expirations of ſome men and beaſts do the like when corrupted; and that one may be particularly ſenſible of the breath of a man in choler, and that the bite of a *red haired* perſon is venomous; moreover, that if a man having waſhed his mouth with vinegar, breathes into a bottle, the wine put into it will ſour; and that a butcher's boy having eat onions or garlick, or having rotten teeth, the beef or mutton by him blowed up the night before will be livid next morning, and worth nothing, &c.

He further obſerves that the breath coming from the ſpongy lungs of vipers enraged, is of greater force than all thoſe he hath ſpoken of, and that it is full of bilious ſpirits when they are angered; and examines whether vipers have a paſſage aſcending from the bladder of gall to the throat, as he affirms it hath been found in ſnakes, and particularly in thoſe of the *Grotto del ſerpi*, near Bracciano, famous for curing ſtubborn maladies, by large ſnakes winding themſelves about the bodies of the ſick expoſed there, of which he affirms to have ſeen the experiment himſelf.

He concludes the whole with obſerving, 1ſt, That as vipers are eaſily provoked, ſo they are very gentle when their bile is not agitated; and that it may be ſaid they know thoſe who attend them, and take them out of their tuns in handfuls, without fear or injury. 2dly, That vipers do exceedingly abound in ſpirits, whence they are ſo proper to reſtore the aged, and prolong their days; and that the heart or liver of the viper is one of the greateſt alexiterics in the world, and admirably efficacious in malign fevers.

The obſervations of the ſpots of the Sun made at the Royal Academy at Paris, continued.*

HAVING formerly communicated the obſervations of the *new ſpots* in the *ſun*, together with Signor *Caſſini's* way of noting their ſituation in his diſk, which hath ſerved to determine the time when they ſhould be viſible on his apparent ſurface, and how long they ſhould remain on his hidden hemiſphere before their re-appearing to us; and laſtly, to calculate the duration of their periodical revolution about his axis; it may juſtly be expected we ſhould give the ſequel of what hath been obſerved ſince the firſt and laſt appearance of theſe ſpots.

It hath been noted in the *firſt* Paper, that in the laſt obſervation, made the 13th of Auguſt, the anterior limb of the miſty crown encloſing all the ſpots, was in the ſame horary circle with the ſun's centre.

In the morning of the 14th of the ſame month, from ſix to ſeven o'clock, there paſſed 15″ of time between the paſſage of the anterior limb of the ſaid crown, and the paſſage of the ſun's centre through the ſame horary circle; and then the ſouthern limb of the crown was a minute and an half diſtant towards the north, from the parallel of the equator, paſſing through the ſame centre of the ſun. The figure of the firſt ſpot was almoſt the ſame with *that* of the day before. The ſecond had taken the form of an heart, the point of which was turned to the north ſide, and its baſe between the ſouth and eaſt. Three other ſmall ſpots, diſpoſed trianglewiſe, ſtood over the ſaid baſe, and were accompanied with two others upon a line turned ſouthward, and they were all encompaſſed with a crown running out into a point on the ſouth ſide; and on the north ſide eaſtward, it had an appendix.

* See page 335.

The 15th, at six in the morning, there passed 27" between the passage of the anterior limb of the crown, and that of the sun's centre through the same horary circle. The southern limb of the same crown was *two minutes* and an *half* distant from the parallel of the *equator* passing through the centre of the sun, whose diameter passed in 2' 9", through the same horary circle. The first spot had a little changed its figure; the second was quadrangular, longer from east to west, than from north to south; it appeared bigger than ordinary, and had withal on its sides, within the compass of the crown, three other small spots. There were also seen four more without the said crown, on the south side.

The 16th, at six in the morning, there were 27" between the passage of the sun's anterior limb, and the passage of the anterior limb of the crown through the same horary circle; and 38" between the passage of the anterior limb of the crown, and the passage of the sun's centre. The southern limb of the crown was 3' ¼ off from the parallel of the equator, passing through the centre of the sun towards the north: and the observation having been made yet more exactly at half an hour past seven of the same morning, this distance was found to be 3' 33". The figure of the first spot in the beginning of the observation differed not much from that of the precedent day; but afterwards it was seen divided into two. The second, which likewise seemed to be the same in the beginning, was afterwards divided into three, accompanied with black and dark points, without the crown on the south side.

The same day, at 15' past six o'clock in the evening, the figures of these spots were much changed, there being then five spots inclosed in the crown. The two foremost were part of that which had been seen in the morning as one; the two others following those two first, were part of the second in the morning; and without there were five points on the south side, and two more a little further to the north; which points were ranged as in another *area* made up of other points, so small that they could scarce be perceived.

The 17th in the morning, immediately after the rising of the sun, there appeared three very dark spots, which formed in a manner these letters F, n, J, posited from east to west, and included in their wonted crown, which stretched out as it were two arms, or two handles, one to the south, and the other to the north. There lapsed 18" between the passage of the foremost limb of the sun and that of the foremost limb of the crown, and

5

47″½ between the paſſage of the anterior limb of the crown unto the paſſage of the ſun's centre. The ſouthern limb of the ſame crown was diſtant 11′ 17″ from the parallel that touched the ſun on the north ſide, and 4′ 38″ from the parallel that paſſed through his centre.

The 18th, at ſeven in the morning, the ſpots which appeared through ſome clouds, had almoſt the ſame ſhape with thoſe of the day before, only with this difference, that they were a little cloſer together, drawing from eaſt to weſt. There is here no particular deſcription exhibited of them, for fear of failing in their exactneſs, by reaſon of the clouds, which hindered their being ſeen diſtinctly. There lapſed 13″ between the paſſage of the anterior limb of the ſun, and that of the anterior limb of the ſpot, through the ſame horary circle; and 52″½ of the foremoſt limb of the ſpot unto the paſſage of the centre. The ſouthern limb of the ſpot was 9′ 13″ diſtant from the parallel that paſſed through his centre. This obſervation was ended between ſeven and eight in the morning.

At 55′ after five in the evening of the ſame day we renewed our obſervations. There lapſed 11″ between the paſſage of the anterior limb of the ſun, through the ſame horary circle, and the paſſage of the anterior limb of the crown, and thence into the paſſage of the ſun's centre 54″½. The limb of the crown next to the parallel paſſing through the centre of the ſun, was diſtant from the ſame parallel 7′ 40″.

From four o'clock to five in the evening of the 19th, the ſpot was obſerved whilſt the ſun was emerging out of the clouds. It then appeared oblong near the ſun's circumference, from which it was diſtant about the breadth of the ſame ſpot: and when we were preparing to meaſure its diſtance from the parallel of the diurnal motion of the ſun's centre, the clouds, which roſe from the horizon, intercepted it from our ſight.

The apparent velocity of the ſpots when they approached to the ſun's centre, gave ground to determine their apparent periodical revolution about the ſun's axe to be about *twenty-ſeven days* and an *half*, ſuppoſing them to be adherent to his ſurface, or at leaſt very nigh to it; and conſequently that from the morning of the 13th of *Auguſt*, when they were near his centre, they ſhould take between ſix and ſeven days to arrive at the limb of his apparent diſk: the which hath come to paſs, conformable to the obſervations ſince that time: for ſince the morning of the 13th unto the evening of the 19th, when they were ſeen nigh the limb, there are 6½ days; and then they were yet ſo far diſtant from it, that it was eaſv to judge they would not come out that day. The clouds and night did then hinder to obſerve them; but on the morning of the 20th, which was not the full ſeventh from the day that they were arrived to the middle of the diſk, they had diſappeared. This likewiſe agrees well enough with what had been practiſed, viz. *that* theſe ſpots during the fourth part of the time of their motion about the ſun's centre, calculated according to this hypotheſis, and upon the firſt *obſervations*, would remain in the *weſtern* quadrant.

The apparent velocity near the centre was ſuch, that if it had continued the ſame, the ſpots would have arrived almoſt in *four* days to the limb of the diſk; but in this hypotheſis this apparent velocity was to leſſen according as the ſpots ſhould remove from the centre, as hath come to paſs in effect. The diminution of the length of the miſty crown was in a manner proportionate to the diminution of the apparent velocity; ſince that, when this crown was in the middle, and in a ſituation wherein its true figure could be beſt ſeen, it appeared oblong, and of the form of an human ear, its greateſt diameter reſpecting eaſt and weſt; but being nigh the limb, this ſame diameter ſeemed to ſhorten; and having appeared greateſt in its firſt ſituation, it appeared leaſt in this, becauſe it was almoſt in a circle that paſſed through the centre of the ſun, whoſe equal arches are by ſo much the more oblique, by how much they approach more to the limb of his diſk, and conſequently appear leſs, according to the rules of optics; mean time the diameter, that was turned from ſouth to north, apparently kept the ſame bigneſs it had near the centre, becauſe it was in a circle almoſt parallel to the horizon of the ſun, which formed the repreſentation of its limb, and whoſe equal arches, (by the ſame optical reaſon) do not appear contracted.

Obſervations concerning Saturn, made in the ſame place with the former.

AT the ſame time that the *new ſpots* in the ſun began to appear, Signor Caſſini obſerved in Saturn alſo ſomething remarkable, in regard to the unexpected change of his figure. Aſtronomers know that this planet is for the moſt part ſeen with arms or anſes joined to the two ſides of his diſk, when he is beheld with ſome great teleſcope; and that he re-taketh not his *round figure* but every fifteenth year. This change was to come to paſs this preſent year, and Saturn to appear in that *round figure*, without his anſes or handles, according to the *hypotheſis* and predictions of *M. Hugens*; which indeed hath ſo happened, but not juſt within the time he had appointed: for this ſpherical figure of *Saturn* ſhould not have appeared, according to his ſuppoſitions, but in the months of July and Auguſt, and ſo continued for the reſt of the time that Saturn was to be viſible at this period, and even for a part of his appearance in the next year; but this roundneſs hath been perceived ſooner, and Saturn hath appeared orbicular ſince the end of May, at a time when he was diſtant enough from the ſun and the horizon to be well obſerved. He hath remained in this figure unto the 11th of Auguſt. The ſaid Signor Caſſini did then obſerve him thus; but three days after he ſaw him with *arms*, though very narrow ones, which do ſtill continue.

Monſieur Hugens having examined theſe appearances, and the cauſe of the difference from what he predicted of them, finds not that they are contrary to his hypotheſis of the *flat* ring about *Saturn*, by means of which he explicates all the changes of his figure; but eſteems that they will ſerve to determine more preciſely than could be done hitherto, the ſeveral appearances of his *round* figure; and becauſe he foreſees that it will ſo appear again within a little time, and at the furtheſt in the then enſuing December, and that the ſame will ſo continue the remaining time of its appearance, he conſiders the return of the arms, which do at preſent appear, as a little interruption of this round figure; which would not ſo much as have been perceived with middle ſized glaſſes of ſix or ſeven feet, like thoſe that were uſed by *Galileo* and *Caſſendi:* which experience may verify, if inſtead of teleſcopes of fifteen or twenty feet long you employ only ſome of theſe ſmaller ones, with which you are not able to diſcern theſe arms becauſe of their tenuity, and that they are but faintly illuminated by the ſun-beams, which do more obliquely fall upon the flat ſurface of the ring.

Monſieur Hugens believed alſo that Saturn would appear the next ſummer, after his conjunction with the ſun, with arms like thoſe he then had, in which he amends his former prediction; having ſeen by theſe laſt obſervations (as he was already aware of it in his ſyſtem) that this round appearance is to be defined to a leſs number of degrees than he had done, in reſpect of great teleſcopes.

Extract of two letters from Derby, Nov. 21, and Dec. 2, 1671, by Mr. Flamstead, touching some late appearances of Saturn.

OCTOBER 12th last past, at my first viewing *Saturn* with my lesser tube, I thought I saw something on each side of him, amidst the colours of my glass and the spurious rays of his body. Directing my longer tube, of 14 feet, to him, I could see his *anses* somewhat more distinctly, but very slender, and to one that thought not of them, scarce discernible.

November 30th (the only clear night we have had of late) I observed Saturn with my 14 feet telescope. He appeared perfectly round, free from rays and colours, and no ansæ to be seen.

A week or two after the observation of Saturn, which I made Oct. 12, I had frequently the same appearance, though in a wider aperture than I use at present, &c.

Further observations about the shining of Glow-worms; by Mr. John Templer.

JUNE 1st. Upon several trials of different positions, I find the glow-worm not to shine sometimes when in motion: but I could never yet see her shine when not in motion of some part.

June 8th. Putting her into an urinal of white glass at nine o'clock at night, she crawled nimbly in it, and extended herself beyond her ordinary length, yet her shining was not so clear as in her box when opened. Putting the urinal into the water for about half an hour, it gave a very delightful irradiation of the water. When this light seemed wholly *extinct*, although the animal was in motion, if I depressed the urinal into the water till the bottom almost touched the bottom of the bason, I could (upon looking in at the top of the urinal) see a very fair light; but upon lifting the glass out of the water, I could discern very little shining. Then putting her into her box, she did, in about a minute's time, almost ten times increase her former shining in the glass.

Anatomy of Vegetables, &c. by Nehemia Grew, M. D. Fellow of the ROYAL SOCIETY.

THE ingenious and learned author of the above tract, confidering with himfelf that the *anatomy* of *vegetables* hath hitherto been much uncultivated, and that yet it very well deferved the labours of diligent naturalifts, hath attempted to make a very particular enquiry into the conftitution and ftructure of plants, and thereupon to found a rational difcourfe concerning the nature of vegetation; which being undertaken by him, he advifes thofe who fhall think fit to examine thefe obfervations of his, not only that they begin, and fo proceed till they end with the *feed*: but alfo that they confine not their enquiries to one time of the year, but to make them in feveral feafons, wherein the parts of a *vegetable* may be feen in their feveral ftates: and then, that they neglect not the comparative anatomy, confronting feveral vegetables and their feveral parts together.

The method he choofes in the profecution of this fubject, is the method of nature herfelf in her continued *feries* of *vegetations*, proceeding from the *feed* fown, to the formation of the root, trunk, branch, leaf, flower, fruit; and laftly, of the *feed* to be *fown again*, or in its ftate of regeneration.

Difcourfing of the *feed* as vegetating, he diffects a garden bean, and fhews the two coats thereof; the *foramen* in the outer coat, and what is generally obfervable of the covers of the feed. This done, he difplays the proper feed itfelf, and therein finds three conftituent, and as it were organical parts of the bean, viz. the main body, always divided into two lobes (though in fome few other feeds into more); and two other appendant to the bafis of the bean; whereof the one is called by him the *radicle*, being that which upon the vegetation of the feed becomes the root; the other the *plume*, which becomes the trunk of the plant; and being divided at its loofe end into divers pieces, (all very clofe fet together as *feathers* in a bunch) thefe pieces are fo many true and already formed, though not difplayed *leaves*, intended for the faid trunk, and folded up in the fame plicature, wherein upon the bean's fprouting, they do appear. Thefe organical parts he finds compofed of thefe fimilar ones, viz. 1ft, The cuticle, extending itfelf over the whole bean, and herein diftinguifhed from the coats; whereas *thefe*, upon fetting the bean, do only adminifter the fap, and then die; the cuticle is with the organical parts of the bean nouriſhed, augmented, and co-extended. 2d, The *parenchyma* itſelf, having ſome ſimilitude to the pith, while ſappy, in the roots and trunks of plants; common to, and the ſame in the lobes, radicle, and plume of the bean. 3d, The inner body, diſtributed throughout the *parenchyma*, but withal eſſentially different from it; called by the author the *ſeminal root*, and diſtinguiſhed from the radicle, in that the former is the original root within its ſeed, the latter is the plant root, which the radicle becomes in its growth; the parenchyma of the ſeed being, in ſome reſemblance, that to the *ſeminal root* at firſt, which the mould is to the plant root afterwards; and the *ſeminal root* being that to the *plant root*, which the plant root is to the trunk. Having viewed theſe parts, he enquires into their uſe, and in what manner they are the fountain of vegetation, and concurrent to the being of the future plant.

Proceeding to the root, which he finds ſubſtantially one with the radicle, (as are the parts of an old man with thoſe of the fœtus) he therein obſerves its *ſkin*, *cortical body*, and *lignous part*, together with the original of each of thoſe, and the *pores* of the two latter, and their proportions; as alſo the pith, and its original, ſometimes from the *ſeed*, ſometimes from the *cortical body*, together with its *pores* and proportions: moreover, the fibres of the lignous body diſperſed through the pith, and the cavity and pith of thoſe fibres. Where he explains how the root grows, and what is the uſe of its parts; how it grows in length and breadth, and how it deſcends; adding the uſe of the pith, viz. for the better advancement of the ſap, and its quicker and higher fermentation, begun in the *cortical body*, inſerted through the *lignous part*, by which inſertions the ſap, like the blood of the diſſeminations of the *arteries*, is conveyed to its intimate parts; and that the deſign whereto all theſe parts are together concurrent, is the circulation of the ſap.

Having thus declared the degrees of vegetation in the root, he next ſhews the continuance thereof in the trunk; the obſervables and parts of which are, 1ſt, The ſkin derived from the cuticle of the ſeed: 2d, The cortical body originated from the *parenchyma* of the ſeed: 3d, The lignous body, being the prolongation of the *inner* body, diſtributed in the lobes and plume of the ſeed: 4th, The *inſertment* and *pith*, proceeding alſo from the *plume*, as the ſame in the *root* from the *radicle*; ſo that as to their ſubſtantial parts, the *lobes* of the ſeed, the *radicle* and *plume*, the *root* and *trunk*, are all one. Here notice is taken of the ſhooting of the *lignous body* in breadth; where are obſervable its fibres, production of *rings*, and eſpecially *pores*; and theſe of three ſorts, *great*, *leſs*, and *leaſt* of all; all continuous and prolonged by the length of the trunk, which he proves by an experiment made by Mr. Hook, by filling up (ſuppoſe in a piece of charcoal) all the ſaid pores with mercury, which appears to paſs quite through them, as is viſible by a good glaſs. The reſult of all is, that the *woody* part of a vegetable is nothing elſe but a cluſter of innumerable and extraordinary ſmall veſſels or concave fibres. He further ſhews the inſertions of the *cortical body* in the *trunk*, and the pores of thoſe inſertions; in none of which *pores* he could obſerve any thing that may have the true nature and uſe of *valves*, the non-exiſtence of which he is aſſerting. He diſcourſes alſo of the *poſition* and *tract* of the *pores*: and concludes this ſection by declaring how the *trunk* aſcends; how its parts, in conſequence of that aſcent, are diſpoſed; how that diſpoſition is conſequent to the different nature and energy of the ſap; what the effects are of that difference; which way, and how the ſap aſcends, viz. by the joint ſubſerviency of the lignous and cortical body in ſome, but in moſt, and principally, of the *lignous body* and *pith*; the latter being here conſidered as a curious filtre of nature's own contrivance: where he examines how the pores of the pith are permable; and renders a reaſon why a piece of *dry elder pith* ſet in ſome tinged liquor, the liquor doth not then penetrate the pores, ſo as to aſcend through the body of the pith.

After this he proceeds to the germen, branch, and leaf, and finds in the two former the ſame parts with thoſe of the trunk, viz. the ſame ſkin, the ſame lignous and cortical bodies, as alſo the ſame inſertment and pith, hereinto propagated and diſtinctly obſervable in it. Further he ſhows the manner of their growth and nutrition, and how the *germen* is ſecured; as alſo the uſe of the *knots*. Then he lays open the parts of a *leaf*, and explains the poſitions of the fibres in the ſtalks of leaves, and the cauſe of their different ſhapes, and of their being flat; and then treats of the folds of leaves, their kinds and uſe, together with the uſes of the leaf itſelf; and here adds an Appendix of thorns, hairs, and globulets, explaining both their conſtitution and uſe.

Next he gives an account of the flower, and its three general parts, the *empalement*, the *foliation*, and the *attire*; explaining the formation, nature, and uſes of all three, but moſt particularly of the attire, which he finds to be of two kinds, ſeminy and flory; the *ſeminy* made up of two parts, *chives* and *ſemets*, the latter of which are hollow, yet not ſo but that they are filled up with minute particles, like a powder. The florid attire is commonly called *thrumbs*, which are ſeveral ſuits, of which this attire is made up; the outer part of every ſuit is its floret, which is the epitome of a flower, and in many plants all the flower. The next part is from within its tube brought to ſight, and is called the *ſheath*, likewiſe concave. The third part, and the innermoſt of the ſuit is the *blade*, which is ſolid, but at its point evermore divided into two halves; upon which diviſion there appears a *powder* of *globulets*, of the ſame nature with thoſe of the *ſemet*. The uſe of the attire he aſſigns to be not only ornament and diſtinction to us, but alſo food to a vaſt number of little animals, who have their peculiar proviſions ſtored up in theſe attires of flowers; each flower becoming their lodging and their dining room, both in one. Though it as yet be not determined wherein the particular parts of the attire may be more diſtinctly ſerviceable, this to one animal, that to another; or to the ſame animal, as a *bee*, whether this for the honey, another for the *bread*, a third for the *wax*; or whether *all* do only ſuck from thence ſome *juice*, or ſome may not alſo carry ſome of the parts, as the globulet, wholly away, &c.

The next head treats of the *fruit*, conſidering the number, conſtitution, and original of the parts of an *apple*, *bean*, *plum*, *nut*, and *berry*; and obſerving that the general compoſition of all fruits is one, that is, their eſſential and vital parts are in all the ſame, and but the continuation of thoſe, which in other parts of a vegetable he hath already taken notice of. To which he ſubjoins the uſes of fruits, both for man and beaſts; as alſo for the ſeed; to which latter it ſerves for ſupply of ſap, and for protection and ſecurity; the whole fruit being, by comprehenſion, that to the ſeed, which the hen, by incubation, is to the egg or chick.

In the concluſion he conſiders the *ſeed* again but in its ſtate of *generation*, as he before examined it in its ſtate apt for vegetation; where occurs what in the other ſtate was either not diſtinctly exiſtent, or not ſo apparent, or not ſo intelligible: as firſt the *caſe* of the *ſeed*, and its *outer* coat, their figures, various ſurface and mucilages; together with the nature of the outer coat and its original: then the original and nature of the *inner* coat, in which the lignous body or ſeed branch is deſcribed. Whereupon he obſerves that all the parts of a vegetable, the root, trunk, branch, leaf, flower, fruit and ſeed, are ſtill made up of two ſubſtantially different; and that as every part hath two, ſo the whole vegetable taken together is a compound of two only, and no more; all properly *woody* parts, *ſtrings*, and *fibres*, being one body; all ſimple barks, piths, parenchimas, and pulps; and for ſubſtance, *pills* and *ſkins* alſo, all but one body. The ſeveral parts of a vegetable differing from each other only by the various proportions and mixtures, and the variouſly ſized pores of theſe two bodies.

But to return, beſides theſe three covers, he finds a fourth, which is the innermoſt, called by him the *ſecondine*, the concave of which membrane is filled with a tranſparent liquor, out of which the ſeed is formed. Through this membrane the lignous *body* or *ſeed branches*, diſtributed in the inner coat, at laſt ſhoot downright two ſlender *fibres*, like two navels, one into each lobe of the bean. Theſe fibres, from the ſuperficies of each lobe, deſcend a little directly down, and preſently each is divided into two branches, one diſtributed into the lobes, the other into the *radicle* of the *plume*.

As for the generation of the ſeed, dependant upon the hiſtory delivered, he ſaith, that the ſap, having in the *root*, *trunk*, and *leaves* paſſed divers concoctions and ſeparations, in the manner by him deſcribed, it is at laſt, in ſome good maturity, advanced towards the ſeed. The more copious and cruder part whereof is again ſeparated by a free reception into the fruit, or other part analogous to it. The more eſſential part is entertained in the *ſeed-branches*, which being conſiderably long, and very fine, the ſap becomes therein, as in the *ſpermatic veſſels*, ſtill more mature. Hence it is next delivered up into the coats of the ſeed as into a *womb*, and the meaner part hereof is again diſcharged to the outer coat, as aliment good enough; the *finer* is tranſmitted to the *inner*, which being a *parenchymoſis*, and more ſpacious body, the ſap therefore is not herein a mere aliment, but in order to its being further prepared for fermentation. The ſap being thus prepared in the inner coat, as a liquor now *apt* to be the matter of the *ſeed-embrio*, by freſh ſupplies is thence diſcharged, or filtered, or tranſpired through the *ſecondine* abovementioned, and the depoſiture thereof, anſwerable to the *colliquamentum* in an egg, or the *ſemen muliebre*, is at laſt made into the concave of the ſame. The other part of the *pureſt ſap*, imboſomed in the *ramulets* of the *ſeed-branch*, runs a circle, and ſo becomes, as the *ſemen maſculinum*, yet more elaborate.

With this pureſt ſap the ſaid ramulets being ſupplied, from thence at laſt the *navel-fibres* ſhoot (as the artery in the colliquamentum) through the *ſecondine* into the aforeſaid liquor depoſited therein. Into which liquor being now ſhot, and its own proper ſap or tinctures mixt therewith, it ſtrikes it thus into a *coagulum*, or into a body conſiſtent and truly *parenchymous*. And in the interim of the *coagulation*, a gentle *fermentation* being alſo made, the ſaid parenchyma or coagulum becomes ſuch, not of any conſtitution indifferently, but is raiſed (as we ſee bread in baking) into a congeries of fixed bubbles; the parenchyma of the whole ſeed being ſuch.

Veins in Plants, analogous to human veins, obſerved by Dr. M. Liſter.

SOME time ago, having made a few obſervations concerning the veins, or ſuch ducts as ſeem to contain and carry in them the nobleſt juices of plants, I am of opinion that they will prove to be veſſels analogous to human veins. Thoſe parts of a plant which Pliny calls by the names of Venæ and Pulpæ, are nothing elſe, in my opinion, but what Dr. Grew calls fibres and inſertments, or the lignous body interwoven with that which he takes to be the cortical, that is, the ſeveral diſtinctions of the grain. But that theſe veſſels are not any of the pores of the lignous body, (to uſe the Doctor's terms) is plain in a tranſverſe cut of *Angelica Sylveſtris* volgatior; the veins there very clearly ſhow themſelves to an attentive view to be diſtinct from fibres, obſervable in the parenchyma of the ſame cortical body together with themſelves; the milky juice ſtill riſing beſides, and not in any fibre. Alſo in the like cut of a burdock in *June*, the like juice ſprings on this ſide and on that ſide of the radii of the woody circle; that is, in the cortical body and pith only. Again, where there is no pith there is none of this juice to be obſerved, and conſequently none of theſe veins, as in the roots of plants and trunks of trees, but ever in the bark of either. Theſe particulars are plainly obſervable in the *ſpodilium*, *cicutaria*, many of the thiſtle kind, &c.

Further, neither are they probably of the number of the pores deſcribed by Dr. Grew, in the cortical body or pith. Not ſurely of thoſe *pores* extended by the breadth, becauſe the courſe of the juices in theſe veſſels is by the length of the plant; as I have ſometimes very plainly traced in the pith of a dried fennel ſtalk, following them by diſſection quite through the length of the pith. It remains, that if *pores*, they are thoſe *pores* of the cortical body, that are ſuppoſed to be extended by the length thereof, which yet ſeems (to me at leaſt) not enough; but we think them veſſels inveſted with their own proper membranes, analogous to the veins of the human body; for theſe reaſons, 1ſt. becauſe they are to be found in the pith, and ſometimes in the cortical body of a plant, not included within the common tunicle of any fibres, as is above noted. That fibres, or the ſeminal roots, are clothed, is plain in ſome plants, as in fern and geranium batrachoides; the fibres of the former are coated, at leaſt in ſome parts of the plant, with a black ſkin, in the latter likewiſe with a red one. And in theſe caſes, had they not, I ſay, their own proper membranes, we ſee no cauſe why the very porous and ſpongy body of the pith, and *cortex*, ſhould not be in all places filled alike with the juice, and not riſe (as moſt plainly it doth) in a few determinate and ſet places only, that is, according to the poſition and order of theſe veſſels. 2d. The experiment I made concerning the effects of a ligature on *cataputia minor lobel*, viz. the ſudden ſpringing of the milky juice out of infinite pores beſides the inciſion, (the cauſe of which phænomenon I take to be the diſſected veins impetuouſly diſcharging themſelves of part of their juice within the porous parenchyma of the bark,) whence it is probable, that if there was no coated veſſel to hold this milky juice, we might well expect its ſpringing upon the bare ligature, as when we ſqueeze a wet ſponge, the external cuticle of the plant, as this experiment ſhows, being actually perforated.

In the next place, it is very probable that theſe veſſels are in all plants whatſoever; for, as it is true of all the other ſubſtantial parts of plants that they are actually in, and common to all plants, though ſpecified by divers accidents in figure and texture; ſo of theſe veins, which, though they be diſcernible moſtly in thoſe plants where they hold diſcoloured juices, yet we may very probably think that they are not wanting where the eye finds not that aſſiſtance in the challenging of them. And in theſe very plants, where they are leaſt viſible, there is yet a time when they are, if not in all, yet in ſome parts of theſe plants plain enough to the naked eye. The tender ſhoots of the greater and leſſer maple, in May, are full of a milky juice, viz. the known liquor of theſe veins. Again to this purpoſe if you apply a clean knife-blade to a tranſverſe cut of the like ſhoots of elder, the gummy liquor of theſe veins will be drawn forth into viſible ſtrings, as is the nature of bird-lime of the bark of holly, or the milk of *cataputia minor lobel.* Further, the leaf ſtalks of our garden rhubarb do ſometimes ſhoot (by what accident we enquire not here) a tranſparent and very pure chryſtalline gum, though the veins that held this gummy juice are by no ordinary means viſible in them; and yet by comparing the nature and properties of this gum, with that of the gums of other vegetables, we cannot doubt but this gum-rhubarb is the juice of thoſe veins, as well as we are aſſured the gum of other vegetables to be of theirs, by the ſame comparative anatomy. Laſtly, we think that even muſhrooms, that ſeemingly inferior and imperfect order of vegetables, are not exempt from, and deſtitute of, theſe veins; ſome of them yielding a milky juice, hot and fiery, not unlike ſome of the ſpurge-kind of *euphorbium*.

The primary uſe of theſe veins is, in my opinion, to carry the *ſuccus nutritius* of plants; becauſe where they are not, there is no vegetation; as it is ſeen if an engrafted branch or arm be bared and deprived of the clay, &c. in *June*, all the courſe of vegetation will appear to have been made only by the bark and not by the wood; that is, in the place only where theſe veins are. A ſecond uſe is the rich furniture of our ſhops; for from theſe veins only it is that all our vegetable drugs are extracted, and infinitely more might be had by a diligent inquiry, and ſome eaſy means which I have not unſucceſsfully put in practice.

To the foregoing obſervations I ſhall at preſent only add, *that* the ſkin of a plant may be cut clear off with part of the ſpongy *parenchyma*, and no ſigns of milky juice follow, that is, no breach of a vein. Again, we have ſtripped the plant of its ſkin, by pulling it up by the roots, and expoſing it to the wet weather, until it became flaccid as a wet thong, without any injury to the veins, which yet upon inciſion, would freſhly bleed. Theſe experiments make againſt the general opinion of *one only* ſap, looſely pervading the whole plant, like water in a ſponge.

In the tranſverſe cuts of plants we ſee, as it were, a certain order and number of the bloody orifices of diſſected veins.

*An obſervation and experiment concerning a Mineral Balſam.**

IN the territory of *Bergamo*, Signior M. Ant. Caſtagana, (upon the confines of his juriſdiction,) accidentally met with an extraordinary ſweet balſamic

* Tranſlated from the Giornale Veneto de Letterati.

ſcent, and following the ſame ſo as to find the ſpirits thereof, it ſtruck his ſmelling more and more ſtrongly. He firſt cauſed that rocky hill, where he then was, to be dug in the place that appeared to him moſt likely to be the ſeat of it, and found that the ſtones thereof harboured the fragrancy he ſmelt, which was ſo ſtrong, and by trials found ſo friendly to the *uterus*, that being applied, they did in a very ſhort time remove many complaints therein. Encouraged hereby to proſecute this work, he made his men dig into the bowels of the hill, and, after much labour and charge, diſcovered holes in ſome ſtones as if excavated by art, of a greeniſh colour, in which he found, as if diſtilled by nature, and kept in veſſels, *that* liquor and balſam which proved the ſource of that ſcent, which was limpid and of a white colour, like the white of an egg, but ſomewhat oleaginous, floating upon all ſorts of liquors like oil. Beſides, he met in the cavities ſome ſmall grains concreted of the ſaid liquor, reſembling that which they call white amber; which, being chemically diſtilled, had the ſame odour with the balſam. This raiſed the curioſity of many, to know what rich ore may be lodged amongſt or under thoſe ſtones.

Two Obſervations made by P. Franceſco Lana, author of the Prodromus.

THE firſt is, that the ſaid Fr. Lana having been informed that the famous *burning concave* of Lions, not long ſince made by *M. de Vilette*, did much ſooner melt iron than gold or ſilver; he eſteems it worth conſidering why a kitchen fire doth the contrary, melting gold ſooner than iron. Whether it proceeds thence, that the aſtral heat of the ſun is drier than our common fire, having much humidity in it; whence gold being moiſter than iron may more reſiſt the dry celeſtial heat of the ſun, than iron and the reſt of the drier metals can do. Or whether gold, being of all metals we know of, the longeſt a producing and perfecting by the ſolar heat, ſo it is alſo the longer diſſolving by the ſame, &c.

The other is, that the ſaid P. Lana having extracted out of a metallic ſubſtance a very white ſalt, the ſame was, upon the application of the gentleſt heat, reſolved into a golden coloured liquor; which being removed from that warmth, as ſoon as it felt the cool air, and even by opening the glaſs wherein it was incloſed, did in a moment ſhoot afreſh into the ſame ſalt;

and that (which feemed oddeft) whilft he was pouring it out of one glafs into another during its fluidity, it was difperfed all over the glafs it was poured into, fuddenly congealing into moft fine threads, many of which were extended from one fide of the glafs to the other, and hanging, as it were in the air, formed like the fubtileft cobwebs, not all rigid, but by reafon of their exquifite fubtility, pliable, and fcarce perceivable by the eye.

New Theory of Light and Colours, by Mr. Ifaac Newton, Profeffor of Mathematics in the Univerfity of Cambridge, addreffed to the ROYAL SOCIETY.

IN the year 1666, (at which time I applied myfelf to the grinding of optic glaffes of other figures than fpherical,) I procured a triangular glafs prifm, to try therewith the *celebrated phænomena* of colours. And in order thereto, having darkened my chamber, and made a fmall hole in my window-fhuts, to let in a convenient quantity of the fun's light, I placed my prifm at its entrance, that it might be thereby refracted to the oppofite wall. It was at firft a very pleafing divertifement to view the vivid and intenfe colours produced thereby; but after a while applying myfelf to confider them more circumfpectly, I became furprifed to fee them in an *oblong* form; which, according to the received laws of refraction, I expected fhould have been *circular*. They were terminated at the fides with ftraight lines, but at the ends the decay of light was fo gradual that it was difficult to determine juftly what was their figure, yet they feemed femicircular.

Comparing the length of this coloured *fpectrum* with its breadth, I found it about five times greater, a difproportion fo extravagant that it excited me to a more than ordinary curiofity of examining whence it might proceed. I could fcarce think that the various *thicknefs* of the glafs, or the termination with fhadow or darknefs, could have any influence on light to produce fuch an effect; yet I thought it not amifs, firft to examine thofe circumftances, and fo tried, what would happen by tranfmitting light through parts of the glafs of divers thickneffes, or through holes in the window of divers bigneffes, or by fetting the prifm without, fo that the light might pafs through it, and be refracted before it was terminated by the hole; but I found none of thofe circumftances material. The fafhion of the colours was in all thefe cafes the fame.

Then I fufpected, whether by any *unevennefs* in the glafs, or other contingent irregularity, thefe colours might be thus dilated. And to try this, I took another prifm like the former, and fo placed it, that the light paffing through them both might be refracted contrary ways, and fo by the latter returned into that courfe from which the former diverted it; for, by this means, I thought the *regular* effects of the firft prifm would be deftroyed by the fecond prifm, but the *irregular* ones more augmented by the multiplicity of refractions. The event was, that the light, which by the firft prifm was diffufed into an *oblong* form, was by the fecond reduced into an *orbicular* with as much regularity as when it did not at all pafs through them. So that, whatever was the caufe of that length, it was not any contingent irregularity.

Then I proceeded to examine more critically what might be effected by the difference of the incidence of rays coming from divers parts of the fun, and to that end meafured feveral lines and angles belonging to the image. Its diftance from the hole or prifm was 22 feet, its utmoft length 13¼ inches, its breadth 2⅝, the diameter of the hole ¼ of an inch; the angle, with the rays, tending toward the middle of the image, made with thofe lines, in which they would have proceeded without refraction, was 44 deg. 56′; and the vertical angle of the prifm 63 deg. 12′; alfo the refractions on both fides the prifm, that is, of the incident and emergent rays were, as near as I could make them, equal, and confequently about 54 deg. 4′; and the rays fell perpendicularly upon the wall. Now fubducting the diameter of the hole from the length and breadth of the image, there remains 13 inches the length, and 2⅜ the breadth, comprehended by thofe rays which paffed through the centre of the faid hole, and confequently the angle of the hole, which that breadth fubtended was about 31, anfwerable to the fun's diameter; but the angle, which the length fubtended, was more than five fuch diameters, namely 2 deg. 49′. Having made thefe obfervations, I firft computed from them the refractive power of that glafs, and found it meafured by the *ratio* of the fines, 20 to 31. And then, by that *ratio*, I computed the refractions of two rays flowing from oppofite parts of the fun's *difcus*, fo as to differ 31′. in their obliquity of incidence, and found that the emergent rays fhould have comprehended an angle of about 31′, as they did before they were incident.

But becauſe this computation was founded on the hypotheſis of the proportionality of the *ſines* of incidence and refraction, which, though by my own experience, I could not imagine to be ſo erroneous as to make that angle but 31′, which in reality was 2 deg. 49′; yet my curioſity cauſed me again to take my priſm. And having placed it at my window, as before, I obſerved, that by turning it a little about its *axis* to and fro, ſo as to vary its obliquity to the light, more than an angle of 4 or 5 deg. the colours were not thereby ſenſibly tranſlated from their place on the wall, and conſequently by that variation of incidence the quantity of refraction was not ſenſibly varied. By this experiment, therefore, as well as by the former computation, it was evident that the difference of the incidence of rays, flowing from divers parts of the ſun, could not make them, after decuſſation, diverge at a ſenſibly greater angle than that at which they before converged; which, being at moſt, about 31 or 32 minutes, there ſtill remained ſome other cauſe to be found out from whence it could be 2 deg. 49 minutes.

Then I began to ſuſpect whether the rays, after this trajection through the priſm, did not move in curve lines, and according to their more or leſs curvity tend to divers parts of the wall. And it increaſed my ſuſpicion when I remembered that I had often ſeen a tennis-ball, ſtuck with an oblique racket, deſcribe ſuch a curve line. For a circular as well as progreſſive motion being communicated to it by that ſtroke, its parts on that ſide where the motions conſpire, muſt preſs and beat the contiguous air more violently than on the other, and there excite a reluctancy and re-action of the air proportionably greater. And for the ſame reaſon, if the rays ſhould poſſibly be globular bodies, and by their oblique paſſage out of one medium into another, acquire a circulating motion, they ought to feel a greater reſiſtance from the ambient æther, on that ſide, where the motions conſpire, and thence be continually bowed to the other. But notwithſtanding this plauſible ground of ſuſpicion, when I came to examine it, I could obſerve no ſuch curvity in them. And beſides (which was enough for my purpoſe) I obſerved, that the difference between the length of the image, and diameter of the hole through which the light was tranſmitted, was proportionable to their diſtance.

The gradual removal of theſe ſuſpicions at length led me to the *experimentum crucis*, which was this: I took two boards and placed one of them cloſe behind the priſm at the window, ſo that the light might paſs through a ſmall hole made in it for the purpoſe, and fall on the other board, which I placed at about 12 feet diſtance, having firſt made in it a ſmall hole alſo for ſome of that incident light to paſs through. Then I placed another priſm behind this ſecond board, ſo that the light, trajeƈted through both the boards, might paſs through that alſo, and be again refracted before it arrived at the wall. This done, I took the firſt priſm in my hand and turned it to and fro ſlowly about its axis, ſo much, as to make the ſeveral parts of the image, caſt on the ſecond board, ſucceſſively paſs through the hole in it, that I might obſerve to what places on the wall the ſecond priſm would refract them. And I ſaw by the variation of thoſe places that the light, tending to that end of the image, towards which the refraction of the firſt priſm was made, did in the ſecond priſm ſuffer a refraction conſiderably greater than the light tending to the other end. And ſo the true cauſe of the length of that image was detected to be no other, than, that light conſiſts of *rays differently refrangible*, which, without any reſpect to a difference in their incidence, were, according to their degrees of refrangibility, tranſmitted towards divers parts of the wall.

When I underſtood this, I left off my aforeſaid glaſs works; for I ſaw that the perfection of teleſcopes was hitherto limited, not ſo much for want of glaſſes truly figured according to the preſcriptions of *optic authors*, (which all men have hitherto imagined) as becauſe that light itſelf is a *heterogeneous mixture of differently refrangible rays*. So that were a glaſs ſo exactly figured as to collect any ſort of rays into one point it could not collect thoſe alſo into the ſame point, which having the ſame incidence upon the ſame medium are apt to ſuffer a different refraction. Nay, I wondered that, ſeeing the difference of refrangibility was ſo great as I found it, teleſcopes ſhould arrive at that perfection they are now at. For, meaſuring the refractions in one of my priſms, I found, that ſuppoſing the common *ſine* of incidence upon one of its planes was 44 parts, the *ſine* of refraction of the utmoſt rays on the red end of the colours, made out of the glaſs into the air, would be 68 parts, and the *ſine* of refraction of the utmoſt rays on the other end 69 parts; ſo that the difference is about a 24th or 25th part of the whole refraction. And, conſequently, the object glaſs of any teleſcope cannot collect all the rays, which come from one point of an object, ſo as to make them convene at its *focus* in leſs room than in a circular ſpace, whoſe diameter is the 50th part of the diameter of its aperture; which is an irregularity ſome hundreds of times greater than a circularly figured *lens* (of ſo ſmall a ſection as the object glaſſes of long teleſcopes are) would cauſe, by the unfitneſs of its figure, were light *uniform*.

This made me take *reflections* into conſideration, and finding them regular, ſo that the angle of reflection of all ſorts of rays was equal to their angle of incidence, I underſtood, that by their mediation, optic inſtruments might be brought to any degree of perfection imaginable, provided a *reflecting* ſubſtance could be found which would poliſh as finely as glaſs, and *reflect* as much light as glaſs *tranſmits*, and the art of communicating to it a parabolic figure be alſo attained. But there ſeemed very great difficulties, and I have almoſt thought them inſuperable, when I further conſidered that every irregularity in a reflecting ſuperficies makes the rays ſtray five or ſix times more out of their due courſe than the like irregularities in a refracting one; ſo that a much greater circumſpection would be here requiſite than in figuring glaſſes for refraction.

Amidſt theſe thoughts I was forced from *Cambridge* by the intervening *plague*, and it was more than two years before I proceeded further. But *then* having thought on a tender way of poliſhing proper for metal, whereby, as I imagined, the figure alſo would be corrected to the laſt, I began to try what might be effected in this kind, and by degrees ſo far perfected an inſtrument (in the eſſential parts of it like that I ſent to London,) by which I could diſcern Jupiter's four concomitants, and ſhewed them divers times to two others of my acquaintance. I could alſo diſcern the moon-like phaſe of *Venus*, but not very diſtinctly, nor without ſome niceneſs in diſpoſing the inſtrument.

From that time I was interrupted until laſt autumn when I made the other, and as that was ſenſibly better than the firſt (eſpecially for day objects) ſo I doubt not but they will be ſtill brought to a much greater perfection by their endeavours, who, as you inform me, are taking care about it in London.

But, to return from this digreſſion, I told you that light is not ſimilar or homogeneal, but conſiſts of difform rays, ſome of which are more refrangible than others; ſo that of thoſe, which are alike incident on the ſame medium, ſome ſhall be more refracted than others, and that not by any virtue of the glaſs, or other external cauſe, but from a prediſpoſition which every particular ray hath to ſuffer a particular degree of refraction.

I ſhall now proceed to acquaint you with another more notable deformity in its rays, wherein the *origin* of *colours* is unfolded: concerning which I ſhall lay down the *doctrine* firſt, and then, for its examination, give an inſtance or two of the *experiments* as a ſpecimen of the reſt.

The doctrine will be comprehended and illuſtrated in the following propoſitions:—

1ſt. As the rays of light differ in degrees of refrangibility, ſo they alſo differ in their diſpoſition to exhibit this or that particular colour. Colours are not *qualifications* of *light* derived from refractions, or reflections of natural bodies (as it is generally believed), but original and *connate properties*, which in divers rays are divers. Some rays are diſpoſed to exhibit a red colour and no other, ſome a yellow and no other, ſome a green and no other, and ſo of the reſt. Nor are there rays only proper and particular to the more eminent colours, but even to all their intermediate gradations.

2d. The ſame degree of refrangibility ever belongs to the ſame colour, and to the ſame colour ever belongs the ſame degree of refrangibility. The leaſt *refrangible* rays are all diſpoſed to exhibit a *red* colour, and contrarily thoſe rays, which are diſpoſed to exhibit a *red* colour, are all the leaſt refrangible. So the *moſt refrangible* rays are diſpoſed to exhibit a deep *violet colour*, and contrarily thoſe which are apt to exhibit ſuch a violet colour, are all the moſt refrangible. And ſo to all the intermediate colours in a continued ſeries belong intermediate degrees of refrangibility. And this analogy betwixt colours and refrangibility is very preciſe and ſtrict; the rays always either exactly agreeing in both, or proportionably diſagreeing in both.

3d. The ſpecies of colour, and degree of refrangibility proper to any particular ſort of rays, is not mutable by refraction, nor by reflection from natural bodies, nor by any other cauſe that I could yet obſerve. When any one ſort of rays hath been well parted from thoſe of other kinds, it hath afterwards obſtinately retained its colour, notwithſtanding my utmoſt endeavours to change it. I have refracted it with priſms, and reflected it with bodies, which in day light were of other colours; I have intercepted it with the coloured film of air interceding two compreſſed plates of glaſs; tranſmitted it through coloured mediums, and through mediums irradiated with other ſorts of rays, and diverſly terminated it, and yet could never produce any new colour out of it. It would by contracting or dilating become more brifk, or faint, and by the lofs of many rays, in fome cafes, very obfcure and dark, but I could never fee it changed in *fpecie*.

4th. Yet feeming tranfmutations of colours may be made where there is any mixture of divers forts of rays; for, in fuch mixtures, the component colours appear not, but, by their mutually allaying each other, conftitute a middling colour, and therefore, if by refraction, or any other of the aforefaid caufes, the difform rays, latent in fuch a mixture, be feparated, there fhall emerge colours different from the colour of the compofition; which colours are not *new* generated, but only made apparent by being parted, for if they be again entirely mixt and blended together, they will again compofe that colour, which they did before feparation; and for the fame reafon tranfmutations made by the convening of divers colours are not real; for when the difform rays are again fevered they will exhibit the very fame colours which they did before they entered the compofition, as you fee *blue* and *yellow* powders, when finely mixed, appear to the naked eye green, and yet the colours of the component corpufcles are not thereby really tranfmuted but only blended; for, when viewed with a good microfcope, they ftill appear blue and yellow interfperfedly.

5th. There are, therefore, two forts of colours; the one original and fimple, the other compounded of thefe. The original or primary colours are, *red*, *yellow*, *green*, *blue*, and a *violet purple*, together with *orange*, indigo, and an indefinite variety of intermediate gradations.

6th. The fame colours in *fpecie* with thefe primary ones, may be alfo produced by compofition; for a mixture of yellow and blue makes green; of red and yellow makes orange; of orange and yellowifh green makes yellow. And in general if any two colours be mixt, which in the feries of thofe generated by the prifm, are not too far diftant one from another, they, by their mutual alloy compound that colour, which in the faid feries appears in the mid way between them; but thofe which are fituated at too great a diftance do not fo. Orange and indigo produce not the intermediate green, nor fcarlet and green the intermediate yellow.

7th. But the moft furprifing and wonderful compofition was that of whitenefs. There is no one fort of rays which alone can exhibit this; it is ever compounded, and to its compofition are requifite all the aforefaid primary colours, mixed in a due proportion. I have often, with admiration beheld, that all the colours of the prism being made to converge, and thereby to be again mixed as they were in the light before it was incident upon the prism, re-produced light intirely and perfectly white, and not at all sensibly differing from a direct light of the sun, unless when the glasses I used were not sufficiently clear, for then they would a little incline it to their colour.

8th. Hence therefore it comes to pass that whiteness is the usual colour of *light*, for light is a confused aggregate of rays induced with all sorts of colours as they are promiscuously darted from the various parts of luminous bodies; and of such a confused aggregate, as I said, is generated whiteness, if there be a due proportion of the ingredients, but if any one predominates, the light must incline to that colour, as it happens in the blue flame of brimstone, the yellow flame of a candle, and the various colours of the fixed stars.

9th. These things considered, the manner how colours are produced by the prism is evident; for of the rays, constituting the incident light, since those which differ in colour proportionally differ in refrangibility, they, by their unequal refractions, must be severed and dispersed into an oblong form in an orderly succession from the least refracted scarlet to the most refracted violet. And for the same reason it is that objects, when looked upon through a prism, appear coloured; for the difform rays, by their unequal refractions, are made to diverge towards several parts of the *retina*, and there express images of things coloured, as in the former case they did the sun's image upon a wall; and by this inequality of refractions they become not only coloured, but also very confused and indistinct.

10th. Why the colours of the rainbow appear in falling drops of rain is also from hence evident; for those drops, which refract the rays, disposed to appear purple in greatest quantity to the spectators eye, refract the rays of other sorts so much less as to make them pass beside it; and such are the drops on the inside of the *primary bow*, and on the outside of the *secondary* or exterior one. So those drops which refract in greatest plenty the rays, apt to appear red, toward the spectator's eye refract those of other sorts so much more as to make them pass beside it; and such are the drops on the exterior part of the *primary*, and interior part of the secondary bow.

11th. The odd phœnomena of an infusion of *lignum nephriticum*, *leaf-gold*, *fragments* of *coloured glass*, and some other transparently coloured bodies, appearing in one position of one colour, and of another in another, are on these grounds no longer riddles; for those are substances apt to reflect one sort of light and tranſmit another, as may be ſeen in a dark room by illuminating them with ſimilar or uncompounded light, for then they appear of that colour only with which they are illuminated, but yet in one poſition more vivid and luminous than in another, accordingly as they are diſpoſed more or leſs to reflect or tranſmit the incident colour.

12th, From hence alſo is manifeſt the reaſon of an unexpected experiment, which Mr. Hook ſomewhere in his Micrography relates to have made with two wedge-like tranſparent veſſels, filled the one with red, the other with a blue liquor: namely, that though they were ſeverally tranſparent enough, yet both together became opaque; for if one tranſmitted only red, and the other only blue, no rays could paſs through both.

13th, I might add more inſtances of this nature, but I ſhall conclude with this general one, that the colours of all natural bodies have no other origin than this, that they are variouſly qualified to reflect one ſort of light in greater plenty than another. And this I have experimented in a dark room by illuminating thoſe bodies with uncompounded light of divers colours; for by that means any body may be made to appear of any colour. They have *there* no appropriate colour, but ever appear of the colour of the light caſt upon them, but yet with this difference, that they are moſt briſk and vivid in the light of their own day-light colour. *Minium* appeareth there of any colour indifferently with which it is illuſtrated, but yet moſt luminous in red; and ſo *Biſe* appeareth indifferently of any colour with which it is illuſtrated, but yet moſt luminous in blue; and therefore Minium reflecteth rays of any colour, but moſt copiouſly thoſe endued with red; and conſequently when illuſtrated by day-light, that is, with all ſorts of rays promiſcuouſly blended, thoſe qualified with red ſhall abound moſt in the reflected light, and by their prevalence cauſe it to appear of that colour. And for the ſame reaſon *Biſe*, reflecting blue moſt copiouſly, ſhall appear blue by the exceſs of thoſe rays in its reflected light; and the like of other bodies. And that this is the entire and adequate cauſe of their colours is manifeſt, becauſe they have no power to change or alter the colours of any ſort of rays incident apart, but put on all colours indifferently with which they are enlightened. Theſe things being ſo, it can be no longer diſputed whether there be colours in the dark, nor whether they be the qualities of the objects we ſee; no, nor perhaps whether light be a body: for ſince colours are the qualities of light, having its rays for their entire and immediate ſubject, how can we think thoſe rays qualities alſo, unleſs one quality may be the ſubject of and ſuſtain another; which in effect is to call it ſubſtance. We ſhould not know bodies for ſubſtance were it not for their ſenſible qualities, and the principal of thoſe being now found due to ſomething elſe, we have as good reaſon to believe that to be a ſubſtance alſo.

Beſides, who ever thought any quality to be an heterogeneous aggregate, ſuch as light is diſcovered to be. But to determine more abſolutely what light is, after what manner refracted, and by what modes or actions it produceth in our minds the phantoms of colours, is not eaſy: and I ſhall not mingle conjectures with certainties.

Reviewing what I have written, I ſee the diſcourſe itſelf will lead to divers experiments ſufficient for its examination; and therefore I ſhall not trouble you further than to deſcribe one of thoſe, which I have already inſinuated.

In a darkened room make a hole in the ſhutter of a window, the diameter of which may conveniently be about the third part of an inch, to admit a convenient quantity of the ſun's light; and there place a clear and colourleſs priſm, to refract the entering light towards the further part of the room, which, as I ſaid, will thereby be diffuſed into an oblong coloured image. Then place a *lens* of about three feet radious (ſuppoſe a broad object glaſs of a three foot teleſcope), at the diſtance of about four or five feet from thence, through which all thoſe colours may at once be tranſmitted, and made by its refraction to convene at a further diſtance of about ten or twelve feet. If at that diſtance you intercept this light with a ſheet of white paper, you will ſee the colours converted into whiteneſs again by being mingled. But it is requiſite that the *priſme* and *lens* be placed ſteady, and that the paper on which the colours are caſt be moved to and fro; for by ſuch motion you will not only find at what diſtance the whiteneſs is moſt perfect, but alſo ſee how the colours gradually convene and vaniſh into whiteneſs, and afterwards having croſſed one another in that place where they compound whiteneſs, are again diſſipated and ſevered, and in an inverted order retain the ſame colours which they had before they entered the compoſition. You may alſo ſee that if any of the colours at the lens be intercepted, the whiteneſs will be changed into the other colours: and therefore that the compofition of whitenefs be perfect, care muft be taken that none of the colours fall befide the lens.

In the annexed defign of this experiment, A B C expreffeth the prifm fet endwife to fight, clofe by the hole F, of the window E G. Its

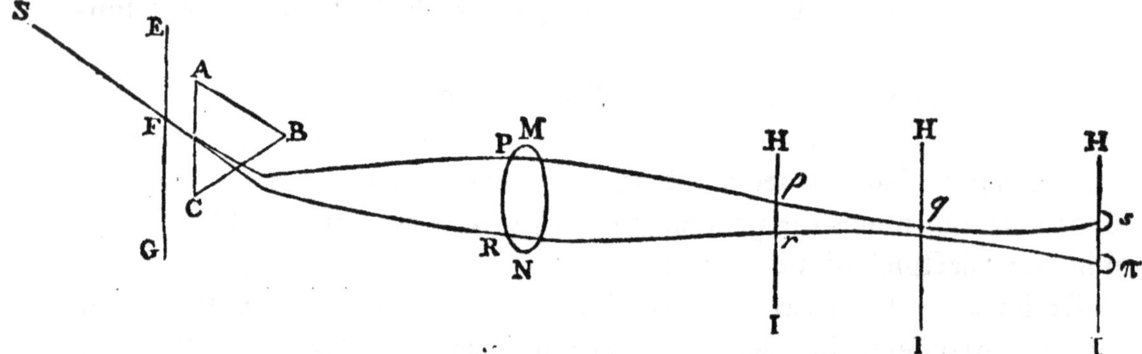

vertical angle A B C may conveniently be about 60 degrees: M N defigneth the *lens*. Its breadth 2½ or 3 inches. S F one of the ftraight lines, in which deform rays may be conceived to flow fucceffively from the fun. F P and F R, two of thofe rays unequally refracted, which the *lens* makes to converge towards *q*, and after decuffation to diverge again. And H I, the paper at divers diftances, on which the colours are projected; which in *q* conftitute *whitenefs*, but are *red* and *yellow* in R r and and s, *blue* and *purple* in P p and π.

If you proceed further to try the impoffibility of changing any uncompounded colour (which I have afferted in the third and thirteenth propofitions), it is requifite that the room be made very dark, leaft any fcattering light mixing with the colour difturb and allay it, and render it compound contrary to the defign of the experiment. It is alfo requifite that there be a more perfect feparation of the colours than after the manner above defcribed can be made by the reflection of one fingle prifm, and how to make fuch further feparations will fcarce be difficult to them who confider the difcovered laws of refractions. But if trial fhall be made with colours not thoroughly feparated, there muft be allowed changes proportionable to the mixture. Thus if compound yellow light fall upon blue *bife*, the *bife* will not appear perfectly yellow, but rather green, becaufe there are in the yellow mixture many rays endued with green, and green being lefs remote from the ufual blue colour of bife than yellow, is the more copioufly reflected by it.

In like manner if any one of the prismatic colours, suppose *red*, be intercepted, on design to try the asserted impossibility of producing that colour out of the others which are pretermitted, it is necessary either that the colours be very well parted before the *red* be intercepted, or that together with the *red* the neighbouring colours into which any *red* is secretly dispersed, (that is, the yellow, and perhaps green too) be intercepted, or else that allowance be made for emerging of so much red out of the yellow green as may possibly have been diffused, and scatteringly blended in those colours. And if these things be observed, the new production of *red*, or any intercepted colour, will be found impossible.

This I conceive is enough for an introduction to experiments of this kind; which if any of the ROYAL SOCIETY shall be so curious as to prosecute, I should be very glad to be informed with what success. That if any thing seems to be defective, or to thwart this relation, I may have an opportunity of giving further direction about it, or of acknowledging my errors, if I have committed any.

So far the *illustrious author* of this *learned* and *celebrated* essay, which has given *light* to colour, and *colour* unto light; and from *whose bright* ideas, as from the sun itself, the most brilliant *emanations* have *irradiated* and *illumed* the philosophic world.

An account of what hath been lately observed by Dr. Kerkringius, concerning Eggs to be found in all sorts of females.

BECAUSE we have not hitherto taken notice of what the inquisitive Kerkringius hath said concerning *ovaria* and *ova* in all sorts of females, yet to excite the greater attention of our eminent anatomists here to a further search into this matter, as those of that profession in many foreign parts, as France, Italy, Holland, &c. employ themselves to find what truth there is in it; we thought it would not be unwelcome to the curious of all sorts of this country to give them here in English a particular description of what the said Kerkringius hath from his own observation delivered on this subject: in doing of which we shall not scruple to follow the French philosophical journals to the following effect.

What Dr. Kerkringius hath from his curious observations advanced, viz.

That man hath his origin from an egg, hath been very differently received, ſome appearing much ſurpriſed at it, others rejecting the opinion, and many being induced thereby to make further enquiry into it. This great diverſity of ſentiments made me think I ſhould do well for the ſatisfaction of all ſorts of people to inſert here the particulars themſelves, obſerved by Dr. Kerkringius, and to add hereafter ſome reflections that may ſeem neceſſary to remove the principal difficulties occurring in this curious matter.

But for the better comprehending the nature and ſituation of the parts where theſe eggs are formed and perfected, a plate is annexed, wherein Fig. I. repreſents a matrix, with its chief dependencies.

B is the matrix; C the bladder of urine faſtened to the neck of the matrix; D D the two teſticuli, or rather the repoſitories which contain the eggs ſpoken of; E E the two tubes of the *matrix*; F F the two *vaſa differentia*, eſteemed by anatomiſts to convey *ſemen teſticulorum in uterum*; G G the two *vaſa præparantia*, for preparing the matter to be perfected *in teſticulis*.

Fig. II. repreſents eggs of different bigneſs, as the doctor found them in the teſticles of a woman.

Fig. III. ſhews a bigger egg, ſuch an one as we have found at *Paris* in a woman of 40 years of age, and in a maiden of 18 years.

Fig. IV. exhibits ſmall eggs, of which we have found a good number in the teſticles of a cow.

Fig. V. repreſents an egg, which the doctor opened three or four days after it had fallen into the matrix of a woman, and in which he ſaw that little embryon marked B, whereof he found the head began to be diſtinguiſhed from the body, yet without a diſtinct perception of the organs.

Fig. VI. ſhews a larger egg, which he opened a fortnight after conception, finding in it theſe particulars:—A a little ſecondine, B B B B the membrane, *Chorion*, divided in four places; C C C C the membrane, *amnios*, divided ſo too; D the navel ſtring, by which the child is faſtened to the ſecondine. E a child of 14 days after conception, in which the face begins to appear, together with the principal parts of the body.

Fig. VII. repreſents the ſkeleton of an infant, found in one of theſe eggs, three weeks after conception.

Fig. VIII. exhibits the ſkeleton of another child, found alſo by the doctor in an egg, a month after conception.

Fig. V. page 382.

Fig. . page 382.

Fig. II. page 382.

Fig. VI. page 382.

Fig. III. page 382.

Fig. IV. page 382.

Fig. IX. page 383.

Fig. VIII. page 382.

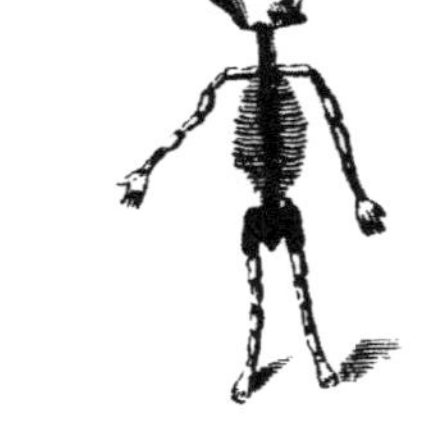

Fig. VII. page 382.

Plate VI. Vol. I.

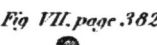

Publish'd by J. Gold, late Bunney & Gold, 103 Shoe Lane, Sept.r 18th. 1802.

Fig. IX. reprefents the fkeleton of an *embryon* found by him in an egg fix weeks after conception.

Though this opinion (*faith Kerkringius*) about the firft formation of man in an egg, as that of all fowl, is not common, yet it is true; and if any one is difficult of belief, he may caft his eyes on Fig. II. where he will fee thofe eggs reprefented after their due appearance, as I have found them myfelf in the bodies of many women opened by me.

Thefe eggs are not only to be met with in the tefticles of women married, but alfo in thofe of maids, even as young hens will lay eggs without any commerce with a cock.

Thefe eggs are of the bignefs of a pea, and they contain a glutinous liquor, which will be hardened by the fire, juft as the white and yolk in other eggs. The tafte of them is flat and unpleafant enough; they are invefted with one or two fine fkins, which ftretch themfelves a little while after the eggs are fallen into the womb, and change into two membranes, called *amnios* and *chorion*: and as thefe two membranes are always found afterwards enwrapping the child, fo it is very probable, that the eggs of women are alfo covered with two fkins from their beginning; though by reafon of their finenefs I could not diftinctly fee them.

It feems that Fallopius hath feen thofe eggs before me, as appears in his Anatom. Obfervations. And as to their ufe they have in generation, it feems eafy to be determined, by reflecting upon what that very expert anatomift Thomas Warton teacheth in his Treatife of Glandulls, chapter 33, concerning the manner of conception: For, according to him, *femen viri penetrat in teftes fœminæ per uteri tubas.* Now, there it is joined with the egg, in fuch a manner, which hath not been explained till now, but is neverthelefs certain, and much refembling what comes to pafs in the other oviparous animals.

The egg being made thus fecund, defcends into the womb through the *vafa deferentia*, and in two or three days grows to the bignefs of a black cherry. When they fall down they are a little bigger than we have reprefented them; but being foft, they are eafily flattened, and never remain round. If in falling they are handled and flightly preffed, there will ftick a little fkin to the finger, which fhews that it is not feed, nor any thing like it, but of fuch eggs as we fpeak of. *Fœminæ dejiciunt hæc ova imprimis tempore menftruorum, vel in iræ vehementia.*

I have had (faith *Kerkringius*) an occafion favourable enough for examining that *germe* of three or at moſt of four days, repreſented Fig. V. A married woman died three or four days *poſt fluxum menſtruum*. I aſſiſted at the opening of her body, and having found in the matrix a little round maſs of the bigneſs of a large black cherry, I took the huſband aſide, and aſked him, *Num a tempore fluxus menſtruorum uxorem cognoviſſit?* And having received for anſwer, *that he had*, I prayed him to let me carry home with me this little ball which I had found in her womb. I was no ſooner come home than I opened it, and found that nature had wrought with ſo much activity in ſo ſmall a time, that one might already ſee the firſt lineaments of a child, ſince we obſerved in it the head diſtinct from the body, and in the head we took notice of ſome traces of its principal organs. As for the reſt of the body, it was nothing as yet but a maſs groſsly wrought, as you may ſee in this figure. But further, the embrio repreſented in Fig. VI. was only of 15 days, when in its head there were noted the eyes, noſe, mouth, and ears; and the body began to have legs and arms, as well diſtinguiſhable as appears in this figure, which repreſents it juſt as it was given me. I durſt not yet attempt to ſeparate the fleſh from theſe little bones, or rather from theſe ſmall cartilages, which in time become bones; all theſe parts being yet too tender to make an accurate diſſection of them.

In Fig. VII. is delineated a child, which is already furniſhed with all its cartilages, though it had been conceived but three weeks. It having fallen to my hands, I attempted to ſever the ſkin and fleſh from the cartilages, holding the place of the bones, and I ſucceeded well enough in it, and keep ſtill by me the ſkeleton thereof, truly repreſented in this figure. The head, wherein the brain is to lodge, and all man's wiſdom, is nothing but a ſimple membrane, inflated with wind or ſpirits. The arms are diſtinct from the body, and the hands have now their fingers perfectly diſtinct. One may eaſily count in this contexture of cartilages how many ribs there will be: and laſtly, the diſtinction of the toes of the feet is as perceptible as that of the fingers of the hands. But we muſt add withal that all theſe parts are no larger than hairs, and conſequently a great dexterity is to be uſed for diſplaying them.

Fig. VIII. repreſents a *fœtus* of a month, having now the whole human ſhape, and the bones thereof firm enough in many places to ſupport the parts. Behold the figure well which repreſents this little engine in its natural ſize. It already in a manner ſuſtains itſelf. The two jaw-bones appear, the clavicles are formed, and all the ribs are very diſtinct, except the firſt and laſt, which are not wont to have even in the ſecond month the conſiſtence of bones. One may ſee in the arms the joints of the ſhoulder bones and of the elbows; as alſo the thighs and both the legs, together with their bones, called *focils*, which I had not obſerved when I wrote my Treatiſe of the *generation of the bones*. All that you ſee of white in this eighth figure, hath at this time the quality of bones: where I have a fair occaſion to enlarge and diſcuſs that great queſtion, whence proceeds the hardneſs of bones? And I could not give a better or more curious reaſon for it than by alledging the doctrine that ſerveth for a ground to all chymiſtry; which is, that there is an *acid ſpirit* univerſally diſpoſed through the world, which giveth ſolidity not only to bones, but alſo to minerals and metals, and to all vegetables; penetrating all, fixing all, and being the Father of the hardneſs and ſolidity of all bodies.

Fig. IX. repreſents a child of ſix weeks after conception; where it is to be noted, that comparing together the bones of ſeveral fœtus's it will be found perhaps to admiration, that *that* which has been conceived but a little after another, hath yet the bones in proportion twice as big. That which is here exhibited by Fig. IX. appears much leſs than another of two months, as appears in my book of the *generation* of *bones*: but the bones are for all that no leſs remarkable; for whatever hath the hardneſs and conſiſtence of bones in *that*, hath already the nature of cartilages in *this*. The inferior jaw-bone is moſt obſervable in this child of ſix weeks, marked A, it being at this age compoſed of ſix little bones, which when it is born are all joined together, and make but one.

If it be aſked how I came to know that theſe degrees of growth come to paſs exactly within thoſe times recited; eſpecially ſince in abortions we often ſee embrios of four months and above, that are not ſo big as thoſe ſpoken of? I might anſwer by repeating all I ſaid before, when I compared the proportions of thoſe different *germs*. To which I ſhall only add, that embrios that miſcarry have often remained a long while in the body before they came forth, or have lived there ſo ſickly as not to draw perhaps half the nouriſhment neceſſary for them, and therefore much leſs than elſe they would be.

So far *Kerkringius*, on whoſe diſcourſe are made theſe reflections by Monſieur *Denys*.

1ſt, That thoſe eggs are generated in fœminarum teſticulis, and thence made to deſcend *per tubam into* the *matrix*, in coitu, *per vim ſpirituoſam ſeminis maſculi, per uteri tubam penetrantis*.

2d, Theſe eggs are of different bigneſſes; ſince thoſe of the third Fig. repreſent one according to the life, as it was found with nine or ten leſſer ones in a woman of 40 years of age. Such as were found by him in the teſticles of a cow, are duly exhibited in Fig. IV. If any do wonder that in ſo big an animal they ſhould be ſo much ſmaller than in a woman, he will have more cauſe to admire that women have them ſo little in compariſon of ducks, hens, &c. the firſt beginning of things not bearing always a proportion to their ſtate of increaſe; as beans and peas, (*e. g.*) whence grow plants of a very middling ſize, have much bigger ſeeds than are the kernels of apples and pears, which do produce large trees. Beſides it may be, that cows when in their heat may afford bigger eggs: meantime the reaſons why the eggs of fowl are always proportionably bigger than thoſe of women and of quadrupeds, is, that they when laid muſt contain the matter not only for forming, but for feeding the young animal.

3d, That this opinion is not new, as ſome imagine; ſince *Fallopius*, in his Anatomical Obſervations, &c. makes mention of them.

But here we ſhall obſerve the true ſtate of the queſtion out of the Journal of Monſieur *Gaulois*, ſaying, that the veſicles or eggs in all ſorts of females are to be conſidered in three conditions, 1ſt, When they are faſtened to the place where nature hath lodged them, as in a repoſitory; 2d, when they are looſened from thence; 3d, when they encloſe the *embrion*. The firſt of theſe, namely, that there are veſicles in all ſorts of females faſtened to their bodies, is certain, and not new, as appears by the authority juſt now quoted. It is alſo certain that after conception that which encloſeth the *fœtus*, is almoſt like an egg; but this is not new either, ſeeing that *Hippocrates* hath obſerved it, and Ariſtotle hath ſaid it more than once. To which alſo the moderns agree, and amongſt others the famous *Harvey*, Exper. 68. de Gener. Anim. The *queſtion* therefore is only whether theſe veſicles, faſtened to the bodies of females, are looſened from it; and whether that kind of eggs wherein the embrion is formed, is one of the veſicles looſened? And here *Kerkringius* aſſerts the affirmative; as hath been ſeen above. Thoſe who are of a contrary opinion ſay, that it is certain that *that* bladder, like an egg, in which the *fœtus* is formed, comes not elſewhere; ſince it is known that it is produced in the place of conception, and even how it is there produced; as appears out of Harvey, ibid. & Tract. de Concept. Beſides, ſay *they*, the veſicles found in the bodies of women are ſo faſtened there, that naturally they cannot be ſeparated from thence; and ſuppoſe they were looſened, there is in the ſame place where there is no paſſage large enough to get through. They add, that if you will give the name of eggs to all the veſicles to be found in the parts of generation, there would alſo be eggs in the bodies of men; it being known that at the ſide of the *vaſa deferentiæ* there are found divers veſicles, which anatomiſts compare to a cluſter of grapes, by reaſon of their figure.

The reader, ſaith this Journaliſt, is left to decide this queſtion. He only intimates that in the many animals diſſected in the Royal Philoſophical Academy at Paris, there were never found any veſicles actually looſe: but that as to a paſſage for them, there had been three years ſince diſſected a woman, and found in each of the *tubæ uteri* a manifeſt cavity going into the bottom of the matrix: adding, that though theſe conduits appear not open ordinarily, they may yet dilate themſelves at the time of conception: as the conduit through which the eggs of a fowl do paſs out of the *ovarium* into the *matrix*, is uſually very cloſe, but yet opens ſometimes.

4th, To return to M. Denys, he obſerveth that all other animals, (not to ſpeak now of plants) are produced by the means of eggs; as birds and inſects of all ſorts, fiſhes, (of which laſt ſort, though whales, ſea-calves, and dolphins bring forth live creatures of their kind, yet they firſt breed them within their bodies in eggs): and why not quadrupeds alſo, and the females of mankind.

5th, As for eggs, ſaid by *Kirkringius* to have been *in virgimbus*, the ſame M. Denys eſteems probable enough: for, *ſays he*, though we had not the inſtance of hens laying eggs without any congreſs of a cock, the place where they are bred ſhows enough that man contributes nothing to their production; all that he can do being nothing but an attraction of the eggs out of their conſervatory, and making them deſcend into the *uterus*, *ut ibi irrorentur a ſemine, & fœcunditatem acquirant*; even as the juices of the earth do vivify all the plants by inſinuating themſelves into their grains, and penetrating their ſkins. And it may be, it is the alteration that befalls theſe eggs when they are retained too long, which cauſeth the abundance of vapours and diſorders which other parts are accuſed of. On which occaſion he alledgeth a notable example of a young maid of quality that lately died in the 18th year of her age, who was ſubject to very frequent hyſterical fits of vapours, with which ſhe was one day aſſaulted ſo violently that it coſt her her life. Her body being opened, *teſticulus dexter erat flaccidus, & figuræ ſolitæ, at ſiniſter ædei tumidus & inflatus, ut ovi anatis æquaret magnitudinem: eoque aperto, ovum fuit intus repertum, olivam figurâ & magnitudine referens, & ſeparatu nequaquam difficile.* This, he obſerves, is ſtill kept by Monſieur Charas.

The opinion of that experienced anatomiſt *Regnerus de Graaf*, relating to this curious ſubject, will be hereafter noticed.

Account of a Stone cut from under the tongue of a man; communicated by Dr. Liſter.

THE patient from whom this *ſtone* was cut, told me that about eight years before it was taken from him he ſuffered an exceeding cold in a winter ſea voyage, which laſted much longer than he expected; and that not long after his landing he found a certain *nodus* or hard lump in the very place whence this ſtone was cut. From that time, upon all freſh cold-taking, he ſuffered much pain, in that part eſpecially; and yet that cold being over, that part was no more painful than the reſt of his mouth. In the ſeventh and eighth years it often cauſed ſudden ſwellings in all the *glandules* about the mouth and throat, upon the firſt draught of beer at meals, which yet would in a ſhort time fall again. But at laſt it began its work with a certrin *vertigo*, which vertiginous diſpoſition continued more or leſs from ſpring till Auguſt; in which month, without any previous cauſe, ſave riding, the place where it was lodged ſuddenly ſwelled, and ran purulent matter at the aperture of the *ductus wartonianus*. But it ſuddenly ſtopped of its running, (which he cannot attribute to any thing but cold) and ſwelled with great inflammation, and very great danger of choaking, it being ſcarce credible what pain he ſuffered in endeavouring to ſwallow any liquid thing. This extremity laſted five days, in all which time the party had ſo vaſt a flux of ſpittle running from him, that it was not poſſible for him to repoſe his head to ſleep without wetting all the bed about him; inſomuch that it was very much queſtioned by ſome friendly viſitants whether he had not of himſelf, or by miſtake, made uſe of ſome mercurial medicine. The firſt day the ſaliva ran thin and tranſparent, almoſt like water, without any bubbles. The ſecond day it ran frothy, it taſted ſalt, (which yet he is apt to think was hot rather than really ſalt, becauſe that day the inflammation was at the height.) The third day it roped exceedingly. On this day a ſmall pin-hole broke directly over the place of the ſtone, and ran with purulent matter as formerly. The fourth day the ſaliva ran inſipid, ſenſibly cold in the mouth, (which again confirms me in that opinion that the former ſharp taſte was the effect of heat, and not the immediate quality of ſalt humour) very little frothy. The fifth day, (which was the day of inciſion) it ran as on the fourth, but left an extreme clammineſs on the teeth, inſomuch that they often cleaved together as though they had been joined with glue.

Upon the inciſion, which proved not wide enough, the membranes or bags wherein the ſtone lay, came away firſt. It was covered over with graſs-green matter, which ſoon dried, and left the ſtone of a whitiſh colour; and was ſo hard as to endure the forceps in drawing it forth. It is but light in proportion to its bulk, weighing about ſeven grains, and is much of the ſhape of our ordinary horſe-beans. There are viſible impreſſions on it of ſome capillary and ſmall veſſels it was bred amongſt. Laſtly, it is ſcabrous or rough, ſand like, although the ſubſtance is tophaceous.

The ſtone is now in the repoſitory of the ROYAL SOCIETY.

Extract of a letter from Dr. Liſter to the Secretary of the ROYAL SOCIETY, *concerning animated Horſe-hairs, rectifying a vulgar error.*

I CANNOT diſcover any thing new and rare in natural philoſophy but I muſt forthwith make you participate of my good fortune, and, I aſſure you, the relation I am about to make you is of a thing very ſurpriſing.

It hath been credibly reported, that *horſe-hairs* thrown into water will become animated, and yet I ſhall ſhew you by an unqueſtionable obſervation, that ſuch things as are vulgarly thought animated hairs, are *very* inſects, even as *ichneumones are* within the bodies of caterpillars.

I will premiſe the particulars concerning this animal, as I find them collected by the induſtry of *Aldrovandus*, and ſave you the trouble of that voluminous author.

This inſect, ſaith he, ſeems to have been unknown to the antients; as it is called by the moderns *ſeta aquotica*, or *vermis ſetarius*, either from the moſt ſlender figure of the body, or becauſe it is thought to be generated of an horſe-hair putrifying in water. The Germans call them by the name rendered *vituli aquatici*.

It is bred in corrupt waters, perhaps of horſe-hair, for, ſaith *Albertus*, upon his own frequent trial, (as I find him quoted by *Aldrovandus*,) theſe hairs, put into ſtanding water, move and are animated, or, as he words it, *vitam & ſpiritum accipiunt, & moventur*. Others have thought them to have their birth from weeds hanging down from the banks into ponds and rivers. Others from locuſts and graſshoppers (*ex bruchis*), which laſt, though it be near the matter, yet is rejected by *Aldrovandus* himſelf as the moſt unlikely.

They have been found in a cold and good ſpring and elſewhere, (which is a wonder, ſaith Aldrovandus) and upon a leaf in a garden. And this, which was there found, was five or ſix fingers breadth long, the thickneſs of a briſtle horſe-hair, with a duſkiſh back, and white belly, and the tail on every ſide white.

I ſaw, ſaith the ſame author, a black one thicker than the whiteiſh one. Other authors otherwiſe deſcribe them, as Bertrutius, Albertus, &c. ſome affirming them to have been a cubit long, others two cubits, others nine inches long at leaſt; that they are white of colour, and ſo hard as ſcarce to be cruſhed with one's foot; to be every where of the ſame thickneſs; that they move not as worms move, but *ſnake like*, and knit themſelves up into knots; that their ſkin is one continued thing without inciſures, and therefore ſome would exclude them from the inſect kind; that they have no head, but ſwim both ways, and therefore may be called amphiſbæna aquatica; that they are poiſon taken into the ſtomach, but not venom to the touch.

And thus much out of *Aldrovandus* concerning the name of this inſect, the place of its birth and original, the place where they are to be found, its deſcription, different ſpecies, nature, poiſon, &c.

Our obſervation is this:—April the 2d, there was thrown up out of the ground of my garden, in digging amongſt other things of this nature, a certain coal-black beetle, of a middle ſize, and flat ſhape, and which I have obſerved elſewhere common enough. Theſe beetles I diſſected upon the account of ſome curioſity, wherein I had a mind to ſatisfy myſelf. But I was ſurpriſed to find in their ſwollen bellies, *of theſe hair worms*, in ſome three, in others but one only. Theſe particulars were carefully noted; firſt, that upon the inciſion they crawled forth of themſelves. Second, that putting them into water they lived in it many days, and did ſeem to endeavour to eſcape by lifting up their heads out of the water, and faſtening them to the ſides of the veſſels, very plainly drawing the reſt of their body forward. Thirdly, that they cannot be ſaid to be amphiſbæna, but do move forward only by the head, which is fairly diſtinguiſhable from the tail by a notable blackneſs. Fourth, that the three I took out of the body of one beetle were all of a dark hair-colour, with whiteiſh bellies, ſomewhat thicker than hogs briſtles; but I took out of the belly of another beetle one that was much thicker than the reſt, much lighter coloured, and by meaſure juſt five inches and a half long; whereas all the reſt did not exceed three inches three quarters.

An extract of a letter, written March 5, 1672, by Doctor Cornelio, a Neapolitan Philoſopher and Phyſician, to John Doddington, Eſq. his Majeſty's Reſident at Venice, concerning ſome obſervations made of perſons pretending to be ſtung by Tarantulas. Tranſlated from the Italian.

Sir,—Now the time approaches, that I may ſend you ſome tarantulas; meanwhile I ſhall not omit to impart unto you what was related to me a few days ſince, by a judicious and unprejudicate perſon, which is, that being in the country of Otranto (where thoſe inſects are in great numbers), there was a man, who, thinking himſelf ſtung by a tarantula, ſhewed in his neck a ſmall ſpeck, about which in a very ſhort time there aroſe ſome pimples full of ſerous humour, and that, in a few hours after, that poor man was ſorely afflicted with very violent ſymptoms, as ſyncopes, very great agitations, giddineſs of the head, and vomit; but that without all deſire of having any muſical inſtruments, he miſerably died within two days.

The ſame perſon affirmed to me, that all thoſe that think themſelves bitten by tarantulas (except ſuch as for ſome ends fain themſelves to be ſo), are for the moſt part young wanton girls, (whom the Italian writer calls dolci di ſale) who by ſome particular indiſpoſition falling into this melancholy madneſs, perſuade themſelves, according to the vulgar prejudice, to have been ſtung by a tarantula. And I remember to have obſerved in Calabria ſome women who, ſeized on by ſome ſuch accidents, were counted to be poſſeſſed of the devil; it being the common belief in that province that the greateſt part of the evils which afflict mankind, proceeds from evil ſpirits.

This brings to my mind a terrible evil, which often enough is obſerved in Calabria, and is called in their language coccio maligno. It ariſeth on the ſurface of the body, in the form of a ſmall ſpeck, of the bigneſs of a lupin. It cauſeth ſome pain, and if it grow not red thereupon, it in a very ſhort time certainly kills. It is the common opinion of thoſe people that ſuch a diſtemper befals thoſe only that have eaten fleſh of animals dead of themſelves; which opinion I can from experience affirm to be falſe. So it frequently falls out, that of many ſtrange effects we daily meet with, the true cauſe not being known, ſuch an one is aſſigned which is grounded upon ſome vulgar prejudice; and of this kind I eſteem to be the vulgar belief of the cauſe of that diſtemper, which appears in thoſe that think themſelves ſtung by tarantulas.

But why ſhould not we rather think, that that diſtemper is cauſed by an inward diſpoſition, like that which in ſome places in Germany is wont to produce that evil which they call chorea Sti Viti, St. Vitas's dance. But of this I hope I ſhall ſoon be able to write my thoughts more fully, which will, I think, be ſufficient to refute that fable of the tarantula.

An account of the Aponenſian Baths near Padua, by a letter from Venice to the Secretary of the ROYAL SOCIETY.

IN the obſervations and hiſtory of nature, poſſibly this may not be unworthy notice. Five miles from *Padua* are the waters called *Aponenſia*, from a town called *Aponum*, famous in antiquity, and among others frequently mentioned by Livy. I will not doubt but that Sir J. F. and D. B. two worthy members of the ROYAL SOCIETY, and who lived long in *Padua*, have informed themſelves moſt exactly of whatever I ſhall be able to ſay on this ſubject; however I do not ſcruple to give you a ſhort relation of it.

The waters are actually very hot. Secondly, they are ſtinking. Thirdly, they yield a great deal of very fine ſalt, of which the natives ſerve themſelves in their ordinary occaſions. This ſalt is the thing, I think, moſt conſiderable there. It is gathered in this manner: the natives, after ſun-ſet, ſtir pieces of wood in the water, and preſently the ſalt ſticks to them, and comes off in ſmall flakes, exceeding white and very ſalt. This never loſeth its ſavour. The people there, with the ſame water uſe to waſh their walls, to render them whiter than ordinary, which it doth even whiter than lime. Such walls conſerve their ſaltneſs ſome few days after, and then become inſipid, even though they ſweat forth a white excreſcence in thin and light flakes like nitre, many years after. But that ſalt which is collected from the ſtones, gravel, and earth, by which the rivulets deſcending from thoſe baths do run, is without any taſte of ſalt, though there be no difference in the form or colour from that which is gathered with the wooden inſtruments.

Concerning the formation of Chryſtals, by P. Franciſco Lana. From the Italian.

IN the laſt month of September, being arrived in the *Val Sabbia*, at a place called *Le Mezzane*, where I knew that chryſtals were generated, I obſerved in a ſpacious round of a meadow, ſeated on a hillock, ſome narrow places bare of all herbs, in which alone, and no where elſe thereabouts, theſe chryſtals are produced, being all ſex-angular, both points of them terminating in a pyramidal figure, ſex-angular likewiſe.

I was told that they were produced from the dews, becauſe (forſooth) being gathered over night, the next morning there would be found others at ſuch a time only when it was a ſerene and dewy ſky; and that upon the herbs of the meadow, and without the bounds of thoſe bare and ſterile places, never any chryſtals were to be found; beſides, that the ground having been in ſome places bared of all greens, and reduced to the condition of thoſe other naked places, yet no chryſtals were ever ſeen to have been formed there. But when I had examined, that in the neighbourhood of that hill, there was no mark at all of any mines, I concluded, that it might be a plenty of nitrous ſteams, which might withal hinder vegetation in thoſe places, and coagulate the dew falling thereon. And that thoſe exhalations were rather nitrous than of another kind I was induced to believe, becauſe nitre is not only the natural coagulum of water, as is manifeſt in artificial glaciations, but alſo that it ever retains the aboveſaid ſex-angular figure, altogether like that of thoſe chryſtals; which may alſo be the very cauſe of the ſex-angular figure in ſnow; this being nothing elſe but water concreted by its natural coagulum, which is a nitrous exhalation. And to make it yet more manifeſt, that theſe are indeed expirations of nitre, I digged up ſome of the earth and drew a ſalt from it which had both the taſte and figure of nitre, though ſome grains of it were of a ſquare, others of a pyramidal figure.

It therefore ought not to be affirmed, that a dewy nature is of itſelf able to be formed into a ſolid gem; becauſe, if that were ſo, ſuch vapours being eaſily carried by any motion of the air from thoſe narrow places, and falling down in dew far from the ſame, chryſtals would be formed in thoſe other places, but they are *only* formed *there*: whence we may very probably infer, that thence are raiſed the exhalations which do concrete the dew, after ſuch a manner as the vapour or exhalation of lead coagulates quickſilver.

A relation of an Inland-Sea, near Dantzick, yielding at a certain ſeaſon of the year a green ſubſtance, which cauſeth certain death; together with an obſervation about white Amber. Communicated by Mr. Kirby, in a letter to the Secretary of the ROYAL SOCIETY, *from Dantzick, Dec.* 19, 1671.

NEAR a ſmall village, called Tuckum, 2½ German miles diſtant from this city weſtward, there is an inland ſea (made by the meeting of three rivulets, ſome ſprings from the adjoining hillocks, and the deſcending rain and ſnow water,) of about half a German mile long and an eighth part of ſuch a mile broad. It ſtretches N. N. W. and S. S. W. About the middle of the bow, on the eaſt ſide, it diſchargeth itſelf with a pretty ſtream, as it alſo doth in another place more ſoutherly. The ſoil of the ground round about ſeems to be ſand mixt with clay. Its ſhore generally ſandy, as is its bottom alſo. Its depth, where deepeſt, four fathoms; but for the moſt part but one, or one fathom and a half. It is ſtored with wholeſome and delicate fiſh, as pearch, roach, eels, &c. and famed for a ſmall fiſh, much eſteemed here, and not much unlike a pearch, only not ſo party coloured, and having a larger head proportionable to its body, called the cole-pearch. The water ſweet and wholeſome;

but only in the three fummer months, June, July, and Auguft, it becomes every year, during the dry weather, green in the middle with an hairy efflorefcence; which green fubftance, being by fome violent wind forced afhore, and with the water drunk by any cattle, dog, or poultry, caufeth certain and fudden death; whereas at the fame time that a knowing and ingenious perfon (who firft acquainted me with it) faw three dogs killed with it, the horfes that were ridden into the water beyond the place, where this green fubftance floated, drunk without any hurt; and that alfo, during the fame feafon, the water in the ftreams that flow from it are wholefome. I fhall endeavour, if you defire it, to procure fome of that ftuff, and get it examined by a chymical analyfis.

One thing more I muft add, that the chief fifher here informed me, that two or three years ago, fifhing in this fea, his net brought up a confiderable large piece of white amber, which as a rarity he prefented to one of the chief fathers of the Olive's Abbey, to which this fea belongs. Now fince this fea is not to be fufpected to come from the ocean, it lying fo high, and about three German miles diftant from the ocean; and fince alfo the neighbouring woods that bear none, but highly refinous trees, cannot be reafonably faid to furnifh fuch amber, that conjecture, which imports that amber is a bituminous fluid fubftance, hardened by the operations of the aqu-aerial particles upon it, may receive fome confirmation from this account.

De Anima Brutorum Exercitationes duæ, prior Phyfiologia, altera Pathologica, Auth. Thoma Willis, M. D. Philof. Natur. Prof. Sidlej. Oxon.

WHAT the learned author of this difficult argument had heretofore promifed, he now in this *tract* with much care performeth: which is the *pathology* of the brain, and the *nervous kind,* explicating the difeafes that affect it, and teaching their cures; together with fome previous phyfiological confiderations of the *fouls of brutes.*

And becaufe it may, by fome, be thought fomewhat paradoxical that he affigneth to that foul, whereby both brutes and men have life, fenfe, and local motion, not only extenfion, and as it were organical parts, but alfo peculiar difeafes and appropriate cures; and becaufe alfo he diftinguifhes this merely vital and ſenſitive ſoul from the rational, to which he makes it ſubordinate, and ſo maketh man a double ſouled animal; he maketh it firſt of all his buſineſs to clear theſe matters, and to free them from what may ſeem offenſive in them.

In the doing of this he denieth not the corporeity of the brutal ſoul, eſteeming, that both by conſiderable arguments, and by very ample ancient and modern ſuffrages, the ſame be evinced; and beſides, that its *bipartition* is by a neceſſary conſequence deducible from the *flammeous* life of the *blood*, and the *lucid* or ethereal ſubſtance of the *animal ſpirits*; both which he hath formerly aſſerted, and endeavoured to prove; for if it be granted him that the *vital* portion of this ſoul, lodging in the blood, be a kind of fire, and the *ſenſitive* part be nothing but an aggregate of animal ſpirits, diffuſed all over the brain and nerves; he draws this conſequence, that the ſoul of a brute, co-extended to the whole body, hath not only many and diſtinct, but alſo ſomewhat diſſimilar parts. And if it be objected that the ſoul of a brute is immaterial, becauſe it perceiveth, or is aware that it feels, matter ſeeming incapable of perception; he anſwers, that that would be very probable if that perception did exceed the bounds of things material, and were of a higher pitch than what is generally aſcribed to natural inſtinct, or *idioſyncraſis*; adding, that none is like to undertake to prove, that the Omnipotent Maker, and Firſt-Mover, and conſtant governor of all things ſhould not be able to impreſs ſuch powers upon matter as might be proper and ſufficient to perform the functions of the ſenſitive life.

And as to what he further aſſerts, that ſome people are more, yea ſooner and rather ſick in their ſoul than in their body; whereas phyſicians do commonly in ſchools refer the principal ſeats of all diſeaſes to the ſolid parts, and the humours, and vital ſpirits,) in this he ſpeaketh conſonantly to his hypotheſis: for, ſince that *that* ſoul hath a material *being* co-extended to the body, and peculiar parts, powers, and affections, he rationally concludeth, that it is ſubject alſo to preternatural affections, and frequently needs the phyſician's aid.

Beſides, he eſteems to have made it out in his *pathology*, that the corporeal ſoul extends her diſeaſes, not only to the body, but alſo to the *mind*, or the rational ſoul; and often involves the ſame in her defects and perturbations.

Moreover, he thinks to have alſo proved from reaſon and authority, that there are in man two diſtinct ſouls, ſubordinately; and eſteems this opinion

4

to be ſo far from being heretical or pernicious, that on the contrary he hopes it will prove altogether orthodox, and conducive to a good life, and a powerful confutation of atheiſm.

But to the end that the author might the better inform us of the corporeal nature, and the *flammeous* and *lucid* parts, and the affection of the ſame, he found it neceſſary both to deſcribe the vital organs of divers animals, by whoſe operation the lamp of life is maintained; and to repreſent alſo the brains of thoſe they call perfect brutes, and of man, diſcovered by him as to their inmoſt receſſes, and their ſecret and ſmalleſt *ducts*. By which manifold and comparative anatomy, as the manifold and wonderful wiſdom of the Creator is manifeſted; ſo are by the ſame diſcovered, even in the ſmalleſt and moſt deſpicable animals, not only mouths and limbs, but alſo hearts; being as it were ſo many altars and hearths to perpetuate this vital flame. In this tract may alſo be met with very ſkilful and accurate diſſections of the *ſilk worm*, oyſter, lobſter, earth-worm, as alſo of divers brains: and firſt, that of a ſheep, in a manner excarnated, to make the madullar ſtreaks, and its inmoſt fabrick to be ſeen. And, ſecondly, of a new one of an human brain; where, a ſection being made through the falx, the *corpus-calloſum* and the *fornix*, and their parts diſplayed and orderly laid open, are exhibited the ſtreaked bodies, as alſo the optic and orbicular prominencies, &c. that ſo by confronting theſe brains, the vaſt difference of the ſoul of a brute, and that of a man, may the better be ſhown.

Some experiments relating to the Viper and its Venom, by Moyſe Charas.

THIS is a ſequel of experiments, made by the ſkill and induſtry of the ſame, that was the author of the tract, entitled *Nouvelles Experiences ſur la Vipre*, formerly deſcribed in page 237, and ſince tranſlated from the French. It is made by the author in his own defence againſt a letter of *Signor Redi*, publiſhed in Italian againſt ſome experiments of the author's former tract. In it M. Charas expreſſeth, that he is ſo far from changing his opinion upon his examining Signor Redi's letter, that he is much more confirmed in it.

The controverſy conſiſts chiefly in this: firſt, that *Signor Redi* will have the yellow liquor contained in the bags of the teeth-gum of vipers to be the only and true ſeat of their venom. Second, that this liquor is indeed not venomous being taken at the mouth, but only when let into a wound, made either by the live animal, or even by a dead one's teeth, thruſt into one's fleſh after it is dead. Third, that the ſame juice drawn from a dead viper, as well as from a live one, is always venomous, if it paſs into a wound and mingle with the blood of the wounded animal, whether it be liquid or dried to powder. Fourth, that it kills generally all ſorts of animals being wounded, and receiving of this liquor into the wound. Whereas M. Charas aſſerts, firſt, that the venom of vipers is only in the enraged ſpirits. Second, that the yellow liquor, as well of a live and even a much angered viper, as of a dead one, hath no venom at all in it, neither in the biting, nor when taken inwardly, or let into a wound and mixed with the blood, nor any other way; and conſequently that it kills and infects no kind of animals, but is a pure and very innocent *ſaliva*.

To make good theſe aſſertions M. Charas affirms to have made new experiments, in the preſence of two or three hundred perſons, phyſicians and others, capable to judge, and of great veracity; and to have found abundant cauſe to adhere to the reſult he had made from his former trials, viz. that never any one animal of all thoſe he wounded, died of the yellow liqour let into the wounds, though drawn hot from the bags of the gums of vipers much enraged. Theſe experiments are at length deſcribed in his treatiſe.

If it be ſaid in favour of Signor Redi, that the diverſity of climates, or of food alſo, may change the nature of vipers, and cauſe that manifeſt difference between the experiments; M. Charas anſwers, that it cannot be, that the nature of the yellow liquor, and that of the ſpirits ſhould be quite ſo changed; becauſe that in France the ſame marks are found in the yellow liquor with thoſe deſcribed in Italy, and that the French vipers do, without an intervention of the ſaid liquor, kill as readily as thoſe of Italy can do. And he adds, that he hath verified it by very many experiments, that all the vipers of France, though taken in very different places, and thoſe often diſtant from one another above an hundred and twenty leagues, do all kill equally.

And, as to the bilious expirations of vipers, which may intervene with the yellow liquor and render it venomous, he ſaith, that is nothing but the angered ſpirits under a diſguiſe.

Now touching the enraged ſpirits of vipers, our author, though he calls them ſpiritual, or not material, and maketh their venom not viſible or palpable, yet certainly he will be underſtood to ſpeak ſo in compariſon to the yellow liquor, which is a *viſible* body; for it is beyond all doubt that thoſe irritated ſpirits are corpuſcles, though not ſuch as may be ſeen and handled like the ſaid liquor, nor ſuch as you may aſſign a particular place to in the body of the viper, where they lodge; though it may be ſaid, that being raiſed and ſevered either from the maſs of the blood, or rather from the whole habit of the body, they rendezvous in the head, being ſtirred up by the concuſſion and great commotion, which the viper feels in her whole body when vexed; whereupon follows an eagerneſs of being revenged for the ill done them, and then a quick and fiery action of the ſpirits thus enraged. Nor can he mean, that theſe ſpirits have neither place nor extenſion; for, how could they part from the viper without having been in her body; and, how could they enter into the body of the animal bitten without being there.

Further, to illuſtrate his notion of the idea of the viper for revenge, he alledges the imagination of terror by a toad impreſſed in a ferret, which having ſeen and been ſeen by that ugly animal, at a certain ſeaſon of the year, and that always in ſummer, cannot avoid running round about it, crying out aloud as if it called for ſuccour, whilſt the toad remains unmoved with its throat open, and being at length by that imagination forced to ſurrender itſelf into that throat, as he affirms to have ſeen, and to have even killed the toad at the very inſtant, and ſo ſaved the ferret, which ran away. He alleges likewiſe a mad-dog who can communicate his malignity to all ſorts of animals, none excepted. And why not then vipers, convey their angry ſpirits into ſuch animals as they meet with, and by them kill thoſe they have bitten? which, he ſaith, they execute by the perturbation and corruption they introduce to the whole maſs of blood, foraſmuch as they obſtruct the circulalation and communication of the natural ſpirits through the body. He adds the example of men, capable to cauſe a gangrene and death itſelf by biting in choler; whereas no ſuch accident comes to paſs when they chance to bite one without choler. He concludeth this diſcourſe with a ſting of a *tarantula*, which he conceiveth to be accompanied with an imagination, ſo ſtrongly impreſſed in perſons that are ſtung by it, as that their ſpirits are perverted and made conform to the agitating nature of the ſame, and conſtrained at certain times by certain tunes to dance, and to return to ſuch motions every year. To confirm which, he relateth an example of a Neapolitan ſoldier, who, he ſaith, hath been theſe four years in the French Infantry, and is ſtill in the royal regiment of *Rouſſillon.* This perſon never failed to feel every year, at a determinate time, (viz. about the 24th of July) the effects of that ſting, which he had received before he came into France. And when the ideas of the ſting were found exalted to a degree capable to produce their effects, he began to dance, and would hear, without interruption, the violins, which the officers of that regiment cauſed to be played for him out of charity; to which he anſwered continually, keeping his time very well, without being tired, during three days, eating and drinking without interrupting his dances, and being very impatient at any diſcontinuance of the play of the violins. But on the fourth day his eagerneſs to dance abated, when he remembered all he had done, and knew all that were about him; after which time he paſſed the remainder of the year without any inclination to dance. This ſoldier, he ſaith, was ſeen thus to dance every year by thouſands of people, and particularly in the camp royal, A. 1670, where the King himſelf and the whole court ſaw him.

A relation of two Stones, the one found in the bladder of a Dog, the other in the body of a Horſe, as mentioned in two Roman Journals de Letterati.

A PRETTY ſpaniel, (in Italy) 2½ palms high, and an excellent ſetter of quails, being kept tied, as ſuch dogs are wont to be, would rather have burſt than urine or ſoil in the place where he was kept. By reaſon of his aptneſs to bite he was cut when he was five years old; and two years after that he began to urine with much difficulty. Whereupon, as often as he was let looſe, he ran preſently into the garden and fell to eat of *pellitory of the wall,* and *fig-leaves*; which *Matthiolus* and others obſerve to provoke urine, and cleanſe the reins. This diſeaſe continued upon him for five years together, ſometimes with that violence that his maſter had him ſyringed and anointed with *oil* of *ſcorpions,* and uſed other remedies to help the poor creature. At length he died at twelve years of age; and, being opened, there was found in his *bladder* a *ſtone* weighing an ounce, of an irregular figure, white, yet here and there with ſome reddiſh ſpecks; and in the bottom of the bladder was found ſtore of ſmall white *gravel*; and in the mouth of the *urinal paſſage* a

www.ingramcontent.com/pod-product-compliance
Lightning Source LLC
Chambersburg PA
CBHW082230180426
43200CB00036B/2707

* 9 7 8 1 5 3 5 8 1 4 1 4 0 *